Autobiography and Decolonization

Wisconsin Studies in Autobiography

William L. Andrews
General Editor

Autobiography and Decolonization

Modernity, Masculinity, and the Nation-State

Philip Holden

The University of Wisconsin Press

This book was published with the support
of the ANONYMOUS FUND
OF THE COLLEGE OF LETTERS AND SCIENCE
AT THE UNIVERSITY OF WISCONSIN–MADISON.

The University of Wisconsin Press
1930 Monroe Street, 3rd Floor
Madison, Wisconsin 53711-2059

www.wisc.edu/wisconsinpress/

3 Henrietta Street
London WC2E 8LU, England

Library of Congress Cataloging-in-Publication Data
Holden, Philip, 1962-
Autobiography and decolonization : modernity, masculinity, and
    the nation-state / Philip Holden.
        p.   cm.—(Wisconsin studies in autobiography)
        Includes bibliographical references and index.
        ISBN 0-299-22610-7 (cloth: alk. paper)
1. Autobiography—Political aspects.   2. Heads of state—Biography.
    3. Decolonization in literature.   4. Postcolonialism in literature.
    I. Title.   II. Series.
CT25.H65   2008
808'.06692—dc22   2007040019

For Yun Sian

Contents

Preface and Acknowledgments

My interest in autobiography and decolonization began in 2000 with a conference paper on Lee Kuan Yew's *The Singapore Story*. Conversations with friends and colleagues convinced me that the first volume of Lee's autobiography was part of a more substantial genre, one widely read yet under-studied. Despite my best efforts to restrict the texts covered in the book to four substantial case studies, the project has been global in scope: it has involved travel to Ghana, India, South Africa, Malaysia, the United Kingdom, and the United States and periods of residence in both Singapore and Canada.

My primary debt in conceiving the book is to George Landow, then dean of the University Scholars Programme at the National University of Singapore, who provided me with inspiration, encouragement, and guidance in embarking on an initially daunting project. Several of my colleagues in the program gave me useful advice, suggestions for further research, and indeed feedback on written work. Stephanie Rupp and Michael Maiwald read an early chapter on Nkrumah, while Johan Geertsema was an invaluable interlocutor concerning South Africa, introducing me to the fiction and criticism of Njabulo Nbedele. Medha Kudaisya first suggested *Biography* as an avenue for initial publication and was also helpful in advising me on sources for Nehru and arranging archival research in New Delhi. The Scholars Programme provided not only intellectual but also financial support, in the form of research grant R-103-000-033-112 from the National University of Singapore's Academic Research Fund.

As my research proceeded, I found myself corresponding with residents of and then traveling to four continents. In the United Kingdom, Nick Barrett did useful preliminary research for me, and I am indebted either through discussion or correspondence to suggestions from Richard Rathbone, David Birmingham, and Elaine Unterhalter. In South Africa, Zabeth Botha helped me navigate the intricacies of the archives in Pretoria; Kgaladi

Kekana and Simphiwe Yako welcomed me and gave assistance at the University of the Western Cape; and Sadie Forman helped me at the University of Fort Hare. I would also like to thank Augustine Mensah and the staff of the National Archives of Ghana; Joellen Elbashir and the Moorland-Spingarn Center at Howard University; Dr. N. Balakrishnan and the staff at the Nehru Memorial Library, and the staff of the National Archives of India; the personnel at National Archives of Singapore and the library staff at the National University of Singapore, who suffered an interminable list of demands for interlibrary loans.

As the project developed, my growing interest in autobiography studies led me to a growing involvement with the intellectual community of the International Auto/Biography Association. I'm grateful to conversations at conferences, emailed advice, or editorial comments and suggestions from Craig Howes, Margaretta Jolly, Gabriele Helms, Zhao Baisheng, Michael Keren, Maria Besemeres, Sue Thomas, David Parker, and Richard Freadman, and also to the IABA itself and its associated listserv in providing a stimulating environment for discussing the social contexts of life writing.

I completed the manuscript during my period as visiting fellow at the Centre for Research in Women's Studies and Gender Relations, University of British Columbia. Tineke Hellwig was helpful in facilitating my visit; on my arrival Sneja Gunew, Valerie Raoul, Margery Fee, and many others made my stay a stimulating one intellectually, while Jane Charles ensured that it went smoothly logistically. Susanna Egan was a careful and insightful reader of two early chapters. At NUS Rajeev Patke also gave me useful comments on the introductory chapter.

I also thank Bill Andrews, the series editor for Wisconsin Studies in Autobiography, and Raphael Kadushin at the University of Wisconsin Press for encouragement and then efficient help in reviewing the manuscript. I would also like to thank the press's two readers, who provided useful guidance and thoughtful suggestions in their reports.

Parts of chapter 1 first appeared as "Other Modernities: National Autobiography and Globalization," *Biography: An Interdisciplinary Quarterly* 28.1 (Winter 2005): 89–103, and an earlier version of chapter 2 as "Missing in Action: The Strange Case of Imperial Autobiography," *a/b: Auto/Biography Studies* 26 (2006): 269–89. An early version of chapter 4 was published as "Modernity's Body: Kwame Nkrumah's *Ghana*," *Postcolonial Studies* 7 (2004): 313–32, and chapter 6 is developed from "A Man and an Island: Gender and Nation in Lee Kuan Yew's *The Singapore Story*," *Biography: An Interdisciplinary Quarterly* 24 (2001): 401–24. Relevant chapters appear here with the permission of the Center for Biographical Research at the

University of Hawai'i, the Institute for Postcolonial Studies, Melbourne, and with thanks to the editors of *Postcolonial Studies, a/b: Auto/Biography Studies,* and *Biography.*

Autobiography and Decolonization

Introduction

This book begins and ends in Singapore. My arrival in the Southeast Asian city-state over a decade ago to teach postcolonial literature at the university level placed a major intellectual responsibility on me. I needed to know Singapore history and society well, to explore the various ways its literatures and cultures expressed its postcoloniality, and to be able to discuss with my colleagues and students the manner in which the postcolonial was woven into the texture of everyday life. Yet the process of knowing Singapore as a postcolonial space confronted me with several paradoxes. The country was on one level apparently deeply colonized, as the Malaysian critic Kee Thuan Chye noted, "more inclined towards the West than the East . . . [,] rootless, culturally vacuous."[1] Malay, the national language, was spoken by only a small minority of the population, while the lingua franca and language of administration and education was English. Road names from the colonial era had not been changed; and the statue of the colonial "founder," Sir Stamford Raffles, remained untouched near Parliament and had been supplemented by the recent erection of a replica at his alleged landing site on the Singapore River. Yet on the other hand most of the built environment of the colonial entrepôt had been swept away: the skyscrapers of the financial district of Shenton Way embodied a governmental discourse that acclaimed Singapore's achievement of a distinctively Asian modernity. Other paradoxes abounded. If Singapore's politics were often perceived from the outside as reflecting an unchanging authoritarianism, from a closer perspective they seemed more like the corporatization of politics toward which Western democracies were rapidly converging: while preparing for power in 1996 Britain's Tony Blair visited Singapore and drew on its housing and pension policies in a speech articulating the vision of a modern "stakeholder society" that would animate his prolonged tenure as prime minister.[2] Singapore had successfully institutionalized multiculturalism as central to the national imaginary in a way that the United States, Canada, and Australia had struggled to do—bilingual education was compulsory, and legal restrictions ensured there was little explicitly racist discourse in the public sphere. And yet such multiculturalism was often rooted in the crudest racial essentialism: when I applied for my identity card, I was asked to nominate a racial affiliation for myself, and after some negotiation was assigned the nineteenth-century racialist category "Caucasian."

The more I researched, however, the more I had a growing conviction that the paradoxes I confronted in Singapore were not entirely exceptional; my experiences in living, teaching, researching and participating in civil society, and my growing dissatisfaction with some of the intellectual frameworks I had inherited from my graduate studies in North America, had resonances with the experiences of many other societies outside Europe and North America—societies that Indian historian Partha Chatterjee pointedly reminds us constitute "most of the world."[3] The complex series of negotiations regarding colonialism, nationalism, and modernity embodied in the paradoxes I observed found parallels, if not absolute convergence, elsewhere. And this growing conviction was complemented by disciplinary changes that suggested other scholars were thinking in similar ways. From the middle of the 1990s, work in postcolonial studies became increasingly historicized, looking at the experience of colonized elites and seeing not simply rupture but also continuities in the transition from the colonial to the national state, stressing transnational rather than merely national histories, and developing an expanded definition of literary texts in order to examine genres such as newspaper essays or life writing, which had been central to the making and unmaking of colonial and national lifeworlds. These transformations were radical enough for many to question the utility of the term "postcolonial" in its continual reference to a now receding colonial past: Gayatri Spivak was not alone in decamping to "transnational cultural studies."[4]

The specific impetus for this project was two parallel events that occurred in the late 1990s, as the gathering Asian economic crisis threatened to undo the narrative of development that had guided Singapore since its independence in 1965. The first of these was a moral panic concerning a 1996 survey conducted by Singapore's Ministry of Education of over two thousand young Singaporeans, which uncovered a startling lack of knowledge of the nation's past. Attempts to rectify this problem led to the institution of a National Education program in schools and also the mounting of a National Education exhibition at the new downtown conference centre at Suntec City in 1997.[5] The highlight of the exhibition, which attracted an audience of 600,000 over its one-month run, was a multimedia show entitled *The Singapore Story* that plotted a national history back into a past before the nation had existed, or was even thought of, and then forward into the future. The second event was the publication in 1998 of the first volume of the memoirs of Lee Kuan Yew, Singapore's first prime minister and elder statesman. Lee's memoirs had the same title as the exhibition, expressing national history as autobiography, mapping the nation's story onto an individual's body, and drawing parallels between scripts of personal and collective awakening. In reading Lee's autobiography I was struck by the almost uncanny inevitability of the narrative. Here was a story that made sense precisely because it followed the contours of an already constituted social imaginary, expressed through the exhibition and the National Education program, but possessing a much longer genealogy. Lee's self-identification as father of the nation, his paralleling of personal discipline with national discipline through the metaphor of regulation of the unruliness of a male body, was already written into Singapore's national narrative. His memoirs were thus not so much a belatedly imposed master story as the excavation of a national unconscious that seemed always to have underpinned the manner in which national history had been publicly recited in Singapore since its independence.

Reading Lee's memoirs, and researching further, I realized that his autobiography was part of—and indeed perhaps one of the last texts in—a much larger and neglected genre, one I came to call national autobiography.[6] Nationalist leaders in the process of decolonization such as Mohandas K. Gandhi, Jawaharlal Nehru, Kwame Nkrumah, Kenneth Kaunda and many others all wrote autobiographies in which the growth of an individual implicitly identified as a national father explicitly parallels the growth of national consciousness and, frequently proleptically, the achievement of an independent nation-state.[7] These texts had—and continue to have—two functions. They demonstrate to an international audience, through the life of a representative individual who is paradoxically also an exceptional leader, the nation's entry into modernity. At the same time, they function within the nation as documents of—and indeed, by being read, incitements to—the production of citizens of the new nation-state. They thus become conduct books of exemplary, although not unflawed, lives.

National autobiographies as a genre clearly display common characteristics and indeed, as Elleke Boehmer has shown, follow a common structural "grammar" of a journey, a time in the wilderness of exile, and then a return.[8] Moreover, they are bound together in a dense intertextual network of emulative self-fashioning that is frequently fraternal or filial in nature.

Many of the author-protagonists knew each other, corresponded with and commented on each other, and modeled their narratives on (or at times distanced them from) those of their predecessors. Yet paradoxically, despite the widespread popularity of these autobiographies, we rarely consider them as literary texts. Two examples might illustrate this. In the 1980s in the United States, other student and community activists and I read Gandhi's autobiography when planning a campaign for our public university to divest itself of investments in South Africa, looking for both inspiration and specific tactics of civil disobedience. In the new millennium, Nkrumah's autobiography is recommended reading for American students departing on study programs to West Africa in order to give them background on Ghana's history. In each of these reading situations, the narrative is mined for content—for inspiration, tactics or for cultural and historical knowledge—while its literariness, the manner in which it is presented to a reader, is neglected.

Yet there are profound reasons we should attend to the literariness of these texts, to examine them as not simply partial records of the past but contributing to the way we understand this past. Literary studies has always, but perhaps increasingly in the last fifty years, emphasized how the way in which a story is told is integral to its meaning; in narratological terms, "discourse" is as central to a narrative as "story."[9] In a parallel movement, auto/biography studies has stressed the importance of narrative to the construction of identity itself—how, in Paul John Eakin's words, "narrative . . . is not merely *about* the self but rather in some profound way a constituent part *of* self."[10] Yet, despite the influence of the "linguistic or narrative turn" in the social sciences, those of us who work in these areas and move increasingly toward interdisciplinarity often meet with skepticism from colleagues working in history, sociology or related disciplines when we make arguments about the manner in which literary and autobiographical texts and the selves they make enter into a larger social world.[11] It is easy to show, for example, that postmodern novels such as Salman Rushdie's *Midnight's Children* utilizing a "historiographic metafictive process" cause an individual reader to contemplate the manner in which history is told, and ultimately to gain what Jean-François Lyotard has called an "incredulity towards metanarratives."[12] Yet it is much more difficult to make an argument concerning the influence of reading practices on larger public narratives such as national history without dispensing with the close reading of the discourse of the text that is central to literary studies.[13]

National autobiographies offer unique possibilities as an arena where the micronarratives of the literary text and the metanarratives of nation and history meet. Reformulating Benedict Anderson's well-known phrase, they constitute the nation not so much as an imagined community as an imagined individual, with newfound autonomy in a public sphere of international relations, ready to "play its part on the stage of history."[14] They describe a past, but they also mould this past, contributing to the making of what Canadian philosopher Charles Taylor has called a "social imaginary," the "normative notions and images" through which various members of a society conceive of their social existence.[15] And as they move from the past to the promise of the future, they meditate on how public and private, individual and collective stories come together, how the construction of a new self is linked to the construction of a new polity, a new world.

What story do these narratives reveal? Each iteration of the genre tells us part of a familiar narrative, a history of the last two centuries. These texts begin in a world of inequality, a colonial world that is also, paradoxically, a modern one. In seeking new futures, they critique the present from two opposing directions. Although they frequently imagine a precolonial past as a time before the disruptions of colonialism, the narratives urge us that such an interruption in history can now be overcome only by moving forward, not backward; these stories thus critique colonialism not simply as disturbing a precolonial order but also as not modern enough, as refusing to take the ideals of the Enlightenment seriously. They thus propose new nationalisms as the Enlightenment's genuine heirs, seizing the baton of modernity from an exhausted West. They tell the story of decolonization and of the hopes for new nation-states in the period immediately after the Second World War. Some end here, but later narratives must cope with a world that has changed again, in which the promises of decolonization have not been realized. They negotiate with new challenges and a new vocabulary—globalization, structural adjustment, reflexive modernity—at a time when the nation-state's borders have become increasingly porous to global capital flows; they arrive, belatedly and sometimes reluctantly, in the world in which we live now.

This story is familiar enough, but these narratives tell it from a different angle than the customary viewpoint of the early twenty-first century, making strategic use of what black American intellectual W. E. B. Du Bois called the "double-consciousness" of the colonized.[16] In doing so, as we shall see presently, they offer the possibility of reviewing the way such national stories are told, and thus of interrogating the critical assumptions of auto/biography studies on the one hand, and postcolonial studies and its successors on the other. These texts operate as a kind of lay theory, offering a critical reading of the history of the present. Yet they are also objects to which theoretical and critical reading practice may be applied: they offer us the possibility of examining the way gender is written into modernities after colonialism and how constructions of the collective, however progressive in intent, also contain exclusions.

To study such national autobiographies, we need two contexts: one critical and the other historical. Chapter 1 provides a critical toolbox, focusing on three key issues: autobiography as a distinctively modern genre, the nature of emergent modernity or modernities—and indeed the utility of the term "modernity" itself—under colonialism and decolonization, and the contested yet central place of gender in decolonization. In doing so, it also makes a critical intervention, contesting the manner in which the absolute difference of the "non-Western" text is frequently assumed in contemporary auto/biography studies, and the manner in which it is then subsumed into a developmental narrative of changing autobiographical practice on a global scale.

The next section of the study begins the work of historicization, and thus comprises two chapters exploring autobiography in the colonial world. The first takes a step backward, looking at the problematic status of imperial autobiography and the manner in which it attempts to project the social imaginary of the colonial state. If canonical nineteenth-century autobiography constructs, as much contemporary auto/biography theory has asserted, an exclusive, rational "post-Enlightenment subject" through strategies of racial and gendered othering, one would expect imperial proconsuls to have written autobiographies that epitomize this paradigm. However, the reality is precisely the opposite: examining four of the most publicly influential exemplars of imperial masculinity who were also prolific writers—Hugh Clifford, Nathaniel Curzon, Frederick Lugard, and Cecil Rhodes—we find a collection of fragments, but no published accounts of a coherent life. We have posthumous wills and testaments, travel writing and anecdotes, autobiography presented as fiction, voluminous autobiographical notes (Curzon) and a suppressed autobiography (Clifford). Through an analysis of such texts, I argue that the inability of most imperial governors to write autobiographies is no accident but is related to the contradictory nature of the colonial state and colonial modernity itself, a contradiction that national autobiographies would later exploit. I have chosen the examples of Curzon, Rhodes, Clifford, and Lugard: their careers were spent in the four areas of the world—India, West Africa, South Africa, and Malaya—that constitute the settings for the texts in the case studies in later chapters.

Chapter 3 brings together three very different narratives, each written in the first three decades of the twentieth century, that provide a textual context for the emergence of national autobiography in the postcolonial world. Joseph Ephraim Casely Hayford's *Ethiopia Unbound*, written in the third person, is the only text in this study that cannot fulfill Philippe Lejeune's autobiographical contract in affirming "'identity' between the names of the author, narrator, and protagonist."[17] I have nonetheless included it here because form is closely related to content, telling us much about the colonial elite environment in which Casely Hayford is writing. Emerging from the Gold Coast in the early years of the twentieth century, *Ethiopia Unbound* is a hybrid text that merges Bunyan, Homer, Dante, Fante tradition and the lives of two reformers, its author and that of "the greatest living exponent of the true spirit of African nationality and manhood," the Jamaican-born Edward Wilmot Blyden.[18] A text that appears— at least in formal terms—postmodern before its time, *Ethiopia Unbound* enhances our understanding of the complexity of the self-fashioning of colonial elites from which, much later, autobiography would emerge. Our second narrative, the autobiography of Marcus Garvey, might promise a reinscription of the tropes and narrative elements of modern masculinity as expressed in canonical autobiography of the nineteenth century. Garvey was committed to self-improvement through work, much in the mode of Benjamin Franklin, and his awarding of himself the title of provisional president of Africa shows an attempt to appropriate the symbols of national authority from the colonial powers. Yet, after a brief introduction— which shows the influence of Franklin, Daniel Defoe, Samuel Smiles, and Horatio Alger—Garvey launches into a self-defense that is also the defense of a failed nationalism. Here the demise of Black Star Line and associated enterprises is largely the result of a failure in integrity on the part of other men, Garvey's partners and subordinates in his enterprise, and the narrative collapses under a burden of relationality.

The final autobiography in the chapter is Mohandas K. Gandhi's *Autobiography*, possibly the most widely read of all the texts in this study. While featuring several disciplinary elements which will become common in the later autobiographies in this study, Gandhi's text is unique in its principled reluctance to accept the terms of colonial masculinity and in its refusal to engage with the formation of a postcolonial state. This refusal has made it something of a puzzle for succeeding writers of national autobiography, and thus more marginal to the genre than its continued popularity might suggest. All three early autobiographical texts are interesting because they are written—for various reasons—before the national state can be fully imagined: they thus occupy, wittingly or unwittingly, a space of free play, with the possibility of presents and futures, or contesting colonial or neo-colonial pastoral power in ways denied to the writers of later texts.

Having established the genre's literary and historical background, we can now move to a series of case studies. The third section of the book thus looks at two autobiographies that might be considered normative or even prototypical representatives of the subgenre: the autobiographies of Jawaharlal Nehru, first prime minister of India, and Kwame Nkrumah, first prime minister and later first president of Ghana. Nehru's stature and Nkrumah's reached their peaks at the time of the Bandung generation, associated with the Asian-African Conference of April 1955; each leader was seen as not just representing a nation, but arguably a continent, and the Bandung conference, the Afro-Asian movement and indeed the movement of history itself seemed to offer the possibilities of a world remade after colonialism. Richard Wright was surely not alone in predicting that the "decisions or lack of them flowing from Bandung [would] condition the totality of human life on this earth."[19] In looking at individual texts, I adopt a different working mode from that of the introductory chapters. Close textual reading is supplemented by substantial archival work in the personal papers of the author, enabling us to see how events represented in the autobiographies were narrated differently by different actors at various historical periods and thus how each autobiographical text remakes the past for the needs of its own particular present.

Chapter 4 thus examines Nehru's autobiography, written during his imprisonment by the British in 1934–35. The autobiography would become almost a template for future generations of nationalist leaders, particularly in the series of homologies it lays out between authorial disciplining of a narrative, the rational control of a male body through discipline, and the manner in which the future postcolonial state might contain and channel the unruly matter of the nation. Yet Nehru's text is also rich and self-reflective, and its dialogical relationship between protagonist and narrator results in life writing that asks a series of questions about the homologies it proposes. Material from Colonial Office and Police files and also from Nehru's own personal papers at Teenmurti House, New Delhi, lets us see how the autobiography's narrative reshapes a past and how it produces a protagonist in opposition to British attempts to disqualify the character of nationalist leaders in India.

Kwame Nkrumah's *Ghana: The Autobiography of Kwame Nkrumah* is the subject of chapter five. Nkrumah's text, hastily dictated to and composed into a narrative by his private secretary, Erica Powell, for the occasion of Ghana's independence in 1957, reiterates and reworks many of the homologies of its Nehruvian precursor, supplementing them with an effort to reclaim ethnography from the hands of the colonizers. Less self-reflexive than Nehru's text, Nkrumah's autobiography is still, like his Indian predecessor's, haunted by the spectacle of a crowd that is not amenable to the disciplinary apparatus of the state-to-be and threatens to overwhelm the autonomy of the protagonist himself. My analysis of Nkrumah's autobiography is informed by archival material from Colonial Office files that documents the discursive environment in which Nkrumah came to power and substantial biographical and autobiographical material from the National Archives of Ghana and the Moorland-Spingarn Center at Howard University.

The final section of the book examines two texts written much later, in the 1990s, that respond to changes in the world in which the autonomy promised by developmental states after colonialism has not been realized. These works are published in a world of late or reflexive modernity, marked by increasingly borderless capital flows and the decline in the sovereignty of nation-states, by continual instability crises and by persistent inequalities that nationalisms after colonization had sought to eliminate.

The first text, Nelson Mandela's autobiography, *Long Walk to Freedom*, shares a complex genesis with Nkrumah's *Ghana*. Although, while incarcerated on Robben Island, Mandela completed an autobiography that was smuggled out to the ANC leadership in exile, the present text is a commercially written autobiography, produced with the assistance of journalist Richard Stengel of *Time* magazine and published on the occasion of the first democratic elections in the new South Africa of 1994. It would be easy to posit that such changes result in a commodification of postcoloniality and revolutionary nationalism for a contemporary audience. Yet I wish to argue that Mandela's autobiography is a complex text that develops a consciously internationalist element already found in Nkrumah's and Nehru's autobiographies, providing its readers with a means to imagine their own places within social imaginaries now threatened by the instabilities of late modernity. I read *Long Walk* with the assistance of archival material from the ANC Archives at the University of Fort Hare, the National Archives in Pretoria, and the Mayibuye Centre at the University of the Western Cape, Cape Town; I also locate it within the context of the phenomenal increase in South African life writing in the last decade.

The second chapter of the section looks at the first of two volumes of the memoirs of Lee Kuan Yew, prime minister of Singapore for the first thirty-five years of its existence as an independent nation-state. Unlike the three previous narratives, Lee's was written almost four decades after his assumption of power and more than three decades after Singapore achieved independence in 1965. Of all the political leaders here, Lee might believe his life to embody the successful achievement of a modernity to which all others so earnestly aspired: he wrote his narrative having voluntarily relinquished the prime minister's office of a developed nation whose per capita income exceeded that of its former colonial master. Paradoxically, however, Lee's narrative is the most haunted by the incompleteness of the project of modernity and is the most relational in the manner in which the author's own persona is created with reference not to women—as Nkrumah's and Mandela's are—but to other men. Lee's own political success has resulted in control over and therefore a paucity of archival sources, and I respond to this methodological challenge by embarking on a thick description of Singapore nationalism and considering other possibilities in the way Singapore history has been and might be told.

In the concluding chapter, I briefly explore ways of writing otherwise: fictional and auto/biographical narratives which respond to and question the paradigms of Lee and Mandela, or provide alternative models for engaging with the nation-state and the social imaginary that citizens inhabit. In the case of South Africa, I explore Elinor Sisulu's composite biography of her parents-in-law, *Walter and Albertina Sisulu: In Our Lifetime,* as an alternative way of memorializing the life of men and women in a national liberation struggle, and examine Njabulo Ndebele's remarkable fictional text *The Cry of Winnie Mandela* for the manner in which it excavates the centrality of gender in the construction of South Africa's national narrative. For Singapore, I examine the recent autobiography of Malayan Communist Party secretary general Chin Peng (Ong Boon Hua) and the manner in which it rewrites the tropes of Lee's narrative to produce a very different "Singapore story," and also consider Lau Siew Mei's novel *Playing Madame Mao,* which contains a caricature of Lee. In considering these narratives, I wish to also question a frequent critical assumption in auto/biography studies that postmodern life writing strategies are necessarily destabilizing or questioning of social imaginaries. While the "decline of the nation-state and the end of colonialism" may have produced a new "crisis of the values it represented" exemplified in postmodern texts, national autobiography has, in a sense, always gained its authority by making visible and then managing crises.[20]

Finally, two caveats about my own location. This study develops insights from recent studies of masculinity that draw upon feminist research and thought. One difficulty in writing about national or state projects involving hegemonic masculinities and related social imaginaries is that one may ascribe too much power to the project itself, mistaking it for an entire social reality. Concentration on influential narratives written by men thus runs the risk of erasing women's agencies. However, gendered social imaginaries have shown remarkable persistence in the new millennium in most of the world. In Singapore, for example, women's participation in civil society organizations such as the Singapore Council of Women and in political parties was high in the era immediately preceding self-rule: four women were elected to the first Legislative Assembly in 1959. Yet it would be forty years before parliamentary representation for women reached that level again, and in a very different social environment in which state fatherhood, although somewhat loosened, is still manifest. We need to register the limits that such national narratives impose, even as we hope to move beyond them.

Second, let me return to the subject with which I began this introduction. My own physical location is the result of a journey which—although much more modest in scope or effect—has parallels with the itinerant movements of some of the protagonists of the autobiographies in this book. After study in Britain and North America—supplemented by teaching and study in China and Taiwan—I have spent my academic career entirely in Singapore. Living the Asian modernity that Singapore embodies—with full awareness of the series of conflicts such a description temporarily elides—I have sought to trace in much of my research over the last decade the manner in which postcolonial criticism and theory and the other disciplinary areas that have emerged in their wake can usefully speak in a Singapore environment. This book represents my first attempt to bring some conclusions and observations based on this experience back out into a larger, comparative realm. Yet Singapore remains an exceptional postcolonial space in both the continued economic success of the development state from 1965 and in the thinness of its political and civil society. To generalize from Singapore's experience concerning the other nation-states in this study would prove as homogenizing as some of the generalizations from North American or British situations that I critique. I hope I am able to use my position as an academic in Singapore not to claim—or indeed appropriate—a spuriously authentic speaking position, but rather strategically to allow that estrangement from the familiar that enables critical thought. At its core, this book describes a place where different national and personal narratives meet: it cannot expect to trace each to its origin.

But in exploring this place of meeting, it may perhaps allow us to think again about the stories we tell about our modernity, and indeed who "we" — both collectively and as individuals within a social body — might be.

1

Starting Points

*Life Writing, Modernity, and Masculinity
in the Postcolony*

As a heuristic device, let us begin with a scene played out repeatedly all over the world in last half-century. A woman stands at a lectern, confidently addressing a nation as its first female president or prime minister. In one respect, she seems to embody the realization of the promise of modernity achieved through the nation, of the equality of all citizens, men and women, embodied in the constitution. And yet her speech, as it progresses, refers less to herself than to an absent figure, centering on a claim not of direct but a deferred authority, an authority gained relationally through her status as wife or daughter of an actual or potential father of the nation.

The list of protagonists in such scenes is long. Indira Gandhi, daughter of India's first prime minister, Jawaharlal Nehru; Guyana's Janet Jagan; Indonesia's Megawati Sukarnoputri; and Bangladesh's Sheikh Hasina Wajed are perhaps the most prominent examples. But the plausibility of other scenes that have not yet taken place hints that these performances are part of a much larger, congruent series of social imaginaries. Aung San Suu Kyi may yet or may never address Burma as a nation, but her status as Aung San's daughter remains a central component of her political capital. Corazon Aquino, as president of the Philippines in 1986, spoke of the martyrdom of her husband, Benigno Aquino, before he had the chance to father a return to democracy in his homeland; she also noted how his return from exile consciously followed the example of a father of another nation, Mohandas. K. Gandhi.[1] Benazir Bhutto's autobiography, *Daughter of the East*, commences with a scene at the grave of her executed father, Zulfikar Ali Bhutto, represented as "the first leader of Pakistan to speak for all the people, not just for the military and the élite"; she feels "the strength and conviction of his soul replenishing me," and when the narrative closes with the protagonist's return to Pakistan in 1986 Bhutto again invokes the father.[2] In Sri Lanka, Chandrika Kumaratunga and her mother Sirimavo Bandaranaike are unique in their status as daughter and wife, respectively, of the country's fourth prime minister, Solomon Bandaranaike. And in South Africa, women prominent in the anti-apartheid struggle were often, to use Mamphela Ramphele's phrase, "political widows."[3] Winnie Mandela, Albertina Sisulu, and indeed Ramphele herself—through her relationship with Black Consciousness leader Steve Biko—were often defined through their relationship to dead or imprisoned potential fathers of the nation.

I do not want to suggest here that women leaders in such situations are discursively imprisoned and devoid of agency but rather that their success—and indeed survival—is dependent upon manipulation of a pre-existing gendered discursive field that bears further investigation. Indira Gandhi was extremely adept at performing her dual roles as Nehru's daughter and her husband's widow; Megawati perhaps less so in utilizing the social capital she possessed as Sukarno's daughter.[4] Surely significant is that this discursive environment is, without exception, a postcolonial one in a very precise use of the term. The nationalisms to which these female leaders appeal, and the developmental states over which they preside or hope to preside, emerged from colonialism. Each has a deferred relationship to capitalist modernity; in Partha Chatterjee's words, they are part of "those parts of the world that were not direct participants in the history of evolution of the institutions of modern capitalist democracy."[5] And the scene described above suggests that gender, and in particular a notion of paternity, is deeply inscribed into popular images of both nation and of the pastoral state that succeeds colonialism, into what Charles Taylor has described as the social imaginary of the nation-state, "the ways people imagine their social existence, how they fit together with others, how things go on between them and their fellows, the expectations that are normally met, and the deeper normative notions and images that underlie these expectations."[6] The notion of the social imaginary, indeed, may be particularly useful to us, because it enables an analytical distinction between the nation and the state and a realization that the relationship between these two elements of postcolonial nationalism are not always in harmony, as much work on gender and nationalism might suggest.

How do such modern social imaginaries come into being? Taylor is careful to acknowledge that his analysis is limited to Europe and North America, noting that modernity is not a "single process of which Europe is the paradigm" (196). Yet he offers suggestions worthy of consideration in other contexts. New practices, Taylor notes, may develop "through improvisation among certain groups and strata of the population," or be "launched by elites in such a way as to recruit a larger and larger base" (30); they are likely to draw on and transform elements of the imaginaries of previous social orders. Furthermore, social imaginaries are given life through narrative. Nationalism, for instance, succeeds because it is presented as the realization of the destiny of a people who have already imagined themselves as a collective subject (176–77).

The autobiographies that are the subject of this book seem central to the kind of transformation of which Taylor writes, producing the narrative of a collective subject from that of an individual life. The texts are the products of improvisation by present or former members of colonized elites, drawing from the heterogeneous, uneven terrain of lifeworlds with relative autonomy from the projects of the colonial state and indigenizing modernity through a strategic reinscription and reclamation of both the past and the future. They feature a twofold movement in which the male protagonist reclaims his place in a collective after a mental or physical exile and then urges fellow citizens of the nation-to-be to undergo a similar process of individuation and reclaiming of a shared past in order to claim citizenship. In all these texts, the double time of autobiography works to enhance this movement. The texts are narrated retrospectively after the achievement of the nation—or, in Nehru's case, after the achievement of a coherent nationalist consciousness—and thus embed their protagonist's narrative into a history of self-realization within a collective narrative; at the same time, they provide readers with a model to follow in self-fashioning as a citizen of the new nation.

To understand the manner in which national autobiographies both document and contribute to the formation of postcolonial social imaginaries, we need to investigate more deeply the terminology used in this introduction. First, we examine both autobiography as a genre and the manner in which it has been associated with modern self-fashioning. Yet this leads to a further issue: we must think through the nature of the "modern," and in particular the unique experience of modern nation-state formation in the postcolony, in Chatterjee's words, "most of the world."[7] Here we need to negotiate the difficulties presented by the term "modernity" itself, as both an indigenous and also an analytical category. Such excavations will enable us to return to a third aspect of these texts that has been most apparent in the opening scene, an embodied masculinity as part of a larger gender politics associated with nationalism and state formation, enabling us to ask why, in a postcolonial context, gender seems to matter so much.

Autobiography and Modernity

Autobiography's relationship to the growth of modern bourgeois subjectivity in Europe and North America has been extensively, and perhaps exhaustively, documented. Forms of life writing fulfilling the first of the terms of Philippe Lejeune's "autobiographical contract"—"a retrospective prose narrative produced by a real person concerning his own existence"—have been produced in many societies at various periods: Hei'an Japan, Tang dynasty China, medieval Europe, or indeed fifth-century North Africa.[8] Much contemporary autobiography studies, however, posits that autobiography—in Lejeune's consciously restricted definition—as a form of life writing that emerged in eighteenth and nineteenth-century Europe and North America is distinctively different from earlier forms, particularly in terms of the second part of Lejeune's pact—"focusing on his individual life, in particular on the development of his personality."[9] Karl Weintraub characterizes this difference in terms of a new notion of "development" that replaces an earlier principle of "unfolding": the story of a life, rather than being seen as developing according to an overall principle "as if by a necessary, predetermined sequentiality," is now about the formation of a self through interaction with the world.[10] Indeed Weintraub's schema, shorn of its civilizational emphasis, dovetails with other accounts of changed senses of time and self under modernity, for instance Benedict Anderson's famous discussion of the replacement of "the medieval conception of simultaneity-along-time" with the modern conceptualization of simultaneity "cross-time" marked not by prefiguring and fulfillment but by temporal coincidence and measured by clock and calendar and also with many other accounts of the rise of the notion of the individual after the Enlightenment.[11]

We will defer for now an examination of the term modernity itself; we may wish, in particular, to express skepticism regarding a simple equation of the modern with a change in consciousness prompted by the philosophical innovations of the Enlightenment. Yet the argument concerning autobiography—in Lejeune's formal, restricted generic definition—as a modern genre is persuasive. Essential features of the genre of writing were noted, if in an uncritical and overly celebratory framework, by "second-wave" theorists of autobiography, such as Georges Gusdorf or Weintraub himself.[12] For Weintraub, autobiography is marked by a retrospective attention to the development of a unique personality through its encounter with the world, through a cultivation of "individuality" in which every "individual existence is but one of the actualizations of . . . [an] indefinitely variable human potential."[13] Thus the growth in popularity in autobiographical writings since 1800 in Europe is not merely due to "mass literacy," but because autobiography, through its focus upon the production of unique, autonomous individuals within a specific environment, is an expression of "the emergence of the particular modern form of historical mindedness we call historism or historicism" (821). For Gusdorf, too, the "awareness of the singularity of each individual life" embodied in autobiography "is the late product of a specific civilization"—here the post-Enlightenment West.[14] Such awareness makes autobiography possible when "consciousness of self" exists and "man knows himself a responsible agent" (30–31). History is thus supplemented by autobiography, in which "the artist and the model coincide, the historian tackles himself as object" (31). Historical evidence would seem to support Gusdorf and Weintraub's assertions: the word "autobiography" is first used in English in the late eighteenth century, and earlier texts we now know as canonical autobiographies, such as that of Benjamin Franklin, were not assembled and packaged as such until the nineteenth century.[15] Yet the phenomenon of "historical mindedness" has perhaps a slightly longer history in a more gradual process of the growth of the bourgeois individual even in Europe: most early European novels, such as Daniel Defoe's *Robinson Crusoe,* were initially presented to the reading public as autobiographical texts.

Later work in autobiography studies has tended to place analysis such as Gusdorf's and Weintraub's in a broader context. The civilisationalist assumptions in second-wave criticism have been rightly critiqued, although surprisingly little work has been done in examining subject constitution in nineteenth-century autobiographical texts outside Europe in areas that increasingly were subject to "development" and became enmeshed in the flows of modern cultures and capital. Much energy has instead been devoted to a critical interrogation of the identities constituted by such autobiographical texts. The genre Gusdorf and Weintraub endorse is no longer uncritically celebrated but seen as enabling the construction of a rational, autonomous, frequently exclusionary subjectivity that is part of a problem, not a solution. Thus in the feminist critique of Julia Watson and Sidonie Smith, the "Enlightenment self" produced in these narratives models a unitary "universal human subject."[16] Canonical autobiographies of this type present what is historically and socially contingent as universal, silencing the heterogeneity of different modes of self-construction, in theory inviting participation from all, but in practice only offering a "constraining template" (xviii). Martin Danahay, among others, has noted the manner in which nineteenth-century autobiography is profoundly gendered, aiming to produce a "feminized other" representative of the "excluded principle of the social," which the notion of individual autonomy attempts to expel.[17] In this account, male autobiographers in the Victorian era frequently aimed, albeit with mixed success, to align themselves with monologism, closing down a play of meaning in the text in order to produce an autonomous individual (5). The production of the individual subject in these texts is thus achieved at great cost. The autonomous subjectivity promised by autobiography in which Gusdorf and Weintraub invest so much, is thus predicated on the exclusion of others. It is not so much emancipation as a new kind of subjection: an entry into a Foucauldian disciplinary regime of power, or Max Weber's "iron cage" of rationality.[18]

Watson and Smith's critique can be readily extended to other areas of inquiry. The series of binarisms reproduced in the making of the self in classical nineteenth-century autobiography: public versus private, rationality versus irrationality, individual autonomy versus the tyranny of community all very much parallel the underlying structures of colonial discourse explored in a growing body of critical work in the wake of Edward Said's *Orientalism.* Yet we might in passing note that canonical autobiographical texts of the nineteenth century have, in Trev Lynn Broughton's words, become something of a "stalking-horse."[19] While the broad outline described above has some plausibility, individual texts frequently exceed the theoretical framework and demonstrate considerable self-reflexivity, as recent criticism has been at pains to show.[20] And Broughton's insight perhaps raises further concerns when applied to the manner in which postcolonial and autobiography studies have come together. For if canonical nineteenth-century canonical autobiography has been unjustly marginalized through certain reading practices, we might say that "non-Western" texts in contemporary autobiography studies have been valorized, read almost solely as a way of escaping from this prison-house of modernity, either through a connection with the premodern or, more frequently, an embracing of the postmodern and the global. As Said and his successors have shown, valorization of the devalued term in a binarism does not in itself challenge the basic discursive assumptions the binarism endorses.

An account of the place accorded to "non-Western" texts might usefully begin with a schema outlined by Sidonie Smith and Julia Watson in their recent—and excellent—introductory text, *Reading Autobiography.* "Although at this time," Smith and Watson argue, "the unitary self of liberal humanism remains a prevailing notion governing Western configurations and disciplines of selfhood, that universal self and narratives through which it has claimed its authority are increasingly open to challenge.

Around the globe, contesting versions of selfhood are posed, above all, in diverse kinds of life narratives that introduce collective, provisional, and mobile subjects."[21] I fully support Smith and Watson's project—to reclaim voices marginalized by previous generations of autobiography studies and to show their centrality to the field of study. However, there are dangers in using the "non-Western," especially when prematurely conflated with the "global," as a means of showing the inadequacy of "the unitary self of liberal humanism." Viewing "a postmodern form of autobiography as an appropriate medium for emancipation and decolonization," studies of "non-Western" texts frequently concentrate upon their postmodern elements, their "fragmentations [,] . . . multiple and contradictory narratives" and stress their production of provisional, performative, communal, or fragmentary selves.[22] The texts chosen as "non-Western" or "intercultural" are frequently narratives largely set or written in Europe or North America that describe migration between different cultural and social environments: they are very important within their own national or community contexts and readily comprehensible within other, similar, contexts, but their concerns cannot be easily magnified to embrace all of the "non-West." Indeed we might, with rather greater charity, apply the criticisms made by Aijaz Ahmad and Arif Dirlik of the state of postcolonial studies in the mid-1990s to the fetishization of the "non-Western" and the global in contemporary autobiography studies.[23] There is a danger, with the best of intentions, of mistaking one's own condition as a diasporic intellectual in Europe or North America for a global condition, and of this unacknowledged misapprehension determining both the texts to be studied and the manner in which they are read.

Much evidence of "non-Western" autobiography and its encounter with modernity would, in fact, cast doubt upon a narrative that ends in performative postmodern texts that, in a newly globalized environment, challenge the hegemony of the nation-state. First, we might note that many of the features of what we now call globalization are not new, and indeed are bound up inextricably with colonialism and modernity. The introduction of information technology to China in the late nineteenth century, for example, in the form of the telegraph, radically transformed the lifeworlds of the Chinese elites in a way that paralleled the effect of the internet a century later, and indeed arguably led to the formation of the notion of a Chinese public.[24] Many of the measures by which globalization is defined—mass migration, for instance, or international trade as a percentage of world Gross Domestic Product—prove, on closer examination, to have been higher in the nineteenth and early twentieth centuries than they are at present.[25] Second, we might note that forms of autobiography have a long history in complex negotiations with modernity by the colonized. These autobiographical writings may draw on premodern written forms and often make use of the hybrid, performative lifeworld of the colonial entrepôt. The Malay writer Abdullah bin Abdul Kadir's autobiography *Hikayat Abdullah* (1843), for instance, set in early-nineteenth-century Malacca and Singapore, draws on the genre of Hikayat, or court history, while radically reworking it to tell the story of an individual life and a rational modernity fully compatible with Islam. Joseph Ephraim Casely Hayford's *Ethiopia Unbound,* written in the colonial Gold Coast in the early years of the twentieth century, is a fascinatingly polyglossic "autobiographical novel" influenced by Bunyan, Homer, folk stories, and contemporary newspaper journalism.[26] While it would be easy to read these texts as reveling in the hybridity or the performative subjectivity of a colonial world already globalized, they frequently attempt to construct "pure," stable, autonomous, modern subjects who have agency to claim an autochthonous modernity. Such texts, and their antecedents and descendants, demand that "non-Western" autobiography be seen not as bearing traces of premodernity or alternatively embodying postmodernity, and thus serving as the West's Other, but as engaged in a difficult and flawed process of the fashioning of modern selfhoods that are not identical to the "the unitary self of liberal humanism" posited as a central feature of "Western" modernity.[27] In the autobiographies examined in this book, we will see this process at work.

Colonial and Alternative Modernities

The references to modernity—and less frequently, modernities—that have provided the foundations for our discussion of autobiography now need further examination. Modernity in the post-Enlightenment European tradition explicated by Gusdorf and Weintraub involves a rupture with the past, a Kantian act of daring to know that enables individuals to gain rational autonomy from a world of unthinking tradition and myth. Modernity has been contested by many social theorists in the twentieth century: to Weber's "iron cage" of rationality and Foucault's vision of a disciplinary regime of power that succeeds through individual subjects' belief they are free, we might add the "subsumptive rationality" of the Frankfurt school, in which the rationality of the Enlightenment begins to cannibalize itself. Under the conditions of late modernity, Max Horkheimer and Theodor

Adorno, argue, "what men want to learn from nature is how to use it in order to wholly dominate it and other men. That is the only aim. Ruthlessly, in despite of itself, the Enlightenment has extinguished any trace of its own self-consciousness."[28] In the late twentieth century and the new millennium, there has been renewed skepticism regarding modernity's ends. Theorists such as Jean-François Lyotard or Jean Baudrillard claim that we are in a postmodern era, marked by an "obsolescence of the meta-narrative" of the Enlightenment featuring "the dialectics of Reason, the hermeneutics of meaning, the emancipation of the rational or working subject, or the creation of wealth," or "an era of simulation" marked by "a liquidation of all referentials" in which all signifiers are now permanently detached from their signifieds.[29] Other social theorists see global transformations after the Cold War as proceeding from the contradictory nature of modernity itself as an ongoing crisis, and marking an entry into what Ulrich Beck has characterized as "reflexive modernity," marked by "an unfinished and unfinishable dialectic of modernization and counter-modernization."[30] In this "fluid modernity" in which all structures built by modernizing projects are again eroded, it still seems possible to deploy elements of Enlightenment narratives strategically; the question is how one might save "the children [of orthodox narratives of modernity] from the outpouring of polluted bath-waters" of the failure of modernizing projects.[31]

While I am personally sympathetic to the latter viewpoint, I wish initially to step back from this debate and think about the various meanings of modernity within the context of nationalism in the colonial world. American historian Frederick Cooper expresses a general trend in contemporary colonial and postcolonial studies in arguing that analyses of contemporary African societies need to move beyond a simple rejection to a carefully situated critique of modernity. While metanarratives such as nationalism or development should be questioned, we also still need to study the various formations of capital and the state, and also see the "violence and oppression that lies in other social formations."[32] Thus Cooper wants to "push capital and the state back in, making them the object of an analysis more nuanced and interactive than attacks on metanarrative and modernity" (24). Cooper's insight can be readily extended to the African, Asian, and Caribbean contexts from which the autobiographies in this study emerged. Modernity is a complex and often abstract concept, simultaneously, as Cooper notes, a "condition" and a "representation," a way of being and a way of seeing the world; it needs specification and embedding within the local.[33] Yet, this in itself is not an argument for abandoning the term. Rather, we need to take what these texts say about modernity seriously, to employ it with caution as both an indigenous and an analytical concept.

Locating modernity as a site of struggle under colonialism and postcolonial nationalism has two advantages in a study such as this. First, it enables comparison between the different social contexts from which our texts emerge; it lets us draw parallels, as well as plot differences that a vocabulary only concerned to specify social particulars would not. Second, it is a contested idea in all the texts we shall study: if Gandhi famously condemned the excesses of "modern civilisation" in *Hind Swaraj,* he also praised in his autobiography the influence of Leo Tolstoy, John Ruskin, and the poet Raychandra on him as three "moderns" who had "left a deep impress on life, and captivated" him.[34] Modernity, then, was a concept important—although in very different ways—to each of the writers of autobiography in this study; for all of them, indeed, the word, and associated notions of "progress" and "development," was a key vocabulary item to express the possibilities and perils of social transformation and freedom from colonial rule. We thus need to work through, rather than sidestep, the nature of modernity under and after colonialism.

One route to thinking of the modernity of the colonized is to move beyond viewing the concept as simply a change of consciousness centered on a new understanding of subjectivity, and instead embed it within discrete material and social contexts. Modernity involves technologies—not just the physical technologies that enable a "developed economy, technological and industrial advancement" but also information technologies, which enable human beings to form new kinds of communities and have changed apprehensions of their lifeworlds.[35] Thus, Arjun Appadurai argues that modernity, as a "general break with all sorts of pasts" is enabled by new electronic technologies and migration, the latter itself an effect of developments in technologies of transportation.[36] Looking at an earlier time period, Benedict Anderson has famously argued that "print capitalism" enabled the formation of imagined national communities through the radically different concept of time that artifacts such as newspapers and popular novels engendered in their readers.[37] Here technology in the outer world matches technology in the inner world, physical technologies work in tandem with those "technologies of the self" that Michel Foucault notes "permit individuals to effect . . . a certain number of operations on their own bodies and souls, thoughts, conduct, and way of being, so as to transform themselves in order to attain a certain state of happiness, purity, wisdom, perfection, or immortality"; these technologies become central in modern society.[38] In accounts of European modernity after the Enlightenment, such technologies are often associated with the self-construction of modern subjects or selfhoods that follow individualizing scripts.

For the colonized, however, such technologies were always inextricably linked to others, which Foucault names "technologies of power," exemplified by the omnipresence of colonial rule. The printing press was frequently introduced through commercial or missionary activity, neither of which was fully consonant with the apparatus of colonial rule, but both of which were nonetheless intimately connected with colonial technologies of power. The telegraph and railway came to both India and China under the aegis of different forms of colonialism as, indeed, did the mechanized loom. We should avoid a tendency of some theoretical models to see colonialism as omnipresent and omnipotent: substantial areas of the earth's surface were never formally colonized, and the imposition of formal mechanisms of colonial rule in colonized areas such as the Kenyan Highlands or Malaysia's Cameron Highlands lasted much less than a lifetime. Each technology we have discussed might also be—and in most cases has been—appropriated by those struggling against or making temporary accommodations with colonial rule. Yet for the colonized, the experience of the technologies of colonial modernity was radically different from the modernity of Enlightenment Europe. For Weber, the primal scene of modernity was a small, self-originating decision by a "putter-out" of textiles, operating under a system that was nominally capitalist, but dominated by traditional practices and an ethos that led to a certain leisured equilibrium to life:

> Now at some time this leisureliness was suddenly destroyed, and often entirely without any essential change in the form of organization, such as the transition to a unified factory, to mechanical weaving, etc. What happened was, on the contrary, often no more than this: some young man from one of the putting-out families went out into the country, carefully chose weavers for his employ, greatly increased the rigor of his supervision of their work, and thus turned them from peasants into laborers. On the other hand, he would begin to change his marketing methods by so far as possible going directly to the final consumer, would take the details into his own hands, would personally solicit customers, visiting them every year, and above all would adapt the quality of the product directly to their needs and wishes. At the same time he began to introduce the principle of low prices and large turnover. There was repeated what everywhere and always is the result of such a process of rationalization: those who would not follow suit had to go out of business. The idyllic state collapsed under the pressure of a bitter competitive struggle, respectable fortunes were made, and not

lent out at interest, but always reinvested in the business. The old leisurely and comfortable attitude toward life gave way to a hard frugality in which some participated and came to the top, because they did
not wish to consume but to earn, while others who wished to keep on
with the old ways were forced to curtail their consumption.[39]

The colonized could tell themselves no such story about the advent of
colonial modernity; for them, such transformations might begin with the
clearing of land for a plantation, or a local agent recruiting indentured
labor, or indeed with the gradual channeling of opportunities of advancement for the comprador classes. The new imperialism of the late nineteenth century coincided with a rapid wave of technological development:
the visible signs of colonial rule were manifested through modern technologies: new buildings (sometimes subtly legitimated by architectural references to indigenous styles); gunboats; railways; factories; the telegraph;
city planning; and, most significantly for us, the various products of the
printing press.

How might the colonized begin to imagine a modernity of their own?
Indian historian Partha Chatterjee has been perhaps the most influential of
a number of scholars exploring such a question. Noting the very different
experience of modernity of colonial subjects from that of European or
North American citizen-subjects, Chatterjee has argued that analytical
concepts associated with modernity, such as nationalism, cannot be simply
transferred in a "modular" fashion from metropolitan Europe to the colonial world. In his earlier work, Chatterjee was concerned with the way nationalism rephrased and reworked "tradition" under colonialism, emerging
as "a different discourse, yet one that is dominated by another," not fully
leaving the discursive frameworks of colonialism behind.[40] In more recent
writings, Chatterjee has become more concerned with the nature of the colonial state, and the problematic legacies it leaves for postcolonial polities.
While, as we will see, Chatterjee's concepts need reformulation in contexts
outside India—the subject of all his scholarly work—they are a useful
starting point for considering the growth of modern nationalist movements in opposition to colonial rule.

Let us begin with the state first. Chatterjee's argument is that the formation of the state and citizenship in "most of the world" differs significantly from the script laid down by North American and European experience, a script that is often taken as normative. The normative "story of
citizenship" in modernity from the American and French revolutions onward moves "from the institution of civic rights in civil society to political
rights in the fully-developed nation state" and then, finally, in modern

capitalist democracy, to a depoliticized "government from the social point of view," a politics that some have felt to be post-national, or expressive of a postmodern condition.[41] We might paraphrase this and say that the notion of the autonomous individual, of the "rights of man," comes before the state: the state then offers the possibility of providing a framework for such rights through its offer of citizenship.

Chatterjee maps this story onto Foucault's concept of two poles of "power over life" manifested in modern society. The first of these is a notion we have already discussed: that of individualized "technologies of the self" through which human beings discipline themselves. The second, "formed somewhat later," is directed not toward the individual body but "the species body," in the regulatory controls imposed on population by the governmental technologies of the state.[42] This is again something we have explored as present in colonial modernity; Foucault elsewhere describes the pole as a series of "technologies of power, which determine the conduct of individuals and submit them to certain ends or domination, an objectivizing of the subject."[43] These technologies might be expressed in many ways: in the spatial organization of the colonial city, for example, or in campaigns focusing on education or hygiene.

In Foucault's narrative of European modernity, crucially, the pastoral power of the state and its attention through "bio-power" to specified populations comes after, not before, the individualized notion of citizenship. Chatterjee's key insight is to note that in Asia and Africa, however, the order in which the poles were manifested was reversed. "Governmental technologies" targeting ethnographically specified populations were first applied by a colonial state that did not recognize popular sovereignty, viewing the colonized as subjects classified into a variety of overlapping racial types, castes, or classes, not as individualized citizens.[44] In their rejection of colonialism, nationalist liberation struggles then emphasized the disciplinary pole of citizenship. However, the new national state could not evade continuing to exercise pastoral power upon populations in the service of "development." As Chatterjee notes, "caste and religion in India, ethnic groups in Southeast Asia, and tribes in Africa remained the dominant criteria for identifying populations as objects of policy."[45] The modern state could never achieve the dream of homogeneity, consisting of citizens interacting freely in civil society, but was rather subject to a "politics of heterogeneity" (22). In this politics, appeals to community and tradition did not simply represent "survivors from a pre-modern past" but were "new products of the encounter with modernity itself" (7). In this politics, the self's relation to the collective is always complex: the self is individuated, yet also a member of a community already recognized by colonial and national polities. In terms of autobiographical texts that do the work of political representation, we must therefore note that individual and collective selves are perhaps less easily separated than one might at first think.[46]

If we move from state to nation, further complexities emerge. Colonial modernity contained inherent contradictions of which colonized elites made strategic use. The new imperialism of the late nineteenth century clothed itself in Enlightenment notions of progress, of the potential equality of human beings, and thus presented itself as—at least partially—a project of uplifting and educating "subject races." Yet colonialism—in its British form, at least—constitutively refused to grant equality to those who fulfilled the very criteria it laid down: indeed, most colonial governments exhibited considerable reluctance to accord non-Europeans the status of British subjects. In the colonies, Chatterjee notes, colonialism was destined "never to fulfill the normalizing mission of the modern state because the premise of its power was a rule of colonial difference, namely, the preservation of the alienness of the ruling group."[47] If it used the rhetoric of modernity, it was, in fact, a feudal order, based ultimately on the threat of violence.

The self-fashioning of nationalist elites in the colonial world thus frequently took place within a progressive narrative of nationhood derived from a reinscribed colonial template: unlike colonial governments, they could, and would, fulfill the "normalizing mission of the modern state" (6). Central to this reinscription, Chatterjee notes, was the notion of tradition, in which the distinction between private and public characteristic of nineteenth-century thought was reworked into a new configuration of tradition and modernity. Anticolonial nationalism attempted to invent a nationhood that was not Western, and exclude the colonial state from the heart of national culture: it did this by the production and purification of a private, spiritual domain of tradition. "The greater one's success," Chatterjee notes, "in imitating Western skills in the material domain . . . , the greater the need to preserve the distinctness of one's spiritual culture" (6). This separation of spheres, we need to note in passing here, was also inescapably gendered: it reprised the Ruskinian division of public and private that formed the basis for nineteenth-century European bourgeois self-fashioning.

Colonial elites might thus claim, with some justification, that they were the true heirs of the Enlightenment, which the West had abandoned through bad faith. Indeed, they might rediscover an underlying rationality in precolonial cultures: Indian nationalism's positing India as the "original home of science," which "unlike the West, . . . had never separated science from religious life and the philosophy of daily living," or Julius Nyerere's identification of the social structure of precolonial African village life, allowing "those who sow [to] reap a fair share of what they sow," with socialism.[48] Claiming the space occupied by civil society in the West, the colonial elites created a political society that laid the ground for the postcolonial state, and claimed the authority to produce national subjects through disciplinary practices.

We can thus see that tradition, nation, citizenship, and state—each a central and yet contested category in the modern world—are inflected differently in a modernity that emerges from the experience of colonialism. Recent discussions of colonial and postcolonial polities have stressed plural modernities and the possibility of the discovery of alternative or "other" ones different from that of the post-Enlightenment West. Such modernities, Lisa Rofel notes, are "neither merely local enactments nor simply examples of a universal model" but rather are "forced cross-cultural translations of various projects of science and management" that do not necessarily converge upon the same outcome.[49] Dilip Gaonkar similarly argues that "modernity always unfolds within a specific cultural or civilizational context and that different starting points for the transition to modernity lead to different outcomes," while Simon Gikandi, writing of Jomo Kenyatta, has criticized a tendency to see colonialism as the only force that "engendered the subject's irruption into modernity."[50] Such arguments provide a useful corrective to Chatterjee's bleak assessment of nationalist thought as a "derivative discourse" that automatically leads to a Gramscian passive revolution through accepting "the very intellectual premises of 'modernity' upon which colonial domination was based."[51] Yet Chatterjee is right that these various modernities share much, and his insights regarding the nature of state formation in areas of the world that were not direct "participants in the history of evolution of the institutions of modern capitalist democracy" are crucial here.[52]

Alternative modernities, while they exhibit differences, have important structural parallels. The radical restructuring of societies and transformations undertaken by colonialism, anticolonial nationalisms, and the postcolonial state, though unevenly applied, do show important congruences, an "unavoidable dialectic of convergence and divergence."[53] My preference in this study is thus to use modernity in the singular, as most of the writers of the texts under consideration did, and to speak of the process of indigenizing modernity. Modernity was a battleground in the colonial world, in which colonized elites drew on indigenous resources, and indigenized others taken both from the colonial state and, through connections frequently forged in the colonial metropolis, from other societies struggling to emerge from colonialism.[54] Yet, it was a process in which new communities were forged or older ones were remade in reaction to the technologies of rule; it was a narrative that people told themselves and saw their lives as participating in, with its denouement always over the horizon of the future. And it was a process of transformation that, in its drawing together of narrative, technology, individual, state and new national community, national autobiography was especially equipped to tell.

Masculinity and (Post)colonial Modernity

We now turn to the third layer of our palimpsest, masculinity, which has never been entirely absent from our discussion. In describing the subject of Western modernity, Weintraub and Gusdorf are unselfconscious in their use of male pronouns; later work in autobiography studies, under the influence of feminism, has noted how this subject is implicitly masculine and, indeed, masculinist. In addition, Chatterjee's discussion of the two spheres formed by nationalist thought among the colonial elites again speaks of the construction of gender roles as a key organizing factor. Men venture forth to engage the public sphere of modernity, while women, in the home, represent the tradition that is central to the narrative of the modern nation: *Bharat Mata,* mother India, the motherland.

As Elleke Boehmer has noted, literary texts are central in dissemination of profoundly gendered nationalist imaginaries, making connections between gender roles in an idealized "modern" family and a larger national community.[55]

Much recent feminist scholarship has been concerned to critique the omission of women from accounts written by nationalist themselves, and by theorists who followed in their footsteps. Activists involved in liberation struggles, such as Frantz Fanon, Amilcar Cabral and Nelson Mandela, often pay tribute to women, but give them only subsidiary roles in anti-colonial praxis in which men are agents.[56] The same might be said of significant literary texts: in a study of African novels produced in the process of decolonization, Florence Stratton has noted that female characters are often reduced to signifiers of deeper thematic struggles: they may be deployed as personifications of tradition or as indicators of "the state of the nation," but they are seldom subjects in their own right.[57] In addition, influential critical and historical discussions of nationalism and postcolonialism, such as Benedict Anderson's notion of imagined communities, or

Homi Bhabha's dialectic of the pedagogic and performative national scripts in *Nation and Narration*, mention gender, but only in a subordinate or illustrative manner.[58]

Feminist scholarship in the last decade has thus been concerned to demonstrate the fact that anticolonial nationalism, and especially the manner in which the nation was imagined, was a gendered enterprise.[59] The gendering of the nation has many dimensions; it is both reliant on a gendered concept of space based on a "prior naturalizing of the social subordination of women and children within the domestic sphere" and on a temporal division, in which women are associated with the authentic but atavisitic body of national tradition.[60] The two faces of the Janus of nationalism are thus, in this reading, gendered: the female one looks back to the past, the male one forward to a progressive future. Other studies have explored the connection between such gendering and bourgeois self-fashioning in specific contexts. Sangeeta Ray, for example, draws on Gyanendra Pandey's argument that there were two distinct phases to Indian nationalism. The first of these, emerging in the nineteenth century, saw the nation in terms of a collection of different castes and communities, while the second, in the early twentieth century, was more aggressively rationalist and secular and opposed "communalism," aiming to create citizens whose primary loyalty transcended community. However, this new layer of nationalist thought was laid down on the sediments of the first phase, sediments in which gender had already solidified. Thus the "woman who had become synonymous with the country in the second half of the nineteenth century was specifically an upper-caste Hindu woman," and this deployment of a class- and religiously inflected symbol continued under a more secular nationalism; a site of contradiction within nationalism was marked by the figure of a woman.[61] Such accounts usefully complicate earlier typologies—such as Chatterjee's—that at times seem to present a symbolic economy that is fixed, without a theory of how change might take place.

Much feminist work on the nationalism, however, has struggled with a central paradox. Women were actively involved in anticolonial nationalist movements of various political complexions and saw them as a means toward achieving social equality.[62] Indeed, as Boehmer notes, the rhetoric of most nationalisms "specifically invites the woman as citizen to enter modernity and public space," in contrast to culturalist imaginings that relegate them to the private sphere.[63] Yet such nationalisms have also "subordinated women . . . by controlling their sexuality, mobility, the trope of motherhood, rights of citizenship and a variety of personal laws."[64] As we have seen, this subordination at one level relies on the association of women with tradition noted by Chatterjee and others: as Caren Kaplan and her fellow editors express it, the "'essential woman' . . . becomes the national iconic signifier for the material, the passive, and the corporeal, to be worshipped, protected and controlled by those with the power to remember and to forget, to guard, to define, and redefine."[65] Yet this is not the whole story: anticolonial nationalism frequently makes use of images of women's emancipation, "interpellating them as 'national' actors: . . . educators, workers and even fighters."[66] Work that merely illustrates how women are discursively trapped within nationalist self-fashioning may well be self-confirming and "depressing," and indeed Chatterjee's schema has been criticized by feminist scholars as representing an "erasure of women's agency."[67] At the same time, an attempt to distinguish between "national-liberation movements" that promote gender equality and a "bourgeois anti-colonial nationalism" that does not, while useful at an analytical level, struggles to account for the fact that gender remains inscribed in social imaginaries of all nation-states after colonialism.[68] Rajeswari Sunder Rajan has recently argued that for analysis that envisions a "more dialectical . . . relationship" between the state and women, in which it is acknowledged that conceptual categories such as "the state" and "women" are formed through "mutual engagement," even though these engagements are always infused with imbalances of power.[69]

While ongoing research into the participation of women in nationalist movements is obviously of central importance, this study might also offer a complementary dialectical investigation. Much feminist work on nationalism, Tamar Mayer notes, has not focused on men, nor considered masculinity as a constructed category.[70] Yet the state is not simply an expression of pre-formed male interests that somehow lie hidden beneath it; it is surely rather an element in the formation of certain styles of masculine self-fashioning. To explore this area, we may wish to pause and consider the nature of modern masculinities.

First, a note of caution. Different forms of "gender order," as R. W. Connell terms them, have existed in many and complex permutations in human societies, and it is important to register differences, not to read every action as converging upon a single modern template.[71] Kam Louie and Louise Edwards, for instance, have noted the presence of a dialectic of *wen* and *wu* in traditional Chinese constructions of masculinity, in which martiality needs to be balanced with scholastic contemplation, and in which "the Chinese tradition of machismo represented in terms such as *yingxiong* (hero) and *haohan* (good bloke) will be seen to be counterbalanced by a softer, cerebral male tradition that is not found to the same degree in the secular West."[72] Yet Louie and Edwards themselves note the radical transformation of this gender order in Chinese modernity, and it would be misguided to adopt a mode of analysis in which we comb representations of masculinity and femininity in national autobiographies solely for the traces of premodern gender orders that serve as others to colonial and indeed what Connell calls contemporary "globalizing masculinities."[73] We will be more interested in the manner in which masculinity—although frequently not named or consciously registered as such—becomes an object of contention and dispute in texts that aim to manufacture modern subjects.

Much work in social history and cultural studies in the last two decades has examined the emergence of modern masculinity from pre-Enlightenment gender regimes. Several broad features can be noted. If the expression of many earlier masculinities often involved excess, what George Mosse has characterized as "modern masculinity" from the late eighteenth century onward stressed discipline.[74] Clothes became more fitted and increasingly monochromatic, and there was an increasing identification of masculinity with work and with control over both the self and the external environment.[75] Herbert Sussman has described the cultural dynamics of essential maleness and manliness in the early Victorian period as paralleling a growing post-Enlightenment separation between self and world. Thus maleness was defined as "the possession of an innate, distinctively male energy" that needed to be controlled by disciplinary technologies of manliness identified with the manner in which industrial technology managed "the natural energy of water and fire."[76] Under the influence of Enlightenment thought and medical discoveries, disciplines such as physiognomy stressed the "linkage of body and soul, of morality and bodily structure."[77] In response, schooling increasingly stressed both physical and moral "hygiene," for men; the aim of such self-vigilant discipline, noted Herbert Spencer, "should be to produce a *self-governing* being; not to produce a being to be *governed by others*."[78] Modern constructions of masculinity and nationalism evolved at the same time, drew upon each other, and contributed to the growth of a "world gender order" commencing in the nineteenth century and based on a "hegemonic masculinity" stressing above all an identification "between masculinity and rationality."[79] These changes were not simply discursive: they reflected profound changes in the way men's and women's lives were lived under industrial capitalism: new relationships grew between leisure and work and between the public and the private.

Such broad brushstrokes, of course, necessitate caveats. Modern masculinities did not so much institute a complete break with past masculinities as they recycled elements of them: figures from earlier gender orders were refurbished and put to new use in modern society. Johann Joachim Winckelmann reworked classical notions of masculine beauty, while the aristocratic, feudal notion of the gentleman was resurrected and transformed to become a largely moral, and increasingly bourgeois, category. Much recent work has stressed the plural nature of masculinities, rather than a single masculinity under modernity: we should not assume that discursive constructions are uncontested or necessarily perfectly congruent with various lived realities. Modernity brought a variety of changes and transformations for men, many emancipatory, and the possibility of a number of different identities and subidentities coalescing around gender and sexuality. John D'Emilio, for instance has demonstrated that while the restructuring of lifeworlds under global capitalism from the nineteenth century onward has discursively sacralized the family; the same process has also made individuals able define an identity around homosexual desire, able to make their living by wage labor independent of the family.[80]

Colonialism was clearly also a gendered enterprise. Commentators from Edward Said onward have noted that the colonial landscape and the colonized were frequently feminized, displaying a fundamental lack with reference to masculine colonizers.[81] The situation was in reality much more complex: certain "martial" races—Zulus, Sikhs, Pathans—in fact became symbols of hypermasculinity, magnificently expressive of male energy. Conspicuous feminization and accusations of unmanliness were often reserved for those who threatened what Chatterjee describes as the "rule of colonial difference," middlemen in the colonial world, such as Eurasians, Straits Chinese, and Bengali "babus."[82] Yet in both cases the colonial production of these others was clearly central to the construction and preservation of the masculinity of the colonizer, based on the technological regulation of innately male energy. If the reality of colonizing masculinity in the late nineteenth century was often prosaic—mounds of paperwork, life in a rigidly segregated quarter of a colonial city, the "incorporation" of colonial wives to keep their husbands morally "up to the mark"—it was romanticized textually.[83] Kipling, Clifford, Haggard, and, more prosaically, G. E. Henty, John Buchan and a host of popular novelists and travel writers, wrote of the empire as a space of masculine invigoration, where an essential male energy that had degenerated in the metropolis might be recovered, and then subject more tightly to technologies of control. Richard Phillips has described nineteenth-century children's fiction in

Britain as plotting a "geography of adventure" in the colonies, which in practice "is restricted to *male* encounters—real and imaginative—with nature and the unknown"; such a space was then imaginatively contrasted to a feminized home country.[84] Such representations were omnipresent in the colonial metropolis, expressed in the various popular cultural representations of figures such as T. E. Lawrence as "Lawrence of Arabia," for example, or indeed in the presence of statues of and monuments to men of Empire in public spaces or parks.[85] All such representations were also gendered forms of narrativization, implying that the path to modernity would be forged by the actions of "great men" of empire engaged in the process of colonization.

Responses by the colonized to this gendered narrative were varied. Much literature on masculinities stresses the coercive nature of the manner in which "local gender arrangements were reshaped by conquest and sexual exploitation, imported epidemics, missionary intervention, slavery, indentured labour, migration, and resettlement."[86] Yet recent discussion of colonialism has explored the complex layers of power and privilege in colonial societies, how the technologies of indirect rule resulted in "alliances with preexisting authorities" and the formation of new comprador elites.[87] It may thus be fruitful to think of colonized elites who produced the great majority of the authors of the texts in this study as engaging in a series of transactions, reshaping and reinventing older indigenous gender orders, as well as having newer ones imposed of writing new scripts for themselves that reframed older ones.

Responses to the system of colonial masculinity from the colonized elites were often made within the discursive constraints of a modern gender order, accepting colonial criticism of the feminized status of colonized men but attributing this to the debilitating effects of colonialism itself and urging the assertion of nationalist or proto-nationalist masculinities that adopted many of the technologies of modern masculinity discussed above. Thus Max Nordau urged the adoption of new training regimes to create "new muscle-Jews [*Muskeljuden*]" who might pursue the course of Zionism. "For too long, all too long," he observed, "have we been engaged in the mortification of our own flesh. . . . Let us take up our oldest traditions; let us once more become deep-chested, sturdy, sharp-eyed men."[88] In colonial Singapore, Lim Boon Keng urged a muscular Confucianism upon young Straits Chinese men who, deprived of "the necessity of manual labour or field work" succumbed to sloth, and a concomitant physical, mental and moral "process of degeneration;" in India, a young Mohandas Gandhi, influenced by discourses of muscular Hinduism and robust Indian masculinity, experimented with eating meat, "to make me strong and daring," so that "if the whole country took to meat-eating, the English could be overcome."[89] Gandhi was to leave such carnivorous episodes behind, but his stress on asceticism as a prelude to political self-rule in *Hind Swaraj,* in which he writes that "Real Home Rule is Self Rule or self-control," still draws—although in a very different and potentially more subversive manner—on the image of an implicitly male human body subject to disciplinary control.[90]

Gandhi is, of course, an exceptional figure in terms of the manipulation of normative masculinities. Controversy continues to rage regarding the fundamental assumptions of his gender politics, yet Ashis Nandy is surely right in noting that he ultimately responded to the "hyper-masculine world view of colonialism" by shifting the terms of debate and emphasizing androgyny rather than trying to "beat the colonizers at their own game."[91] Yet Gandhi's choice here was very different from that made by most others engaged in the anticolonial struggle. "Reading many of your articles in *Young India*—your autobiography, etc.," wrote Jawaharhal Nehru to Gandhi, "I have often felt how very different my ideals were from yours."[92] We shall explore this difference further later; for now, we may just note that Gandhi, unlike Nehru, refused to participate in an inescapably gendered arena of struggle: the formation of the new nation-state.

The new nation-state and the social imaginary associated with it are the sites at which this contested modern masculinity condenses. We might here remember Chatterjee's point: the new national state distinguishes itself from the colonial state through a renewed stress on the disciplinary formation of citizens. The people will no longer be seen solely as populations (although this element of governance can never vanish) but must now enter the public sphere as self-governing beings who express popular sovereignty. Clearly the new state will establish a new gender order: it will no longer be complicit with older patriarchies made use of by colonial mechanisms of indirect rule, with the "mummified fragments" of reinvented traditions critiqued by Frantz Fanon, or content to roam what Pramoedya Ananta Toer's protagonist Minke calls "colonialism's special nature reserve."[93]

The new state thus offers very real emancipatory possibilities to women, but within certain scripts. To understand the limits it imposes, we might here return to the normative story of European and North American modernity and the manner in which gender is always already inscribed into it. The implicit contract through which the sovereign people cede power to the state is in itself gendered: in Carole Pateman's influential formulation, it involves "a change from a traditional (paternal) form of patriarchy to a new *specifically modern* (or fraternal) form: patriarchal civil society."[94] Women are not simply left behind in a Hobbesian "state of nature" that the social contract supersedes, but they enter a "civil body politic . . . fashioned after the image of the male 'individual,'" an individual predicated on the "separation of male reason from female body" (115–16). The new body politic that comes into being, Pateman notes, is inescapably gendered: a new fraternity of men "give birth to an artificial body, the body politic of civil society; they create Hobbes's 'Artificial Man, we call a Commonwealth,' or Rousseau's 'an artificial and collective body,' or the 'one Body' of Locke's 'Body Politick'" (115). Gender is thus central to ways we think about the representative politics of the nation-state itself.

The exact terms of the responses, and the elaboration of disciplinary masculinity within each national—and indeed individual—context, show great variation, as we will presently see. Yet there is perhaps one common thread that may be related to Pateman's and Chatterjee's insights. Autobiographical narratives exemplifying anticolonial and postcolonial masculinities focus closely on the male body itself. Much nineteenth- and early-twentieth-century representation of British and colonizing masculinity denies the somatic: the male body frequently becomes invisible, a center point for contemplation of a rationalized world, much as Maupassant, according to the story, used to take his lunch at the Eiffel Tower because it was the only place in Paris from which he could not see the hated structure.[95] In texts written by the colonized, the body is rarely absent: as an interface between inner and outer worlds, it bears the marks of colonization, yet its training, refurbishment, and redecoration, provide, on the smallest of scales, a vision of the possibilities that await the social space of the nation subject to parallel processes of reform. In texts written by members of the colonial elites we are often presented by a series of events that write an autobiography of the individual body as social body. First, there is a sudden registering of corporeality, a realization by a member of the elite of the impossibility of disembodiment, of evading colonial power applied directly to the body, Nehru's realization in a demonstration of "a feeling of exhilaration that I was physically strong enough to face and bear *lathi* blows."[96] Second, there is a focus on training and rigorous discipline of the body itself, the elimination forever of the "limp body and a flabby look" of the colonial subject as a metonymic representation of the construction of the new social body of the nation (76). Yet this training is never quite completed: there is always tension, a fear that the crowd, the population, the feminized energy of the nation, may overwhelm the governance of the body, the citizen, the state. If the body of the state is artificial, it must also realize something now coded as natural: tradition, the nation, those vari-ous populations that the colonial state interpellated and that now speak with their own voices.

This reinvented body may, of course, be imagined in different ways, within a constantly shifting dialectic of discipline and desire. At times, it may itself be reinfused with "traditional" energy, as in Sukarno's deft and selective use of elements of Javanese culture in his self-portrayal as a great lover of women. At others, a reinvented tradition may become discipline, as in Nkrumah's own homophobia articulated through an insistence that "in his society a man would be killed for" participating in a homosexual acts and his reimaging homosexuality as symptomatic of colonial deca-dence and decline, a trope later extended by Robert Mugabe.[97] Yet it can never quite be absent; moments of crisis in the narrative frequently return us to the corporeal.

These questions of autobiography, modernity, and gender will reappear in various forms in the analysis to follow. In conclusion, let us recall a few points. First, analysis needs to revisit the manner in which auto/biography studies have viewed "non-Western" texts and, indeed, dispense with the term "non-Western" to engage in a more situated reading practice. Read-ing the autobiographies in this study requires a strategy that avoids realiz-ing contemporary critical desire to comb the texts for traces of difference, for modes of self-fashioning that are different from an essentialized West. Equally, we should avoid a specific culturalism that maintains the incom-mensurability of each context. Rather, our practice should be to historicize the conditions of emergence of each text, to show both the commonalities and the differences of their circumstances of production in hybrid colonial and postcolonial worlds.

We have seen the importance of some of these commonalities: first, the fraught and contested nature of modernities that seek to leave colonialism behind; second, the complex manner in which the nation and, crucially, the state are imagined in a way that diverges from a European or North American script; and third, the imbrication of gender and corporeality into national social imaginaries, especially in the imagining of the complex relationship of the individual to the collective. And these commonalities demand that we start not with a fetishization of the precolonial but at the heart of the colonial state itself, with the autobiographical writings of im-perial governors and proconsuls.

2

Missing in Action

The Strange Case of Imperial Autobiography

In their recent *Reading Autobiography*, Sidonie Smith and Julia Watson provide a succinct and persuasive historiography of autobiography criticism in the last half of the twentieth century. Early approaches to the subject, Smith and Watson argue, emphasized the transparency and representativeness of individual autobiographical texts and aimed to delineate a canon of life writing. A second wave of critics and theorists were more conscious that autobiography was a matter of construction of self through narrative, rather than a simple transcription of the past; such criticism, nonetheless, was informed by "an ideology of . . . autonomous selfhood," which in turn influenced "the texts privileged and the practices of self-creation valued" by critics.[1] Now a third wave of autobiography criticism challenges "the concept of a unified, sovereign subject" that founds "Western" narratives of progress and reason. If the "unitary self of liberal humanism" still has power in a new millennium, Smith and Watson suggest, it is increasingly being challenged by non-Western narratives that resist, and that emphasize different kinds of subjectivity—performative, community-based, or flexible selves (135). This new wave of autobiography criticism, then, drawing on the apparatus of contemporary literary theory—in particular poststructuralist, postcolonial, and feminist readings—is very much in line with a concomitant expansion in practices of life writing.

Challenging some of the assumptions on which Smith and Watson's account is based will clear the ground for a discussion of an important subgenre of "non-Western" life writing.[2] Auto/biographies written in the last century outside North America, Western Europe, and the most prosperous of their former settler colonies in the twentieth and twenty-first centuries have engaged with narratives of progress and reason as much as "Western" writing has, attempting to explore the possibility of cultural autonomy within modernity. They have thus followed paths in which unitary sub-jecthood, on the one hand, and community, performativity, and hybridity, on the other, do not automatically fall into easy opposition in the manner Smith and Watson suggest. As we will see in examining national autobiog-raphies in the colonial world, "resistance" is a highly unstable category in a time of huge institutional and political change: a revolutionary autobiog-raphy that is an "out-law genre" under a colonial regime may be employed to incite a unitary subjectivity for citizens of the nation-to-be.[3] Colonial-ism, as we have previously noted, prefigures and interrogates the "global" that Smith and Watson celebrate as a contemporary and recent phenome-non: who, after all, might have a more flexible selfhood than an indentured laborer, whose identity might be more performative than that of a member of a colonial comprador class?[4] Indeed, as we shall see, Jawaharlal Nehru and Kwame Nkrumah attempt in their autobiographies to create unitary national subjects in opposition to colonialism's discredited appeal to com-munity: British manipulation of communalism in India, or its indirect rule through traditional chiefs in the Gold Coast. Selves that acknowledge community may thus not automatically be emancipatory; flexibility and performativity may at times be a matter of reluctant participation, rather than celebration.

If we go further, more wrinkles become apparent in the assumptions about the history of autobiography that underlie Smith and Watson's criti-cal historiography. The manner in which Jean-François Lyotard's "meta-narratives," to which Smith and Watson refer, come to reside in individual texts is complex: it is not simply a question of readerly realist texts mim-icking these narratives in miniature, and postmodern and other writerly texts challenging them through a series of micropractices.[5] If there is a close connection between conventional autobiography, which stresses uni-tary subjectivity, and Lyotard's Western metanarratives, then one would expect the autobiographies of imperial proconsuls—British colonial gover-nors, governors-general and viceroys—to be prototypical autobiography, occupying a nexus at which coincide many of the narratives that are now contested. In the figure of the imperial proconsul, a variety of unitary selves come together: a racialized self, a gendered male self, a rational self committed—although contradictorily—to a grand narrative of the spread of reason. Yet, no imperial proconsul produced an autobiography, and their life writing was transmuted into other genres—travel writing, testa-ments, thin fictionalizations. Closer discussion of such autobiographical efforts and failures has much to tell us about imperial and colonial moder-nities and the manner in which imperial governance was imagined. More usefully, such discussion may also lay a foundation for an understanding of the discursive conditions from which (post)colonial national autobiographies would emerge, and their relationship to new national social imaginaries and the promise of development embodied in the nation-state.

Rethinking Imperial Autobiography

The discursive association between imperialism and large cultural narratives of development and progress toward reason in the late nineteenth and early twentieth century is well documented. Intellectual justifications of colonial rule from the 1850s onward had to negotiate with the uncomfortable fact that notions of individual rights and autonomy that were fundamental to political reforms in Europe and North America in the nineteenth century did not extend to the colonies. While casual and institutional racism were common in colonial governance, theoretical elaborations of colonialism in the later nineteenth and twentieth centuries tended to eschew an absolute endorsement of racial difference for a stress on tutelage under which the colonized would move at a glacial pace toward autonomy. Frederick Lugard was candid on this point in his study *The Dual Mandate*, which formalized previous practices and in turn influenced a generation of colonial civil servants: "As Roman imperialism laid the foundations of modern civilization, and led the wild barbarians of these islands along the path to progress, so in Africa to-day we are repaying the debt, and bringing to the dark places of the earth, the abode of barbarism and cruelty, the torch of culture and progress, while ministering to the material needs of our own civilisation."[6] British colonialism in Africa might be motivated in part by a civilizing mission, but Lugard's last clause is significant—colonial rule was "for the mutual benefit of her own industrial classes, and of the native races in their progress to a higher plane" (617): if it enabled the putative development of Africa, it also crucially enabled the continued advancement of the narrative of European civilization. In Pateman's terms, fraternity might only very slowly replace the patriarchal order of colonialism, and such fraternity would not automatically be beneficial to what William Howard Taft referred to as the colonial powers' "little brown brothers."[7]

The British Empire, as many commentators have noted, was represented discursively as not only a rational space but also a masculine one. Martin Green has described the close association between the growth of Britain's empire and its representation in adventure fiction featuring a male protagonist. Robinson Crusoe's prudence, piety, and frugality is replaced in late-nineteenth-century texts with figures such as Kim O'Hara, Captain Lingard, and or Alan Quartermain, who engage in deeds of masculine self-assertion on a vanishing frontier.[8] Plotting the development of imperial fiction for boys, Joseph Bristow has examined the manner in which the feudal fantasy of "a romanticized tradition of medieval knights in shining armor, aristocratic masculinity" became domesticated through these texts as central to male bourgeois self-fashioning in the metropolis.[9] Such English masculinity was increasingly constituted in opposition to other racial masculinities, ranging from the martial Sikh to the effeminate Bengali.[10] Central to this process was the reinvention of the English gentleman from an aristocratic to a bourgeois figure, from a landed property owner to the possessor of moral qualities that distinguished late-Victorian masculinity: rationality, emotional continence, somatic control. Indeed the notion of the gentleman effectively addressed a potential crisis in late Victorian and Edwardian masculinity. Victorian masculinity was, as noted in the introduction, often represented in terms of the technological control over powerful natural forces, the fostering yet channeling for productive use of Charles Kingsley's "manly *thumos*."[11] From the late nineteenth century onward, however, the fear of degeneration brought about by increasing urbanization threatened the notion of a vital male energy. The notion of the gentleman appealed to a feudal, precapitalist "natural order" in opposition to degeneration, while at the same time the series of disciplinary techniques it incited embedded capitalism within the micropractices of individual lives.

Colonial civil servants, Anthony Kirk-Greene has recently argued, could be seen as the epitome of this Victorian and Edwardian bourgeois masculine ethos. Unlike diplomatic and military posts, positions in the Indian Civil Service and the Colonial Administrative Service did not require private wealth. They thus appealed to a generation of bourgeois gentlemen who were the products of public school: the positions attracted men whose class position came not from landed family, but emerged out of "class formation, of elitist moulding," the products "not of birth but of nurturing."[12] As Kirk-Greene notes, such an insight resonates with Peter Cain and Anthony Hopkins's notion of a "gentlemanly order" of gentleman capitalists as the motor for empire.[13] Imperial proconsuls epitomized such an order.

The so-called imperial proconsuls did not usually emerge from one of the colonial civil services. Many were politicians—frequently from landed gentry families—or military men, but they came to share the ethos of the civil services that they oversaw.[14] We will consider four prominent figures from the late nineteenth and early twentieth centuries—Cecil Rhodes,

George Nathaniel Curzon, Frederick Lugard, and Hugh Clifford—whose names are associated with areas are central to the national autobiographies that form the central element of this study: South Africa, India, West Africa, and the Malayan Peninsula. In the case of each man, we can distinguish a clear pattern to his life that is expressive of some of the central tenets of gentlemanliness within imperial development. Manly adventures on the frontier of the kind that would excite the readers of whom Kirk-Greene writes were followed by a more sedentary administrative career. While they had philosophical differences—Clifford, for instance, was much more ambivalent about large-scale capitalist colonial development than Rhodes—all four men shared a commitment to an imperial vision, an acceptance of racialist ideologies, and a deep investment in ideals of character and discipline which were central to Victorian and Edwardian notions of manliness.

Narrative Failures

As its various subsequent fictionalized and biographical representations have shown, the life of Cecil Rhodes is particularly suitable for narrativization. Rhodes perhaps represented imperialism at its most naked: in twenty brief years he rose from subsistence cotton-farming in Natal to holding the position of prime minister of Cape Colony, while simultaneously gaining control over the world diamond trade. The imperialist and industrialist's crude beliefs in racial superiority appealed to populist sentiments among European populations in Southern Africa and in Britain: of all Britain's colonial legacies, his was perhaps the most difficult to undo. His life, commencing with frontier adventure and ending not long after he overreached himself in sponsoring the Jameson Raid, would fit into the grand narratives of progressivism and the expansion of empire with which Smith and Watson implicitly associate autobiography. Additionally, his intense homosocial attachments to younger men—such as Neville Pickering, Harry Currey, and Philip Jourdan—would seem to suggest a performance of mentorship that might easily be textualized for a wider audience.[15] At the same time, Rhodes's belief in his imperial mission was matched by brooding introspection induced by an awareness of his own mortality after a heart attack when he was nineteen. His ownership and manipulation of the press in Cape Colony showed a clear appreciation of the power of print media, and he found time to write influential formulations of imperialism that drew on his own experience, most notably his much-revised *Last Will and Testament.*[16] Yet he did not write an autobiography.

Frederick Lugard, perhaps to a even greater extent than Rhodes, would seem a likely candidate for autobiographical self-representation. The imperial proconsul's early military service in India, passionate love affair, and subsequent adventures in East Africa would seem fertile material for life writing. Lugard's career was supplemented by periods in colonial administration, to his final and most prestigious posting as governor-general of Nigeria from 1914–19. The contrast between what his biographer Margery Perham called the "years of adventure" and those of authority would seem an ideal spur for the retrospective construction of Lejeune's "double subject" of autobiography, split between past protagonist and present narrator.[17] Lugard was, like Rhodes, a prolific writer and produced substantial studies, from *The Rise of Our East African Empire* in 1893 to the influential *The Dual Mandate* in 1922, that, as we have seen, embedded imperialism and colonialism within an Enlightenment narrative of progress toward reason. Married for the latter part of his career to the journalist and writer Flora Shaw, the imperial administrator was aware, again like Rhodes, of the power of print media, and in his quarter-century retirement from colonial service he continued to write voluminously on colonial affairs. Nor was Lugard lacking raw material, having kept several diaries of his expeditions in East and later West Africa in the last decade of the nineteenth century, which would have formed an ideal basis for an important section of an autobiography. He insisted, however, that his brother, Edward, burn them before the latter's death.[18] In the last years of his life the autobiographical impulse was still absent, and he spent much time fruitlessly revising *The Dual Mandate* to fit a much changed world.[19]

To the cases of Lugard and Rhodes, we can add a third failed autobiographer. George Nathaniel Curzon's life was also split between youthful deeds on the frontier and a later, more sober, political career. From 1898 to 1905, Curzon was viceroy of India, occupying the most prestigious of proconsular positions. Again, we have a published writer, already the author of travel narratives and nonnarrative reflections of empire, who feels that his life story personally embodies the narrative of imperialism. In Curzon's case, an almost religious identification with the imperial mission was enhanced by the strange coincidence that Government House in Calcutta was apparently modeled after Kedleston Hall, his ancestral seat.[20] As in the case of Lugard and Rhodes, Curzon showed the retrospective impulse common to autobiographers. Indeed, he went further than the two other imperial proconsuls in that he wrote a series of autobiographical notes, apparently for the use of a biographer, which attempt to reconstruct and reinterpret his childhood in the light of later experience.[21] Like Lugard, however, Curzon

would also need to wait for the attentions of a devoted biographer to produce a coherent narrative of his life as an act of imperial service.[22]

Of the four imperial proconsuls discussed here, Hugh Clifford perhaps
came closest to publishing an autobiography. Occupying various administrative positions in Pahang in the last years of the nineteenth century, Clifford produced several novels and collections of short stories and sketches
of Malay life.[23] He continued his writing career, albeit with a much dimin-
ished output, during postings to the Caribbean, West Africa, and Ceylon.
Letters Clifford wrote to his friend Henry Clodd from Accra when governor of the Gold Coast reveal that he embarked on an autobiography, pro-
visionally entitled *The Notebook of a Colonial Civil Servant*.[24] By late 1916,
Clifford had produced a manuscript of 90,000 words, which he asked
Clodd to comment on, while stressing, "the book is one which I should
never dream of publishing until I have retired from the Service, for from
first to last it contains too many unorthodox opinions, and too many
home-truths, about Colonial Administration."[25] By the next year, however, the governor had undergone a change of heart. His correspondence
with Clodd is unfortunately unrevealing as to motive, but by May 1917 he
had decided to abandon the work, while early the following year, in response to an inquiry from Clodd, he noted, "You ask after my note-book.
I have scrapped the *whole* of the work I did."[26]

It might, of course, be argued that the publication of any memoirs or
autobiography by public figures was unusual in late-Victorian and Edwardian England. Both Curzon and Clifford refer to the need for reticence
about political matters as a powerful brake on the impulse to produce life
writing. Among nineteenth-century British prime ministers Salisbury,
Rosebery, Gladstone, and Disraeli (despite the last's obvious literary tal-
ents) failed to publish either autobiographies or memoirs, leaving H. H.
Asquith and Arthur Balfour (posthumously) to pioneer the genre in the
third decade of the twentieth century. Yet imperial autobiographers surely
had more compelling raw material than Asquith's—epitomized by his
memoirs' title, *Fifty Years in Parliament*—on which to work, especially
given the widespread popularity of fiction with imperialist themes. And
autobiographical reticence on the part of imperial proconsuls did not end,
as that of prime ministers did, in the 1920s: it persisted until after World
War II, by which time, in a world changed by both improvements in communication technology and incipient anticolonialism, there were no real
proconsuls left.

A more detailed analysis of writings by Curzon and Clifford that have
autobiographical elements suggests another reason for the impossibility of

coherent imperial autobiography: a fundamental contradiction in the construction of the manly imperialist as subject, and indeed a series of splits among the narratives of race, gender, and rationality which Smith and Watson's schema would suggest are inseparably fused. The contradiction exists not just at the level of the individual subject but also extends to the manner in which the colonial state and colonial governance are imagined through the telling of an individual life story. Since the polities over which Curzon and Clifford governed were complex and incoherent (India was split between provinces and princely states, Malaya among the Federated Malay States, Unfederated Malay States, and the Crown Colony of the Straits Settlements) we cannot really speak here of a colonial or imperial social imaginary. Yet for a clear illustration of the contradiction, we might look first at Curzon's autobiographical writings, which can be divided between published travel writing and unpublished notebooks recounting his early life.

Curzon and the Limits of Narrative

Curzon's unpublished autobiographical notebooks consist of two different texts, both describing his childhood, and apparently written later in his life.[27] The first is a largely static, nonnarrative account of his experiences on frequent visits to London as a child and a young man in the second half of the nineteenth century; the text is retrospective and at times elegiac in tone, describing features of the metropolis that have vanished or been transformed in the narrative present. The second is a series of four fragments, one of which is titled "Note for Biography," and which describe in turn Curzon's "Baby Days," schooling with a governess, preparatory school, and experiences at Eton, the last-mentioned section being by far the longest. The manuscripts are substantial and written apparently with little effort: there are a few minor revisions, and some—presumably later—interpolations.

The notebooks, and in particular the narrative manuscript, share features with canonical nineteenth-century autobiographies of the type Gusdorf and Weintraub describe. In the latter text, Curzon the protagonist moves from being the object of other's attention and ridicule to expressing greater autonomy and individuation. Thus, the early sections of the manuscript describe teasing directed at the young Curzon on account of his abnormally large "moonface" and the various humiliations inflicted on him by his governess and at Wixenford School (4 recto). There is at times a

Rousseauesque confessionality and intimacy to these accounts, which is missing from the later descriptions of Eton: the future viceroy recalls the "horrible moment when I saw the fly and white horse drive away [from Wixenford on his first day] carrying my mother, who was dearer to me than anyone in the world" and also confesses to a "delicious feeling of warmth" spreading through the body after a spanking (22 recto, 25 verso). The account of Curzon's earlier childhood is more corporeal, concerned with embodiment, and indeed some events that focus closely on Curzon's own body and which occurred at Eton—such as continued teasing about his physical appearance—are related proleptically in this earlier part of the narrative.

In the section of the narrative concerning Eton, the body becomes less visible, Curzon stressing mental growth and the development of individual autonomy through the construction of character. Thus he describes many of his difficulties and triumphs at public school as stemming from "features or faults of character which years afterwards seem to me to stand out quite clear": a "tendency to represent myself as worse than I was," an innate rebelliousness, and a "passionate desire to win and be the first in whatever I undertook" (10 recto). Curzon's growth as an individual comes, he implies, from an ability to manage these traits in public life. And if the time of the narrative itself never goes beyond the protagonist's Eton days, there are hints that the story is working toward a denouement enacted on a much larger stage. When recollecting the sound of a master's voice, the narrator notes that it "was rather like the 'waugh-waugh' I afterward heard tigers make when wounded in the Indian jungle," while in another passage he describes a friendship at both Eton and Balliol with St. John Brodrick and its destruction years later when the latter, while overseeing the India Office from 1903 until 1905, and "to gratify a certain latent jealousy of my superior success in public life," allowed Curzon little autonomy as viceroy, precipitating his resignation (13 recto, 20 verso, 21 recto).

A further feature that makes Curzon's narrative similar to much canonical nineteenth-century autobiography is its gradual movement away from the body. As a child, Curzon as protagonist is aware of his body; indeed, the narrator shapes the narrative so that later incidents that exhibit awareness of corporeality are told in the "Baby Days" section. At Eton, however, and during most of the extended descriptions of London, the protagonist is reduced to a seeing eye for the narrator, who then explicates a growth of consciousness; there is much greater stress on the visual and little sense of embodiment. This again has parallels in nineteenth-century autobiographies that "almost completely efface the bodies in which the lives they describe were lived," reflecting cultural assumptions that opposed the masculine, rational, and artificial to the feminine, emotional, and "natural."[28] Curzon's notebooks would thus reinforce an orthodox account of the evolution of autobiography such as Smith and Watson's, but for one key fact. The former viceroy did not complete the drafts and, from all the evidence we have, twice abandoned an attempt to represent the story of his life beyond young adulthood.

To understand the Curzon's struggles with autobiography as genre, we might turn to his published works. The two volumes *Tales of Travel* and the posthumous *Leaves from a Viceroy's Notebook* are representative of his published autobiographical writings and consist of a miscellany of texts: a mixture of tales drawn from Curzon's travels in the mid-1880s and 1890s and anecdotes from his time as Viceroy of India, supplemented with more factual accounts, such as "The Great Waterfalls of the World," in which narrator and protagonist "I" are only fitfully present. Curzon's brief narratives are largely set outside Europe, and they apply a scrupulously rational narrative framework to the incidents they record. Several stories stress the exhaustive observation and then application of inductive logic to understand the world. Thus "The Voice of Memnon" is an exhaustive analysis of how one of the two Colossi of Thebes might have been capable of spontaneously generating sound. Such anecdotes as "The Death-Bed of Sir Henry Lawrence" and "The Billiard Table of Napoleon" show a narrator who notes with an almost Holmesian relish "the carelessness with which people observe, or rather fail to observe, that which is daily and even hourly under their eyes."[29] This can be overcome, Curzon as narrator argues, by "accurate observation" facilitated by "acquainting oneself, as far as possible, with the facts of a case or the features of a scene before coming in contact with it" (160). Thus Curzon as protagonist discovers through rational calculation that the plaque showing where Henry Lawrence, one of the British combatants in the 1857 Indian Revolt, died, is misplaced in the residency in Lucknow—he also tracks down Napoleon's billiard table in St. Helena through a series of sharp observations. In *Leaves from a Viceroy's Notebook,* in contrast, Curzon is contemptuous of the irrationality of Chinese monks in Fujian province who chant Sanskrit and Pali sutras transliterated into Chinese characters, manifesting "ignorant repetition of unmeaning sounds."[30] In all these narratives the ability of European men to engage in rational self-governance implicitly forms a justification for colonial or quasi-colonial governance.

Curzon's writings, however, do more than merely provide an implicit endorsement of colonial power through a binary opposition between rational occidental observer and irrational Oriental landscape. Indeed, most of their affective power is channeled elsewhere and invested in the pleasure of a recollected past of adventure and its contrast with an overly rationalized and bureaucratic present. In his introduction to *Tales of Travel,* Curzon notes, "if in rare moments I seek literary distraction, it is in the perusal of works of travel and exploration that I am certain to find it."[31] If political events cause too many difficulties, "recreation and repose come stealing in upon me from memories of the past. I am once again in the wilds of Asia, or on the mountain-tops, or amid the majestic monuments of bygone ages" (4). Elaborating on the point, Curzon pictures himself as a "middle-aged and sedentary politician" who can recall tales that "belong to a past that is quite dead, not merely by reason of the change in my own environment, but also because of the revolution in the conditions of travel, or in the state of the peoples and lands which I visited. For instance, in some countries where I rode thousands of weary miles on horseback, the traveller now proceeds rapidly and comfortably by carriage or motor, or even by train" (5, 6). The paradox here is that the death of the past in which Curzon has so much investment has been brought about by a process of "development" in which he himself has been a prominent agent. The bureaucratic rationality of the colonial state, which targets populations, contradicts with the masculine subject's desire for autonomy. Rather than running in parallel, gendered and colonial narratives here diverge and then become tangled: it is impossible to superimpose one on another with any congruence.

A further illustration of the split nature of colonialism is the brief anecdote "The 'Pig and Whistle' at Bunji," published in *Tales of Travel* in 1923, concerning a journey Curzon made thirty years previously. In an expansive opening two paragraphs, the narrator praises the "character and spirit of the young men who on the outskirts of our Indian Dominions are upholding the fabric and sustaining the prestige of the British Raj": "In the remote mountain fastnesses, amid wild tribes, far from civilisation, in a climate sometimes savagely hot, at others piercingly cold, with no comforts or luxuries, often amid cruel hardships, they face their task with unflinching and patriotic ardour, dispensing justice among alien populations, training and disciplining native forces, and setting a model of manly and uncomplaining devotion to duty, which reflects undying credit on the British name" (225). A better illustration of the manner in which Empire, nation, and masculinity work in parallel in colonial narratives would be hard to find: the discipline applied to an individual male body stands metonymically for the manner in which India is subject to imperial discipline. The narrative then narrows to a specific incident, the protagonist's visit to a small, remote bungalow in the Himalaya that, "seeking to invest this dingy meeting-place with the simulacrum of a tavern, its frequenters had christened . . . the 'Pig and Whistle'" (226). Surveying the walls of the bungalow, Curzon's protagonist notices that a series of pictures of "famous English beauties" are pinned on the walls—many of these women are known to him personally (226). The protagonist is invited to follow the custom practiced in the "hostelry" of signing his name and voting for the most beautiful: he does so, but the narrator's voice now intrudes to note that "wild horses" would not induce him to reveal his choice in the present (227).

In a more playful way, the short anecdote reveals some of the tensions that Curzon works out more explicitly in his introduction. The narrator's reticence places a hermetic seal between past and present, between the time of the events themselves and the time of their retrospective narration. The time of the incident—India in the autumn of 1894—is made mythic through Curzon's explicit, if playful, comparison of his choice of "beauties" to the choice of Paris; this is a homosocial, Homeric world where heroic masculinity is still possible. This world can, of course, be represented in the place and time of narration—metropolitan England of the 1920s—but this can only be done by an implicit contrast between the colonial frontier as a space of putatively premodern masculine freedom and the metropolis and its associated mechanisms of government as a place of restriction. It is difficult to see how such a binarism could accommodate the whole career of a colonial administrator, dedicated to colonial "development."

Clifford and Fictionalization

This element of contradiction that memory opens up in Curzon's texts can be illustrated more precisely by looking at Clifford's autobiographical fragments, particularly the short stories and sketches that arise from Clifford's early experiences in Pahang in the 1880s. Taking up a cadetship in the Protected Malay States in 1883 at the age of seventeen, Clifford initially spent three years as private secretary to Hugh Low, resident of Perak. In 1887 he was dispatched on a mission to Pahang, a state on the more remote east coast of the Malayan Peninsula, in order to begin to bring it under British influence through a treaty requiring the presence of a British agent. After a successful mission, Clifford returned to Pahang and occupied a variety of official positions, including that of resident, from 1887–99. The capital, Pekan, and the new administrative center of the state, Kuala Lipis, rapidly developed into settled colonial outposts. In the administrator's 1893 diary, it is clear that his life revolved around office work, meetings, and lawn tennis played with other members of the European community: the work of "development" was gradually replacing the frontier adventures of the late 1880s. In 1896, while on leave in England, Clifford married, and his wife accompanied him back to Pahang. At this time he also began to write and publish fiction and sketches, most of which celebrate his early experiences of the frontier, eliding the domestic present and the daily administrative round.

Clifford's series of essays and short stories, published in volumes such as *In Court and Kampong* and *Malayan Monochromes,* adopt a complex series of strategies with reference to their status as life writing. They play with the notion of an "autobiographical pact," at times acknowledging their status as autobiography, at others resorting to thin—and evidently transparent—strategies of fictionalization. Clifford's preface to his third collection, *In a Corner of Asia* (1899), uses an autobiographical "I" and stresses referentiality, noting that he has "sacrificed dramatic effects in the cause of truth" and that the descriptions "owe nothing at all to . . . imagination," embodying a "scrupulous" "fidelity to [their] models."[32] However, the stories themselves have a variety of relationships to autobiography and to Lejeune's notion of an autobiographical contract, which promises "'identity' between the names of the author, narrator, and protagonist."[33] Some stories, such as, "A Daughter of the Muhammadans," are told in the first person by a narrator whom the reader is encouraged to identify with Clifford (he is a European and a colonial officer with authority over the village headmen, is addressed as "Tuan" by the Malay villagers, and claims to know Islam better than the Malays do themselves) even if he is not explicitly named. In other stories, brief parenthetical comments [such as "so men who knew him tell me"] make readers fleetingly aware of a narrator who authorizes a text as something more than a Malay folktale: again, Clifford's autobiographical preface suggests to the reader that this narrator should be identified with the author himself.[34] Other stories, however, are presented as fiction rather than autobiography. The opening story, "At the Court of Pelesu," is presented to the readers through a third-person narrator and features a protagonist called Jack Norris; yet it is an extremely thinly fictionalized account of Clifford's initial visit to Pahang, the details of which would have been very familiar to his initial audience in the Straits Settlements.

The thinness of the fictionalization in Clifford's writings can be corroborated from two independent sources. The first of these is the series of annual reports Clifford wrote while resident of Pahang in the 1890s. These frequently describe incidents in which he is involved which will later become, substantially unchanged, the subject matter for the stories and sketches.[35] Second, while governor of Nigeria in 1924, Clifford annotated several volumes of his Malayan writings, apparently as a gift to a younger woman, Eveline Hall, with whom he had become infatuated. The annotations again clearly show the extent to which the stories are related to Clifford's own experiences and indeed his construction of himself as an imperialist. Thus the author identifies himself as the anonymous "white man who is a political agent" in "Bushwhacking," and in further annotations insists that many of his stories are "autobiographical."[36] Clifford is, of course, here making notes over thirty years after the incidents on which the stories were based occurred: we have no way of knowing the accuracy of his reflections or the extent to which they were rhetorically shaped and exaggerated to impress his correspondent. Yet what is most apparent in his comments is a continued insistence upon referentiality, of the central importance of the stories as accounts of the formation of a self which are now to be shared, with explanatory annotations, with a love object.

Clifford's writings thus confront us with a paradox. The writer's authority to narrate, established in a series of prefaces and indeed by his contemporary reputation, is based on some level on the stories' referentiality. Yet the manner of the presentation of the stories frequently evades or obscures an autobiographical contract with their readers. Rather than creating a unitary subject through a conventionally autobiographical narrative representing in a condensed fashion grand cultural narratives of race, gender, and development, then, Clifford's texts are evasive about their status as autobiography or life writing.

This reticence, and its connection to the operation of memory noted in Curzon's texts, can be best illustrated through the close reading of a single story, "At a Malayan Court." Published as "His Heart's Desire" in the author's first collection, *In Court and Kampong*, the tale seems to have been a particular favorite of Clifford's and was republished and retitled in the later collection *The Further Side of Silence* (1916). The plot is vintage Clifford, involving a framing narrative in which a white man "whose name does not matter" is invited in the dead of night to an empty fishing boat which lies beached in a Malayan river.[37] He is met by a young woman, Bedah, and a broken, degenerate man, Awang Itam, whom he has previously known as one of the most handsome of the *budak raja,* the followers of the sultan of the state. Shocked, he asks why Awang Itam has been reduced to these circumstances. In a nested narrative we now learn that Awang Itam fell in love with Iang Munah, a "temporary" concubine of the Sultan. His childhood companion and immediate chief, Saiyid Usman, at the same time caught the eye of the Sultan's daughter, Tungku Uteh. Both men carried on their love affairs simultaneously, and remained undiscovered until Tungku Uteh capriciously and clandestinely relieved the saiyid of his dagger, which she placed as a trophy in her bedroom. Unable to revenge himself immediately upon the saiyid because of the latter's noble birth, the sultan thus exacted revenge by torturing Awang Itam, before having the saiyid killed on a hunting expedition. Bedah, the woman present on the boat, is the saiyid's widow and has arranged the meeting between Awang Itam and the white man. At the end of the story, Awang Itam confesses that his torture does not matter so much to him as the knowledge that Iang Munah has again become a "temporary" concubine of the sultan.

The context in which Clifford's story was read, and indeed clues in the text itself, suggests to the reader an identification between the colonial official of the frame narrative and Clifford himself. The "white man whose name does not matter" is fluent in Malay and is well acquainted with the members of the sultan's household. Yet this association is also mediated in a complex way: at the time of writing, Clifford is recounting and fictionalizing an incident that presumably occurred a decade previously. Through his official reports, it is possible to reconstruct the discursive position he occupied when in Pahang at the time the story is set—since the "white man" is powerless to intervene in the case unfolded in the story, it is clearly set at a time soon after his arrival in the state.[38] Looking at Clifford's reports preserved in Colonial Office files does not, of course, give us access to an original story of events before the embellishment of discourse. The reports do, however, provide an insight into how a very different situation of writing results in the production of a very different sense of self, a self which cannot easily be reconciled with that of the later stories.

Contemporary accounts written by Clifford in the early years in Pahang are produced in an official context and thus stress the need for British colonization, with Clifford himself as an autobiographical actor engaged in the making of history. "No government as we shd. understand the word really exists in Pahang," Clifford wrote in an 1887 report. "There are no Courts of Justice, no Police, no Code of Laws," continued the agent, repeating stories of oppression "told to me by trustworthy Malays & Chinese" as evidence for the need for active intervention.[39] In particular, Clifford concentrates upon the sexual appetites of Malay rulers as evidence of this lack of government:

> The one offence wh. H.H.[40] cannot forgive is his followers having connection with any of the women about his palaces—H.H. sends for[?] every girl, who lives near Pekan, when she comes of age, if she is

reported to be pretty, & he then keeps her in his palaces together with his concubines—these girls are not allowed to marry, & are given nothing except their food and clothing. During the day they sometimes return to their relatives, but they are guarded all the time, & are brought back at night. The people complain bitterly of this custom, as their daughters cannot marry, [. . .] & the girls dislike it, as they may not marry, & are subjected to the most fearful tortures if they go wrong with any body—In a case of this sort the man is almost always killed. No proof is required.[41]

Here Clifford explains the issue of "temporary" concubinage, which is central to "His Heart's Desire" and, indeed, gives a general context to the story. The relationship between narratives of masculinity and imperialism here seems quite clear. Sultan Ahmad's failings as a ruler are similar to his failings as a man: both arise from a lack of restraint. In terms of manliness, Ahmad does not show the control of natural forces so crucial to Victorian masculinity; in terms of governance, his state has no legal apparatus to restrain despotism and the abuse of power. Only the intervention of a new, rational order can thus bring Pahang into the modern world. It is significant that when, a few years later, Clifford writes of improvements in Pahang, he again illustrates his account with a discussion of masculine morality. "At the present time," Clifford writes in his 1893 report, "the rights of the peasant are fully recognised. His wives and children, his land, and the fruits of his labour are at length really his own, and the knowledge that this is so has bred a spirit of independence in him which quells the dread of his superiors which formerly caused him to suffer in silence."[42] Pahang has rejoined a narrative of progress toward modernity, with sturdy yeoman peasants, now resisting the excesses of feudal rule. Significantly, Clifford's idealized peasants now resemble more the Victorian bourgeois family, secure in its ownership of property and with women occupying the private sphere, than their counterparts in early modern England.

Clifford's early reports exemplify in embryo what Johannes Fabian has called "allochronic discourse," a splitting of temporality in representation in which the anthropological subject of the text is placed in "another Time" from that of the narrator and the observer and so made amenable to analysis.[43] Pahang is repeatedly compared to medieval Europe, while Clifford himself occupies modern, progressive time. Yet it is important to emphasize that this split is only embryonic: unlike the anthropological texts and, more recently, travelogues that Fabian has discussed, the split is not—or at best is only marginally—embedded within the structure of the narrative itself. There is as yet little narrational retrospection in these stories, which proceed from the present moment. Clifford's "At a Malayan Court," however, written a decade later, is clearly different. Here the framing narrative imposes a clear temporal distinction between the world of the "white man" and that of the Malay Court: the affective power of narrated events is contrasted with the cool detachment of the time of their narration, just as "native fashion" is distinguished from "white men's methods."[44] Indeed, the transparent pretence of the protagonist's anonymity and the coy transformation of the narrative into a short story featuring third-person narration serve to enhance this effect. The story acquires an exemplary meaning beyond its immediate environment, the narrator noting that "where and when these things happened does not signify at all," just as readers are exhorted to "have no concern" about the identity of the protagonists (299). The story here acquires the representativeness that Smith and Watson note as central to the judgment of "second-wave" auto/biography theorists. Such a quality enables Clifford's story to exemplify a larger narrative in which empire, reason, and masculine detachment run as parallel threads; yet, paradoxically, the narrative gains representativeness not by remaining autobiography but by becoming fiction.

Closer examination raises other paradoxes. The discussion above represents only a partial reading of the story. For if the frame narrative introduces separation between "white man" and Malay protagonist, other elements of the text hint at what they share—the "heart's desire" of the title is not only Awang Itam's desire for his lover but the white man's desire to be a Malay man. Awang Itam, in his memory, has been a "fine, clean-limbed, upstanding youngster, dressed wonderfully in an extravagantly peaked kerchief and brilliant garments of many-coloured silks"; he has lived in a world of martial homosociality, under a "code of honour" that cannot refuse any "challenge to his manhood" (303, 310). Awang Itam thus represents a spectacle of medieval chivalry which the gentleman-administrator white man identifies—he, too has an "appetite for adventure," and yet his function here is merely to provide an audience to the tale. While Clifford's text is circumspect, it is clear to a reader familiar with his works that Awang Itam's mutilation involves castration. Saiyid Usman, we might remember, is robbed of his phallic dagger by Tunku Uteh, which is then placed upon a "tall erection of ornamental pillows" (314). When the nameless white man first sees Awang Itam, he is disgusted at his "air of abject degradation" and the "humiliation of its broken manhood"—the absence of a personal pronoun in the second clause indicating that Awag Itam is now not a man, but an "object" (302, 303). When Awang Itam describes the "nameless tortures" inflicted on him to "wreck his manhood," his listener begins "writhing in sympathetic agony, . . . assailed by a feeling of horror so violent that it turned him sick" (318). Here we have a moment of identification by two men separated only by temporality. Clifford presents the saiyid's death on the hunting expedition as heroic, as he stood on the sandbank defying the sultan's men: in reply to Awang Itam's account of his mutilation, however, the white man replies that it would be "better far to die than to endure such excruciating pains, and thereafter to live the life which is no life" (318). The contrast between the two men's fates seems to thus represent, in a condensed fashion, the contrast between the time of narration and the time of writing, between heroic deeds of adventure on the frontier and the sedentary, deskbound life of a colonial administrator, between a past "wild life" and the present reality of dealing with "vast piles of official correspondence," which Clifford would later describe as "working in chains."[45]

Clifford's published texts, thus, like Curzon's, give even as they take away. Even as on one level they introduce a structuring series of binarisms—rationality/irrationality, masculinity/unmanliness, white man/native—at another level the affective response produced by the text tends to break this down. Colonial discourse is here marked by "ambivalence," to use Homi Bhabha's phrase, but it is not so much a universalized psychic condition as a product of particular historical contradictions.[46] Colonialism described itself as a modern form of power, as a kind of Foucauldian "governmentality" in which individual colonial subjects might be incited toward rational self-development, but in the last resort, as Ranajit Guha notes, it was a premodern form of power based on the threat of violence expressed through "the coercive apparatus of the state."[47] Colonialism pictured itself, in Lugard's terms, as "bringing to the dark places of the earth, the abode of barbarism and cruelty, the torch of culture and progress," yet in fact, through selective adaptation, set about manufacturing "barbarous" indigenous traditions on an unprecedented scale.[48] It claimed a tutelary function, yet its inherent "rule of colonial difference" made it despise the products of that tutelage and deny them advancement.[49] Clifford and Curzon, then, have a profound emotional investment in and identification with imagined properties of the societies that they are committed to "develop" and thus destroy.

Conclusion

From these circumstances, the contradictory nature, and thus the impossibility of imperial autobiography emerges. We have noted Weintraub's

notion of autobiography as "centered upon an aware self aware of its relation to its experiences" and the world, as well as Gusdorf's celebration of
autobiography as made possible only by historical consciousness, a genre
in which "the artist and the model coincide, the historian tackles himself as
object."[50] We have also seen how Watson and Smith, and many other contemporary scholars of autobiography studies do not so much directly rebut
second-wave assertions as place them in a larger framework in which their
celebratory culturalist rhetoric is questioned. The individual whose arrival
Gusdorf and Weintraub celebrate is seen as raced, gendered, and the product of a specific moment of modernity.

Yet for imperial autobiography the individual's relationship to "history" and "historical consciousness" is not unproblematic. Colonial texts
may, as Fabian suggests of anthropology, attempt representation of the colonized by denying "coevalness," by placing the observer in progressive
time and the observed in the cyclical time of the past.[51] In the examples
here, the observer and the observed are in effect the same individual, Gusdorf's "artist and the model," occupying different, incommensurable times.
The manly adventurer identifies with an imagined precolonial culture,
while the imperial administrator imposes the strictures of "development"
on this culture: these two positions cannot be reconciled within a narrative
of individual development and growth, and a coherent life narrative becomes impossible to sustain. What emerges in imperial life writing is a series of texts that individually may seem to be readerly, to observe realist
conventions, but collectively form a series of mutually contradictory fragments drawing on a variety of fictional and nonfictional genres, with no
central explicatory narrative. As a whole, then, each of these efforts by imperial proconsuls to represent their lives begins to look remarkably writerly, postmodern: there is in fact no coherent narrational principle to hold
the life together.

These features of imperial autobiography are not merely representative
of discursive ambivalence visible only to the eyes of a twenty-first-century
literary critic or theorist: they were features of life writing that the colonized exploited.[52] Joseph Ephraim Casely Hayford's *Ethiopia Unbound*
thus explodes the genre of autobiography, fundamentally challenging the
division between premodern and modern time through its intercutting of
past, present, future and a mythic time that is coeval with, not prior to,
the present. Mohandas K. Gandhi, taking a different tack, refuses homologies between male energy and primitivity, and masculinity and modernity. Later anticolonial autobiographers, possessed with a vision—or indeed the reality—of a postcolonial state, could appropriate the project of

modernity: Nehru and Nkrumah were able to write autobiographies that aligned an individual life with the grand narrative of the nation about to be born. In these narratives the crooked is made straight, the past reclaimed as part of a narrative interrupted by colonialism. The individual's story of personal growth is "a remarkable personal fusion of what was initially given, what his world brings to him, what he selects from this, how he builds this into his makeup, and how he in turn affects the world."[53] In national autobiographies experiences in the colonial world take Nkrumah and Nehru back to a reflection upon and reinterpretation of an "initially given" cultural past, and thus inspire action in a world through the liberation of the nation. Nkrumah's autobiography is thus titled *Ghana;* while trying "to trace . . . [his] own mental development," Nehru discovered he had produced "a survey of recent Indian history."[54]

If imperial autobiography teaches us something about imperialism and colonialism, then, it may enable us to unlearn something about the critical study of autobiography. In particular, we might be more cautious about an uncritical mapping of the smaller narratives constituted by individual examples of life writing onto Lyotard's grand narratives, and to an invocation of "non-Western" narratives as either resisting modern grand narratives or subverting them. First, Western modernity—and particularly the history of colonialism, central to the production of the modern West—is itself flawed and contradictory. We cannot look to the "non-West" only as a source of premodern or nominally postmodern critiques of the West: we need to respect and explore "non-Western" narratives of modernity on their own terms. Indeed, popular biographical writing on the shelves of bookstores in contemporary Accra, Delhi, or Singapore seems as much, if not more, modern, expressive of "governing . . . configurations and disciplines of selfhood" as that sold in New York or London: if many of these exemplary narratives are in fact Western—biographies and autobiographies of politicians and captains of industry—the configurations and disciplines they promote are embedded in various local productions of modernity that have a degree of autonomy from those of the West.[55]

Second, we might recognize that unitary selfhood is not only a feature of Western autobiography; nor is autobiography, even in the narrow canon Weintraub and Gusdorf explore, unconcerned with community and the community-defined nature of the self. Indeed, autobiography, John Sturrock notes in a study of canonical autobiographies, is perhaps best seen as a series of negotiations between "apartness" and "association": in its invitation to readers to share in a life, it is perhaps "the most sociable of literary acts."[56] In the nation emerging from colonialism, there can be no simple opposition between individual and community. Communities within the nation—populations interpellated or solidified by the ethnographic colonial state—cannot be ignored by the new nation-state, no matter how much its leaders may wish to erase their boundaries. Representative individuals may stand for a new national community, while the nation-state itself, as we have seen, is often metaphorically represented as a sovereign individual now enabled to act with autonomy on an international stage.

This insight into autobiography as a space of negotiation between individual and community may also cause us to rethink critical-reading strategies, and here we may usefully employ recent insights in autobiography studies, particularly those arising from feminism. In a pathbreaking essay in 1994, Nancy Miller argued that many feminist insights into women's autobiographies could also illuminate those written by men. Feminist critics of the 1980s, Miller noted, stressed that women's autobiography was different from men's because self-representation in the former occurred in relation to others, communities, not in terms of an isolated individual.[57] While maintaining that there were clear differences between men's writing and women's, Miller emphasized that insights regarding the relational formation of the self could be applied to men's autobiographies too and that reading practices inspired by these insights would give new perspectives on canonical autobiographies. Paul John Eakin has more recently taken up and amplified this point in his influential argument that "we are . . . relational selves leading relational lives" and his reading of a variety of autobiographies written by men and women in this light.[58] Inspired by the constitutive contradictions of imperial autobiography, we can perhaps aim for a similar insight into national autobiographies in the postcolonial world that may seem at first to replicate the strategies and structures of canonical autobiography. First, however, we need to look in the next chapter at a series of interstitial narratives that occupy ground between the ruins of imperial autobiography and the monuments of new national autobiographies, works that emerge from the colonial world and engage colonialism in situ. As with all interstitial narratives, they are polyglossic, hybrid, uneven texts. They have much to teach us about the recovery of self from colonialism, and they will constitute the subject matter of the next chapter.

3

Absent States

Casely Hayford, Gandhi, Garvey

I am not writing the autobiography to please critics. Writing it is itself one of the experiments with truth.

Gandhi, *An Autobiography*

This chapter examines three transitional autobiographies in the colonial world, written from 1910 to the early part of the 1930s, well before the era of decolonization. The autobiographies of Joseph Ephraim Casely Hayford, Mohandas K. Gandhi, and Marcus Garvey are very different from each other and can by no means be brought together under the rubric of shared generic conventions. Yet they each respond to both the discursive contradictions of colonial autobiography discussed in the last chapter and to the complexities of the colonial lifeworld: they insert themselves at key points in various narratives and open up spaces of exploration and contradiction.

The specific locations of these texts will be of ongoing relevance to this study. The setting of Casely Hayford's *Ethiopia Unbound,* West Africa, provides a useful connection back to Lugard. More profoundly, the text's shuttling between the colonial Gold Coast and the imperial metropolis foreshadows a similar movement in the autobiography of Kwame Nkrumah. Despite his exceptionality, Gandhi's engagement with the idea of India in his autobiography allows us to make a generational—if not philosophical—link between Curzon and Nehru. Garvey's text's territory is very different, triangulating Jamaica, the United States, and the United Kingdom, but his concern with diasporic networks and the circulation of capital foreshadows a subterranean element of the autobiography of Nelson Mandela that comes to light more explicitly in Lee Kuan Yew's *Singapore Story.* We also here see the beginnings of an interpersonal and intertextual network that would tighten in the later texts. Casely Hayford was acquainted with Clifford; Gandhi uses his experience of Curzon's durbar as a touchstone to meditate on the pomp of empire as a spectacle of degraded masculinity—"Maharajahs bedecked like women," their elaborate costumes "insignia not of their royalty, but of their slavery"; Garvey's text—not without some hubris—will make parallels between his life and that of Gandhi.[1]

The narratives are further united by a concern with textuality. Each of their writers learned from young adulthood, as Nehru, Nkrumah, Mandela, and Lee would do later, the profound connections between various narrative and nonnarrative texts and imperialism. Like the majority of writers in this study, Gandhi and Casely Hayford trained as lawyers, and indeed much of their early activism was as legal professionals concerned to demonstrate how far social and political colonial governmental practice did not live up to legislated British principle. In so doing, they also emphasized the right of colonial subjects to be treated as full, autonomous individuals—as British subjects fully protected by the law. They did so by preparing legal briefs and representing clients but also, increasingly, by writing books and pamphlets and developing other strategies to mold and, indeed, at times create public opinion. For both, the modernity they sought to engage with needed to be narrated, brought into being through written and spoken narratives. Garvey's path was slightly different, moving through apprenticeship and employment in printing to labor organization in Kingston, but his writings continually attach his own political project to a variety of other master narratives: nationalism, Zionism, Ethiopianism, Messianic Christianity, and the progress of capitalism.

Gandhi and Casely Hayford's lives are easily—although certainly not unproblematically—recuperated within Indian and Ghanaian nationalism respectively: after a period of exile, each returned to the country of his birth and participated in a widening of public space and a critique of colonialism that prepared the ground for—and in the case of Gandhi, realized—national independence. Garvey's life story is much less easy to narrativize in this way. It is the story of a failed nationalism, of successive exiles, a tragedy rather than a romance. And for Garvey perhaps the greatest irony might be that he was claimed by Jamaican nationalism in 1964, his remains reburied in the Marcus Garvey Memorial in Kingston: he and, indeed, Gandhi and Casely Hayford—through his founding of the National Conference of British West Africa—had participated in projects that emphasized much wider social and political changes than simply the formation of a nation-state in each postcolony.

Writing before the achievement of independence and at a point where national movements were either nascent or not yet fully fledged, these writers have deferred relationships to the nation-states that will be the central objects of attention for their successors. Their narratives of self-making thus take very different turns, as they sought to create new selves in a world marked by colonialism. Casely Hayford resorts to nonrealist techniques, and, crucially, interrupts and reinscribes the elaborate stratification of time, the allochronism that we have seen is so tortured a feature of colonial texts such as Clifford's and Curzon's writings. Gandhi, in a very different narrative, which is much closer—despite its initial protestations to the contrary—to classical nineteenth-century autobiography, writes an autobiography that refuses homologies between masculinity, modernity, and the state. Yet he produces other technologies of the self that, particularly in their stress on public and private hygiene and bodily governance, look both back to colonial governmentality and forward to the disciplinary mechanisms of national autobiographies to come. Finally, Garvey's "Autobiography," like Gandhi's, initially published as a series of articles, attempts, as one might expect, to produce a Horatio Alger–style narrative of self-help through frugality and devotion to work that is transformed into an oppositional narrative through racialization. If the first few pages of the autobiography begin in this manner, however, they are quickly superseded by a relational narrative in which Garvey exposes the weaknesses of other male characters as a strategy to defend the integrity of an increasingly besieged protagonist. Garvey's text, through its failure as a narrative, will thus provide an important opportunity to amplify the notion of relationality, introduced in the previous chapter, which is a marked feature of the national autobiographies that will follow.

Casely Hayford: *Ethiopia Unbound*

The inclusion of Casely Hayford's *Ethiopia Unbound* in a study of autobiography and decolonization needs some preliminary contextualization. Published in London in 1911 and set largely in the Gold Coast in the early twentieth century, *Ethiopia Unbound* is usually discussed as one of the first African novels in English, rather than as an example of life writing. The text makes no pretense to present itself as autobiography in a normative sense, as "a retrospective prose narrative produced by a real person concerning his own existence," and indeed has been considered an "autobiographical novel" rather than autobiography.[2] Casely Hayford's narrative follows, albeit in a nonlinear manner, its protagonist Kwamankra through his experiences in a proto-nationalist struggle in the Gold Coast, and its setting moves between London, America, the Gold Coast, and a parallel spirit world. Yet despite the fictionalized presentation of the text it clearly constitutes a form of life writing; connections between Casely Hayford and Kwamankra are undeniable, and would have been very apparent to a contemporary reading public. Like Casely Hayford himself, Kwamankra comes from an elite Gold Coast family whose ancestors were received into the Methodist church and baptized with the name Hayford, has edited a Gold Coast newspaper, studied in Cambridge and qualified as a barrister in London, lost a wife in childbirth, and returned to the Gold Coast to work for "race emancipation."[3]

Ethiopia Unbound merits consideration here for two reasons. First, as much current research has shown, literary writing in English in Africa and elsewhere under colonialism emerged in a variety of hybrid or paraliterary forms—journalism, pamphlets, missionary-inspired exemplary biographies, and autobiographies.[4] To insist on purity of genre here may thus cause us to lose sight of texts like *Ethiopia Unbound* that occupy key places within their own colonial discursive fields: attention to them, in contrast, may enable us to see life writing in the process of being made in a colonial world. Second, the presentation of life writing as a third-person fictional narrative here has a tactical function: it enables Casely Hayford's protagonist to become a prototypical nationalist hero, merging individual biographies into collective life writing. Some of Kwamankra's later speeches, for instance, are peppered with extensive quotations from the Pan-Africanist pioneer Edward Wilmot Blyden. Given the wider scope offered by a fictional narrative, *Ethiopia Unbound* ends in an imagined denouement in which a mutually beneficial "truce" has been established between black and white races, with the black races having "learnt to run along their own natural lines of development," achieving an indigenous modernity different from that of Europe (208). It thus perhaps represents not so much the story of a life lived as the fulfillment of the best possible life available to its author, and the space provided by its presentation as fiction, rather than as autobiography, enables this gesture.

Casely Hayford's "autobiographical novel" is thus, as are all the texts discussed in this book, the product of a particular series of historical circumstances. *Ethiopia Unbound* emerges from the world of the Gold Coast elites in the early twentieth century, where educated Africans in a growing para-colonial public sphere found themselves increasing drawn into confrontation with the unitary colonial state that replaced previous informal arrangements of rule.[5] Rising nationalist consciousness—although ideas concerning the extent and inclusiveness of the nation were hotly contested—confronted more exclusionary colonial governance, again sharply illustrating Chatterjee's rule of colonial difference. The "men of light and leading both in America and Europe," as Kwamankra caustically comments early in the text, governed a colonial state that was constitutively unable to fulfill Enlightenment principles, and this failure in turn led to colonial hostility against the Gold Coast African elites who demanded greater representation (1). "With the best of intentions," noted a 1909 editorial in the *African Mail,* "we are repeating in Western Africa the disastrous mistake pursued during the past thirty years in India, of Westernising the native races. We are busy manufacturing black and brown Englishmen—turning them out by the score, and cursing the finished article when the operation is complete."[6] Edmund Morel's perception of the contradiction of colonial rule (even if couched in nostalgia for Orientalism in the nineteenth-century Anglo-Indian sense) illustrates the complex manner in which identity and power are imbricated. If Casely Hayford's world is a world of hybridity, then, it is one in which such hybridity is contested, rather than unproblematically celebrated. The act of imagining a nation aims to construct and reclaim identity, even though the nation-state itself is still beyond the immediate political horizon.

Ethiopia Unbound seems on first inspection to be very different from the classical autobiographies of the nineteenth century: it is closer in form at least to a late-twentieth-century postmodern or postcolonial novel, to Ben Okri's *The Famished Road,* for instance, or indeed Salman Rushdie's *Midnight's Children,* although it is certainly less playful than most postmodern works. The text is linguistically hybrid: it is attributed to "Casely Hayford (Ekra-Agiman)," contains attempts to both to transliterate Fante and represent the sounds of Gold Coast English, and is accompanied by a glossary of Fante words and phrases. Such hybridity extends to structure. The narrative is fragmentary and at times recursive, eschewing the austerely realist progression of classical autobiography, Virginia Woolf's "series of gig lamps symmetrically arranged."[7] Yet it is not modernist in the manner of Woolf's predecessors and Casely Hayford's contemporaries such as Conrad. We have no literary impressionism, elaborately orchestrated diegetic levels, or "delayed decoding" and the text does not seem, as is much early European modernist writing, ultimately skeptical of the possibilities of modernity itself.[8] The narrative's fragmentation seems, if anything, more eclectic than that of high modernism: individual episodes range in form from Socratic dialogues, domestic incidents which verge on melodrama, acutely observed scenes dramatizing colonial racial prejudice that observe the conventions of realism, and visits to a parallel spirit world described in a mythic style that draws on Homer, Dante, and Bunyan.

In contrast to the colonial writings that preceded it, and like the national autobiographies that would succeed it, *Ethiopia Unbound* explores the personal transformation necessary to claim an indigenized modernity. In Kwamankra, its author attempts to produce a figure of an "Ethiopian gentleman" whose status as "the scion of a spiritual sphere" enables him to realize a true modernity abandoned by "Western nations [that] . . . have exhausted their energy" in the pursuit of material gains (2). Casely Hayford thus seeks to embed models of heroic masculinity within a modern African present. The text continually appeals to contemporary and past masculine models. When we are introduced to Kwamankra, the narrator notes that "three continents were ringing with the names of men like Du Bois, Booker T. Washington, Blyden . . . and others;" Christ and Buddha as exemplars of manliness mix with historical figures such as Toussaint L'Ouverture and Marcus Aurelius, fictional characters such as Hamlet, and deities such as "the Father of all, call him *Nyiakropon, Zeus, Ra, Jupiter*" (2, 41) Thinking again of Carole Pateman's formulation, we might see Casely Hayford as attempting to reform patriarchy and introduce a modified fraternity: to produce a modern reformulation of "tradition" in which the mythic penetrates the everyday. Space is gendered in the text; most public discussions are between men, with conversations with women taking place either within the confines of the home or in the parallel spirit world. Paternal transmission of values is stressed, especially in Kwamankra's educational activities and in his didactic discussions as "paterfamilias" with his "precocious" son Ekra Kwow, and he frequently gives advice to other African men, drawing them as junior brothers into a modern fraternity (199).

In contrast, European men such as Kwamankra's friend in London, Whitely, are shown to be weak, lacking in intellectual and moral autonomy, and thus unable to resist the transformative pressure of the colonial state. In London, Whitely is morally and intellectually shallow but courteous to his African friend. When he initially comes to the Gold Coast he is disturbed by the inequalities of colonialism, noting in conversation with another European "how spoilt you Colonials are!" and asking sharp questions about the colonial order of things. After "a few months of coast life" he has fewer questions, allowing Africans with better education than him to do most of his work for him, but disdaining social contact with them (81). At times, Kwamankra's advocacy of African masculine discipline through contrast with such a fallen European masculinity takes on a messianic quality. "If my people are to be saved from national and racial death," he notes at one point, "they must be proved as if by fire—by the practice of a virile religion, not by following emasculated sentimentalities which men shamelessly and slanderously identify with the holy One of God, His son, Jesus Christ" (75).

Casely Hayford's reformed male subject exists in modern time. The many non-realist elements of Casely Hayford's text have received some critical attention, but a neglected aspect of the text that responds most explicitly to the discursive context of the book is its manipulation of time and concomitant appropriation of modernity.[9] Colonial texts, we have noted, following Fabian, frequently indulge in allochronism, a denial of coevalness between the mythic time of indigenous cultures (and of early colonial contact) and the progressive time of the West (and by extension, of colonial administration): this makes the process of life writing fraught for a colonial administrator who must simultaneously identify with and disavow indigenous cultures in the colony. In Casely Hayford's text, there is no such temporal division. *Ethiopia Unbound* begins in medias res, at "the dawn of the twentieth century" accompanied by the anticipation of a renaissance for "the black man" enabled, in its first stages, by the departure to the "universities of Europe and America" of "the sons of Ethiopia in quest of the golden tree of knowledge" (1, 3). The focus then narrows to London, and a dialogue between Kwamankra and Whitely. We will, as the narrative progresses, go back to recall Kwamankra's past and also move forward, to see how Whitely and Kwamankra's relationship is transformed in the colony itself and the eventual success of the latter's protonationalist project. Time here is more flexible and allows the expression of agency: we do not merely have Curzon's and Clifford's elegiac analepses into a now-lost mythic time. If Curzon's and Clifford's protagonists are prisoners of modern, progressive time, drawn, like Walter Benjamin's reading of Paul Klee's angel, inexorably forward while still gazing at the rubble of the colonial modernity they have created, Kwamankra looks forward, enabled and given agency by a historical process he claims as his own.

The process of reclaiming of agency through time explains an element of the book that many readers have found unsatisfactory, the interruption of fictional narrative by long passages of direct exposition on various topics relating to race and colonialism. As often as the text narrows to a narrative exemplum of a particular point, as it does in chapter 1, it also pulls back to make a larger comparison. A character interacting with another may give a two- or three-page speech on a particular topic, after which a didactic point has been made, but narrative momentum has been lost. Yet this continual

movement from abstract to concrete and back serves a particular purpose—
it emphasizes the place of the small individual part within a larger whole.
In a sense, it duplicates on a global scale the "simultaneity" across time,
"marked not by prefiguring and fulfilment, but by temporal coincidence,
and measured by clock and calendar" that Benedict Anderson sees as a distinctive feature of such cultural artifacts as the newspaper or the novel.[10] In
Anderson's analysis, of course, such a changed temporality is central to the
formation of the nation: for Casely Hayford, writing before the nation,
and indeed still seeking a "degree of free and democratic life, which will
enable us to develop according to the genius of our race within a free
United British Empire," this simultaneity has a different function.[11] Kwamankra's struggles are seen as part of a larger, progressive movement of
history that is global and irreversible. In particular, in a prefiguration of
the Afro-Asian solidarity movement of the 1950s and 1960s, late Meiji-era
Japan, fresh from its 1905 victory over Russia at Tsushima Strait, is put forward as an example of the possibilities that lie ahead for Africa. Through
his use of Ethiopianism, Casely Hayford draws Africans and Japanese together through a subtle emphasis on the "Oriental" aspects of Kwamankra's behavior. "While a student in London," the author writes of his protagonist, "a thrill of Oriental pride used to run through the writer when he
brushed against an Asiatic in a garb distinctively Eastern. They aped no
one. They were content to remain Eastern" (172). Japan's ability to achieve
modernity while maintaining a distinctly Japanese language, dress, "the institutions and customs of . . . ancestors, and . . . an intelligent past" are
both a model for Africans, and signs of a movement in world history that
will favor Africa (170). And the requirements of modernizing movements
rephrasing tradition such as Bushido that "disciples . . . submit to a strict
physical and mental discipline" provide a possible model for the constitution of modern African subjects (75).

The phrase "intelligent past" also reveals the second element of *Ethiopia Unbound*'s reclamation of time. In Casely Hayford's text, mythic time
is not relegated to the premodern or prehistoric: it is not mourned as an in-
accessible golden age but exists in parallel with the progressive time of the
present. Early in the book, Kwamankra, under the influence of anesthesia,
enters "another sphere" of existence, visiting a parallel world in which his
deceased wife, Mansa, has now become a deity, living with a daughter who
died in infancy (44). Her words give him courage to continue his struggle
in the "work-a-day world" (64). The description of the city where Mansa
lives, "surrounded by a great lake whose water was as clear as crystal,"
draws heavily on Bunyan's *Pilgrim's Progress* and other canonical European

texts: this mythical time, then, unlike its representation in Curzon and Clifford's writing, is thus not simply the time of the colonized (44). To further emphasize this point, Casely Hayford's most lengthy explications of Fante culture occur in the narrative present. The form of a Socratic dialogue is used, Kwamakra, for instance, instructing a reluctant and spiritually confused Whitely in the intricacies of Fante theology and philosophy. Whitely's theological difficulties, Kwamankra suggests, may be "due to the limitations of your language" (8) The West is "drifting, drifting, drifting away from the ancient moorings that you Westerners built in sand," and African cultures may well now have their place in the sun (8–9). In chapter 10 Kwamankra, talking to his son, discusses the similarities between Fante culture and the various cultures of ancient Greece; the implication again is that Europe has fallen away from the purity of the civilization it takes as its model, whereas African social practices parallel Hellenic ones. Drawing on nineteenth-century and earlier European appropriations of Greece as a precursor to European modernity, Casely Hayford thus claims modernity as African—the "anatomically perfect" Greek sculptural ideal of male beauty expressed by Winckelmann is now realized in an African body (2).

Casely Hayford's manipulation of realist and colonial conventions of time remains one of the most powerful elements of *Ethiopia Unbound* and is matched, as we have seen, by the placement of a modern African protagonist at the center of the narrative, a man who has the autonomy to become Gusdorf's "historian of himself."[12] In a speech given not long after the publication of *Ethiopia Unbound* to welcome the new governor of the Gold Coast—the very Hugh Clifford whose Malayan short stories we examined in the previous chapter—Casely Hayford stressed the importance of modern subject-formation. The people of the Gold Coast, he noted, could not remain "for ever hewers of wood and drawers of water": future colonial governments should inculcate the values of citizenship, "so that the people of this country may take their true place as citizens of the British Empire."[13] Yet in taking on the discourse of citizenship, Casely Hayford still struggled to articulate a position in a discourse that was not his own: "the Ethiopian gentleman" was perhaps an oxymoron, in that African identities, taken seriously, themselves challenged normative discourses of respectable sexuality in which Casely Hayford himself had invested so much. The fault lines of contradiction in Casely Hayford's text are nowhere clearer than in its representation of interpersonal relationships between men and women.

In the middle of *Ethiopia Unbound*, Kwamankra engages in a discussion regarding marriage with Tom Palmer, a young member of the "black

aristocracy"—the educated African costal elites—in Accra. Palmer is thinking of getting married, but for most of the chapter it is unclear as to what
exactly is holding him back. Kwamankra's pronouncements are equally nu-
minous: he advises Palmer not to look for "Parisian skirts and Regent
Street high heels" but to aim for "sympathy," noting that love, "like the
wind . . . bloweth where it listest" (131, 132, 133). To the modern reader, perhaps less sensitive to nuances than Casely Hayford's Gold Coast contemporaries, the subject of discussion only becomes clear in the concluding
paragraphs: Kwamankra notes, "You may have a child, a poor nameless
one, in some out-of-the-way corner of the world. You needn't be shy about
it. All of us do it" (136). The protagonist then concludes with an endorsement of "polygamy"—more properly polygyny—as a means of protecting
women who would otherwise be unmarried: "In Africa, she is protected;
she is a wife. Call it polygamy, if you like. In so-called Christian countries
she is despised, a prostitute, a leper" (136).

Casely-Hayford's argument—voiced through the mouthpiece of
Kwamankra—prefigures similar, later ethnographic expositions by Jomo
Kenyatta and Kwame Nkrumah. It answers back to European discourses
regarding excessive African sexuality and to claims that colonial governments and indeed European ideologies of "decency" protected women
from being victimized by traditional practices by emphasizing that polygyny is a viable and moral "conception of family life."[14] Yet such an endorsement of polygyny—rather than polyandry—is also reliant on a reinvention
of traditional patriarchy that is ambivalent about the place of women as
modern subjects. Women in this episode in *Ethiopia Unbound* are objects,
not subjects, relegated to a domestic sphere—none of Tom Palmer's new
wives, we hear, "sought to be a leader in society, and he was well content"
(137). Yet the text also seems slightly uneasy in its claim that urban elite men
who, like Tom, have "come to . . . [their] heritage" can represent women
better than colonial power can through their reclamation of tradition (137).

Ethiopia Unbound thus does not merely follow well-worn discursive
grooves in relation to gender, adopting a new problematic while maintaining the thematic of colonialism.[15] In touching on polygyny, it explores a
complex fault line in the modernity of the Gold Coast elites. In a study of
the Brew family, from which Casely Hayford's mother came, and several
members of which he would work with closely, Margaret Priestley notes
how an emphasis on a male line of descent, individualist "property attitudes" and "Christian marriage with literate wives" interwove with an
Akan lifeworld featuring a wide kinship network, observation of social ob-
ligations, and "polygamy and unions contracted by customary law" since

"it was not uncommon for the Brews to have domestics or family dependants as wives."[16] Missionary narratives and ideologies of respectability within the emerging colonial public sphere made such cultural hybridity an object of contention and focused in particular on monogamous marriage: European Christian missions opposed polygyny, while more syncretic African-led churches embraced it.[17] Yet the opposition between polygny and monogamy was not a simple one between colonial discourse and indigeneity. Debates arising from the Marriage Ordinance of 1888 and its subsequent modifications were not only about the preservation of "tradition" but also about the autonomy of women as subjects, exemplified by their ability to inherit a husband's property.[18] As Stephanie Newell notes, much creative writing among the coastal elites in the first half of the twentieth century concentrates on the effect of ordinances mandating monogamy upon gender relations, and feminist agitation in the 1950s was concerned primarily to clarify the legal situation of women in various forms of marriage.[19] *Ethiopia Unbound* responds to this debate; while there is an explicit theoretical defense of polygyny, as we have seen above, it is undercut by events in the plot: the formation of affective bonds with women and the relationship of these bonds to normative masculinities remains a fraught process for at least two of the major characters.

The first of these is the protagonist himself. Kwamankra performs heroic resistance to colonial power in the public sphere, and yet these actions are separated narratively from his activities as a husband and a father in the domestic realm.[20] A widower through Mansa's death, Kwamankra apparently does not remarry—or, at the very least, his remarriage is not mentioned—and what domestic aspects of him we see are entirely devoted to the remaining member of a nuclear family, his son, Ekra Kwow. Mansa is educated but also seems very much the idealized Victorian angel of the house: when Kwamankra courts her, he asks her to "teach" him "the way of duty" (34). The mundane elements of their marriage, married life, and Mansa's death in childbirth are relegated to two pages, while Kwamankra's visit to the "Goddess Mansa" in the spirit world of Nanamu-Krome (translated by Casely Hayford as "the abodes of the gods") occupies a whole chapter. Kwamankra's personal experience of modern companionate marriage thus seems to exclude polygyny, even as it develops masculine identity in opposition to an idealized femininity in the manner of the Victorian division of gendered spheres. And yet even this is not the whole story: in his teaching his son, Ekra Kwow, Kwamankra reads to him the description of Nausicaa from the *Odyssey,* commenting on the many similarities between Homeric Greece and contemporary "Fanti-born" society. The story shared between men is one of masculine vagrancy. Penelope waits, while Ulysses engages in a series of love affairs before he returns home. The epic world naturalizes polygyny—or at least a serial infidelity in which the figure of the legal wife is never abandoned—yet, curiously, this is the one cultural parallel never explicitly commented on.

The paradoxical nature of such vagrant masculinity is also shown in the story of Kwamankra's friend Tandor-Kuma, which is woven as a subplot into the main narrative. When we first meet Tandor-Kuma, his relationship with his wife seems to be a foil to that of Kwamankra and Mansa. In a chapter entitled "Sowing the Wind," he and his "wife . . . [,] at least before God," Ekuba, are introduced. He has succeeded in his studies while she, having accompanied him to England, is "a nurse-maid"—her presence at social events in colonial Gold Coast society on his return will, Tandor-Kuma meditates, constitute "a most difficult situation," since she is not educated enough to fulfill the role of a companionate life-partner (13). In a scene that shows perhaps the greatest narrational endorsement of female agency in the text, Ekuba condemns her lover's "cant" and leaves him, in order "not to give you the opportunity of dismissing me like a cur" (14).

The narrative does not return to the couple until much later, in a chapter entitled "Reaping the Whirlwind," which immediately follows Kwamankra's discussion of polygamy with Tom Palmer. Here we find Tandor-Kuma has contracted a legal marriage and become a "most respectable member of society": on a trip along the coast, however, he contracts malaria and is nursed back to health by Ekuba, whom we now learn has given birth to a child he has disowned after their separation. "Confronted with the same forbidden fruit of his earlier days," Tandor-Kuma attempts to resist, but is overcome by passion in a scene in which Ekuba enters his room, bolts the door, and flings herself at his feet (140). "The next moment," Casely Hayford's narrator tells us, "he completely broke down. Erring love had conquered, that was all" (146).

As in the presentation of the story of Nausicaa to Ekra Kwow, the most puzzling element of the story of Tandor-Kuma and Ekuba is the ambiguous narrational attitude to its events. The chapter titles suggest a moralistic Christian judgment, based on biblical injunctions against any kind of extramarital sexual relationship. In the first of the two chapters in the story we feel sympathy for Ekuba; it is possible to see her as a victim of social circumstance, much like women in late Victorian fiction such as Thomas Hardy's Tess Durbeyfield. Yet both chapters are focalized entirely through the male character, and the second seems to endorse Victorian masculinity, expressed as the restraint of natural forces, even as it shows some sympathy for Tandor-Kuma's weakness. But the obvious argument, which would surely have occurred to Kwamankra—that polygamy might allow Ekuba a social place that a rigid adherence to monogamy does not—is never made. In a very real sense, then, the theoretical expositions on, and practices of masculinity and respectable sexuality in, *Ethiopia Unbound* contradict each other: a theoretical reclamation of polygyny is matched by an enactment of the respectability of monogamy within the plot itself.

This ambivalence regarding masculinity and sexuality is symptomatic of a larger ambivalence, concerning modernity, at the center of Casely Hayford's text. African characters such as Tandor-Kuma and Kwow Ayensu, a student "of several years standing at the Charing Cross Hospital" nicknamed "the Professor" partly because of his over-Westernization, are often foils to Kwamankra, visibly lacking the features that make the latter an exemplar of "Ethiopian" modernity. These characters' actions thus construct Kwamankra's persona by negative definition, yet positive definition of Kwamankara as modern subject proves elusive: despite his founding of institutions, such as a university, we have little sense of how he might be an agent of social, rather than simply moral, change. *Ethiopia Unbound* certainly represents a tactically astute form of life writing. The comparison made with postmodern fiction earlier in this discussion is not solely a matter of textual form and appearance but also of function. Like a postmodern text, Casely Hayford's book seizes on the gaps and contradictions in its discursive environment, here colonialism in the Gold Coast in the early years of the twentieth century: it magnifies them, points out their absurdity, and offers alternative futures. Yet in *Ethiopia Unbound,* for all its uniqueness as a text written under colonialism, we do not yet see an attempt to bring a reinvented spiritual domain into the material space of colonialism, or an equivalence made between individual and territorial self-government. The colonial state oppresses, corrupts, but—beyond a general exhortation to self-improvement through education—we have no sense of what strategies of self-rule might replace it. For this, we must turn to Gandhi.

Gandhi's Experiments with Truth

Unlike *Ethiopia Unbound,* Mohandas K. Gandhi's *Autobiography* needs no special pleading to be included in a study of autobiography and decolonization; it is perhaps the best known of all the autobiographies in this book. Like Nelson Mandela's later *Long Walk to Freedom,* Gandhi's work has achieved wider recognition than the autobiographies of figures such as

Nkrumah or Nehru: his book is read internationally not so much as political or personal history as an inspirational text concerning the triumph of the human spirit. As Joseph Alter has noted, Gandhi has been successfully—and through considerable amnesia regarding many elements of his life story—assimilated into a liberal humanist tradition as a "personification of Truth": his autobiography has been read as an exemplary life of struggle of an individual claiming a destiny in the face of oppression.[21]

There are further reasons why Gandhi's autobiography might justifiably be accorded a more prominent place in this study. To a greater extent even than Casely Hayford, Gandhi was a central participant in an explicitly anticolonial struggle, and his methods of nonviolent resistance were made use of, if seldom completely endorsed philosophically, by succeeding waves of anticolonial activists, finding an echo in such campaigns as Nkrumah's call for "positive action" against the colonial government in the Gold Coast a generation after the publication of *Ethiopia Unbound.* Furthermore, Gandhi's ideas and strategies of leadership have been central—although contested—objects of study of theorists of gender and anticolonial nationalism. While the extent to which Gandhian politics empowered women remains debatable, Gandhi undoubtedly made a significant intervention into the sexual politics of nationalism, in particular in the gendering of a nascent national social imaginary.[22] Gandhi's politics and writings clearly refuse a simple anti-colonial masculinity which simply answers back within a "hyper-masculine world view," drawing strength from their association of reworked Indic and European concepts of femininity and androgyny as resources for the reconstruction of self.[23] Yet, as we shall see, Gandhi's autobiography is unique in that it does not anticipate the structure of a new national state; *swaraj,* or self-rule, for Gandhi is fundamentally a series of technologies of the self. If Gandhi would become the father of the Indian nation, Nehru would become the father of the Indian state, and Gandhi would remain an enticing yet frustrating puzzle to Nehru himself and the series of national autobiographers who would follow in the latter's wake.

To understand Gandhi's autobiography within the concept of a recessive colonial modernity and a newly emergent national modernity, we need to use two strategies to look at it afresh. First, we consider it as a text that follows within and yet pushes against the limits of its chosen genre. Second, and following from this, we should consider its vexed nature as a modern text. Rejecting "modern civilisation," Gandhi's *Autobiography* is nonetheless modern in the manner in which it attempts to construct and test a science of the self through personal and community-based "experiments": it is a text from which future autobiographies would learn, even if—as we shall see—they frequently chose not to follow its example.[24] And if we look closely at the technologies of the self which form the core Gandhi's of text, we may be rather surprised at the nature of our findings.

Written in Gujarati, and published over the course of three and a half years from late 1925 to early 1929, the *Autobiography* was simultaneously translated into English, and Gandhi seems to have exerted close supervision over its final form in translation.[25] While its author expresses some ambiguity about whether the text should properly be called an autobiography in both a preface and in correspondence, the text follows the generic conventions of canonical autobiography much more closely than Casely Hayford's.[26] It is told in the first person and proceeds largely in a linear fashion through its protagonist's life. Several of its features, indeed, will become paradigmatic in later national autobiographies: the focus on the maternal in a description of childhood, for example, and a period of exile that prompts self-recognition in the colonial metropolis.

Yet two features of the text seem surprising in retrospect. First, over half of its length is occupied by events during Gandhi's long sojourn in South Africa, despite the fact that its narrator notes that he has already written a history of the *satyagraha* struggle in South Africa (339). Second, the text ends in 1921, having devoted only one of its five sections to events after Gandhi's return to India, and his early involvement in struggles that lead inexorably to an engagement in nationalist politics. Gandhi's narrator's repeatedly stresses that his autobiography should not be read as history.[27] Yet his final comment that since 1921 his life "has been so public that there is hardly anything about it that people do not know" and that his "experiments" over the past seven years had all been made through Congress—essentially stating that his life has merged with the history of the nationalist struggle—contradicts this assertion (466).[28] Later national autobiographies always end with the confluence of personal and national narratives, with the time of the story reaching the time of narration: Gandhi's proclaims this identity of personal and national narratives, but does not enact it through the discourse of the narrative itself.

Some of the puzzling strands of Gandhi's *Autobiography* may be unraveled through a focus on an element of narrative that has proved productive in the analysis of *Ethiopia Unbound:* time. As we have seen, at first sight Gandhi's text seems conventional here—we follow the protagonist from birth through to maturity, and the narrative concentrates on his character to the exclusion of others. Kasturbai, his wife, plays only a minor role, and there are no other major characters to serve as relational foils to the protagonist. Yet there is a key difference between Gandhi's own autobiographical practice and that of canonical nineteenth-century biographers. For him, time is not progressive, but immanent: the narrative is a journey with a goal—"self-realization, to see God face to face, to attain *moksha*"—but it is a goal that the narrative itself does not realize (90). "The more I reflect and look back on the past," Gandhi notes, "the more vividly do I feel my limitations" (90).

Gandhi's *Autobiography*, like *Ethiopia Unbound*, challenges the temporal division of texts such as Clifford's and Curzon's, but it does so in a different way, flooding the text with a single, non-progressive notion of time, which is similar to the "simultaneity-along-time" that Anderson identifies as characteristic of premodern—or at least prenational—narratives.[29] The path followed by Gandhi's protagonist thus seems closer to what Weintraub calls "unfolding," in which the life is seen as developing according to an overall principle, rather than "development," characteristic of modern autobiography, in which the self is formed through interaction with the world.[30] From childhood, Gandhi the narrator notes, "passion for truth was innate in me," and his experiences represent encounters with relative truths that serve as "my beacon, my shield and buckler" in the absence of "Absolute Truth" (90, 91). Gandhi the protagonist may make plans, but these are only comprehensible in their relationship to God and to Truth: his plans to return early to India from South Africa do not come to fruition, for instance, because "God disposed otherwise" (186). In the national autobiographies that follow Gandhi's the narratives turn on moments of climax and revelation: Nehru's realization of the condition of the Kisans in the United Provinces, for example, or Lee Kuan Yew's precipitous plunge into the world of the Chinese-educated in Singapore. Moments that promise a similar climax, and indeed would be made into moments of anagnorisis by later biographers—such as Gandhi's involvement in tenancy disputes in Champaran—are narrated in a manner that describes their overall historical significance but gives little sense of personal transformation on the part of the protagonist. As Gandhi repeatedly asserts, we do not have history here but a series of "experiments with truth."

A contemporary auto/biography studies reading informed by these observations might stress the "non-Western" features of Gandhi's autobiography and the manner in which it preserves premodern concepts of time and self within a modern narrative form. Yet such a reading produces a caricature of the text, reprising, albeit with a more affirmative inflection, George Gusdorf's dismissal of Gandhi as one of "those men [who] have been annexed by a sort of intellectual colonizing to a mentality that was not their own. When Gandhi tells his own story, he is using Western means to defend the East."[31] Searching for traces of the premodern in the "non-Western" may result in a neglect of the complexity of texts such a Gandhi's; indeed, we have already seen the complex interpenetrability of mythic and modern time in *Ethiopia Unbound*. Much contemporary research has noted the uneven nature of modernities after colonialism and how rupture and disjunction between different concepts of space and time are foundational to them, rather than simply a manifestation of an encounter between the modern and the premodern.[32] Gandhi himself had a more sophisticated reading than a simple identification of "modern" as "Western." In a much-quoted letter to H. S. L. Polak in 1909, he noted that there was "no such thing as Western or European civilisation, but there is a modern civilisation, which is purely material" and should be resisted on the grounds that it denied the spiritual.[33]

The manner in which *An Autobiography* approaches modernity is thus a bifurcated one, but the bifurcation is not centered on an identification between the Western and the modern. Gandhi as protagonist displays a distaste for material things, including the feats of civil engineering that would be so beloved of Nehru and Nkrumah. In an early visit to the Paris Exhibition of 1890, he is shocked by the vulgarity of the Eiffel Tower, which he describes as "a good demonstration of the fact that we are all children attracted by trinkets" (150). His text does not, however, reject modernity as such but in fact uses an element of modernity Gandhi admired — the rigor of scientific reasoning arising from the scientific method — as a presiding image for its narrative method.[34] The description of the book as a series of experiments is not a casual one, rather one Gandhi elaborates in his introductory discussion. "I claim for them," he writes, "nothing more than does a scientist who, though he conducts his experiments with the utmost accuracy, forethought and minuteness, never claims any finality about his conclusions, but keeps an open mind regarding them" (90). What we have here is a framing of modern science within an Indic philosophical context: Gandhi seeks *moksha*, true knowledge, through *jnana*, the rigorous application of logical thinking.[35] And his experiments do not have their primary objects within the material world, but rather in the inner world: they are not Foucauldian "technologies of production" but rather "technologies of the self, which permit individuals to effect . . . operations on their own bodies and souls, thoughts, conduct, and way of being, so as to transform themselves in order to attain a certain sense of happiness, purity, wisdom, perfection, or immortality."[36]

Gandhi's experiments commence with an attempt to answer back within the discourse of colonialism, exemplified by his secret trials of meat eating to gain physical strength to resist the British and his later pursuit of "the all too impossible task of becoming an English gentleman."[37] In this they resemble Kwamankra's stress on the perfectability of the physical form and the insertion of the "Ethiopian gentleman" as protagonist into the narrative of modernity. Yet Gandhi quickly moves away from these efforts to appropriate colonial masculinity. If Casely Hayford chooses to engage with sexuality, Gandhi moves from it: youthful sexual desire in marriage and outside it is retrospectively distanced through an understanding of the narrative as a series of experiments with "non-violence, celibacy and other principles of conduct" (91). As Leela Gandhi has convincingly shown, Gandhi's involvement with the vegetarian movement in London is a crucial turning point in his expression of Indic cultural resources as "affective anti-colonialism," in developing a concept of *ahimsa,* stressing compassion above Utilitarian rationality.[38] If, as Gandhi himself remarks, the "experiments in England were conducted from the point of view of economy and hygiene," they are retrospectively narrated as part of a larger system intimately related to Gandhi's vow of *brahmacharya,* chastity or "complete self-restraint," in which internal discipline parallels external discipline, where the regulation of the individual body becomes a representation of a peculiarly modern form of social regulation (139). And this, in turn, is tied to the possibilities of national liberation: "Real Home Rule," Gandhi would write in *Hind Swaraj,* "is Self Rule or self-control."[39] Colonialism becomes figured as excess, as a decadent indulgence in consumption in opposition to the disciplined body of the colonized seeking self rule. What is discovered through experiments in such control, indeed, is the enhanced autonomy of the body. Thus walking rather than taking public transport keeps the protagonist "practically free from illness throughout my stay in England" and produces a "strong body," while changes in living arrangements result in more time for self-improvement.[40]

Yet Gandhi's comment on the importance of "economy and hygiene" also hints at the limits of this autonomy. Indeed, hygiene and economy are two of the neglected elements in many readings of the text which focus on the austere askesis of *brahmacharya.* The autobiography dwells consistently on issues of sanitation as a mark of a community's moral standing. Thus it notes the cleanliness of the poor in Bombay as opposed to the filthy state of the upper classes' latrines and links sanitary reform in Durban's Indian community to gaining "the esteem of the authorities": here "self-purification" and the desire to "ventilate grievances and press for rights" go hand in hand (218, 253). At the 1901 Congress in Calcutta, the protagonist is repelled by both the persistence of caste divisions and poor sanitary facilities:

There was no limit to insanitation. Pools of water were everywhere. There were only a few latrines, and the recollection of their stink still oppresses me. I pointed it out to the volunteers. They said point-blank: 'That is not our work, it is the scavenger's work.' I asked for a broom. The man stared at me in wonder. I procured one and cleaned the latrine. But that was for myself. The rush was so great, and the latrines were so few, that they needed frequent cleaning, but that was more than I could do. So I had to content myself with simply ministering to myself. And the others did not seem to mind the stench and the dirt.

But that was not all. Some of the delegates did not scruple to use the verandahs outside their rooms for calls of nature at night. (258)

Gandhi's *Autobiography* teems with such scenes: he is overwhelmed by "swarming flies" outside the Kashi Vishvanath temple at Varanasi, appalled at having to "wade through urine and excreta" on a boat to Rangoon, and disgusted to "see people performing natural functions" that "desecrate the sacred water of the Ganges" near Hardvar (272, 378, 383). Frequently, unsanitary practices are seen as complicit with colonialism's denial of self-hood to the colonized: the filth on third-class railway carriages in India is critiqued as the "indifference of the railway authorities . . . combined with the dirty and inconsiderate habits of the passengers themselves," while the absence of sanitation in the Indian quarter of Johannesburg results from both the "criminal negligence of the Municipality and the ignorance of the Indian settlers" (270, 305).

Gandhi is here in many ways operating within, or in parallel with, colonial discourse. European colonial town planning and medicine in the late nineteenth and early twentieth century was profoundly concerned with notions of hygiene and sanitation.[41] Indeed, in urging that hygiene should not be limited to the civil lines or European areas of colonial towns but extended everywhere, Gandhi reiterates and indeed amplifies the projects of colonial governmentality in the early twentieth century that aimed to reform the lifeworld of the colonized, moving from "curative medicine and disease control to public health."[42] As a trainee teacher at Achimota College, outside Accra, in the late 1920s, Kwame Nkrumah would have participated in weekly patrols to neighboring villages to instruct the inhabitants "to clean up their villages and keep them clean"; in Nelson Mandela's time at the South African Native College, Fort Hare, students would regularly visit nearby villages to discuss hygiene and "village sanitation" with their inhabitants.[43]

Gandhi's stress upon the body of the colonized as a site for reformatory practices is thus not unique. Nineteenth-century and colonial autobiography, we have seen, makes the body of the protagonist invisible; such autobiographies "almost completely efface the bodies in which the lives they describe were lived."[44] Yet for the colonized the body was not so easily escapable — it carried the visible marks of colonialism's refusal to admit colonized subjects into the public sphere. And the body also became the target of colonial governmentality: it was a site of colonialism's effort to use the law to stigmatize the cultural practices of the colonized and to increase penetrability to colonial development.[45] In appropriating the discourse of hygiene — in making colonial rule "dirty" — Gandhi holds out the possibility of reform through self-rule. The body becomes a site of transformation, in which reform, resistance, and autonomy might take root through a series of micropractices: gesture, dress, speech. As we have seen, Gandhi's autobiography repeatedly returns to the body, its diet, its training, the suppression of its appetites. In his autobiography, and indeed in the performance of his life itself, Gandhi linked such practices back to social transformation: governance of the body was a political act, and personal hygiene, "nocturnal emissions," and masturbation might be discussed in the same breath as politics.[46] Yet in the autobiography, the discourse of hygiene seems to frequently be almost patrician in tone: Gandhi attends not to his own body, but to reforming the practices of recalcitrant populations. There is an ambiguity here: does the narrative of hygiene represent a radical displacement of colonial governmentality — colonialism now figured as the cause of, rather than a cure for, social ills — or does Gandhi's appropriation of such a narrative represent only a reiteration of a derivative discourse?

Indeed, Gandhi's protagonist's and narrator's concerns with hygiene are paralleled by a second disciplinary regime, a Franklinesque concern with economy and frugality. Experiments with economy, Gandhi notes, commenced during his sojourn in England: they are acts of modern individuation in the absence of the community of the family that he left behind. In London, his protagonist develops a system for accounting for every "farthing I spent . . . Every little item, such as omnibus fares or postage or a couple of coppers spent on newspapers, would be entered, and the balance struck every evening before going to bed. The habit has stayed with me ever since. . . . Let every youth take a leaf out of my book and make it a point to account for everything that comes into and goes out of his pocket, and like me he is sure to be a gainer in the end" (131). This careful bookkeeping seems very much in the mold of Benjamin Franklin, or indeed

Horatio Alger or Samuel Smiles, and continues throughout the autobiography. In London, Gandhi glosses his efforts to economize by walking rather than taking public transport and changing his residence and diet. While initially inspired by the thought of reducing the financial burden on Gandhi's family, this frugality, like Franklin's, has a larger significance. In South Africa, Gandhi explains, organizational success is made possible by his refusal to run the *satyagraha* (nonviolent resistance) campaign with permanent funds, since a "permanent fund carries in itself the seed of the moral fall of the institution" (238). And in South Africa, too, he aims for a "simple life," freeing himself from "slavery to the washerman" and "dependence on the barber" through starching his own collars and cutting his own hair. Recalling Samuel Smiles, Gandhi explicitly calls this strategy "self-help" on several occasions, and later reveals that he abhors debt (250, 263, 310, 372, 374, 289).

It seems almost sacrilegious to think of Gandhi as, like Franklin or Alger, embodying Weber's productive spirit of capitalism. Indeed, the freedom he desires is an escape from a reliance on markets: his later taking up of the production of homespun *khadi* was with the aim "to clothe ourselves entirely in cloth manufactured by our own hands" (456). Yet, although Gandhi's aim is very different from his proto-capitalist predecessors, the technologies he uses are similar. He aims to produce an autonomous individual through disciplinary techniques and does so through "experiments"—analogous to science. And this realization—the parallel between those two apparent opposites, the subject of capital and the revolutionary subject—will persist as an important, if subterranean theme, in the later autobiographies we will encounter, reemerging seventy years later with greater vigor in the autobiographies of Lee Kuan Yew and Nelson Mandela.

Gandhi's concern with the regulation of the individual and social body would be taken up, although transformed, in the national autobiographies that followed his. Ashis Nandy, as we have seen, has argued that Gandhi refuses to enter the discursive field of colonial masculinity by stressing androgyny. Rather trying to "beat the colonizers at their own game" and emphasize "hyper-Ksatriyahood," Gandhi makes, in this reading, "the ability to transcend the man-woman dichotomy" a key virtue.[47] Yet it is noticeable how, even in Nandy's reading, femininity is associated, through Gandhi's rereading of Indic traditions, both with uncontrollable and potentially destructive energy and with the maternal. Gandhi's rephrasing of tradition within his modern experiments, then, does not fully escape the disciplinary masculinity of colonialism, and in some ways his writing reiterates it. The figure of the female sex worker, for instance, recurs throughout Gandhi's autobiography as a figure for lack of self-governance. Gandhi is "moved . . . to lust" by a prostitute in Portsmouth, "disgusted at . . . [his] weakness" in entering a brothel in Zanzibar (145, 168). His discovery of a prostitute in his house in Natal warns Gandhi against "infatuation" with the "evil genius" of an erstwhile friend (213). This and other moments of the *Autobiography* represent an identification of women with untrammeled desire, very much part of the discourse of colonial and postcolonial masculinity in which later national autobiographies would participate. And in his retrospective desire to educate Kasturbai, having awakened "from the sleep of lust," Gandhi also predicts the manner in which women's education—subordinated to the national struggle—would become a marker of the legitimacy of anticolonial struggles.[48]

We might summarize some of the difficulties in Gandhi's text around hygiene, economy, and gender by thinking of the nature of the "series of experiments" that Gandhi undertakes. In a sense, he makes strategic use of the "double consciousness" of which Du Bois wrote, placing himself quite consciously as both the subject and object of modernity, the scientist who experiments and the object of such experiments. Yet it is never quite possible for him to maintain both positions simultaneously, to merge individual with social body. What distinguishes Gandhi's narrative from those that would follow it is its lack of interest in the formation of a centralized postcolonial polity. His homology between individual and national self-rule thus remains an abstraction in relation to the future postcolonial nation-state. Later he was to call for the dissolution of Congress upon independence, and the formation of a nation of autonomous villages, linked together in widening circles of authority. In his autobiography, he does not storm the commanding heights of colonial modernity and claim them for the new nation. Indeed, it might be felt that he decamps to a new and radically innovative modern territory. Yet, on closer inspection, many of the contours of this territory look familiar; the elisions of Gandhi's narrative around gender, hygiene, and economy, and above all in the narrative's negotiation between being a subject or object of modernity, rehearse the engagement with colonial modernity continued and extended in later narratives of self-fashioning.

Garvey's Experiences in America

From February to May 1930, the *Pittsburgh Courier* carried a series of autobiographical articles by the Universal Negro Improvement Association leader, Marcus Garvey. Like Gandhi—to whom, indeed, he explicitly compared himself in one of the articles—Garvey was at the time a well-known figure; like his Indian counterpart he attempted to publish an auto-biography in installments and broke off without bringing it successfully to the narrative present.[49] Yet the contrast in fate between Gandhi's and Garvey's autobiographies could not be more extreme. Gandhi's, as we have seen, achieved the status of an international best-seller. Garvey's vanished and was only belatedly published, as a historical curiosity, in a collection of Garvey's writings released by an academic press in the 1980s.

The failure of Garvey's autobiography is all the more surprising given the possibilities open to its author. We have seen that the negotiation in Gandhi's text between Indic and Victorian technologies of the self, between the social and the physical body, is complex and at times contra-dictory, as its author seeks and only partially finds a plausible counter-discourse to colonial modernity. For Garvey, things were much clearer: there was a basic homology between individual and community. "As of the individual," he wrote, "so it should be of the race and nation. . . . The glit-tering success of Rockefeller makes him a power in the American nation; the success of Henry Ford suggests him as an object of universal respect, but no one knows and cares about the bum or hobo who is Rockefeller's or Ford's neighbor. So, also, is the world attracted by the glittering success of races and nations, and pays absolutely no attention to the bum or hobo race that lingers by the wayside."[50] There is no endorsement of Casely Hayford's vagrant masculinity here: the mobility of the "bum" or "hobo" must be sacrificed for the austere disciplines of production. For Garvey, "the Negro" might be made "independent from an economic point of view and later from a political point of view" through an appropriation of nineteenth-century narratives of self-making; the future national narrative would be built through an infinitely replicable series of Horatio Alger–style stories of individual self-improvement (95).

Yet, despite the apparent easiness of the task ahead, Garvey's narrative collapses. The introductory account of childhood, maturation, and then exile so important in Gandhi's and all succeeding national autobiographies is truncated, skipped over in little more than a page that contains echoes of the robustly capitalist pseudo-autobiography of Defoe's *Robinson Crusoe*. Narrative pressure drives Garvey too precipitately to his autobiography's climax, the Universal Negro Improvement Association's 1920 International Convention of the Negro Peoples of the World, when 25,000 delegates from Africa, the Caribbean, and South and North America gathered in

New York. His account of an occasion that "reminded one of the great ceremonials at the courts of Europe, or one of the coronation celebrations at Westminster Abbey, London" now engulfs the narrative, as narration of the event itself proceeds at a slower pace (40). And after this prolonged moment of climax, the narrative bifurcates. The majority of it is devoted to Garvey's own defense of his personal integrity in the wake of the financial collapse of UNIA-sponsored Black Star Line; this element of the text resembles what might be called an autobiography of defeat, in which a vanquished political figure attempts to a rehabilitation of self through a stress on personal integrity.[51] At the same time, Garvey returns twice more to the history of the UNIA and events leading up to the moment of triumph in 1920, at each time holding out the promise of a complete narrative that is never written.

Garvey's narrative fails largely because of the incommensurability between its model and events on the ground. In 1920, he had declared himself provisional president of Africa, and the UNIA used many of the trappings of nationhood, attempting to gain diplomatic recognition from a number of nation-states, and petitioning the League of Nations. Yet by 1930 Garvey's life could no longer, even with the greatest ingenuity, be narrativized on an upward trajectory. His efforts to take on global capitalism on its own terms had collapsed in a welter of accusations of fiscal impropriety; he had then been imprisoned and then expelled from the United States, and the UNIA had split. Given this, however, the terms of Garvey's failure are instructive, as is the manner in which he attempts to construct the self in the face of such failure. As with its colonial counterparts in chapter 2, we may learn more as much from Garvey's narrative's collapse as from the success of those of Gandhi and Casely Hayford.

Garvey's autobiography, as we have seen, increasingly turns aside from recounting the story of a life to engage in a series of critiques of men who have, in his view, prevented the progress of a narrative of emancipation. These range from personal acquaintances, employees, and fellow activists in the struggle to potential rivals such as W. E. B. Du Bois, dismissed for his "hypocrisy" in declining the invitation to attend the 1920 Convention, and then accused by association as one of the "influential" "forces aligned against me" in Garvey's 1922 trial for mail fraud (42). In parallel with the Franklinesque narrative of thrift and responsible self-government, the failings of Garvey's real and perceived antagonists are presented as specifically masculine failings. Women against whom Garvey as narrator might justifiably construct retrospective complaints—such his private secretary

Gwendolyn Campbell, and indeed his first wife, Amy Ashwood Garvey, whom he divorced in 1922—are marginal figures to the narrative and are presented as led astray by more powerful and persuasive men.

Garvey's attacks certainly did not go unnoticed. The subject of his most vitriolic character assassination noted in a protest to the journal's editor that the text had "departed from the legitimate purpose of an autobiography and . . . used . . . your journal as a means to defame, attack, libel and denounce those whom he dubs his 'enemies.'"[52] Yet the feature Domingo isolates here as not "legitimate" is not unusual: Garvey's construction of his self in opposition to others, and in particular to other men, represents an extreme manifestation of a common strategy in national autobiography. If he aims to produce in his text a protagonist as an autonomous self encountering the world and progressing through devotion to work, he singularly fails: the protagonist of the text is ultimately almost entirely defined by his relation to others. Earlier, I have briefly mentioned and indeed at times employed the notion of "relational selves," a term popularized by Paul John Eakin that is receiving increasing attention in autobiography studies. It is time to explore Eakin's concept more thoroughly and think of its use in examining national autobiographies in which individuals and various communities, perforce, can only be thought of in relation to each other.

In his 1999 text *How Our Lives Become Stories: Making Selves,* Eakin notes that we easily "forget that the first person of autobiography is truly plural in its origins and subsequent formation."[53] Plotting the discussion of the nature of the self in autobiography studies, Eakin examines the importance the writings of George Gusdorf and the early Philippe Lejeune place on "unique selfhood" and individualism as a product of the Enlightenment. He further notes that a generation of feminist critics, such as Mary Mason and Domna Stanton, rightfully critique this model in their assertion that female autobiographers, in contrast to the male writers of Gusdorf's canon, emphasize the relationships of their protagonists with others in the formation of autobiographical selves (47–48). Eakin takes this insight and, returning the gaze to canonical male autobiographies, notes that they also feature such relational qualities: that we do not notice them may say more about our reading practices than the content of the autobiographies themselves (50). It may well be, Eakin notes, that "the conceptual legacy of a culture of individualism . . . has blinded us to the relational dimension of identity formation" (63–64). Analysis of autobiographical texts clearly should not write out gender—relationality applies "*equally if not identically* to male experience"—but it should endeavor to escape a series of binarisms which place terms such as male-authored, individual, autonomous, and readerly in simple opposition to female-authored, collective, relational and writerly (50).[54] Aware that in a sense all autobiographies are potentially relational, Eakin seeks to limit the term by applying it to autobiographies centrally concerned with either "an entire social environment" or "key other individuals" (69).

The current popularity of Eakin's concept in autobiography studies perhaps demonstrates the difficulty of his attempts to limit its applicability: there is a danger, I think, in analysis that merely discovers the relationality of a self constructed in an auto/biographical text and then automatically presumes that the text is in some manner discursively destabilizing. Yet what is most interesting in Eakin's analysis is that despite his refutation of binary oppositions regarding gender, he endorses a deeper binarism based on culture. To his credit, he does not, as some readings inspired by his work do, see relational selves as always exemplified in non-Western life writing in opposition to the autonomous subjects of Western autobiography. Yet there is another binarism here. As we have seen, Eakin divides relationality into two aspects—first, relation to the social environment, and second, to "proximate" other individuals, frequently members of the protagonist's family. Curiously, his examples of narratives emerging from "relational environments" are all from minority cultures in the United States, predominately Native and African American contexts; those concerning "key other individuals" are narrated predominately (although not exclusively) by European or, American subjects. More curiously, when explored closely, some elements of this binarism begin to break down; when discussing Henry Louis Gates's *Colored People,* for example, Eakin notes that the text is split between focus on "individual life" and the "story of a community": while Eakin does not say this, his account suggests that rather than seeing the text as a simple expression of relationality, we might think of it rather as a complex negotiation between collective and individualizing narratives of identity (77, 75).

This insight that hints at the particular relevance of Eakin's schema to the autobiographies under discussion. Such texts, written in the process of decolonization and anticolonial nationalism, are always already relational in both of Eakin's senses. They are perforce centrally concerned with social environment and community: the colonial subject seeking autonomy achieves legitimacy by embodying community and speaking for it in a way the colonizer cannot. And yet the narratives to which this community must be attached are narratives of modernity—nationalism and, contradictorily, capitalism—that speak of individuation and autonomy. And in their shuttling from individual to community in subject formation the narratives will frequently come to rest on other men as individuals, members of a fraternity, each of whom is engaged in the individual task of writing his own modern narrative.

In Garvey's narrative, then, other men such as Du Bois, Joshua Cockburn, and Samuel Duncan, are attacked for "hypocrisy," dishonesty, and deceit that is seen as unmanly, contrasted with the "very fine type of man" whom Garvey seeks to lead the UNIA (42). Garvey portrays himself consistently as transparent and honest, laboring in morally improving productive work to support emancipation through the accumulation of capital. Excessive consumption, fashionable clothes, and having "women around" are condemned, while honest hard work and frugality are privileged (67). And, as we have seen, Garvey's protagonist is not merely conceived of relationally to other men: comparisons between men are related to "racial dishonesty," to a stalled narrative of community that would otherwise enable "the race [to] go forward to success" (63, 64).

What are we to make of these various contrasts and comparisons, the complex strands of filiation between communal and individual narratives in Garvey's narrative and also in the narratives of his predecessors? What is happening here is perhaps best explicated by returning to Benedict Anderson's famous phrase: race and nation (and for Casely Hayford and Garvey, at least, these two categories are not yet entirely distinct) are constituted as imagined communities. Yet such communities can only be embedded in a modern narrative by their transformation into "imagined individuals" through the discipline of writing. The nation, like the individual, has a story to tell, one of growing autonomy and freedom to act within the market of international relations without the restraints of colonialism. Racial and national communities as actors and agents need to be constituted through specific disciplines, with institutions such as Congress or the UNIA, and later the apparatus of the state, acting on the body of the nation just as disciplinary self-fashioning works on the individual male body. As we have seen, this process seems almost inevitably gendered, even when a writer such as Gandhi makes a principled attempt to contest hegemonic masculinities.

This realization is a point at which the three narratives discussed in this chapter meet. Each resists colonialism through an appeal to community, and each draws parallels between elements of the self-governance of embodied individuals (sexuality with Casely Hayford, hygiene with Gandhi, fiscal responsibility with Garvey) and the strength of communities that wish to emerge from the colonial world. For each, however, the precise disciplinary mechanism by which such communities might be brought into a narrative of modernity remains unarticulated. Casely Hayford cannot yet imagine an independent nation-state, Gandhi turns away from one on principle, and Garvey can only survey the ruins of a national project. For national autobiography in its classical form, drawing a homology between the party/state, masculine self-government, and the discipline of writing itself, we need to look to Jawaharlal Nehru.

4

Nehru and the National Sublime

Nature has a way of writing history in her rocks and stones, and all who wish to may read it there. It is a kind of autobiography—that is, one's own history.

Jawaharlal Nehru, *Glimpses of World History*

O ur home," wrote Vijaya Lakshimi Pandit, "was divided into Indian and Western sections. The reception and dining rooms and Father's offices were in the front of the house overlooking the garden. It was here that Western-style parties were held. Indian social life went on in another part of the house, which was run in the traditional manner with a Brahman cook and Hindu servants. Although this was Mother's domain it was her elder sister who really attended to all the details."[1] Few descriptions can match for precision Jawaharlal Nehru's sister's account of the material separation of spheres of colonized elites, the public domain masculine, rationalized, aggressively modern, where nationalism engaged colonialism within a discursive framework initially set by the latter, the "inner domain of sovereignty" of national culture feminized and associated with a rediscovered tradition.[2] Nehru's early life was marked by this division in many ways. Studying at Harrow, England, and later at Cambridge University, the young Jawaharlal would write to his mother, Swarup Rani, in elementary Hindi, but to his father, Motilal Nehru, in an English of growing sophistication.

Yet the house Nehru's sister described would, like India, not long remain in so divided a state. After the Calcutta Congress in 1920 Nehru's father unified the residence, Anand Bhawan, as part of a boycott of foreign goods, reducing the number of servants, eliminating crystal, china, and burning much "foreign finery."[3] The transformation of Anand Bhawan was part of a larger transformation, "a total break with [a] past life and a new fashioning of it," which united the two spheres through the creation of national citizens in embryo.[4] Nationalists reformed dress habits, emphasized disciplinary practices, and brought a reenvisioned tradition into the public sphere in various and complex ways, displacing the tawdry finery, the "badges of impotence" of the imperial durbars.[5] Nationalist leaders such as Nehru, Mohandas K. Gandhi, and Vallabhbhai Patel performed the exemplary role of citizen-to-be, in which outer performance corresponded with inner regeneration. Nehru insisted on the North Indian *sherwani* being recognized as formal dinner wear at Indian hotels, while Gandhi strategically contrasted his slight, *khadi*-clothed figure with the ponderous ornamentalism of the viceregal residence.[6]

Nehru's *Autobiography*, written in the heat of anticolonial struggle, also performs this work of regeneration, occupying a liminal space between inner and outer worlds. The book as a material artifact would circulate widely both within India and internationally and would become a template for future anticolonial nationalists writing their own national autobiographies. Yet it also looks inward, examining the reconstruction of the self and internal transformation of an individual in parallel with the construction of a national narrative. Nehru's own accounts of the purpose of the text are contradictory: it is at various times a conduct book for future national citizens, a demonstration of a distinctly Indian modernity to an international audience, and a private means of disciplining and working on the self.[7] In a sense, it is all three things: it draws elaborate parallels among the discipline of writing and constructing a text, the regulation of a male body through rationality, and the action of the state on a nation in the quest for modernity. In its attempt to appropriate and indigenize a peculiarly modern literary form and to put it to use for, through, and ultimately beyond the nation-state, Nehru's text realizes some of the possibilities latent in the autobiographical writings examined in chapter 3. Embedding his text skillfully within a discursive field marked by colonialism and then extending this field through his reference to revolutionaries such as Lenin, Nehru attempts to narrate the arrival of a revolutionary subject into a modernity wrested from the colonizer. Even as it envisions this modernity, however, Nehru's text is troubled by tensions between state and nation, individual and community, embodiment and disembodiment, masculinity and femininity, rationality and affect: the personal narrative bleeds into, contaminates, but can never quite run parallel to the grand project of the nation's—and ultimately modernity's—story.

Written during his imprisonment in Dehradun Jail, Naini Central Prison, Allahabad, and, from June 1934 until early February 1935, in Almora Jail, Nehru's six-hundred-page narrative was produced long before the achievement of the full independence of India in 1947. The *Autobiography* initially follows a fairly even-paced chronology, describing its protagonist's Kashmiri ancestors' migration to the Mughal court in Northern India and Nehru's own childhood, his study at Harrow and Cambridge, and his return to India in 1912 as "a bit of a prig with little to commend me" (26). Nehru's protagonist is rescued from the "utter insipidity" of national life by developments in national politics—the return of Gandhi, his organization of the Satyagraha Sabha to oppose the suppression of civil liberties in the 1919 Rowlatt Bills, and the massacre of peaceful protestors by British troops in the Jallianwala Bagh in Amritsar in the same year (28). These pivotal events in the national narrative are matched by other parallel incidents that implicate him personally: his fortuitous yet transformative involvement with the *kisan* (peasant) movement in the United Provinces and his imprisonment at Nabha, one of the "princely states" that had nominal independence in British India.[8] After this crucial turn in the narrative, the *Autobiography* becomes the unfolding story of the quest for Indian independence, in which Nehru's personal life merges with a national narrative. Events such as its protagonist's accession to the presidency of the Indian National Congress in 1929, his taking of the pledge of independence in 1930, and his participation in civil disobedience are described in detail and interspersed with analysis of their political and social implications; there is also considerable reflection on the process of political reform and revolution, and on internal conflicts within the independence movement and within the Congress itself. The reflective element of the autobiography is enhanced by elements within the narrative it tells: Nehru's visit to Europe in 1926–27 and his seven terms of imprisonment encourage a process of distancing and self-analysis that is largely carried out through the medium of writing, culminating in the writing of the text of the *Autobiography* itself as we reach the narrative present.

The latter part of the *Autobiography* is clearly influenced by Nehru's long periods of imprisonment in the 1930s. There is no substantial personal story to tell as part of the narrative of struggle, the protagonist's "brief periods outside prison" now having "a measure of unreality about them" (184). Indeed, the working title for the book was *In and Out of Prison*.[9] While the narrative of the quest for national independence continues, there is more reflection, and accompanying discussion is thematic and wide-ranging, rather than relating to specific incidents. Thus the momentum of the autobiography slows to a glacial crawl when events close in on the narrative present. The forward movement of the plot is subsumed by two competing nonnarrative writing strategies. First, Nehru uses contemporary events as starting points for discursive essays that consider policy issues to do with an emergent nationalist movement—the extent to which compulsion might be used in effecting revolutionary change, for example. Islands of carefully structured argument are interleaved with a second kind of writing, in which Nehru shows much less certainty, concentrating on intimate relationships in which affect predominates. Thus the book, in closing, returns to the "paradox" of Gandhi's putative irrationality yet his unavoidable centrality to the independence struggle. Gandhi—and, as we shall see, a very different Gandhi from the protagonist of Gandhi's own *Autobiography*— has been a constantly present figure in the text, sometimes engaged with, at others resolutely defended from criticism. But he is not the only figure who returns at the conclusion of the narrative. Kamala Kaul, Nehru's wife, also grows in importance. The composition of Nehru's *Autobiography* was marked by the "peculiarly distressing circumstances" of her long illness, and through Nehru's dedication of the text, upon publication, to "Kamala, who is no more," by her death, which occurred just after Nehru completed revising the text (559).[10] The affective power of the relationship with Kamala, submerged throughout the autobiography and yet emerging at its end, is also mapped onto Nehru's relationship with a feminized Indian nation, "a . . . lady . . . occasionally . . . perverse and obstinate, sometimes even a little hysteric," and his tortured negotiation between state and nation, rationality and affective bonds.[11]

Before looking at the way personal and national narratives intersect, examining Nehru's autobiography in terms of both its narrative projects and their ultimate contradictions, we need first to explore the manner it occupies a position within the discursive field it enters, working on its readers' various horizons of expectations, entering into a discourse not its own and yet wresting elements of it into a new configuration.

Remapping the Discursive Field

For all his protestations that in writing his autobiography he "was hardly thinking of an outside audience," Nehru had long been aware of the power of writing to contest and reframe discursive contexts (559). The text was first published in England in 1936 by the Bodley Head, and Nehru's correspondence with his representative in London, V. K. Krishna Menon, indicates a profound concern about the way the book was presented on publication. Nehru acknowledged in an epilogue to the autobiography that he had "become a queer mixture of the East and the West, out of place everywhere, at home nowhere," and perhaps the most apparent element of the autobiography in the British context is the way Nehru makes strategic use of his hybrid position (596). The text thus answers attempts by the colonial power to disqualify the character of its protagonist by indicating deficiencies in individual integrity and self-control.

As we will see in greater depth with Nkrumah, British official discourse attempted to connect the nationalist objects of its surveillance as closely as possible with Communism, and, by extension, "disreputable" conduct.[12] Official correspondence from the 1920s and 1930s regarding the Congress leadership thus disparages Nehru as a "temperamental person" who "may go off the deep end before too long," and, in a highly public case the 1933–34 Bengal Government's Administrative Report indulged in what a group of concerned British citizens called an attempt to "destroy the personal character" of the nationalist leader by suggesting that he had appropriated funds for work on untouchability for other uses.[13]

With his Harrow and Cambridge background, Nehru was adept at playing the character game, and in this context his *Autobiography* succeeds wholly: it creates a uniquely reflective protagonist, conscious of his own failings and yet a committed actor within history. Nehru's protagonist is frequently self-deprecatory and is committed to austere self-discipline; in creating the central figure of his autobiography, Nehru reiterates many of the central elements of Victorian and indeed colonial masculinity. His protagonist is thus differentiated by relational strategies from two other men, Gandhi and his father, whom Nehru describes as Walter Pater's saint and epicure: "the man of religion, who went through life rejecting what it offers in the way of sensation and physical pleasure, and . . . an epicure, who accepted life and welcomed and enjoyed its many sensations," seeking a middle way between asceticism and indulgence (65).[14] The narrative thus emphasizes bodily discipline as a means of forming character. In jail, he adopts an elaborate regimen of self-care, adhering "to a strict time-table" in order to appreciate "the value of work and exercise . . . , for without them one is apt to go to pieces" (348). He shaves regularly every morning, in contrast to others: "as a rule, people gave it up and slacked in other ways" (348). At another point he attributes his good health to his avoidance of "rich and excessive" food of the Indian middle classes, sunbaths in prison, and exercises (396). At the same time, some of Gandhi's more radical experiments with truth on his own body are dismissed. Nehru sees his elder colleague's bad health while fasting, his letting "himself to go down hill," for instance, as an eccentric personal indulgence (398).

An important feature of Nehru's account of masculine self-fashioning illustrated above is how, as in Victorian texts such as those of Herbert

Spencer or Samuel Smiles, accounts of bodily discipline quickly move beyond the body and take flight into figuration, in which the physical stands for the moral or spiritual. The quest for integrity and trimness thus quickly extends even to the choice of reading matter: "I occupied myself with my books, going from one type of reading to another, but usually sticking to 'heavy' books. Novels made one feel mentally slack, and I did not read many of them" (352). And it becomes a powerful metaphor for the discipline necessary to resist colonialism:

> [Gandhi] did succeed amazingly in giving backbone and character to
> the Indian people. There were many, however, who developed neither
> much backbone nor character, but who imagined that a limp body
> and a flabby look might be the outward semblance of piety.
>
> It was this extraordinary stiffening-up of the masses that filled us
> with confidence. A demoralized, backward, and broken-up people
> suddenly straightened their backs and lifted their heads and took part
> in disciplined, joint action on a country-wide scale. (76)

Here Nehru deploys the vocabulary of the British public school, mens sana in corpore sano, to describe—and indeed give agency and coherence to—a disciplined nationalist movement emerging from a "demoralized" national populace. Gendered notions of character, images of bodily integrity, and the nascent nationalist movement are continually woven together by Nehru's metaphors: writing of the humility needed for party leadership of the masses, he notes that "conceit, like fat on the human body, grows imperceptibly, layer upon layer, and the person whom it affects is unconscious of the daily accretion" (206). What is needed here is conscious control, continual discipline, and trimness.

Such adoptions and reworkings of character and discipline were certainly effective discursively; in London the autobiography received favorable reviews that concentrated less on the subject matter of the book than on the integrity of the narrator and protagonist. "It is a sincere book," noted a review in the *Times,* "written in an easy, almost conversational style, a book to be read, however much one may disagree with the outlook of the author."[15] The government of India briefly considered banning the *Autobiography,* then allowed its distribution after it had been reviewed by a government officer from the Home Department, who noted, "Nehru is a clean and honest fighter and one point which struck me about the book is that it is written without any bitterness"; "incidents tending to reflect discredit on Government are described objectively and without any undue exaggeration of language."[16] Here the integrity of the narrator enables an entry into and agency within a history already marked out by the colonizer.

The most devastating comment that the new viceroy, Lord Linlithgow, could make on the book was that it was "very dull."[17]

Yet it would be a mistake to see Nehru's text as simply answering back as a loyal opposition within a discourse that contains it, focusing all nationalist struggle on the austere disciplining of the effete bourgeois body. In becoming a "historian of himself" Nehru moves, as his predecessors and successors would frequently do, beyond colonialism and particular nationalisms to a larger movement of history, and in particular to the celebration of a certain style of heroic masculinity as a history's cynosure. One example may suffice here: At the time of writing his *Autobiography*, Nehru had recently finished the series of articles that became the pamphlet *Whither India?* Clearly influenced by his visit to Russia in 1927 and by subsequent reading of Trotsky, Marx, and writings on the Soviet Union in prison, Nehru urged those fighting against imperialism to choose between the politics of the "magic or of science" and to cast aside "religious or sentimental processes which confuse and befog the mind."[18] Outlining a vision of imperialism informed by Lenin's *Imperialism: The Highest Stage of Capitalism* (1916), Nehru noted the "living incentive and inspiration of the Russian Revolution" in the "evening of the capitalist system" (6:7, 9). The nationalist movement, largely bourgeois in inspiration, would be superseded by a profound social revolution, a movement "to national freedom within the framework of an international cooperative socialist world federation" (6: 16). India would thus join the inevitable progress of world history.

What is interesting about *Whither India?* is that the science, "logic," and "clarity of thought" such change demands is embodied in an implied narrator, a "newcomer from prison" who can "see the realities under the surface of ever-changing phenomena" (6:1). This is obviously a transparent reference to Nehru himself, but, given the Leninist nature of the essay itself, it also seems to draw a parallel with the Lenin of 1917, newly returned from exile and able to dictate the strategic direction of the revolution. In a series of letters to his daughter, Indira, written from 1930 to 1933, Nehru had praised Lenin as "wholly without self-consciousness . . . [;] the very embodiment of an idea": "There was no doubt or vagueness in Lenin's mind. His were the penetrating eyes which detected the moods of the masses; the clear head which could apply and adapt well-thought-out principles to changing situations; the inflexible will which held on to the course he had mapped out, regardless of immediate consequences. . . . The hour had produced the man."[19] Lenin as described here epitomizes the revolutionary subject on which Nehru would attempt to model the protagonist of the *Autobiography*. He is pure rationality, all "eyes," "mind" and "head," without corporeality. And while Nehru's interest here is also driven by his interest in the 1930s in socialism and a command economy, Lenin is also a type for a masculine "subject of freedom" with potentially much wider resonance. The many letters Nehru received from readers show this. A correspondent from the United States wrote that he found the book "not a biography of a world figure, it is an epic of India; but even more, the portrayal of our entire Age, from a certain—and I think the most valid—viewpoint, that of a Scientist tussling with 'Man, the Unknown'"; another concentrated on the autobiography as conduct book, noting its role in a personal transformation, a realization that "the most important thing in life is the preservation of ideals."[20]

The skill with which Nehru's autobiography allows its protagonist to claim a place within a grand narrative of history and to wrest the story of modernity from colonialism can perhaps be best illustrated through microanalysis of an early chapter in the text, entitled "An Interlude at Nabha." This describes Nehru's brief imprisonment with companions in 1923 in Nabha, one of British India's quasi-independent "princely states." In narratological terms, as its title suggests, it is a satellite with little function in advancing the action. It does not provide an Aristotelian moment of recognition to the protagonist, in the manner of Nehru's early, life-changing encounter with peasant movements in the United Provinces in 1920. Yet the chapter is interesting because the events it describes were extensively narrativized elsewhere: by Nehru at the time through correspondence with his father and in two statements to the court, and by the colonial state—if this is not a misnomer in the Indian context—in Home Department files.

The facts of the incident that all versions of the narrative agree on are these: Nehru went to the princely state with two Congress colleagues because of Sikh protests inspired by the British deposition of the previous ruler of the state, and connected to the larger Akali social reform movement. Unknown to him, an order had been issued by the Nabha authorities prohibiting his entry to the state. This order was duly served on Nehru and his companions at the town of Jaito, and they were arrested and transferred to Nabha jail. After two weeks of imprisonment and court proceedings, which Nehru, with his legal training, found "Gilbertian," he and his companions were sentenced to thirty months of "rigorous imprisonment"; the sentences were then apparently suspended, and they were instructed to leave Nabha immediately (111).[21]

Each account, of course, has its own discursive context. In the police office files, the administrator of Nabha, J. Wilson Johnson, struggles with the contradictions of indirect rule in his letters and telegrams to his superiors. He is worried about a potential "outcry in the press as to the conditions in the State jail," and he urges prosecution of newspapers and heavy sentences for Nehru and his companions, but is contradicted by the guarded realpolitik of the larger interests of a colonial state that is aware of Congress's adroit ability to make use of the media.[22] As Nehru would perceptively note in his autobiography, the administrator is bound by the contradictions of indirect rule, by a "combination of feudalism and the modern bureaucratic machine with the disadvantages of both and the advantages of neither" (114). Nehru's own initial draft statement stresses individual agency as part of a larger movement of history; it mocks the administration of Nabha as feudal and aligns its narrator's experience with that of Darbara Singh, a Sikh companion arrested with him who has already suffered during the *Komagata Maru* incident in which Indian immigrants on a ship were turned away from Canada. Yet this version was not presented in court. "I would make a plain simple statement of the facts and eliminate all personal references . . . or attacks" commented Nehru's father, Motilal, on reading this draft, and Nehru's revised statement to the court follows this advice.[23] Darbara Singh now vanishes: Nehru's statement operates within a narrowed discursive context, making the court into a theatre of modernity, and demonstrating how far the administrative practice of the state, sanctioned by colonialism, shows "a remarkable disregard of all rules of law and procedure."[24] Finally, the retrospective narrative of the incident in the autobiography places it within a personal and historical narrative that now, after the Congress's 1930 declaration of independence, hints more strongly at the formation of the nation-state to be.

Yet we should not be limited entirely by the contextual pragmatics of each document; each also negotiates a central tension between the individual and the collective, and the manner in which the social is imagined. Wilson Johnson's text is the product of an ethnographic state that acts on Foucauldian "populations"—the Akali movement becomes a purely internal matter within a Sikh community, without other significance, and Nehru and his companions, as individualized outside agitators, thus a threat to a shared "public tranquility." We might see this expressed in the choice of transport by the Congress members: in Wilson Johnson's account, which follows a carefully graded hierarchy, "Jawahar Lal . . . riding a horse . . . [and t]he other two gentlemen . . . seated in a bullock cart."[25] Nehru's first statement folds individual action into collective opposition to the colonial state: its protagonist rejoices: "I am being tried for a cause the Sikhs have made their own" and finishes with the cry "Sat Sri Akal!"[26] In this narrative, bullock cart and horse (and it is never clear who makes use of each) are discarded two or three miles from Jaito, as Nehru and his companions "walk along in . . . [the *jatha*'s] wake," following the group's progress as the individuals here become submerged within the masses (1:371). His second statement adopts a different tactic: the individual submits to the colonial state as an individual but demands the fulfillment of its deferred promise of rights, which it is, of course, constitutionally unable to fulfill. And the autobiography makes a further, and perhaps more comprehensively appropriative gesture: it aligns both individual and collective experience with a larger narrative of state formation. Nehru and his companions arrive in a "country cart," following but "keeping apart" from the *jatha*: it is unclear at what point, if any, they resort to walking (110). The text of the *Autobiography* thus manages the contradiction of being both "a personal account" and a representative one, a "wholly one-sided and, inevitably, egotistical" narrative by "a person who . . . became merged" into a wider movement of history so that it "represents, in a large measure, the feelings of many others": Nehru and his companions are here a part of a movement of people with historical significance, and yet they still retain their status as distinct individuals (xii, v).

Further strategies work to enhance the spectacle of a representative individual as the focus of a grand historical narrative. The particularity of the individual is emptied out; as in much of the *Autobiography,* personal relationships with family and friends and the emotions they incite are elided. The detention at Nabha precipitated a violent disagreement between India's future prime minister and his father, Motilal Nehru, who came to Nabha jail to interview him and arrange for his legal defense: this is extensively documented in Home Office accounts and in Nehru's own correspondence. Motilal's role in the *Autobiography* is reduced to a single paragraph, and the confrontation between father and son, which was clearly very intense emotionally, is omitted.[27]

In parallel to this, "An Interlude at Nabha" also reworks the historical narrative in which the protagonist as individual is placed, poaching it from the control of colonialism. The colonial state, far from being enlightened and developmental, is shown to work through feudalism. The presiding magistrate at the court is illiterate, the jail "unwholesome and insanitary," the legal proceedings farcical (111). In giving all authority in Nabha to a British administrator, the government of India has only succeeded in producing "a tightening-up of all the feudal and autocratic bonds" (114). If the colonial state is regressive and cannot realize the historical project of modernity, nationalism, Nehru's narrative suggests, is the vehicle through which modernity may be achieved. Through a series of rhetorical sleights of hand in the first page of Nehru's account, a particular incident is made the center of a series of widening circles of significance. The struggle of Sikhs in a single princely state is first attached to the reformist Akali movement, and this movement is then attached to the "general awakening" of nationalism (109). This chain of connections exemplifies a tendency noted by the Subaltern Studies Collective for Indian "elite historiography" to accredit "popular mobilizations" to a swelling narrative of nationalist emancipation, guided by the Congress.[28] And Nehru even now looks to a wider circle of world history, beyond the nation. In both the testimony he wrote at the time of his trial, and in the *Autobiography*, we have seen, Nehru and his companions are guided to Jaito by a Sikh who has been involved in the *Komagata Maru* incident of 1914, in which a ship of Indian—largely Sikh—immigrants challenged Canadian exclusionist immigration laws. In Nehru's testimony in 1923, he and his companions meet Dabara Singh, and are guided by him. In conversation, they come to know of the Komagata Maru connection.[29] In the *Autobiography*, written a decade later, Dabara Singh is not named and remains a more shadowy figure: Nehru only learns of his *Komagata Maru* connection well after release from Nabha jail. In both narratives a connection is made beyond the national struggle itself and a larger movement of world history: in the *Autobiography*, however, this connection recedes more deeply into a "narrative unconscious." There is a sense in which world history is occurring independently of the protagonists, and the text suggests that they must become aware of it through analysis and investigation before acting in unison with it.

Yet the *Autobiography*'s re-framing of the incident at Nabha, though skilful, is not without ambivalence; in a manner which is typical of many episodes in the succeeding narrative, the "interlude" ends not with certainty, but with a reflexive backward glance. The connection and yet contradiction between individual and collective history is central to the narrative of the *Autobiography*, and yet aligning these histories results in a certain narrative violence. Darbara Singh, in the autobiography, is reduced to anonymity, and although Nehru hastens to reassure us that he is "not forgotten," narrative pressure has its own amnesia. He is left behind by Nehru and his companions to sink "into the oblivion of a provincial prison" and we hear no more of him (115). A. T. Gidwani, one of Nehru's companions, we are told, returned to Nabha six months later: he was rearrested. "I felt inclined to go to Nabha myself," Nehru writes in the *Autobiography*, and "allow the Administrator to treat me as he had treated Gidwani." But practicalities intervened, "friends thought otherwise and dissuaded me . . . , and I have always felt a little ashamed of thus deserting a colleague" (116). The merging of "representative" individual and national narratives here writes other individuals' narratives out.

Nehru and his companions took an "unpleasant companion" away from Nabha: typhoid, contracted in the jail cell. Yet the Congress leader took away another companion, a realization of the way a necessary narrative of national liberation would write out other histories, the necessity and yet the violence of this telling of stories, the shaping, casting of "awakening" into the frame of a vanguardist party that would found the new state. It is to Nehru's credit that he, to a much greater extent than his successors, was aware of the pain of this contradiction; the energy expended in trying to overcome it, indeed, accounts for much of the power of the narrative.

Imagining India

To explore this tension between individual and collective more fully, we need to move back from the microanalysis of an individual incident to reconsider the imaginative geography of the *Autobiography*. Nehru's narrative is structured through an opposition between the heat of the Indo-Gangetic plain and the South on one hand, and the cool mountainous landscapes of the Himalayas and the North West Frontier—and, by extension, the icy landscapes of Norway and Switzerland—on the other. This opposition leads to others and also creates a series of homologies between binarisms such as the personal and the collective, and the individual body and the body politic, suggesting ways personal and national narratives might be mapped onto each other as part of a grander narrative of modernity.

Nehru's narrative begins—and ends, if one considers the 1940 addition "Five Years Later" as an integral part of the text—in Kashmir. The mountains of Kashmir and the Himalayas in general are associated with freedom, and the cool rationality with which Nehru elsewhere invests modernity. The title of the *Autobiography*'s first chapter, "Descent from Kashmir," is deliberately punning—it looks back to Nehru's Kashmiri ancestors, but it also dramatizes a fall into a "sea of Indian and non-Indian humanity" (13). Nehru's narrative is punctured by attempts—either actual or vicarious—to return to these heights: he describes in detail a visit to the snowy landscapes of Norway while at Cambridge, and the chapter "My Wedding and an Adventure in the Himalayas," describing events in 1916, contains only one paragraph referring to the former event, and much discussion of the latter, describing the protagonist's "strange satisfaction in these wild and desolate haunts of nature" (37). The "mountain-top" of the Swiss sanatorium in a 1926 visit, "surrounded by the winter snow" provides a space of "far freer human relationships," while the Himalayas continue to be a source of inspiration throughout the narrative (148). When he is moved to Almora prison to be nearer his ailing wife, Nehru rejoices in "a sense of exhilaration. Higher and higher we went: the gorges deepened: the peaks lost themselves in the clouds: the vegetation changed until the firs and pines covered the hill-sides" (568) "Five Years Later," we have noted, ends with a return to Kashmir, which closes the narrative: Nehru returns to his homeland after an absence of twenty-three years. "I wandered about the Valley and the higher mountains and climbed a glacier, and felt that life was worth while [*sic*]" (611).

The landscape of Kashmir takes on a metaphorical valence for Nehru both inside and outside the text of the *Autobiography*. In his first epilogue to the volume, the author compares both his own life and the project of the realization of the nation to mountain climbing. His own struggle, Nehru notes, has been marked by a "spiritual loneliness"; he is "a stranger and alien in the West," but also has "an exile's feeling" in his own country: "The distant mountains seem easy of access and climbing, the top beckons, but, as one approaches, difficulties appear, and the higher one goes the more laborious becomes the journey and the summit recedes into the clouds. Yet the climbing is worth the effort and has its own joy and satisfaction" (596–97). This metaphorization of a solitary individual in a mountain landscape also recalls Nehru's use of mountain climbing to describe the process of reading and acquiring knowledge in a letter to his daughter, Indira, written while he was completing revisions to the *Autobiography*. "Books," Nehru writes, "give us the experiences and thoughts of innumerable others, often the wisest of their generation, and lift us out of our narrow ruts. Gradually as we go up the mountainsides fresh vistas come into view, our vision extends further and further, and a sense of proportion comes to us."[30]

On one level, Nehru's investment in mountain landscapes and the sublime might be seen as an appropriation—and, through his fascination with the Himalayas, an indigenization—of Romantic tropes which became associated with colonialism. The Romantics, Maurice Bernal notes, "longed for small, virtuous and 'pure' communities in remote and cold places," and, paradoxically, transposed their qualities—associated with discipline and rationality—onto Greece, thus othering Africa and occluding Africa's role in Europe's past.[31] Richard Dyer goes further, noting the association of such landscapes with racialized discourses of whiteness, and their thus coming to epitomize "the white character, its energy, enterprise, discipline and spiritual elevation, even the white body, its hardness and tautness (born of the battle with the elements, and often unfavorably compared with the slack bodies of non-whites), its uprightness (aspiring to the heights), its affinity with (snowy) whiteness."[32] In this context, Nehru's reclamation of the landscapes of Kashmir and the Himalaya in general might be placed as part of a larger effort to establish a specifically Indian rationality as a foundation for modernity. Indian tradition as expressed in the Upanishads is not based on "blind dogma" but on the quest "for knowledge, for enlightenment"; the science of socialism might strip away the accretions of "routine observance of dead forms or ritual and creed" and enable the emergence of a scientific attitude that was uniquely Indian and indeed emancipatory (429, 430).[33] In his later years, Nehru's investment in the sublime landscape of Kashmir would be supplemented by an equal awe for a technological sublime, exemplified by the austere modernity of Le Corbusier's Chandigarh—diminishing forever the tawdry colonial modernity of Lutyens's New Delhi—or the massed concrete of the Bhakra-Nangal dam.

Nehru's use of the alpine sublime in the *Autobiography,* however, is more complex than this. In one sense, the sublime of Kashmir is Burkean—it excites "ideas of pain and danger," Nehru's first experience of climbing in Kashmir resulting in an accident which nearly ends his life.[34] Yet the confrontation with the sublime also, crucially, produces the individuation necessary, in Nehru's schema, for modernity. Immanuel Kant noted that a "Savoyard peasant" would have "unhesitatingly called all lovers of snow mountains fools": "true sublimity," indeed, should "be sought only in the mind of the judging subject."[35] Nehru's sublime is Kantian in this sense, encouraging the application of an individual subject's faculty of reason in the face of the unknown. His accounts of the Himalayas and other mountain landscapes always stress the solitary individual uncontaminated by collective responsibilities and, perhaps above all, free from affective bonds to others. The movement from the single paragraph description of his wedding to the extended narration of "an adventure in the Himalayas" is prototypical of this: the emotion of an intimate relationship is displaced by a solitary encounter with nature. "I am here in the Himalayas," wrote Nehru in a letter written while the *Autobiography* was being composed, "perched up on a ridge, communing with the sky and the clouds."[36]

One further element of Nehru's investment in the Himalayas and in mountainous frontier landscapes suggests itself; mountains seem to be an arena for the rediscovery of a heroic masculinity that has vanished from the heat of the plain. Nehru read accounts of exploration avidly while in jail. In a 1932 letter subsequently published in a collection by Sonia Gandhi, he noted that he had "been reading travel books and with their help I have crossed great deserts and vast glaciers," entering a heroic age, following the paths trod by "Chengiz Khan and Timur."[37] Similar sentiments occurred to him on a visit to the North West Frontier in 1938. Writing to his daughter, Nehru again saw Frontier Province as an epic place, full of "fine upstanding men and women."[38] He celebrated crossing "the Indus almost at the very spot where Alexander is supposed to have crossed" (364), having on an earlier occasion expressed a liking for the vitality of "the Frontier People—simple, childlike, brave, and rather primitive."[39] Nehru's investment here seems in many ways to tie in with his avid consumption of mountaineering and exploration narratives: the mountainous frontier enables one to imagine an epic or heroic narrative in which the interests of protagonist and history are perfectly aligned.

The arena for the independence struggle was not, however, Kashmir or even Simla, but rather the cities of the plains—Lucknow, Amritsar, Delhi, Calcutta, Karachi, Rawalpindi—the countryside, and the plateau of the Deccan stretching South. In the imagined geography of the *Autobiography*, this is a very different India; distinguished not by solitude and contemplation but crowds whose enthusiasms threaten to engulf the protagonist. In his early, life-changing involvement with kisan agitation in the United Provinces on which the *Autobiography* turns as a narrative, Nehru travels into the countryside around Allahabad, noting how it is "afire with enthusiasm and full of a strange excitement" (51). Ever after, he notes, "my mental picture of India always contains this naked, hungry mass." In Nehru's retrospective construction, the plunge into the peasantry is a time of unmediated contact: "I spoke to them, man to man, and told them what I had in my mind and my heart" (57). The mass expresses the essence of the Indian nation; Congress must come closer and closer to "peasant" India, become "more and more the representative of the rural masses" (255, 416). When elected president of Congress in 1929 Nehru experiences "overflowing enthusiasm" from crowds "for a symbol and an idea, not for me personally; yet it was no little thing for a person to become that symbol, even for a while, in the eyes and the hearts of great numbers of people, and I felt exhilarated and lifted out of myself" (201). The crowd here animates the leader, driving him forward on a quest to realize the nation.

Even this passage, however, hints at a certain uneasiness; Nehru frequently, and increasingly as the narrative progresses, expresses discomfort at being "lifted out" of himself, at the crowd's corrosive effect on individuality.

In a letter to Indira just after the *Autobiography* was published, he described being overwhelmed by a "mass of seething humanity" on a temple visit; such "multitudes" are associated with feudalism, but with a regressive and petrified stasis rather than the heroic or epic narrative of the mountains, the crowd's fraught emotions amplifying "the power of the priesthood."[40] The mundane crowd of the plain embodies India, an India associated with an oceanic femininity, "*Bharat Mata,* Mother India, a beautiful lady, very old but ever youthful in appearance, sad-eyed and forlorn, cruelly treated by aliens and outsiders, and calling upon her children to protect her" (431). Nehru acknowledges the power of this mundane India and yet remains necessarily distanced from it: as the narrative progresses the time of an unmediated contact with the masses becomes a textual imaginary, sometimes approached, often remembered, but never quite recaptured.

This constitutive ambivalence can best be illustrated by a memorable scene from the *Autobiography.* In Allahabad in 1930, Nehru finds that his house attracts "crowds of pilgrims" who stop off on their visit to Allahabad for the Kumbh Mela; he responds initially by greeting them, but, as this proves "an impossible undertaking," he decides to "hide" from "prying eyes" (203). When asked by a friend what he thinks of this popular adulation he receives, the Congress leader typically indulges in introspection:

> The crowd had filled some inner need of mine. The notion that I could influence them and move them to action gave me a sense of authority over their minds and hearts; and this satisfied, to some extent, my will to power. On their part, they exercised a subtle tyranny over me, for their confidence and affection moved inner depths within me and evoked emotional responses. Individualist as I was, sometimes the barriers of individuality seemed to melt away, and I felt that it would be better to be accursed with these unhappy people than to be saved alone. But the barriers were too solid to disappear, and I peeped over them with wondering eyes at this phenomenon which I failed to understand. (206)

There is a sense here of the need to resist the crowd's corrosive effect on individuality, which leads back to emotion and the inner depths of, presumably, the premodern. Crucially, Nehru chooses to remain behind the barrier, to maintain autonomy from the enthusiasm of the crowd: he decides to be "saved" rather than "accursed." Yet the temptation—and the contradiction it represents—will not go away. It has both a political dimension, in that national enthusiasm is necessary but needs to be trained in order to realize the project of modernity will give Indian a "new garment," and yet it also has a personal element, as if the imaginative geography of

India is written internally and intimately into the body of the narrator himself (432).

Nehru's metaphors of hardness and softness, solid barriers and melting oceans—which we have seen here attached to gendered landscapes—are connected to nationalism and, indeed, the place of nationalism within a larger narrative of modernity. Yet the Congress leader uses them also to talk about his own self-fashioning. In a moment of vulnerability in the early 1940s, he wrote to Indira about the strain of keeping emotions in check. His shell of restraint, Nehru noted, was a means of "self-protection":

> Yet, I fear, this hardness is only at the surface and underneath lies a sea of sentiment which has often frightened me. A life-time of disciplined living and deliberate training of the mind and body to make them efficient instruments for the purpose I had in view, has thrown a hard shell over this turbulent mass and on the whole I feel fairly sure of myself. This has given me a certain degree of self-confidence and usually a crisis or difficulty makes me clearer-headed and calmer. Yet on occasions the shell bursts to my great discomfiture.[41]

Drawing on a metaphor taken from the current war in Europe, Nehru described this shell of defense as a "mighty Maginot Line which could after all be so easily turned" (11:592). Yet if in his autobiography Nehru seems increasingly wary of venturing beyond his personal Maginot line, he finds a way to compensate for this: his relationship with the most important character in the *Autobiography,* Mohandas K. Gandhi, vicariously and relationally elaborates his need to guide and yet embody the masses.

The Paradox of Gandhi

Gandhi is a central figure in the *Autobiography.* The early narrative turns on the arrival of Nehru's senior colleague from South Africa and his undertaking of agitation against the Rowlatt Bills in 1919. Gandhi provides the impetus that rescues the young Nehru from the torpor of bourgeois life in Allahabad, offering "a way out of the tangle, a method of action which was straight and open" (41). Early in the narrative, Gandhi is subsumed within the same Victorian and bourgeois disciplinary masculinity that marks the book's creation of its protagonist's "character." Thus, in describing his father's affection for Gandhi, Nehru recalls that he "did not admire Gandhiji as a saint or a Mahatma, but as a man. Strong and unbending himself, he admired strength of spirit in him. For it was clear that this little man of poor physique had something of steel in him, something rock-like which did not yield to physical powers, however great they might be" (129). One might, of course, link this description to Gandhi's own explication of *swaraj* as self-discipline, not merely external independence: "Real Home Rule is Self Rule or self-control."[42] Yet it seems Nehru here is reading Gandhi's strategies of corporeal experimentation back into a "hard" national masculinity, writing out the androgyny to which, as Ashis Nandy has demonstrated, the later Gandhi appealed. Later in the text, Nehru also explicitly defends Gandhi against charges of "muddle-headed" thinking, noting that his methods are those of "a man of action, a man of wonderful courage," and designed to achieve "practical results" (289). The perception of Gandhi outside India as quaintly antimodern, he suggests, may be motivated by a stereotype of the "mysterious East" that frames discussions. Foreign journalists, in particular, misapprehend Gandhi, Nehru notes, because "of the ineradicable impression of their childhood that the East is utterly different and cannot be judged by ordinary standards" (289). This is not the first time that Nehru anticipates the concerns of postcolonial theory and criticism later in the century: the mode of thought he describes here is prescient of Edward Said's analysis of the discourse of the Orient in *Orientalism*.

Even here, however, Nehru's defense of Gandhi is not without contradictions. In a 1933 letter, Nehru responds to Aldous Huxley's concern at Gandhi's dismissal of modernity by making a point similar to that discussed above, noting that Gandhi's "attitude to science is very far from being hostile."[43] However, Nehru then makes a further argument which undercuts the first, noting that Gandhi's views are not representative of Congress policy or general feelings among Congress activists. Clearly still troubled by Huxley's questions, he attempts a third strategy—an elaborate justification of practices initiated by Gandhi, such as the production of cloth through hand-spinning, in terms that seem very far from Gandhi's own thought. Thus hand-spinning is not "the rival of machinery," but functions as a reserve means of production that might be useful in war or a prolonged economic blockade (5:512). "I believe in the machine and would have it spread in India," Nehru notes, "but I believe also in the social control of it" (5:513). The argument begins to collapse under a series of recursive contradictions.

Nehru cannot, however, indefinitely sustain such intellectual tightrope walking. In the text of the *Autobiography* itself, vigorous defense of Gandhi is tempered by a growing disillusionment that is perhaps more on the part of the narrator than the protagonist. Nehru as protagonist undergoes a number of changes in his relationship with his erstwhile mentor, in which disagreements that approach acrimony, such as their conflict over the exact tactics to be followed by the independence movement in early 1928, are followed by periods of reconciliation.[44] Nehru the narrator, however, always commenting retrospectively on the text, occupies a different time, that of the writing of the *Autobiography* over eight months from June 1934 onward, under "peculiarly distressing circumstances" caused not only by his wife's illness, but also, and indeed perhaps primarily, by Gandhi's "monstrous" and "immoral" reasoning in his withdrawal of civil disobedience (559, 505). It is this latter, retrospective reconstruction of the relationship with Gandhi that dominates the *Autobiography*, and gives a clue to the function of the character of Gandhi within the text as a relational element in Nehru's own exemplary subject formation.

For Nehru, Gandhi is a paradox who embodies his conflicts about India itself.[45] Even early in the *Autobiography*, the narrator recounts puzzlement with Gandhi among the Congress leadership, and in particular his "frequent reference to *Rama Raj* as a golden age which was to return" (72). All find him "a very difficult person to understand. . . . Often we discussed his fads and peculiarities among ourselves and said, half-humorously, that when Swaraj came these fads must not be encouraged" (73). Gandhi has no theory of the state, no concept of "the modern idea of a party which is built up to seize the State power in order to refashion the political and economic structure" which is central to Nehru the narrator, the Nehru of *Whither India?* (252). His frequent references to religion irritate Nehru, and in the last part of the *Autobiography* the critique becomes stronger. Indians cannot, the narrator argues, take "refuge in vague and emotional phrases, but must face these facts and adapt ourselves to them, so that we may become the subjects of history instead of being its helpless objects" (527). Gandhi's methods give no possibility of agency in modernity, and, while he pushes nonviolence as a creed, he accepts the institutional violence in social structures such as the land tenure system. Ultimately, Nehru notes, economic interests weigh more than moral convictions when governing individual and collective behavior: modernity may only be born through a complete economic and political restructuring of society, and Gandhi's vision of this is regressive, based on idealization of the backward environment of the village (544).

Nehru's growing aversion to Gandhi's politics is expressed more viscerally in his narrative by an increasing focus on Gandhi's body. Nehru's investment in notions of character and heroic masculinity, we have earlier noted, involves a stress on trimness and balance, on bodily discipline and order, and the application of disciplinary rules that subordinate the body to the will. "More and more I feel," he wrote to Indira, "that health comes from the inside rather than the outside, from the observance of the simple rules of life and activity, and at the same time from almost forgetting the body rather than tending it carefully like a hothouse plant."[46] Such self-care, Nehru stressed should avoid a "morbid interest in my body"; yet Gandhi's asceticism promotes such interest as readily as the indulgent epicureanism of the middle classes.[47] Gandhi's stress on sexual abstinence is thus "extraordinary." "If he is right," notes Nehru, "I am a criminal on the verge of imbecility and nervous prostration" (512). "Sex," he elaborates, "has played its part in my life, but it has not obsessed me or diverted me from my other activities. It has been a subordinate part" (513). For Gandhi's junior colleague, balance is all.

Nehru's critique extends to other ascetic practices. "I understand and appreciate simplicity, equality, self-control, but not the mortification of the flesh," he writes while discussing Gandhi toward the end of his narrative: "Just as an athlete requires to train his body, I believe that the mind and habits have also to be trained and brought under control. It would be absurd to expect that a person who is given to too much self-indulgence can endure much suffering or show unusual self-control or behave like a hero when the crisis comes. To be in good moral condition requires at least as much training as to be in good physical condition. But that certainly does not mean asceticism or self-mortification" (510–11). "Self-mortification" here can lead to weakness rather than strength, to a turning inward rather than preparing the protagonist to venture out into the public sphere.

For all this, however, Gandhi remains an attractive figure to Nehru even at the end of his autobiographical narrative, one he cannot let go. While Nehru's reading of Gandhi is sophisticated—he sees him not as a simple embodiment of tradition but as a modern man of "the keenest intellect, of fine good feeling and good taste, wide vision"—he clearly sees him as representing India, having an almost instinctive connection with the people with whom Nehru himself has a more ambivalent relationship (253). Gandhi manages to "represent the peasant masses of India; he is the quintessence of the conscious and subconscious will of those millions"; thus his coming revived India's "ancient and half-forgotten memories, and gave her glimpses of her own soul" (253, 254). Even when at his most critical, Nehru acknowledges Gandhi to be "a wonderful man . . . , with his amazing and almost irresistible charm and subtle power over people. . . . He came to represent India to an amazing degree and to express the very spirit of that ancient and tortured land. Almost he was India, and his very failings were Indian failings" (508). Gandhi and the Indian nation cannot be divided.

For Nehru, then, Gandhi represents a paradox; in Nehru's portrayal of him, Gandhi has the unmediated access to the feminized India associated with crowds, masses, "the people," to embody their will. The colonial state has imposed itself on this India. The British have "seized her body and possessed her, but it was the possession of violence. They did not know her or try to know her. They never looked into her eyes" (429). Gandhi seems to offer the solution of knowing this India intimately, but it is a knowledge that precludes action, a surrender to the "infinite charm" of the nation that forestalls an attempt to embed nationalism within a progressive narrative of modernity or subject national enthusiasm to the individualizing disciplines of a postcolonial state (602).

The notion of the state enclosing and disciplining the nation, we have seen, is also enacted at the level of the body itself. Nehru's *Autobiography* differs from Gandhi's in its uses of corporeality: there is no elaborate siting of modernity in "experiments" conducted on the body. Rather like the canonical nineteenth-century and early-twentieth-century biographies that precede it, it moves away from the male body, changing the body into a metaphor—or, at best, metonym—for objects amenable to rational control. And yet Nehru's own situation under colonialism means that he cannot, even if he wishes, escape the corporeal. Colonialism works on the body in many ways. Bodies are foundational to the rule of colonial difference, as Nehru's protagonist learns early in the narrative. Despite his "sheltered" childhood, he is aware that railway compartments and benches in parks are reserved for Europeans, and one of the family stories he tells is of how an uncle was nearly arrested when his aunt was mistaken for an English girl by British soldiers, being "very fair, as some Kashmiri children are" (6, 2). The threat of physical violence, too, is never far away. The most memorable elements of Nehru's account of imprisonment at Nabha are those that most vividly dramatize the physical restraints of colonialism: Nehru and his companions being led, shackled, through the streets of Jaito, or the physical discomfort of Nabha jail.

Anupama Rao and Steven Pierce have argued that disciplinary techniques that made the body their target were a central feature of colonialism, and yet also note that violence enacted on the body of the colonized was also an act in which colonialism's contradictions became apparent. Chatterjee's "rule of colonial difference," in this reading, ultimately sanctioned violence, since, rather than seeing "natives as subjectified and thus open to enlightened socialization, . . . colonialism relied . . . on corporeal regimes that reconfigured native bodies as legitimately susceptible to the exercise of violence in the interests of good governance."[48] Yet such violence directed at the body also called the civilizing mission of colonialism into question, since it seemed, if anything, to resemble the "primitive savagery" that colonialism sought to eradicate.

Leadership in the nationalist movement brings Nehru into situations where the violence of colonialism acts directly on his body; as Rao and Pierce suggest, such violence also provides an opportunity for thinking beyond colonialism. In an extraordinary passage, he experiences a defamiliarizing double consciousness when facing his first lathi charge in Lucknow in 1928:

> I felt stunned, and my body quivered all over but, to my surprise and satisfaction, I found that I was still standing. . . .
>
> The bodily pain I felt was quite forgotten in a feeling of exhilaration that I was physically strong enough to face and bear *lathi* blows. And a thing that surprised me was that right through the incident, even when I was being beaten, my mind was quite clear and I was consciously analysing my feelings. (178, italics in original)

In one sense, the disassociation Nehru here feels represents a triumph of the will over a "desire to hit out": in this and a subsequent incident his "long training and discipline" distinguishes the protagonist from "European sergeants" who administer the beating, their faces "full of hate and blood-lust, almost mad, with no trace of sympathy or touch of humanity" (180). Savagery is now the property of the colonizer, rationality the source of strength for the colonial subject seeking freedom. And yet, as happens frequently with Nehru, the chapter in which he recounts the incident ends in a reflexive manner, suggesting that the body and the emotions that he associates with it are not mastered. "Probably," he notes, "the faces on our side just then were equally hateful to look at" (180). He, his fellows, and indeed the British themselves, Nehru's narrator notes, are the "blind tools" of "strange and powerful forces which held us in thrall and cast us hither and thither," working not through rationality but through "desires and passions" (181).

The contradiction expressed above is central to Nehru's text. Nationalism in the *Autobiography* individuates Indian subjects by drawing them away from practices advocated by "communalists" into the rationality of modernity (472). As a mechanism for the production of the modern, it will eventually be replaced by socialism; if in the present "religion recedes into the background and nationalism appears in aggressive garbs," behind nationalism are "other isms which talk in social and economic terms" (472). Yet anticolonial modernity is always already relational—it cannot be simply an act of Kantian self-constituting Enlightenment, a simple act of individuation, of daring to know. To be a modern anticolonial subject means that one must become individualized but then as an individual, as a citizen now, not a subject, become part of the larger community of the nation through which the culture of the colonized may be reclaimed, packaged, and achieve the autonomy necessary for the national liberation and entry into the modern world. Thus in Nehru's national autobiography, as in others of its kind, there is a simultaneous need to be both unique and representative, part of and yet separate from the masses, to combine, in Mulk Raj Anand's words, "prophecy and autobiography," to point "out the path to himself and to others."[49] At the end of the *Autobiography,* Nehru summarizes this tension: "I have been one of a mass, moving with it, swaying it occasionally, being influenced by it; and yet, like the other units, an individual, apart from the others, living my separate life in the heart of the crowd" (595).

The Discipline of Prison

The greatest of paradoxes is that Nehru seems to find a resolution to the tensions and conflicts enacted in the *Autobiography* in the one place he is most subject to the discipline of the colonial state: prison. Nehru was jailed nine times between 1921 and the end of the Second World War and in the years from 1930 to 1935, during which the *Autobiography* was conceived and written, was rarely out of jail. As his stature increased, the colonial authorities were increasingly mindful of both Indian and British public opinion regarding the treatment of political prisoners and often—although inconsistently—provided him and other Congress leaders with separate quarters and the opportunity to read and write. Prison thus becomes for Nehru a space for contemplation, in which he may reconstruct the self through disciplinary practices. As a place where one's personal narrative is suspended, prison provides the opportunity for meditation on the place of the individual within the larger narrative of history that continues outside the prison's walls.

On one level, prison offers itself as a ready metaphor for the state of India under colonialism—indeed the working title of Nehru's *Autobiography, In and Out of Prison,* forces the reader to consider the compromised nature of colonial "freedom." At one point in the narrative Nehru explicitly compares Naini Prison to British India, an outward show of efficiency masking a regime "with little or no care for . . . human material," which aims to break inmates so that they "may not have the least bit of spirit left in them" and is maintained through the complicity of stool pigeons who keep the inmates divided (224–25). As in British India, the prison's apparent governmental modernity—its regulations that hint at self-improvement and reform—masks a feudal order in which underpaid warders extort money from the inmates, and make no effort to "consider the prisoner as an individual, a human being, and to improve or look after his mind" (221).

Yet Nehru's own recounting of his experiences in prison concentrates only occasionally on the politics of incarceration. He is concerned, for example, about the treatment of ordinary Congress activists, and David Arnold is surely right that the Congress leader's encounter with the "lifers" in prison perhaps represents discovery of the "real India" comparable to his early contacts with the kisans.[50] The Congress leader is also aware of the physical discomforts of prison, and indeed complains about overcrowding. In a 1931 note, for instance, he writes that it was "a sore trial to have to live with people in a barrack. Always together—no privacy—and the same persons from morning to evening—day after day—time without end! It is terrible at times and one is tempted to prefer solitary confinement even."[51] However, the preferred alternative—solitary confinement—is in fact a more rigorous form of imprisonment. There is some truth in Motilal's caustic observation, after his attempts to assist his son in Nabha jail had been rebuffed, that his visit had interrupted the "even tenor of your happy jail life."[52] Motilal's concluding comment, "I am as happy outside the jail as you are in it," again is perhaps more accurate—and indeed prescient— than Nehru's father realized (29).

"I do firmly believe," Nehru once wrote from jail, "that prison life for a period is good discipline. Physically it ought to do the body good, that is, if one does not break down under it! . . . [A] certain calmness, a peace of mind comes, and a power to detach oneself a little from the passing show and watch it almost as an outsider."[53] As we saw earlier in this chapter, prison offers the *Autobiography*'s protagonist unique opportunities for instituting a regime of self-care that will establish mental mastery over the body. During his accounts of prison terms, Nehru's narrator thus repeatedly stresses the importance of a program of regular exercise, hygiene, and a program of reading "heavy" books, avoiding the mental slackness encouraged by novels (348–52).

Prison in the *Autobiography* creates an environment in which such disciplinary work on the self can be performed. In Naini prison, Nehru notes, he and his companions were "out of it, and yet in it," their imprisonment constituting a part of a narrative of resistance, and yet inevitably cutting them "off from the strife outside" (324). This very situation solves Nehru's dilemma of wishing to be part of the crowd and yet separate from it. There is no need for a personal Maginot line, since this is provided by the prison wall: if Nehru's own personal narrative is now suspended, his imprisonment merges effortlessly with those of countless others in the narrative of national awakening. Indeed, while Nehru does not explicitly state it, the situation of the political prisoner provides a ready metaphor for the realization of modernity through the nation. Indian prisons make little attempt at reforming the prisoner—they are more like the oubliette, the place of incarceration and the infliction of pain—of a Foucauldian regime of sovereignty. Yet each prisoner—in imaginary terms for Nehru, though, of course, not in actuality—is separate; this opens up the possibility of enacting an individual reformatory project subject not to the Foucauldian surveillance of the prison but the larger and more diffuse gaze of the nationalist movement: in this sense nationalism becomes a "carceral network."[54] Disciplinary practices of normative subject formation, "a new modality of power," will be turned against the masters of the prison, against the colonial state; each prisoner, through enacting them, will become a citizen of the nation-to-be, leading a separate life as part of the new community of the nation (305). Finally, prison offers the possibility of writing a narrative that will inaugurate, or at least more firmly establish, this new social imaginary: the merging of personal and national narratives—nation as individual, individual as nation—provided in the *Autobiography* is in itself a product of prison and the ten-month disciplinary regime necessary for the composition of a manuscript.

If we retrace some of the ground covered in this chapter, we can appreciate the centrality of prison to the construction of Nehru's persona. The Indian sublime which forms one half of the binarism through which Nehru imagines India is frequently only encountered from the confines of prison. In a prototypical moment when transferred to Dehradun jail in 1932, Nehru rejoices that he can gaze at the "towering Himalayas[:] . . . these mountains that I loved"; similarly, it is while entering the "solitary grandeur" of his barrack in Almora prison that the narrator reflects on the opposition between the mountain and the plain: "The snowy peaks of the Himalayas stood glistening in the far distance, high above the wooded mountains that intervened. Calm and inscrutable they seemed, with all the wisdom of past ages, mighty sentinels over the vast Indian plain. The very sight of them cooled the fever in the brain, and the petty conflicts and intrigues, the lusts and falsehoods of the plains and the cities seemed trivial and far away before their eternal ways" (353–54, 569). It is as if the confines of prison here heighten, or even constitute the conditions necessary for, the appreciation of the sublime. Some ten or twenty times in the *Autobiography*, Nehru returns to a similar scene. The prisoner walks out of his cell into the jail compound: he looks up and sees the splendor of the mountains, clouds or stars in the sky, or even the strange beauty of airliners passing over on their way to Batavia.

The apprehension of the sublime in prison is supplemented by another feature of the narrative which seems enhanced behind the walls of the jail — an openness to affect. In a letter to his daughter looking back on the composition of the *Autobiography*, Nehru admitted that the expression of emotion had been hard for him. "I suppressed much that filled my mind and heart," he wrote. "To that extent I was untruthful"; public action in the narrative, we have seen, privileges the rationality and observation of a disembodied protagonist who is all "eyes," "mind" and "head."[55] Yet prison forces a realization of the corporeal on Nehru in ways that cannot be appropriated by the disciplinary practices of regimes of self-care. The protagonist's imprisonment, thus, often results not only in abstract contemplation but also an inescapable registering of the physical: the size of the cell or compound, the sounds of daily routine. Some of the most intimate and appealing sections of Nehru's narrative occur in prison and involve a slowing down of time and a concrete encounter with his environment that cannot be easily drawn into the abstract. Many readers of the *Autobiography* remember, for instance, the protagonist's encounters with animals in prison, his caring for abandoned baby squirrels with a fountain-pen filler or nursing a sick puppy (356–58). M. G. Hallet, appointed by the political section of the Home Department to review the text of Nehru's autobiography and judge whether it should be banned, noted that the "chapter 'Animals in Prison' is very human," while Nehru's supporter Ellen Wilkinson also praised the intimate observations of animals and birds; correspondents writing to Nehru after the publication of the text made similar observations.[56] Animals, perhaps, can never be part of the community of the nation: here Nehru can express and be moved by affect within the walls of the prison, without the need to maintain his carapace of individuality in the face of the crowd.

Kamala

Prison, and Nehru's experience of prison as a scene of writing, brings us to the focal point of the *Autobiography*, his relationship with his wife, Kamala. Nehru intimately associated the text with her: he wrote it during her long illness and indeed — through the dedication of the text, upon publication, to "Kamala, who is no more"—it is marked by her extratextual death. Toward the end of the narrative Nehru notes that his autobiography has been "written under peculiarly depressing circumstances when I was suffering from depression and emotional strain"; a few pages later he confesses guilt for his "semi-forgetful, casual attitude" to his marriage caused by his commitment to the independence struggle (559, 562). This association between Kamala and the autobiography grew over the ensuing years. When preparing to write a sequel to from jail in 1941, Nehru's thoughts again turned to Kamala. Despite his "agony of soul," he noted in a letter to Indira, he had been "untruthful. Especially this was so in the last few chapters dealing with my personal life."[57] In drafting the new volume of the autobiography—which later became *The Discovery of India*—he grew more impassioned. "Fundamental problem," he wrote in his notebook, "of human relationships," and then, of Kamala "Did I know her? Did she know me? . . . Was it our fault or fault of this environment we lived in?"[58]

The text of the autobiography as written enacts both neglect by the protagonist and belated remembrance. For most of the narrative, Kamala is a shadowy figure. The marriage ceremony is dismissed in a paragraph, and while Nehru expresses pride in her taking part in picketing of shops in Allahabad, and in her determined support for him in prison, she is not an actor or a fully realized character in the way Motilal Nehru and Gandhi are (214, 567). Even when her illness brings her to the foreground, she seems less an actor than a touchstone to provoke thought in—and at times stiffen the resolve of—the protagonist. Yet the manner in which she is central to the text can be surmised from a further comment in Nehru's 1941 notebook: "K. symbol of Indian women to me—in a sense of India."[59]

We have seen how in the *Autobiography* masculine technologies of body discipline here become metaphors for party discipline, channeling and trimming the forces of history. Femininity in the *Autobiography* comes to represent the waywardness of the nation itself, Nehru, naturally enough, utilizing the image *Bharat Mata*, of the nation as a woman—and a "specifically an upper-caste Hindu woman" at that—which was common in Indian nationalism from the nineteenth century onward, and indeed parallels a pervasive feature of many nationalisms.[60] This feminized Indian nation is "two-faced like Janus," looking "both backwards into the past and forward into the future" and trying "to combine the two" (254). Nehru, even at moments of intimacy, cannot help but actualize the disciplinary relationship of state to nation moving toward modernity in his autobiography through his relationship with Kamala. Extratextual comments by Nehru amplify what in the autobiography itself is very much a subterranean role. Despite his deep concern for Kamala, India's future prime minister was also deeply disturbed by her return to "superstition" as her death approached. "Long talks with K," he noted in his prison diary in 1935, "sometimes irritating and disturbing; at other times soothing. How very child-like she is!"[61] Nehru saw her growing religious inclinations as "all rather vague" and "a type of hysteria": he recounts that he talked with her "of science, psychology, religion, politics & economics in the larger sense" but felt his "efforts had wholly been in vain."[62] Kamala here becomes representative of India's intractability when nationalist discipline is applied; "India is so like a woman," he had noted in a previous letter, "she attracts and repels."[63] The narrative of modernity through the nation is now all-consuming. Even if he wishes to separate the stories of self or nation, to discover a place for private affect, which will resist narrativization, Nehru is no longer able to do so.

Yet if the narrative is all-consuming, it is still open to relentless questioning. In the years after the publication of the *Autobiography* and before the duties of prime minister claimed him, Nehru would continually return to life writing, trying on personas, struggling to bring personal and national narratives together. In an anonymous article entitled "The Rashtrapati," published two years after the publication of the *Autobiography,* Nehru wrote of himself in the third person, painting a picture of a Machiavellian figure performing on the "public stage with consummate artistry": "He stands on the seat of the car, balancing himself rather well, straight and seemingly tall, like a god, serene and unmoved by the seething multitude. Suddenly there is that smile again, or even a merry laugh, and the tension seems to break and the crowd laughs with him, not knowing what it is laughing at. He is godlike no longer but a human being claiming kinship and comradeship with the thousands who surround him."[64] Here again we have the dialectic of the individual and the multitude, seen now from the outside. The narrator of Nehru's article has no access to the Congress leader's consciousness and thus must speculate about his motive, wondering whether the object of his description is driven by the "will to power, of which he speaks in his *Autobiography,*" whether he might whisper to himself: "I drew these tides of men into my hands / and wrote my will across the sky in stars" (8:521). The quotation from T. E. Lawrence's *Seven Pillars of Wisdom* here is matched by a second quotation later in the essay, and the comparison is one that continued to have resonance for Nehru. During his imprisonment in 1941, he again read Lawrence's *Seven Pillars of Wisdom,* and noted that Lawrence's "problems and difficulties with himself" were "not unlike mine in some ways," and then adding, as if for reassurance, that there was "little in common between him and me."[65] Lawrence and Nehru share a feeling of exile in both Asia and Europe, of being immersed in and yet separate from the crowd; Nehru indulges in a continuous "trying on" of heroic masculinities, while at the same time remaining acutely aware of how they are contaminated by colonial power.

Ultimately, Nehru's questioning extends to the nature of writing itself. Although the Congress leader never continued his *Autobiography* after 1935, he added a series of postscripts and, in 1940, the chapter "Five Years Later." In 1941, he began a second volume, planning it meticulously, yet writing took him elsewhere, the manuscript eventually forming the basis for *The Discovery of India*.[66] In most surviving comments, Nehru felt that the narrative was complete in itself, written seemingly by "some other person . . . long ago," yet he continually came back to it when he had the opportunity: the narration of the nation as individual could never quite be complete (599).

Writing in Hindi in Almora jail soon after the completion of the *Autobiography*, Nehru meditated on the "meaning of words." Language, he noted, was "semi-frozen thought—imagination converted into statues": it served the twin functions of disciplining thought and of conveying meaning to others.[67] Many words, Nehru noted, were "nomads," wandering without any meaning "anything in special," and encouraging minds to be "semi-learned and less disciplined" (448). And the most prominent of these were phrases used by Gandhi—"God, the truth, or ahimsa"—they indicated a lack of "mental precision" (449). Again the paradox raises itself: what is most nomadic, uncontainable by the grid of the text, the structure of the narrative, the discipline of the party, are the very words whose affective power is central to the independence struggle.

The narrative of the *Autobiography* would be returned to not only by Nehru but also by his successors in the decolonization struggle, seeking a pattern by which to compose their lives. Kwame Nkrumah, as anticolonial activist in the Gold Coast, took inspiration from both Gandhi and Nehru and felt that he knew Nehru "well through his writings, his personal letters": when they finally met, the Congress leader was "all that I imagined he would be."[68] Lee Kuan Yew recalled reading Nehru's writings as a boy in the 1930s in colonial Singapore and being "moved by India's struggle for freedom, as he told it."[69] His political rival, who represented a very different kind of modernity, Malayan Communist Party secretary general Chin Peng, read Nehru avidly in parallel with Marx and Mao Zedong. Nehru's successors would grapple with the paradoxes contained within Nehru's text in imagining nations of their own, with greater certainty, perhaps, but never with greater sophistication.

5

Modernity's Body

Kwame Nkrumah's Ghana

Without discipline true freedom cannot survive.
Kwame Nkrumah

In March 1935 a young schoolteacher from the British colony of the Gold Coast applied for admission to Lincoln University, Pennsylvania. "I neither know where to begin nor where to end," he wrote in the required autobiographical essay on the application form, "because I feel that the story of my life has not been one of achievements. . . . In truth, the burden of my life can be summarized into a single line in ' The Memoriam' [*sic*] quoted by Cecil Rhodes 'So much to do[,] so little done.'"[1] Sixteen years later, the same student would return to Lincoln University to receive an honorary doctorate. As Kwame Nkrumah, leader of Government Business of the Gold Coast, the young teacher had become a key actor in and theorist of one of the great achievements of the twentieth century, decolonization. In 1957, as prime minister, he would lead his country to independence as Ghana; C. L. R. James would praise him as one of four "men who have substantially altered the shape and direction of world civilization in the last fifty years."[2] For Nkrumah, life writing would remain a central concern. His 1957 autobiography, *Ghana: The Autobiography of Kwame Nkrumah,* enacts Ghana's independence, realizing possibilities latent in Nehru's earlier autobiography, and has become an exemplary life story for a generation of anticolonial nationalists.

Nkrumah would return to Rhodes, and indeed Tennyson via Rhodes, at other times in his career. In testimony to the 1949 Watson Commission investigating his role in "disturbances" in the Gold Coast, Nkrumah— with heavy irony and a strong sense of theater—remarked that his dream of a liberated Africa was "in nature like young Rhodes at Oxford dreaming of South Africa."[3] In a fragmentary autobiography apparently written in the 1940s for a more sympathetic audience, he returned directly to Tennyson, writing, the "story of my life can be summed up in the words of the poet: 'So much to do, so little done.'"[4] And the phrase would echo in a key speech in 1953 calling for full independence for the Gold Coast. Again summoning a vision of disciplined masculinity in the service of nationhood, the Gold Coast's prime minister envisioned that the "heroes of our future will be those who can lead our people out of the stifling fog of disintegration through serfdom, into the valley of light where purpose, endeavour and determination will create that brotherhood which Christ proclaimed two thousand years ago, and about which so much is said, but so little done."[5]

By the 1950s, of course, Nkrumah had no need to tactically ignore Rhodes's racist imperial ethic and his commitment to monopoly capitalism: history had transformed the Ghanaian leader into the South African imperialist's antithesis. Yet the protagonist of Nkrumah's autobiography, his identity defined by discipline, asceticism, and unceasing work, moving through a journey that reaches its moment of arrival in the founding of the nation itself, seems very much like Max Weber's Benjamin Franklin, the "unified, sovereign subject" of nineteenth-century autobiography, and thus not so far from Rhodes himself.[6] As Nkrumah's career progressed, he would call on other models of masculinity. He would repeatedly name Nehru and Gandhi as influences; meeting Nehru in 1958 he spoke of his political awakening as motivated by "the inspiration which I personally have found" reading the Indian leader's books.[7] In the preface to his autobiography, he would refer, somewhat more eclectically, to "Hannibal, Cromwell, Napoleon, Lenin, Mazzini, Gandhi, Mussolini and Hitler," praising Nehru as "one who, pledged to Socialism, was able to interpret Gandhi's philosophy in practical terms" (viii). And Nkrumah's own welding of his narrative of personal growth would prove an attractive precedent for the fashioning of other social imaginaries in Africa. Just as Ghana was—or at least hoped to be—the model for the national liberation of most British and French colonies in Africa in the decade after the country's independence in 1957, so Nkrumah's *Ghana* formed a ready template for a number of African leaders to write the stories of their own lives.[8]

If *Ghana* clearly shows the influence of Nehru's *An Autobiography* in imagining the nation through the story of an individual life, it confronts similar discursive contexts to Nehru's: the need to reestablish masculine "character" in the face of colonial discourse's feminization of the colonized, for example, and the need to reinvent and possess national traditions. Yet there are also new challenges. The end of the Second World War hastened the process of decolonization; by 1950, India, Pakistan, Burma and Ceylon were all independent nations. In parallel, groupings such as the embryonic Non-Aligned Movement resulting from the Bandung Asia-Africa Conference in 1955 gave more concrete expressions to older social imaginaries—such as Pan-Africanism—that went beyond the nation-state, even as the process of decolonization showed the potential frailties of such imagined commonalities and alliances under a new world order that Nkrumah would call neocolonialism. Finally, we should not forget Nkrumah's own remarkable position in the wake of the collapse of the modernizing projects of so many postcolonial developmental states, including Ghana's own, from the 1960s to the 1990s. In a world of "structural adjustment," of the "postcolonial misery" of Africa's unfinished and uneven negotiation for a place within a globalizing modernity, Nkrumah's name has taken on the appearance of a floating signifier, representing everything from the excesses of corruption and megalomania to the messianic possibilities of a renewed commitment to modernity through the nation.[9]

Nehru had the solitary discipline of prison to compose his narrative. Nkrumah suffered only one prolonged period of imprisonment, under harsher conditions, and channeled all his energy while incarcerated into political action. Once released after his election victory in 1951, he was immediately absorbed in the business of government, and thus the structure of *Ghana* betrays its hasty genesis. The autobiography was hurriedly composed for the occasion of Ghana's independence in 1957, largely dictated by Nkrumah to his personal secretary, Erica Powell, and then edited on its publisher's advice to prevent libel suits by Nkrumah's political opponents.[10] It tells a story with structural parallels to Nehru's autobiography, commencing with Nkrumah's birth in Nkroful, in the extreme southwest of the Gold Coast, in 1909, recounting early childhood, schooling at Achimota College, and its protagonist's twelve-year sojourn as a student, preacher, and political activist in the United States and England. The vast majority of the narrative, however, concentrates upon events after Nkrumah's return to the Gold Coast in 1947: his assumption of the post of general secretary of the United Gold Coast Convention (UGCC), his growing involvement in direct political action, which led to his split with the UGCC's "reactionaries, middle-class lawyers and merchants," and his founding in 1949 of the Convention People's Party (CPP) to lead "the politically awakened masses" (62, 108). The autobiography now proceeds at a more leisurely pace, and moves through Nkrumah's two periods of detention by the colonial authorities to his assumption of power after his party's dramatic victory in the 1951 general election. Over half of Nkrumah's text describes events during his tenure as leader of government business and later prime minister of the Gold Coast between 1951 and full independence in early 1957, and the narrative concludes with the announcement, if not the realization, of that independence. Like Nehru's *Autobiography*, *Ghana* is thus marked by an exponential slowing down and stretching of time as the nation enters modernity. Its later pages contain transcriptions of speeches, and digressions that have little to do with the narrative itself, sometimes misplaced in terms of chronology: a whole chapter, for instance, is devoted to Nkrumah's three-week vacation on the Holland West Africa Lijn's *M.V. Nigerstroom* in September 1955, and this precedes a description of the consequences of the 1954 general election.[11] For the most part, however, as the autobiography's title suggests, Nkrumah's personal narrative now merges with that of the nation-to-be—looking back, he might have concurred with Nehru's comments that what started out as an effort "to trace . . . my own mental development" had ended up as "a survey of recent [national] history."[12]

In Nkrumah's autobiography we might identify a series of levels upon which this mapping of individual onto national life may be explored. *Ghana*—like Nehru's *Autobiography*—responds to its discursive environment through an appropriation and reinscription of a colonial masculinity that already drew parallels between political governance of a territory and an individual man's governance of his body. Here we need to register the complexities of the context of Gold Coast nationalism while still noting that it is possible to talk of a "hegemonic masculinity" to which the text responds. In many ways, Nkrumah's construction of the character and integrity of his protagonist parallels Nehru's, although it has its own particular inflections. *Ghana*, we will note, stresses in particular the disciplining of appetites of the body, and the development of character through sojourn, Nkrumah's long exile in the United States and London forming a key element of the narrative.

Yet Nkrumah's initial answering back to colonialism takes him elsewhere. *Ghana* moves beyond a direct address to colonial power to a series of other strategies in its production of a new social imaginary. First, it attempts an autoethnography in which it tries to place an individual's tradition and culture—both in themselves contested words—within a new and uniquely Ghanaian realization of modernity; in this aspect *Ghana*, as do other African national autobiographies, departs from the Nehruvian template. Second, it maps Nkrumah's own experiences as a student and educator, and the disciplinary element of colonial education institutions such as

Achimota College, onto the discipline required in the construction of national subjects. Third, Nkrumah's attempted congruence between national and individual life results in the autobiography's construction of a relational self through the portrayal of the figures of Kwegyir Aggrey and the author's own mother as Mother Africa, paralleling in many ways Nehru's self-construction in relation to Gandhi and to Kamala. Like Nehru, Nkrumah also writes a series of parallel antimonies of masculine/feminine, reason/affect, state/nation, individual/crowd. As in Nehru's case, we also see irresolvable tensions between these, expressed in Nkrumah's protagonist's intoxication with the Ghanaian masses and his simultaneous fear of their feminized subaltern enthusiasm, which threatens to overwhelm the individual's body and cannot be contained by the party or the state. And yet, finally, Nkrumah's autobiography differs from Nehru's in that it finds no place in a public narrative for affect that it codes as private. There is thus no parallel to Nehru's final turn to Kamala. In contrast, in *Ghana* Nkrumah's struggles—never quite successfully—to write out the protagonist's intimacy with women characters from the narrative, and elides the central role of Erica Powell in its production.

National Masculinity

At our first level, then, Nkrumah's autobiography attempts to talk back to colonialism, to provide a textual clearing of the ground upon which the nation is to be built. Like Nehru, Nkrumah was faced with a discourse concerning the character of the colonized—here targeted against the West African coastal elites who contested colonialism and, through such organizations as the Aborigines' Rights Protection Society and the National Congress of British West Africa, began to think of modern social imaginaries beyond the colonial order of things.

Such discursive constructions were very firmly entrenched. Frederick Lugard, writing in the 1920s, condemned the political ambitions of "Europeanised Africans" while simultaneously noting that it was "extremely difficult at present to find educated African youths who are by character and temperament suited to posts in which they may rise to positions of high responsibility."[13] As we have seen already, West African writing in English that interrogates colonial discourse, such as Casely Hayford's *Ethiopia Unbound* and *William Waddy Harris: The West African Reformer, the Man and His Message* (1915) make sophisticated use of life writing to construct heroically masculine protagonists to oppose the "national and racial death" threatened by colonialism, and to urge a return to "the practice of a virile religion," involving "a strict physical and mental discipline" to counteract the "emasculated sentimentalities" propagated by missionaries.[14] Indeed, Casely Hayford's identification of religion, masculinity, and work is not accidental. Much West African life writing in English was influenced by missionary activity, and by the production of exemplary conversion narratives that emphasized the imitation of Christ in a very nineteenth-century mode, through the taking on of nineteenth-century technologies of masculinity and an entrance into the world of productive labor, and the representation of life as a journey. Despite his critique of missionary activity, Kwamankra is at times very close to John Bunyan's Christian.[15]

Nkrumah's own context needs a more precise elaboration. The future president of Ghana had attracted the close attention of the Colonial Office soon after his arrival in Britain in 1945, and he was closely monitored by the colonial government after his return to the Gold Coast in 1947. Colonial Office documents, as well as newspaper articles and other public accounts written during this period, contain many character sketches and assessments of Nkrumah, constituting a form of life writing to which the nationalist leader's own autobiography had, perforce, to respond.

Given the insights of postcolonial studies from the 1980s onwards regarding the structure of colonial discourse, the relative insignificance of "race" as a discursive category in accounts of Nkrumah written before 1951 is initially rather surprising. The Gold Coast was considered by the Colonial Office to be the most developed of Britain's African colonies, and a series of proposals concerning constitutional reform was made, all giving greater—although still very limited—representation to Africans. It may well be in this environment that directly articulated racism and an emphasis on a supposedly innate African lack in temperament would undermine the rhetoric of reform: certainly much initial response to Nkrumah is couched in a different discursive context: that of the emerging cold war.

As in representations of Nelson Mandela three decades later, initial accounts of Nkrumah attempt, obsessively in retrospect, to connect him to communism and to demonstrate if not that he was a card-carrying member of the British Communist Party, at least that his sympathies were broadly communist. Colonial Office correspondence describes Nkrumah as "a Communist of extreme views," while investigations into the Accra "riots" of 28–29 February 1948, which led to the detention of Nkrumah and five other UGCC members, repeatedly stressed the importance of communist affiliations.[16] Cross-examinations of both Nkrumah and J. B. Danquah by the Watson Commission, set up to report on the disturbances, focused repeatedly on the question of communism, with Danquah being asked, for example, why Nkrumah would begin a letter addressed to him with the salutation "Dear Comrade" and end the letter with the word "Fraternally."[17] Nkrumah, too, was repeatedly pressed on his links with communist organizations, and the presence of blank British Communist Party membership and subscription cards among his belongings.[18] The final report of the Watson Commission had few doubts: "Mr. Nkrumah boldly proposes a programme which is all too familiar to those who have fallen the victims of Communist enslavement" and explicitly identifying Nkrumah as a "communist among whose papers have been found a Communist Party membership card."[19]

"Enslavement" is a key word here: communism is presented as a failure of self-government and individual autonomy, a surrender to forces outside the self. Through a focus on communism, the discourse on character is preserved, and its racial and culturalist elements go underground, only to reemerge later. After a brief honeymoon period following the CPP's 1951 election victory, colonial discourse began to reiterate critiques of Nkrumah during the diarchy of colonial and Gold Coast leadership from 1951 to 1957. These, rather than associating "communism" with character, return to the specter of an innate cultural lack within the constitution of indigenous inhabitants of the Gold Coast: "race" and "culture" here gain discursive prominence. This is true even in articles written immediately after the 1951 election that are supportive of Nkrumah. An article in the *Times* on the Gold Coast's new government, for instance, praised Nkrumah's "personal prestige" as a "great asset" in the "practical implementation of policy," remarking that "the semi-religious emotionalism of the African invests him with an almost Messianic aura."[20] By 1952, the asset was represented as a liability: Nkrumah's fear of "the slightest threat of opposition," Arden-Clarke commented, was a "weakness . . . not peculiar to him" but "a common Gold Coast characteristic." "The notion of the delegation of responsibility," the governor continued, was "foreign to the Gold Coast." The result was, again, a lack of integrity, a lack of correspondence between surface and depth, and a susceptibility to "pressures."[21] Dominion Office inquiries into growing corruption in Ghana noted that the Prime Minister had "personally, indulged in practices which would be regarded as unethical in more civilized countries."[22] Later Foreign Office and other reports and briefings brought together culturalist and character-based explanations to indicate why Nkrumah's Ghana had fallen away from the project of modernity. Nkrumah was "inclined to Fetishism," "still the 'show boy,'" manipulated by intriguers and "juju."[23] Culture was now conflated with the "unmanly" character traits that had formed a discursive common sense in such life-writing all along. Nkrumah was a "prima donna," "emotional rather than rational" in argument, with considerable personal charm.[24] He was also unreliable, lacking in integrity, and unable to keep confidences.[25]

These critiques also need placing within the political context of the first half of the 1950s. Nkrumah's political opponents consisted of a nascent alliance between traditional rulers—particularly in Asante—and the elite members of the UGCC, which Nkrumah had left. If many British Colonial Office documents portray Nkrumah as reverting to "Gold Coast" character traits in the absence of tutelage, criticism from his political opponents might come from another angle—his lack of respect for the institutions of "traditional" societies. Thus Nkrumah becomes associated with "verandah boys," "youngmen," and the tensions emerging in the social fabric of the Gold Coast immediately after the World War II.[26] In *Ghana,* then, Nkrumah's emphasis on masculine asceticism as a means of creating an autonomous subject is not enough. He needs to enfold his subject within, and indeed make his life exemplify, a distinctively Ghanaian expression of modernity that will answer both colonial critiques of innate cultural deficiency and appropriate "tradition" from the hands of the chiefs.[27]

Ghana responds to colonial and nascent nationalist critiques by creating a masculine protagonist who sees "laziness as a crime" through a stress upon self-governance and ascetics (91). A presiding feature of *Ghana* is its focus on the male body, and the disciplining of its appetites as a representation of modernity. Nkrumah puts little stress upon the muscularity of male bodies here—there is no Ghanaian equivalent of Max Nordau's "Muskeljuden," nor of muscular Confucianism or Hinduism.[28] Physical labor, indeed, becomes a source of weakness rather than strength, the "huge muscles" of the men who unload cargo through the surf in Accra seemingly testifying to their being "on the face of it . . . strong and healthy men" but concealing an inner exhaustion, a susceptibility to disease and early death (236). Nkrumah's accounts of his own work as a student in the United States make a similar point—the autobiography's protagonist emerges not strengthened from backbreaking work in a soap factory, but rather depleted of vital energy (36).

Ghana thus emphasizes discipline applied to the male body not in the form of training but rather in terms of asceticism and privation, the denial of the appetite. Early in the autobiography, the young Nkrumah recalls a parting comment given by Kwegyir Aggrey, vice principal of Achimota College, before his untimely death. "So far," Aggrey notes of his attempts to raise the consciousness of students at the College, "I have been able to make you hungry but I have not been able to satisfy your hunger" (15). Here hunger is a metaphor for the desire for self-rule, but the metaphor becomes strangely literalized and transformed in meaning in Nkrumah's text. After Aggrey's death, the young Nkrumah is "unable to eat for at least three days," but this in turn brings a realization of his own indifference to food—"I made the discovery that even on an empty stomach I seemed to have more than enough energy to carry on with my studies" (15). Nkrumah glosses this realization as a valuable insight that enables him to survive periods of extreme poverty in both America and England, but it also suggests parallels with other moments in the text. He has earlier recalled how he was reluctant to take food as a child and later mentions fasting in prison, going without food as leader of Government Business, and finally the transformation of hunger into fasting as a spiritual process (127, 144). If in Aggrey's metaphor hunger would be satisfied upon independence, in Nkrumah's appropriation of it the disciplining of the male body through hunger, the denial of appetite, becomes a metaphor for the insatiability of the project of modernity: modernity is continual hunger, surveillance of the appetite, and its denial. Retreats into the wilderness to fast, indeed, became a key element of Nkrumah's public persona as prime minister and later president of Ghana.[29]

The motif of a retreat into the wilderness hints at another motif underlying Nkrumah's protagonist: the imitation of Christ. The CPP made substantial use of Christian motifs that implied connections between its leader and Christ, pictures and cartoons appearing of him with Jesus or angels, and one postcard showing him in the act of receiving from Christ the keys to heaven.[30] At times, Nkrumah's language in *Ghana* contains biblical echoes: when urged to resign from the UGCC by his supporters, for instance, Nkrumah represents his protagonist as saying, "This very day I will lead you!" (107). The Christian elements of the narrative amplify the focus on asceticism in their stress on suffering, poverty and the notion of life as a pilgrimage or a journey. "All my worldly goods—two suits, two pairs of shoes and a few underclothes," Nkrumah writes of his time as an activist in the Gold Coast before independence, "could be easily stored in one small suitcase" (74).

There is a further aspect to the stress on ascetic practices in the text of *Ghana*. The privations of Nkrumah's protagonist in *Ghana* are gendered through a contrast between male and female bodies, the latter expressing primordial desires ungoverned by technologies of masculinity and modernity. Early in the autobiography, the protagonist confesses a fear of women from an early age, "a dread of being trapped, of having my freedom taken away or being in some way overpowered" (12). On his first trip to England, he is repelled by the spectacle of prostitution in the Canary Islands, and in particular by a woman who "to my utter horror and embarrassment . . . came over, planted herself on my knee, and began stroking my hair and generally enveloping me with her limbs" (26). While serving as a bellhop on a ship, he responds to a call from a cabin and is confronted by "a most attractive woman reclining on her bunk almost completely naked": he needs a reassurance of safety before he is willing to enter (38). Above all, women represent extravagance in the narrative, embodying the possibility of the protagonist being pulled away from the course of his narrative journey and losing autonomy. They should, Nkrumah notes, "play a very minor part in a man's life"; if they gain "the upper hand, man becomes a slave and his personality is crushed" (12). Representation of women, as we will presently see, is a key point of narrative instability in *Ghana*; for now, we should perhaps just note their relational function on the rhetorical surface of the text in creating masculine autonomy.

Ethnography and Double-Consciousness

Nkrumah's autobiography goes beyond merely answering back to colonialism, and also implicitly addresses contemporaneous nationalist critiques of his attitudes to tradition, by writing an autoethnography. As are many texts of its kind, *Ghana* is lyrical concerning its protagonist's early childhood. Most of Nkrumah's recollections are pleasant ones—he remembers a "wonderful life for us children with nothing to do but play around all day" and the supportive community formed by an immediate family and a larger circle of relatives (7). In this aspect the text is similar to Nehru's narrative. Yet the lyricism of these descriptions is supplemented by interpolated passages more classically ethnographic in tone and content. Nkrumah's birth, for instance, provides the pretext for a discussion of Akan customs surrounding childbirth. The fact that it occurs after his grandfather's death provides a means of a further digression into funeral ritual, and his descriptions of his parents and the community of which they form a part leads to parenthetical elaboration of kinship and marriage. In the manner of Kenyatta's description of Gikuyu culture in *Facing Mount Kenya*, Nkrumah's narrator implicitly—and at times explicitly—wishes to illustrate the fundamental rationality of the Nzima lifeworld from which his protagonist emerges. In describing polygamy, for instance, the narrator makes an explicit address to an implied reader who is a cultural outsider, noting that while "this way of life" may appear "unconventional and un-satisfactory . . . to . . . confirmed monogamists, . . . it is a frequently ac-cepted fact that man is naturally polygamous. All the African has done is recognise this fact" (6). Nkrumah as narrator also notes the relative lack of divorce in Akan society, despite the fact that it is easily obtained, and em-phasizes the value placed on hospitality in the community (7). The im-plicit comparison here is between Akan and Western society, and it is a comparison that finds the corrosive individualism of the West wanting.

Nkrumah's ethnography, however, does not simply have the West as its audience. One noticeable feature lacking in Nkrumah's ethnography of Akan culture is a description of structures of leadership—"chiefs" are not mentioned, and the household seems to be the focus of authority and governance. There is also a fluidity between different communities, and it is at times unclear which group is the focus of Nkrumah's ethnography: it is sometimes the Nzima people, sometimes the "Akan tribe," and some-times, increasingly, "Africans." While providing a positive ethnography, then, Nkrumah de-emphasizes the "tribal" categories that the British had utilized to administer indirect rule and that were utilized by the opposi-tion, while at the same time suggesting, from the narrator's perspective of 1956–57, communities beyond the "tribe" that might more readily claim modernity.[31]

Disciplinary Institutions

The institution in *Ghana* in which the past is placed within the present, tradition within modernity, and the ethnographic framework of national modernity is developed, is Achimota College. Simon Gikandi has de-scribed Christianity as the "vestibule of a modern identity" for many Africans under colonialism.[32] The same is true in *Ghana*: Nkrumah is drawn into the Catholic Church and then into teaching at a mission school. Yet if Catholicism was, for Nkrumah, a vestibule, Achimota was, to extend Gikandi's metaphor, a substantial, if not grandiose, entrance hall. Estab-lished in 1926 as an autonomous educational institution by Gordon Gug-gisberg, the governor of the Gold Coast, Achimota was a liminal place between colonial and national modernity. In many ways it resembled a Brit-ish public school, with students' time regulated from a 5:30 a.m. rising bell until lights out at 9:30 p.m.[33] Physical training was emphasized, and under the influence of the Tuskegee Institute in the United States, emphasis was put upon agricultural work: training college students, such as Nkrumah, spent "one whole day each week working on the farm and gardens."[34] Achimota might thus be seen as an element of a colonial governmentality intended to produce self-disciplining subjects. A. G. Fraser, the principal of the college, certainly saw the inculcation of self-regulation as one of its goals, noting that school discipline could not "be based on force, which is ephemeral, but must approximate to the discipline of a family whose ties never die, and which has in it the seeds of ever fresh life": it should "be rooted in self-regulation and not in restraint if it is to be permanent," and continue outside the institution.[35] Other commentators were more explicit as to what such discipline might achieve. "In every village and town," noted a report on social service produced just after Nkrumah left Achimota, "there are discharged teachers and unemployed clerks waiting for something to turn up. What a lot of their energy is directed into palavers and letters to the press. And what a fruitful ground for the agitator!"[36] Achimota would produce responsible colonial subjects who would work in their communities to prevent alienation of this kind from the colonial state.

Achimota, however, was not simply a place for the donning of "masks of conquest"—it was a place fostering a new, modern lifeworld that was a precursor to nationalism, and it did so in a way that makes it difficult to speak unproblematically of complicity with or resistance to colonialism.[37] Each of the members of the largely European Achimota staff had to learn a language spoken in the Gold Coast, and both Akan and African history were taught. The college had its own printing press, and students in the teacher training course would create teaching texts in languages such as Twi, Akan, and Ewe as projects: an inspection committee arriving two years after Nkrumah had left noted that "higher-grade work includes the collection, editing, and dramatization of folk stories, the making of reading-cards, and the translation of reading-books and grammars."[38] The assistant vice-principal of the college, Kwegyir Aggrey, despite the "subordinate position" assigned to him through ongoing discrimination, spoke of seeing at Achimota "a New Africa in process of being born," while Fraser remarked that the purpose of such training was part of "an effort to hasten the transference of leadership in African education into African hands."[39] The college coordinated "regular weekly visiting by patrols of students to all the villages around Achimota. . . . In these visits the students persuade the villagers to clean up their villages and keep them clean."[40] These projects were colonial in inspiration, but they had a developmental trajectory that foreshadowed similar rationalizing activities in nationalist movements that were later enacted by the independent nation-state.

It was at Achimota, Nkrumah notes, that "my nationalism was first aroused" (14). He recalls taking the lead role in a student play in which a returned student, now a doctor, plays his part in overcoming superstition by besting a witch doctor who has failed to cure a patient. Here Western science triumphs over indigenous superstition, and Nkrumah as narrator is wryly ironic in recalling how such a conclusion was "to the delight of everyone" (18). Yet he also took part in "tribal drumming and Asafu dancing" and, with other Nzima students, founded a cultural society. After graduating from Achimota, much of Nkrumah's energy before his departure to the United States appears to have been spent in founding and running organizations that codified Nzima culture as part of a modernizing project. As general secretary of the Nzima Literary Association in Axim, for instance, he presided over a project of standardization of the Nzima language, and the script in which it was represented, while presenting this project as "the preservation of purity of language."[41]

We might, indeed, see Achimota in Nkrumah's text as providing structure that makes autoethnography possible through a disciplinary creation of new modern subjects. *Ghana,* like many other African political autobiographies, represents the experience of colonial schooling in a much more positive manner than a reader in the new millennium might expect; such representations cannot be simply dismissed as misguided nostalgia.[42] Accounts of colonial education in these texts tend to stress two positive elements. First, the student gains autonomy through a discipline that is "rooted in self-regulation and not in restraint," the protagonist becoming a modern, self-regulating subject.[43] Second, the student/protagonist becomes aware of a community beyond that of family, class, or ethnic group, one that presages a new national community that will come into being. The disciplinary practices of the schoolroom (and indeed the school playing field) become the model for the practices necessary to create citizen-subjects of the new nation who will then participate in the construction of a national community.

Achimota's influence, indeed, can be seen in Nkrumah's lifelong interest in the transformative possibility of educational institutions. Nkrumah's Ph.D. dissertation draft completed in the United States a decade later, entitled "Mind and Thought in Primitive Society: A Study in Ethno-Philosophy, with Special Reference to the Akan Peoples of the Gold Coast, West Africa," attempts to combine the disciplines of philosophy and anthropology to show that many features of the "primitive mind" are also possessed by the "civilized mind." He begins with an extended discussion of "theories of mind," drawing on both philosophy and psychoanalysis.

The thesis then abruptly moves to a more classical ethnography of the Akan peoples of the Gold Coast, told in a manner that predicts his auto-biography. The focus is now upon attempting to show that Akan beliefs, philosophy and aesthetics are not themselves "irrational," and to problem-atize the distinction between primitive and civilized, especially in terms of any kind of evolutionary perspective in which the primitive represents a forerunner of the civilized. Nkrumah's conclusion, drawn from his 1943 ac-ademic article, "Education and Nationalism in Africa," would have been unexceptional to Aggrey or Fraser—what was needed was the creation of a "new class of educated Africans imbued with the culture of the West but nevertheless attached to their environment" that could push for self-determination through a realization of African rationality.[44] And yet there is still a central paradox here. In ethnography the "culture of the West" and the African "environment" do not have equal status. Nkrumah must still struggle with a deferred relationship to modernity, in which his new African subject is both modernity's subject and its object.

The Mother and the Masses

This uneasiness of a deferred relationship to modernity—Du Bois' "double-consciousness"—and thus an awareness of being both subject and object of ethnography and other modern technologies, is most clearly il-lustrated in Nkrumah's portrayal of his mother, Nyanibah, in *Ghana*. As Partha Chatterjee's formulations would suggest, the mother is associated with the private sphere of tradition (here a series of widening cultural communities—Nzima, Akan, Ghana, West Africa, Africa) and becomes the object of nationalist pedagogy. Inevitably a key figure in the early part of the autobiography describing the protagonist's childhood, she reappears at other important points in the narrative. Before he departs to study at Lincoln University, Nkrumah visits his mother and is struck by the "peace-ful picture of African rural life" she represents: she tells him for the first time of his claim to two chief's stools, defining his place within the com-munity he is about to leave (25). Nkrumah says his goodbyes to her on the bank of the Ankobra River: his crossing over in the direction of the port of Takoradi indicates a final departure from the community of his childhood.

Nkrumah's mother retains for him a close association with Africa, and with the Ghanaian nation-to-be throughout the course of the autobiogra-phy. She is never given a personal name, and thus in many ways takes on the role of the Mother Africa that would be part of the future Ghanaian president's rhetorical repertoire.[45] His protagonist's closeness to death in America after a severe bout of pneumonia provokes a longing "to see my mother again more than anything else in this world," which parallels the connection between America and Africa Nkrumah attempted to invoke in his conducting traditional Akan funeral rites for Aggrey, in which he charged "the spirit of Aggrey to leave . . . foreign soil . . . and go back home to Africa" (34).[46] On his return to the Gold Coast in 1947, Nkrumah almost immediately goes to his mother, and he overcomes her initial inability to recognize him: again, this can be read as the overcoming of alienation from Gold Coast society, and a recognition of belonging on new terms. Her reservations overcome, Nkrumah's protagonist notes, "hitherto wonderfully controlled emotions broke through the barrier and, as she clutched me to her, I felt her body vibrate with deep sobs" (67). The renewed relationship between mother and son is entirely based on affect, Nkrumah noting that he did not discuss "my political ideas for the future" with her (67). This again seems to accord with the division of spheres within nationalist thought. The nation, embodying tradition, is coded as female, while the party, which seeks to found the state, domesticates such tradition through disciplinary action, much as the male body suffers ascetic privations. In a rational modernity, some of the legacies of "feudal power" and "age-old tribalism," which have provided the British with purchase to carry out indirect rule can be cut away, but an innate Africanness must also be maintained (220, 105). The "tide of history" propels Ghana forward onto an ocean of modernity that is also expressive of the "glory" of a Ghanaian past before the arrival of colonialism (202, 198). "Our people must be made to walk, forced draft, into the twentieth century," wrote Richard Wright to Nkrumah after a visit to Ghana: only nationalism could "sweep out the tribal cobwebs" and, implicitly, restore the splendor of the house.[47]

Such a schematic reading of Nkrumah's relationship to his mother, however, neglects key moments later in the autobiography. After Nkrumah's assumption of power, indeed, *Ghana*'s representation of his mother seems much more ambiguous. She reappears in the same role as a witness, but not a full actor, at two more crucial moments in the autobiography. When a first assassination attempt is made on the then prime minister's life, Nkrumah rushes "downstairs to find my mother whose room was very near the explosion. The poor woman was speechless and there were tears in her eyes as she clutched hold of my arm. 'Oh, you are safe!' she said with relief" (220). There is a strange moment of transference here, the mother voicing the feelings of the son—the reader expects Nkrumah himself to utter the words, since anxiety has driven him to search for her. This transference is paralleled in a final incident, which occurs toward the end of the autobiography, on the eve of Ghana's independence in 1957. After a restless night following news from Governor Charles Arden-Clarke of the date of Ghanaian independence, Nkrumah's first action is to go downstairs "to greet my mother" (283). Nkrumah's autobiography rarely allows us into the consciousness of others, even on a speculative basis, but here he senses that she knows that he is "restless and keyed up" and yet accepts that he will not tell her his anxiety's source. This realization in turn prompts the narrator's admiration: "'What an excellent wife she must have been!' I thought to myself, 'No questions, no hints, no suspicion!'" (283).

If the last sentence attempts to restore symmetry to the text, relegating the mother to the domestic and the private, it cannot quite undo what has gone before. The transfer of emotion between Nkrumah and his mother speaks also of the difficulty of "alternative" modernity: the position as both subject and object of modernity means that one cannot, even if one wishes, freely choose what to take and what to discard. Even as the disciplinary elements of Nkrumah's text separate framework and content, modern state and the life of the people, so the realization comes that the former cannot completely contain the latter. If Nkrumah's protagonist is, following Paul John Eakin's terminology, a "relational self," formed through contrast with his mother, his text can never quite escape this realization, never quite construct an autonomous individual subjectivity, and never quite maintain symmetry between individual and national narratives.

If Nkrumah's mother embodies a "tradition" that can never quite be codified within the nation, we can also see how the *askesis* of Nkrumah's male protagonist maps, equally imperfectly, onto the disciplinary mechanisms of the party and the state. Nkrumah's stress upon party discipline is well-known. While still in London, he was instrumental in forming the vanguardist "Circle," an organization dedicated to West African independence with elaborate rules of conduct for members: he reproduces the document, along with the constitution of the CPP, as an appendix to *Ghana*. During his last term of imprisonment, Nkrumah's correspondence to his lieutenants in the CPP, which was smuggled out of prison, stresses party discipline above all else. "Anything set up outside the machinery of the Party is politically dangerous," Nkrumah writes, while "humility and loyalty to the Party at all times is the key to our success."[48] The technology of the party and the state it founds will contain the nation: writing on the need to refuse an offer of Dominion status to Ghana by the British, Nkrumah urges that the CPP "cannot under any circumstances leave the country in the midst of a stream; we must ferry it over, yes, over the shore."[49]

Nkrumah's concern with vanguardism and party discipline is, of course, Leninist, influenced by the classic formulation of the revolutionary party in "What Is to Be Done?" Yet it is also clearly influenced by other elements— freemasonry, shown in the coded handshakes in the Circle document, and Nkrumah's concern with the "cipification" of the country in his prison correspondence; residual elements, too, of Achimota's vision of a disciplined, elite class of Africans to move the Gold Coast toward modernity. And what is unique about it, again, is its stress upon the individual leader as embodiment of the party: members of the Circle had to swear to "accept the Leadership of Kwame Nkrumah," while the prison correspondence emphasized the need for party members to "be made to swear allegeance [*sic*] to Kwame Nkrumah."[50] Even outside of the text of the autobiography itself, party discipline again focuses on an individual both unique and representative, who, in C. L. R. James's words, "in actuality and symbolically . . . fulfills and completes the strivings of the Ghanaian people to become a free and independent part of a new world."[51]

To the party, we might add the state. The colonial state, we have seen, portrayed Nkrumah's activism as corrosive to a social order uniquely suitable for the "Gold Coast native." A leader in the *Times* thus proclaimed that Nkrumah was a "fanatical hater of all things European" and an "enemy of responsible African leadership."[52] "Certain men," the governor Charles Creasy noted in a broadcast in March 1948, "have . . . been attempting to stir up agitation and violence in this country in order that out of the chaos and misery that would thereby be caused they might be enabled to seize power themselves." The arrests of the then UGCC leadership thus, while regrettable, were "like the quarantine which is imposed on people who have caught a dangerous infectious disease." With Nkrumah, Danquah and their colleagues detained, the governor looked forward to "steady progress towards self-government in the Gold Coast" built upon "the long established . . . respect for law and order in this country."[53] Fanaticism and individual character failings are here countered by an appeal to "responsible" government that is manifest through the colonial state's apparatuses: medicine, the law courts, and by implication the security forces.

For Nkrumah the reconstruction of the state, enabled by a vanguardist party, offers the possibility of a Ghanaian modernity that the unrepresentative colonial state could never achieve. Accepting office in 1951 under a revised constitution that still fell short of independence, Nkrumah's protagonist urges CPP members of the Legislative Assembly to work beyond the structures of a still semicolonial state by keeping "contact with those who gave birth to and nurtured the Party" (141). In contrast to the colonial state, Nkrumah's government achieves its legitimacy through its representativeness, its ability to embody the nation. Thus Nkrumah's New Deal for Cocoa, involving the elimination of trees infected by the swollen shoot disease is presented as proceeding with "voluntary effort and absence of compulsion from the Government" since it represents the will of the people (153). The success of the CPP and its reconstruction of the colonial state is thus because of its embodiment of the will of the masses through discipline. "A middle-class élite," Nkrumah notes, "without the battering-ram of the illiterate masses, can never hope to smash the forces of colonialism. Such a thing can be achieved only by a united people organized in a disciplined political party and led by that party" (215). Leader, party, and masses exist, in this schema, as elements in a series of homologies.

In the text of *Ghana*, however, this identity of purpose between individual, party, and the masses is never completed. The protagonist of Nkrumah's autobiography, very much like Nehru's protagonist, is always in awe of the energy of the crowd, disconcerted yet drawn to its ultimate irrationality that threatens the autonomous, ascetic persona the text so elaborately creates. On his release from prison, Nkrumah, in a much disputed account of events, depicts himself as overwhelmed by the enthusiasm of the crowd that greets him:

> I was hoisted shoulder high and carried to an open car that was standing nearby. It is difficult even now to describe all I experienced as this car moved at a snail's pace like a ship being dragged by an overpowering current in a sea of upturned faces. To look at this locked mass of struggling figures and to listen to the deafening clamour of their jubilant voices made me feel quite giddy. The only way I could steady myself was to keep my eyes averted and to gaze at the mighty expanse of sea and sky, until I was able to adjust myself and acknowledge the greetings of the people. (135–36)[54]

The ship, sea, and sky here predict the conclusion of *Ghana*, with its image of the newly independent country as a ship launched on the sea of history for the first time, but the image is subtly transformed. Nkrumah is not on the bridge here, but rather "overpowered" by the current. And the text itself struggles to accommodate this moment: the retrospective glance, which orders a life, and places it within the context of a national narrative, cannot focus on the scene: "It is difficult even now to describe all I experienced."

The image of the crowd's irrationality corroding the individual autonomy of the protagonist is repeated several times in the autobiography. When returning from his visit to America, Nkrumah describes the awaiting crowds in Accra as "so dense that it was almost impossible to penetrate them. . . . They were panting and groaning as their bodies were crushed one against the other and everywhere I looked I could see people fainting" (168). The emotion of the crowd provokes a corresponding light-headedness in Nkrumah's protagonist. When he returns from a state visit to Liberia in 1953 his reception at Takoradi is disorientating: "Never have I seen such a mass of people. They were almost delirious with excitement, waving arms, flags or garments, singing, shouting, dancing and drumming. Looking down on them I felt giddy at the sight; with the swaying of the bodies to the rhythm of the drums it was as if we were about to disembark on to a moving raft in a strong swell" (187–88).

In the 1956 election campaign, Nkrumah again experiences the sensation of being lifted up by the crowd, "snatched from the platform" on which he has been speaking by a forest of arms in an experience that causes an initial "flutter in my stomach," and, while enjoyable, also causes him to wish for "the secure embrace of a safety belt" (269). Finally, in one of the most remarkable passages in the autobiography, he disguises himself with a red cap and mingles "with the excited crowds" awaiting the results of the 1954 General Election, experiencing the "pleasure of being one of the crowd and sharing with them the thrill of Election Night" (211).

These passages challenge the ascetic persona Nkrumah creates as an embodiment of the party and state in two ways. First, they remove a sense of individuation and separation: Nkrumah's protagonist becomes part of the crowd and is moved by it, not by his own volition. Second, as in Nehru's tale, there is frequently a certain pleasure in such surrender, often expressed in terms of giddiness or light-headedness, in a temporary suspension of *askesis* and a mingling with the people; this contrasts strongly with the ascetic persona of the protagonist, the "very normal man with probably more than average self-discipline" (42). As in Nehru's *Autobiography*, the crowd in *Ghana* is feminized. Market women did form a core element of Nkrumah's popular support, and when the crowd needs to be personified through a representative individual, a woman is frequently chosen. When the protagonist of *Ghana* makes his decision to quit the UGCC, "one of the women supporters" jumps "up on the platform" and commences singing the hymn "Lead Kindly Light," which would later become associated with the CPP (107). In the early days of the CPP, Nkrumah remarks on the "fervent" support of women, learning that "at a rally in Kumasi a woman party member who adopted the name of Ama Nkrumah . . . got up on the platform and ended a fiery speech by getting hold of a blade and slashing her face" (109).

Women, Narrative, Affect

The significance of gendered binarisms in the Nkrumah's narrative, how-ever, does not stop with representations of the mother and the crowd; the way gender is deployed in the text also influences what the narrative does not—and indeed perhaps cannot—say. To begin to understand this, we might return to one of Nkrumah's narrator's early comments regarding the place of women in his life, sections of which we have already seen: "I was afraid . . . that if I allowed a woman to play too important a part in my life I would gradually lose sight of my goal. Few people have been able to under-stand this attitude of mine and I have been described by various people as a Don Juan, an impotent man and even a eunuch! Those who know me, however, regard me as a very normal man with probably more than average self-discipline" (42). Even given the rhetorical imperative here to produce the figure of a "normal man" by contrast with the extremes of rumor, it seems strange that Nkrumah could be described as both "Don Juan" and "a eunuch." While rumors of affairs were circulated by political opponents in Accra, most accounts of Nkrumah himself by those who knew him in Ghana strongly stress an ascetic personality that seem to preclude this. Ac-counts by Erica Powell, Genoveva Marais, and A. K. Barden, whatever their differences in other respects, all emphasize Nkrumah's capacity for work, self-discipline and lack of personal emotional attachment to others, in a manner that recapitulates Fraser's description of Aggrey: "He was almost an ascetic. He ate only a light breakfast, and would often eat no more till the same breakfast hour next day. He got absorbed in work to the complete for-getfulness of meals."[55] Yet many accounts also stress Nkrumah's charm: what evidence there is suggests another life, one of emotional intimacy—sometimes, though not always, through sexual relationships—which is written out of the narrative of *Ghana*.

The first relationship that seems consciously absent from *Ghana* is its protagonist's with Portia Duhart, whom Nkrumah knew during his decade in America. Accounts by Nkrumah's friends and colleagues in New York and Philadelphia supplement *Ghana's* representation of Nkrumah's sojourn in America as "hard times" with a fuller picture (35–47). J. Newton Hill, Dean of College at Lincoln University, recalled Nkrumah's flirta-tiousness with women, while Beverly Carter, later United States ambassa-dor to Tanzania went further: "He was very attractive to the opposite sex and there were many weekends when we travelled to Philadelphia and he combined a preaching assignment on Sunday and a social engagement on

Saturday evening. He appeared to have no hang-ups."⁵⁶ In *Ghana*, Nkrumah presents himself as a naive protagonist, ultimately rejected by potential girlfriends to whom his obsession with politics is a "disappointment," always having to fend off the unwanted attention of women (36). While Nkrumah mentions that Portia was a "special friend," his account of their relationship occupies less than a page, yet correspondence suggests that they were, in fact, close to marriage, and that indeed he maintained contact via letters with her during his years in the United Kingdom and in Ghana (41).⁵⁷ Indeed, Portia seems to have had astute knowledge of the limits of Nkrumah's own self-fashioning through a narrative of emancipation. In a perceptive comment in a letter to the Ghanaian leader, Portia noted that Nkrumah should not neglect the "spiritual" side to his character, since in his quest for West African self-rule he was "not going to be dealing with human mechanisms but with hearts and souls."⁵⁸

A second elision in *Ghana* concerns Florence Manley, Nkrumah's landlady in London from 1945 to 1947. In Nkrumah's autobiography, Florence is not named, Nkrumah only telling the story of how he and his coworker and later comrade in the liberation struggle, Ako Adjei, found lodging with "a young woman" after being consistently refused accommodation because of racism (50). Indeed, Nkrumah disarms any possible suspicion on the part of the reader by referring to the anonymous landlady's husband, and later a whole "family" (51).The role of Mr. Manley remains obscure; in a 1973 interview Florence noted that Nkrumah had been a "perfect gentleman," and had "lived as one of the family," her daughter Christina describing him as "like a father to me."⁵⁹ Yet the Manleys here were being disingenuous; Florence's relationship to Nkrumah was certainly closer than this. In a letter sent to the Gold Coast in 1948 that was intercepted by the authorities and then presented as evidence at the Watson Commission hearings, Florence thanked Nkrumah for his "sweet letters" and joked, "I hope you love me as equally as your mother, not next to her as you said (are'nt [*sic*] I jealous. Smiles)." She also discussed plans to come to the Gold Coast to be with him: "I shall add another light dress or two and a very pretty negligee for our first night together. . . . Yes, Kwame I feel so happy planning. I will inform you and let you be happy with me in all I plan and do. Please soon as you are settled send for me. I belong to you remember all that took place between us, nothing can break that one very special bond. (do you remember)[?]"⁶⁰ Yet the Watson Commission hearings also show how the public narrative of self–making writes out such intimacy. When confronted with Florence's letter and asked "Is it not a letter of a rather different type to the other letters we have been looking at?" Nkrumah admitted that it was that of "a woman writing to somebody she loves" and that he "had girl friends in England." In reply to a suggestion that "she was doing a little hero worshipping" Nkrumah attempted to dismiss his relationship with Florence, appealing to male solidarity with the Chairman, Aitken Watson: "You know what women are like."[61] Yet he continued to correspond with Florence intimately over many years.[62]

If Nkrumah writes two relationships that might, in Aitken Watson's words, be characterized as "romantic" out of the text of *Ghana,* his most conspicuous omission is surely a different, equally important relationship, that with his English secretary Erica Powell. Powell had the strange experience of working on both sides of the diarchy: she arrived in Ghana in 1952 and became personal secretary to Governor Charles Arden-Clarke. A friendship with Nkrumah developed, and she became his secretary after being dismissed by the governor, doggedly maintaining her position into the 1960s despite attempts by Nkrumah's Africanist colleagues to have her dismissed. Even if we approach Powell's own representation of her relationship with Nkrumah in *Private Secretary (Female)/Gold Coast* with some caution, it is clear that it was a close one. Surviving correspondence between Nkrumah in Conakry and Powell in Britain illustrates this: Nkrumah addresses Powell by her first name, ends his letters by giving his "love," and inquires about intimate matters such as her weight, noting on one occasion that "I yearn for the day I could see you." Powell reciprocates by reminiscing about their ages when they first met, and signs her letters with "much love."[63]

Powell perhaps more than anyone illustrates Nkrumah's need to erase private affect from his autobiography and indeed all representations of his life. On receiving the manuscript of her memoirs in Conakry, Nkrumah did not explicitly contradict Powell's accounts of events in Ghana, but rather suggested revisions for consistency, much as one might to a fictional character. "Many things I have been quoted as saying," he wrote to her in a letter "are out of character; some statements and views attributed to me are extremely unlikely," and he noted that "accounts of incidents and conversations of a 'demeaning' nature should be avoided." He was particularly insistent on consistency with regards to the composition of *Ghana.* Regarding the autobiography, he wrote insistently, "bad references connected with my auto-biography and the use of 'we' give wrong impression and false indication."[64] Nkrumah would be sharper with other correspondents—he told Hanna Reitsch, all "references to my personal beliefs or to my thoughts should be deleted" from a planned translation of a book about the gliding school she established in Ghana—but his reaction to Powell is particularly interesting, given her role in the composition of the autobiography.[65] From Powell's testimony, it is clear that her role was more than simply that of amanuensis; she accompanied him on a research trip to his birthplace, for instance, to "get some background material for the book."[66] Yet, apart from an initial brief acknowledgement as the person "to whom I dictated most of this book," Powell is absent from the text of *Ghana* (xii).

Yet if Powell vanishes, she does not do so without a trace. In her own memoirs, she recalls an incident in which Nkrumah, agitated on the evening of the 1954 election, comes to visit her for dinner. In response to his wish to "be an ordinary person again" and "to go down to the polo ground and mix with the crowds, to be one of them, to feel the throb of excitement," Powell proposes that he disguise himself with a red beret and allow her to drive him to "the hub of things" in Fifi, her tiny green Fiat (40). Nkrumah acquiesces, and enjoys the experience immensely, his eyes "glowing with satisfaction, gratitude and pleasure" (41). The scene is reproduced in *Ghana,* and yet Powell is erased, Nkrumah only mentioning a conversation with an anonymous friend who enables him to experience the "pleasure of being one of the crowd and sharing with them the thrill of Election Night" in 1954 (211).

If we take Nehru's internal "Maginot line" as a powerful metaphor for his construction of a modern self, Nkrumah has unconsciously provided us with an equally resonant image. On election night, Nkrumah is part of but apart from the masses, anonymous only because he remains "hidden in the confines of a baby Fiat car," separated from the "thrill" of a crowd that flows onto the streets and envelops the traffic (211). Within the car and the tight confines of a disciplined self, affect may be admitted but must also simultaneously be disavowed. Powell's presence as a friend is initially acknowledged—although as "my friend" she is stripped of identity and indeed of gender—but then entirely forgotten in the protagonist's meditations, his pleasure in "sharing" the emotion of the crowd and yet remaining separate from it, negotiating the place of the individual and the collective within an incipient modernity. Nkrumah's fear that if "I allowed a woman to play too important a part in my life I would gradually lose sight of my goal" might be taken retrospectively, indeed, to apply not so much to the living of a life as to the retelling of it, a process of narration that removes affect and thus makes austere self-discipline a metaphor for the disciplinary action of the state (42).

Conclusion

We have seen how *Ghana* negotiates its mapping of individual onto national life, how its response to colonialism and its attempted creation of a new social imaginary results in a relentless shuttling between individual and collective, technologies of government and technologies of the self. Nkrumah's life story, however, took on an afterlife after his exile to Conakry in 1966 and indeed his death of what Amilcar Cabral would call "the cancer of betrayal" in a Romanian hospital in 1972.[67] If the 1950s and early 1960s saw much hope placed in the modernizing projects of newly independent African states, the last three decades of the twentieth century saw the failure of those projects, failures frequently represented within the discursive framework of national autobiography as a lapse in "character" by national fathers.

The relationship of Lee Kuan Yew, prime minister of an independent Singapore from 1965 to 1990, is illustrative here. In 1966, Lee wrote to Nkrumah in Conakry of his sadness over the latter's overthrow: he expressed admiration for the now overthrown Ghanaian president's "vision and leadership" and the hope for "a united Africa and a great Ghana."[68] Nkrumah could still afford a slight condescension in his reply, expressing support for Lee but urging that he read *Neo-colonialism: The Last Stage of Imperialism* in order to understand "what neo-colonialism is and what it is up to in the world of imperialism," hinting subtly at the accommodations Lee had made with British colonial power and with international capital.[69] Lee would have the final word; writing his memoirs a decade after he stepped down as prime minister in a country whose per-capita GDP would soon match that of its erstwhile colonial master, he would refer to Ghana's failure as arising from an absence of the "discipline of modern government," reducing its people to the status of "paupers."[70] Lee's construction is part of a much larger way in which the postcolonial African state is imagined through an individual. Much contemporary media representation of Robert Mugabe, for instance, blames his lapses of character for contemporary Zimbabwe's economic collapse rather than a confluence of factors; popular movies such as Sidney Pollack's *The Interpreter* (2005) see imagined but representative African crises as arising from the moral failure of a national father.

Yet Nkrumah stands for both disappointment and for hope. In present-day Accra, the concrete modernist monuments of Nkrumah's state still stand, in sometimes rather tattered glory: the State House, or the National Museum, its garden containing mutilated statues of Ghana's first

President that were toppled on his overthrow in 1966. To them are now added a collection of newer structures built from the 1990s onwards, their paucity a testimony to the fact that an alternative route of two decades of IMF-sponsored economic restructuring has not brought Ghana much closer to the autonomy Nkrumah desired but conspicuously failed to achieve. And Accra is also marked by other structures that hint at Nkrumah's contested legacy: Danquah Circle, for instance, commemorates the most tenacious of his political opponents. One of the newest buildings, just opposite Parliament House, is the grey marble Kwame Nkrumah Mausoleum, surrounded by a park. Ghanaian politicians of all philosophies cannot but refer to Nkrumah's precedent. Modernity, indeed, now lies in the past, with Nkrumah's heritage not so much remembered as selectively reimagined by many as a time of Ghanaian autonomy and dignity. It is not so much the case now, in Ayi Kwei Armah's phrase, that "the beautyful ones are not yet born," as that they have already passed away. In such an environment, one can surely neither uncritically accept the messianic quality of Nkrumah's text, nor simply celebrate its contradictions and failures.[71] In many African and other uneven, necessarily incomplete modernities, there is still so much to do, so little done.

6

Nelson Mandela's Long Walk

On 11 February 1990, it seemed the whole world was watching as the African National Congress leader Nelson Mandela, at the end of the best part of three decades in detention, walked out of the gates of Victor Verster prison. The object of little international attention in the 1970s, by the 1980s Mandela had become an international symbol of opposition to racism and social inequality, and by extension of the incompleteness of decolonization as part of a global project of modernity.[1] National and local governments, trade unions, and a myriad of other organizations throughout the world had critiqued apartheid by showering the fruits of modern society on the world's most famous political prisoner. Having studied part-time for years to painfully acquire educational qualifications, he was inundated with honorary degrees; still imprisoned and unable to vote, he was elected honorary president of a wide number of institutions; absent in South Africa because of a prohibition on the publication of prisoner's photographs, his image was widely disseminated abroad in magazines, newspapers, and sculptures and other artworks and his name attached to buildings, public squares, and roads.[2] After the fall of the Berlin Wall and the unraveling of the divided fabric of the cold war world, Mandela's release offered a return to an earlier time, when the emancipatory possibilities of decolonization had seemed more certain. His early interviews on his release appeared, in Rob Nixon's words, to conjure up "the high era of anticolonialism, of the early Nkrumah and Kenyatta, of Nyerere, Nasser, Gandhi, Nehru and King."[3] For Ngũgĩ wa Thiong'o, who had suffered the attentions of a later Kenyatta, Mandela's experience embodied that of South Africa, which in turn provided "a mirror of the modern world in its emergence over the last 400 years."[4] South Africa's integration into global capital flows, Ngũgĩ noted, had brought "classical colonialism, neocolonialism, slave wages, racism and the usurpation of a people's sovereignty" (19): Mandela's release now, at a time of international change, offered the possibility of genuine popular control in cultural, economic, and political spheres.

As the events since the fall of the Berlin Wall in 1989 have shown, however, the time of Bandung had not come again. Only four years after Mandela's release, the ANC would achieve Nkrumah's "political kingdom," taking power in South Africa's first multiracial general elections, yet would find possession of the economic kingdom more difficult to gain. The growing reach of international capital flows meant, perforce, the withering of economic sovereignty and the scaling back of large-scale redistribution of wealth through programs such as the Reconstruction and Development Programme in favor of neoliberal economic policies.[5] If Mandela's messianic aura remained undiminished until his retirement in 1999, several of his comrades in the struggle were to fall from grace, and his successor, Thabo Mbeki, would receive much less sympathy from the international media. The new South Africa a decade later, in its successes and failures, is a part of a global present very different from Nehru's 1936 or Nkrumah's 1957.

It is in the light of this ambivalent modernity, in which narrative of the nation must seek accommodation in a very different contemporary reality, that we should read Mandela's 1994 autobiography, *Long Walk to Freedom*. The story it tells seems similar to Nehru's and Nkrumah's, a narrative of an individual subject moving through the widening circles of home, ethnic group, schoolroom, city, and nation in succession. It tells of personal suffering and discipline as metonyms for a series of privations and sacrifices each citizen must make to realize the new nation-state. And yet the text's presentation of itself as the product of a single individual is something of a mirage. While the text purports to be based on an earlier autobiography, *The Struggle Is My Life*, written on Robben Island, its relationship to that work is more tenuous than Mandela's preface in *Long Walk to Freedom* implies.[6] The autobiography we have is a composite production caught, like the new South Africa, in global capital flows. Like most contemporary commercial autobiography, it is assembled through a complex process of recorded interviews, transcription, and narrative shaping by a major American publishing house.[7] These facts should not make us dismiss the autobiography as in some way inauthentic—Nkrumah's *Ghana*, we might remember, was also the product of a collaborative writing process—but they should remind us that it, too, is imbricated in the present, and in the desires of not merely a national but international reading public.

In order to examine how Mandela's narrative creates parallels between individual life, the formation of a new nation-state, and the production of a transnational social imaginary very different from that of Bandung, our analysis in this chapter will follow and tease out the implications of its structure. Like Nkrumah's *Ghana, Long Walk to Freedom* begins with an extensive auto-ethnography that frames the later narrative. While it develops the theme of its protagonist's entry into another's modernity through colonial schooling, it also seeks signs of the future in the "democracy in its purest form" practiced by abeThembu of his childhood.[8] The narrative then follows its protagonist in a movement from the country to the city of Johannesburg. In contrast to earlier narratives such as those of Nehru, Gandhi, and Nkrumah, the city in *Long Walk to Freedom* is not a place of exile and sojourn: rather, its space enables the protagonist to negotiate a place as a subject of capital, his migration mimicking that of thousands of others before and after him. It is also in Johannesburg and its satellite "non-European townships," in Alexandra and Sophiatown that the new community of the nation can be imagined. The third part of the text is perhaps iconic: it covers Mandela's imprisonment on Robben Island, far more prolonged than that of Nkrumah, and in far less comfortable conditions than those Nehru endured in the various jail terms. Using contemporary and retrospective accounts of imprisonment on the island, we can begin to understand how in Mandela's narrative it becomes a site of writing the nation. The final section of this chapter departs from the chronology of *Long Walk to Freedom* to consider how the many moments of repeated autobiographical summary and testimony in the text rehearse modernity for a transnational audience. We might think of the autobiography as responding to some of the crises of late modernity; its popularity beyond the nation, and indeed far beyond an audience that, in the 1980s, might have been concerned that Mandela be released, hints at its role in imagining a fusion between revolutionary and bourgeois selves, in managing the crises of contemporary risk society.

Boyhood and the Ethnography of Modernity

"As you know," Mandela wrote to Fatima Meer from prison in 1988, "there are 2 Transkeis":

> One is the political entity which emerged in the mid-50s & which sparked off ugly polemics, turning, in the process, friends, relatives, idols and their admirers into irreconcilable opponents & even enemies. This is the Bantustan whose capital you recently visited & whose head you met.

> But there is the Transkei about which I often have the most pleas-
> ant recollections and dreams; the Transkei of my childhood where I
> hunted, played sticks, stole mealies on the cob . . . ; it is a world which
> is gone. A well-known English poet had such a world in mind when
> he exclaimed: "The things which I have seen I now can see no more."⁹

By 1994, of course, the first Transkei would have also vanished, now part of
Eastern Cape Province on the map of the new South Africa. Yet Mandela's
recollection of the second Transkei, of a country childhood that he had left
behind over half a century previously, would remain an important element
in imagining national and cultural presents and futures. As with Nkrumah
and his other African predecessors, Mandela's description of his childhood
in *Long Walk to Freedom* serves as a form of auto-ethnography, reclaiming
an African cultural heritage from the denigration of the colonizer and later
of Afrikaner nationalism. Yet it is also a retrospective reconstruction of a
cultural past, with significant omissions, that serves the needs of the nation
in the present. The presence of the quotation from the English poet Wordsworth also hints at another element of this reconstruction: it is enabled by
certain technologies of the self appropriated from the colonial schoolroom.
If the Great Place of Mqhekezweni seems to initially stand in opposition to
the mission school, the narrative surreptitiously draws parallels between
the two cultural sites that condition the young protagonist's bifurcated
existence.

Like Nkrumah's *Ghana,* then, *Long Walk to Freedom* devotes a crucial
introductory section to childhood and youth. Life in Qunu, where Mandela spends his boyhood, is described in loving detail, accounts of games
and adventures supplemented by passages more ethnographic in tone,
introducing a reader to the extended family of "African culture" or describing the "custom, ritual and taboo" of Thembu life (10, 13). Yet there is
never a prelapsarian moment in the narrative: Qunu for the protagonist is
already marked by a wider history, transformed into a "village of women
and children" because of the departure of young men to the mines of Johannesburg (10). The narrator also works to fold the events of the narrative
into a larger historical process. Thus Mandela's birth date is located on the
first page of the autobiography as occurring at the end of the Great War
and preceding the visit of an ANC delegation to the Versailles peace conference (3). As the narrative progresses, Mandela as protagonist moves to
Mqhekezweni, "the provisional capital of Thembuland" on his father's
death; he encounters both technological modernization—in the form of a
"majestic" Ford V8—and also becomes more knowledgeable about

Thembu history and tradition (19). As he grows older, further journeys follow: the young Mandela continues his education at the mission schools of Clarkebury and Healdtown and, finally enters the African Native College at Fort Hare.

Mandela's entry into a colonial school system might be portrayed as promoting what Ngũgĩ has called a "dissociation of the sensibility" of the protagonist, a separation from his cultural roots.[10] *Long Walk to Freedom*'s protagonist finds his body progressively and awkwardly clothed in the accoutrements of a modernity he does not own: he recalls wearing a cut-down pair of his father's trousers on his first day at school in Qunu, first using a knife and fork, and the awkwardly wearing boots for the first time (28, 39). At Fort Hare, he wears his first suit and appreciates the "self-discipline and patience" taught by participation in sports. As a member of the Student's Christian Association, he visits neighboring villages to conduct Sunday Bible study. In Mandela's account of such activity, one can almost hear the earlier voice of Alexander Kerr, principal of the college:

> On such occasions, in addition to religious talks or teaching, discussions might be held on topics of public interest, such as the use of land, or crops and vegetables, or pure water and village sanitation, or on the incidence of the commoner diseases. It was always a wonder to me that villages within easy reach of well-organized and active educational institutions could exhibit such primitive habits and customs as were still found, indicating how slowly new social practices establish themselves in rural communities.[11]

Yet Mandela's narrative does not, of course, dismiss Xhosa culture as "primitive habits and customs"; on the contrary, it suggests that the court of the regent at Mqhekezweni represents "democracy in its purest form" in which "all men" are "free to voice their opinions and . . . equal in their value as citizens" (24). Before he leaves for residential school, the young protagonist listens in fascination as Thembu elders tell stories of the precolonial past of the amaXhosa and of resistance to colonialism by a variety of African leaders. The narration here is strongly retrospective: as protagonist, the young Mandela questions why stories are told about non-Xhosas: only later, the narrator notes "was I moved by the broad sweep of African history, and the deeds of all African heroes regardless of tribe" (27).

Throughout Mandela's education at mission schools and at Fort Hare, indeed, a series of interruptions challenge a colonial worldview: the Xhosa poet Mqhayi's challenge to the "false gods of the white man" at Healdtown, or Nyathi Khongisa's condemnation of Jan Smuts as a racist (48, 58). In each case, the interruption does not automatically change the opinions of the protagonist at the time of its occurrence, but it is highlighted retrospectively by the narrator as a marker of a historical movement with which the protagonist will eventually align himself. The strategic interruptions thus have two functions: first, they suggest that there is a larger and longer movement of history than simply that of colonialism; in a longer perspective, indeed, colonialism may well be a temporary aberration. Simultaneously, they identify African, and in a particular Xhosa culture, with a project of modernity. Knowledge of specific histories promotes a quest for freedom, and the new nation of the new South Africa—conjured here by the narrator's speaking in the narrative present of 1994—will realize the natural democracy exemplified by Thembu society, exposing the contradictions of colonial modernity as it does so.

Yet at a deeper level, in the subject's own understanding of himself and his relationship to the world, there seems to be a profound connection in the narrative between the lifeworlds of the schoolroom and of Thembu society. Fort Hare was certainly a place of student activism, growing political and national consciousness; in the 1940s there were a series of strikes and protests, and Mandela was one of the many students expelled or suspended from the college.[12] Yet, as in Nkrumah's (indeed, as we shall see in Lee Kuan Yew's) narrative, *Long Walk to Freedom* shows a deep investment in the disciplinary elements of the colonial schoolroom that is difficult to explain away in analysis that simply looks for "resistance." Fort Hare is a masculine society that molds men, and Mandela was indeed perhaps more influenced by it and the mission schools than it is narratively appropriate for his protagonist to admit. One omission from *Long Walk to Freedom* is Mandela's fondness for W. E. Henley's poem "Invictus," which he taught from memory to Eddie Daniels on Robben Island, expressing a Victorian masculinity surely honed in the colonial schoolroom:

> It matters not how strait the gate,
> How charged with punishments the scroll,
> I am the master of my fate:
> I am the captain of my soul.[13]

It is of course impossible to know where Mandela encountered Henley for the first time, but certainly this investment in a solitary disciplinary masculinity would persist throughout his life, influencing both his autobiographical manuscript written in prison and later speeches given as president of South Africa.[14] In *Long Walk to Freedom* he simply mentions the lessons of "self-discipline and patience" he earned from participation in sports, and then applied to other areas of life.

The emphasis on masculinity as discipline is paralleled in Mandela's account of Thembu society as—like Fort Hare—a predominately male-centered space in which women are "deemed second-class citizens" (24). Traditional rituals marked on the male body also establish masculine autonomy: Mandela devotes a substantial section of his account of "a country childhood" to circumcision as the beginning of an entry into manhood. The circumcision ceremony and succeeding seclusion take place in a landscape still unmarked by the overgrazing and social disintegration that racial capitalism and later apartheid would produce. When he returns from seclusion Mandela looks down on the Mbashe River, watching it "meander on its way to where . . . it emptied into the Indian Ocean." If he still knows of nothing that lies beyond the river, he is conscious of the presence of "a world beyond it . . . that beckoned me that day" (36). The autonomy the protagonist associates with modernity here comes not come from external sources but from resources and an internal dynamic within Xhosa culture; it is presented as a field awaiting narrativization, a blank page on which the bildungsroman of the self will be written.

Mandela's presentation of circumcision as a marker of the creation of autonomous selfhood is very much in accordance with what we know of Xhosa cultural practices at the time of his childhood. Concepts of masculinity among the amaXhosa, Ann Mager notes, using research from a slightly later period, made a clear distinction between "boyhood and manhood, marked by circumcised bodies."[15] Boys were traditionally strong and undertook tasks such as cattle herding and stick-fighting, while men were "restrained by knowledge of *umthetho* rules and *isiko* (Xhosa law)," and would thus be fluent public speakers and display good leadership qualities, laying aside sticks "in favour of the law" (658, 660). Mandela's text is interesting in that, unlike Nkrumah's or, indeed, Nehru's, it does not code the culture of childhood as maternal or feminine, but rather as enabling masculine discipline in parallel with the disciplinary apparatus of the school.

Yet there are also occlusions. The presentation of Xhosa culture in *Long Walk to Freedom* is crucially different in another way from an earlier generation of autobiographers' accounts of cultural origins: the portrayal of Akan culture in Nkrumah's *Ghana* and in his unpublished doctoral thesis, for example, or Kenyatta's description of the lives of the Gikuyu in *Facing Mount Kenya*. Kenyatta and Nkrumah, like Mandela, each attempt a positive ethnography of their birth culture through a description of its inner logic and rationalities. In doing so, Nkrumah and Kenyatta are concerned to stress and defend the ways that the African cultures they describe are radically different from those of the West, especially in the ways they mold and contain a cultural element that has been long viewed in post-Enlightenment Europe as intimately concerned with liberation and the truth of the self—sexuality.[16] Nkrumah explicitly defends polygamy, while Kenyatta goes farther, defending the institution of *ngweko* (fondling), in which unmarried boys and girls may sleep together overnight, but not overstep certain boundaries of intimacy.[17] In contrast, *Long Walk to Freedom* is coy on the issue of sexuality, mentioning traditions only to deny individual participation in them. "The tradition," Mandela's narrator tells the reader, "was that one should sleep with a woman, who might later become one's wife [after the circumcision ceremonies are over], and she rubs off the pigment with her body. In my case, however, the ochre was removed with a mixture of fat and lard" (34). Mandela's narrative mentions polygyny in passing but is otherwise silent on Xhosa cultural practices surrounding sexuality, particularly the manner in which the promiscuous sex play—largely *metsha* (external sex)—of boys would give way to an expectation on men to "form more serious relationships with a view to marriage."[18] Rather, the narrative emphasizes the closeness of the extended family and refers to conventionally monogamous attractions and love affairs with women both before and after its narrator's circumcision (28–29).

Part of Mandela's silence can readily be explained by the fact that the society in which his protagonist lives was in flux. The churches, for instance, discouraged public sex play, so that as their influence grew, boys and girls chose "new codes for courtship and love affairs"; these were often highly individualized, featuring "secret love affairs and private erotic spaces" that "encouraged individualising practices," and it may well be that the narrative, under the influence of the Methodism that Mandela was exposed to through family and at all three educational institutions he attended, responds to these factors (662, 657). Yet whatever its source, the text's pruning of Xhosa cultural practices emphasizes their similarity to the disciplinary actions of the school; both tend to act on a commonsense understanding of the self as always already seeking autonomy and freedom. Indeed, Mandela concludes his narrative with a final vision of being born free in the Transkei but then realizing the limitations on his freedom, leading him to place his own quest within a large quest for national liberation; the echoes of Rousseau here are unmistakable (750).[19]

Two acts of rebellion conclude the first part of Mandela's narrative: his refusal to take a place on the Student Representative Council at Fort Hare due to its limited powers—leading to his expulsion from the college—and his refusal to participate in an arranged marriage, which leads to his flight from the country to the city of Johannesburg. Each of these is presented as emerging naturally from an unfolding sense of autonomy, yet each is also elaborately coded within the terms of its discursive environment. Students at Fort Hare in the 1940s were already highly politicized, but Mandela codes his refusal and his confrontation with Fort Hare's principal not in terms of politics but of "moral principle" and "good conscience," miming the language of the colonial schoolroom (61–62).[20] Mandela's refusal of the arranged marriage is explicated in a more complex manner; there is indeed some self-deprecatory irony in the narrator's refection: while "I would not have considered fighting the political system of the white man, I was quite prepared to rebel against the social system of my own people" (64). Yet the protagonist's "romantic side" has already been made into a commonsense foundation of the narrative: relationships mentioned with women such as his early girlfriend Winnie and Mathona at Clarkenbury have been shown to be individualizing, drawing out a sense of autonomy (28–29, 39–40). "With women," the narrator recalls, "I found I could . . . confess to weaknesses and fears I would never reveal to another man" (40). At the same time these relationships suggest, embryonically, the importance of a domestic space coded as private in the protagonist's self-constitution. The rebellion against arranged marriage is thus retrospectively naturalized.

Mandela's account of his youth in the Transkei, then, differs crucially from the accounts in autobiographies such as those of Nkrumah. Two extratextual factors—the narrator recalling the events from a much greater temporal distance and the changed audience that the text addresses—result in significant changes in the way the past is remembered. The otherness of Xhosa culture to a largely non-Xhosa reading public is not explicitly foregrounded and defended, but rather elided and, through some judicious pruning, its technologies of the self paralleled surreptitiously to those of the colonial schoolroom. The result is a commonsense understanding of the protagonist's subjectivity as motivated by a masculine journey for self-realization, in which monogamous relationships and friendships with women have a crucial but largely private relational role; this understanding will persist as the narrative develops, and it will become metaphorically attached to new social imaginaries encountered and created in Johannesburg.

City, Capital, Family

Mandela's protagonist's arrival in the "city of light" of Johannesburg from the rural Cape is metonymic of a pattern of migration on a national and international scale in the twentieth century (69). Throughout South Africa—and, indeed, in what are now independent states to its immediate north—rural societies were transformed by the migration of young men to work on the mines. Social orders reinvented in the mine compound existed in an atmosphere of violence; "new forms of masculinity emerged amongst African men which included notions of work and ethnicity."[21] At the same time, wage labor transformed the order of rural societies. Power struggles between "aged fathers and their adult sons" when migrant workers returned to their birthplaces in areas such as Kwa-Zulu Natal, causing the "subdued patriarchy" presided over by older men for most of the year to be displaced by the "rowdy public masculinity" of the returned workers in the Easter holidays, have a genealogy going back to the early twentieth century.[22] Yet migration to the city offered other possibilities: chances, outside the racial exclusivity of the compound, of making cross-ethnic alliances and meeting others also opposed to the colonial order of things, and opportunities, through organizations and affiliations, of devising new kinds of community beyond those of family and ethnic group. This pattern, indeed, repeated across the South in the twentieth century.

Unlike Nehru or Nkrumah, Mandela did not experience exile in the colonial metropolis—his only trip abroad before his long imprisonment was a tour of African and European countries to seek support for the ANC. His city is very different from that of his literary predecessors; it is—although elaborately divided—an African city, a place where he will remain, and in which the new nation will be brought into being. Unlike Nehru or Nkrumah, Mandela is not troubled by the formlessness or enthusiasm of the crowd. Rather, the crowd offers tactical possibilities: it is emplaced in the elaborate racial topography of the city, squatter camp, or the residential area; but its fluidity offers the possibility of resistance and transgressing boundaries. The failures of mass action that lead to violence are glossed as failures of leadership but do not arise from the nature of the crowd itself: there is no sense of the crowd corroding individuality, as in earlier narratives.

As it works on the public spaces of the mines, the city, and the crowd, this section of Mandela's narrative also molds the private space of the household. Although Nehru and Nkrumah are reluctant to acknowledge the place of women—and in particular close affective relationships with female partners or friends—in their narratives, Mandela's takes an opposite tack: despite the presence of an extended family: it sacralizes the nuclear family life produced in the process of migration and presents such life as disrupted by the racial capitalism that will evolve into formal apartheid.

The father of the nation thus becomes the family man who can never fulfill his private responsibilities because of the prevailing social order: normal family life can only be achieved through the realization of the new South Africa. "A happy family life," Mandela noted in a letter 1979 to Winnie from Robben Island, "is an important pillar to any public man."[23] Here the Victorian bourgeois family becomes a precondition of male public activism.

The narrative momentum of the section of Mandela's autobiography before his long imprisonment is first provided by his growing politicization and later by his actions as part of a politics of liberation, his individual story joining a grand narrative of history so that its fourth section is aptly entitled "The Struggle Is My Life." This initial transformation is enabled by the public space of the city of Johannesburg, which is associated with masculinity and modernity. Mandela first attempts to find work in the mines. His protagonist feels "like a millionaire" after a few days' work; yet the narrator notes how the Witswatersrand Reef's success is built on "cheap labour in the form of thousands of Africans working long hours for little pay and no rights" (73).

If the mines of the reef succeed through "segregation" and the exploitation of "factional fights between different [African] ethnic groups," the city of Johannesburg, despite its segregated residential areas, offers more fluidity (74). It is a "combination frontier town and modern city," growing rapidly in population to provide workers to support the Allied war effort (78). In the city, for the first time, Mandela encounters Africans who have skills such as typing; through his growing relationship with Walter Sisulu, he comes to know African property owners, businesspeople, and people working in the paralegal and paramedical professions. Townships such as Alexandra are, because of their neglect by the municipal authorities, very different from the "city of light" seen on the horizon on the protagonist's arrival in the metropolis. In some ways their modernity is perilous—the protagonist fears "*tsotsis* [gangsters]" who imitate "American movie stars" by wearing "fedoras and double-breasted suits and wide, colourful ties," although he perhaps exaggerates his own sartorial inadequacies (88). Yet Alexandra is also "a kind of heaven"; it is a place where Africans can own property and, more significantly, a site where urban living begins "to abrade tribal and ethnic distinctions" (89). One of the protagonist's early relationships here, indeed, is with a Swazi woman: the space of the township encourages an individuation, in which the self is remade in relation to society (92). Mandela finds he cannot rely on "royal connections or the support of family" but rather must forge "relationships with people who did not know or care about my link to the Thembu royal house"; he owns his "own home," and gains the necessary "self-reliance" to make his way in the world (94).

The hybrid urban society of the township continues to have a central place in Mandela's narrative. He later celebrates Sophiatown as the home of artists, professionals, and gangsters, marked by poverty but also "charm" and a "special character" (178–79). With the growing governmental racialization of space in South Africa after the Second World War, the township becomes a place of resistance, offering at least the potential of a different kind of urban modernity. Yet we need perhaps to attend less to the external environment than the effect that the public space of the city has on private self-constitution, how Mandela becomes "a man of the city" (186).

Mandela's arrival in Johannesburg in 1941 came at a crucial turning point in the evolution of non-European middle-class life in South Africa. Increasingly racialized governmentality and the decline of liberalism put under pressure modes of bourgeois self-fashioning such as those of the nineteenth-century "Black Victorians" in the Eastern Cape, while the urban middle classes remained "stunted and repressed" by legislation and discriminatory practices that prevented many educated Africans from finding skilled employment.[24] Whereas the political project of Mandela and his colleagues in the Youth League aimed to transform the ANC from an advocacy of middle-class reformism into a mass movement demanding radical social change through direct action, it is noticeable how the aspirational values of the African bourgeoisie shape the narrative unconscious of *Long Walk to Freedom*. The work tends to sacralize a nuclear family, centered initially around Mandela's first wife, Evelyn Mase, and then around his second wife, Winnie Nomzamo Madikizela. When Mandela's protagonist obtains his own house with Evelyn in Orlando East, he rejoices—without any narrational gloss—that a "man is not a man until he has a house of his own"; it is Evelyn's emptying of the family home when she leaves him that he finds most shattering (120). Visits from an extended family are mentioned but downplayed: the protagonist's psychic life centers on his relationships with his wife and children. He sees apartheid above all as disruptive of family life, which can only be reconstituted in the national imaginary of a new South Africa. A central feature of Mandela's self-fashioning both within the text of *Long Walk to Freedom* and outside of it is thus the repeated regret that he neglected his own family in taking on the role of the father of the nation.[25]

The creation of a revolutionary protagonist embodying both heroic and bourgeois masculinity also explains a feature of *Long Walk to Freedom* that many commentators have noted—its exclusion of women from the public sphere. The book tends to portray the world of political work as a male one, into which only a few women temporarily intrude on special terms, as "honorary men," through especially heroic actions, and as the "gentle intimates" of men who work in the political arena.[26] Thus the breakdown of Mandela's first marriage to Evelyn is presented as a conflict between public and private duties; he cannot accept her religious faith, while she cannot accept that politics, in the words of Mandela's narrator, constitute "an essential and fundamental part of my being" (240).[27] While Winnie, Mandela's second wife, is clearly a more politicized figure than Evelyn, in its representation of her the narrative in many ways repeats its division between public and private. In a manner similar to Nehru's portrayal of his relationship with Kamala, the protagonist's courtship and marriage with Winnie are compressed into a few pages. Like Nehru, Mandela expresses pride but also a deep ambivalence—"mixed emotions"—at her growing involvement in political activism, warning her of "the seriousness of her action" and the consequences that the loss of her income will have for the family if she is arrested (258). Winnie, in testimony admittedly mediated, has a different perspective. She notes that their "life as a family" was "abnormal," that Nelson was "an economic disaster at home," and explains her ambivalence at joining anti-pass demonstrations as arising from the fact that Mandela was not earning a wage, not from her husband's warnings about the dangers of a situation she knew only too well.[28] As Unterhalter has noted, Winnie continues to be associated with the private sphere during Mandela's imprisonment; she is "associated with the soft world outside prison" marked by "silk dressing gowns, care for children, [and] family connections," despite her growing stature as an activist as the narrative progresses.[29]

Unterhalter's observations are telling, but we might see them in a larger context; the manner that women are represented in *Long Walk to Freedom* is part of an extensive gender economy within the narrative of the autobiography and that of the national liberation for which it stands. Mamphele Ramphele has described—partly from the personal experience of her relationship with murdered Black Consciousness Movement activist Steve Biko—the expectation that female partners perform the role of "political widows" during the struggle against apartheid, enacting the presence of a dead or detained husband. The political widow, Ramphele notes, in many ways became "an honorary man," and while her agency was not eliminated, it was limited—she had to renegotiate the manner in which she related to the public. Ramphele, indeed, mentions Winnie Madikizela-Mandela as an example of this, playing her role as political widow to the hilt, and indeed moving beyond it.[30] However, her public place after Mandela's release indicated that there was "no properly elaborated ritual for her return to the private sphere," and so the "public space became contested territory between the hero and his erstwhile stand-in," with Winnie refusing to retreat into invisibility (114).

If Mandela was able to align his personal narrative with that of the nation, Winnie was less successful. In particular, we might return here to the representation of sexuality: in Mandela's case, it is folded into and buried in a national narrative, whereas in Winnie's case it remains a disruptive force. The most vituperative attacks on Winnie concerned her liaisons with younger male political activists, which were anathema within the discourse of political widowhood.[31] Yet *Long Walk to Freedom* does tease the reader with hints of its young male protagonist's sexuality as a "man of the city" driving a "colossal Oldsmobile"; one wonders at the reasons that cause Evelyn to suspect that her husband is "seeing other women" while attending ANC meetings, and he certainly courts Winnie before the divorce with Evelyn is finalized (186).

The manner in which Mandela's self-fashioning underpins a larger narrative of resistance can perhaps best be seen from a brief biography devised by the ANC for an international audience in the early 1960s, apparently while Mandela was still underground before his arrest in 1962. Mandela, it notes, has grown from a "young, rather 'slick' man, to a mature and deep leader of men," marked by a "magnetic" personality: "He is a man of great courage and strength of character who has kept his spirit high in the face of constant persecution and loss of his living as a lawyer. He is supported and encouraged by his wife, Winnie, a beautiful social worker and somehow they have been able to give their small children a secure home."[32] Mandela of course, would have had no control over this representation, apparently produced to appeal to an American reading public still unconscious of the consequences of the middle-class division of labor critiqued in Betty Friedan's *The Feminine Mystique*. In its summoning of a masculine maturity based on depth, on making a living, and the support of a secure domestic sphere presided over by a loyal wife, however, it illustrates much of the underlying common sense of *Long Walk to Freedom*, written three decades later.

Such a rhetoric of self-fashioning, indeed, is not simply adopted to appeal to others. Natasha Erlank has recently demonstrated how masculinist rhetoric was common across the whole spectrum of ANC political belief in the 1940s and 1950s, from the liberal and reformist Alfred Xuma's comment that Africans should reach "the full status of manhood" to the young radical Anton Lembede's description of South Africa as a "young virile nation."[33] While Lembede, Mandela, and other founders of the Youth League would move the ANC itself in a new direction, and women were admitted as ANC members and indeed often took on organizational roles within the movement, a persistent underlying rhetoric surrounding familial responsibility undercut their independence. Changes would, of course, occur because of the prominent role of women in the anti-apartheid struggle and in the founding of the New South Africa, culminating in the appointment of Phumzile Mlambo-Ngcuka as South African Deputy President in 2005. Yet in Long Walk to Freedom the underlying discursive common sense persists. Women are not so much excluded from or reluctantly admitted to the narrative—as in the case of Nkrumah and Nehru—but rather emplaced. The austere disciplines of Nehru and Nkrumah are to an extent maintained, but they are now seen as part of a modernity as return, realizing the potentialities of African cultures; simultaneously, and paradoxically, they are embedded within the site of the nuclear family. The father of the nation is now a man of property, a family man; the social imaginary of Mandela's nation-state-to-be is as deeply gendered as, but differently from, those of Nehru and Nkrumah.

Prison and the Arrival of the Nation

The third and, in many ways, most iconic section of Mandela's narrative describes his three decades of imprisonment, most of which was spent in the high-security prison of Robben Island. Much commentary on Mandela's prison writings and others emerging from Robben Island has seen the remarkable stories of human endurance as a triumph of collective over individual narrative, a refusal to submit to the Foucauldian surveillance of the prison through the forging of powerful community ties.[34] While this is true on a tactical level, on a higher, strategic level Long Walk to Freedom continues the process of aligning individual and national narratives: it prepares the ground for the nation by stressing reconciliation, and molds new citizens by emphasizing self-discipline, in contrast to the "struggle masculinity" of earlier narratives.

South African Robben Island prison writing published during the 1970s and 1980s, before apartheid began to crumble, tends to emphasize the brutality of the prison regime—and, by extension, of the state. Neville Alexander's 1974 Robben Island Dossier consciously aims to write out "anger" through "a certain pedantic meticulousness"; in its cataloguing of abuses, Alexander notes, "on occasion, my real emotions broke through the screen of academic precision" when the recollection of brutality and everyday humiliation became too forceful.[35] Other accounts make no such attempt at distance: Moses Dlamini's *Hell-Hole, Robben Island* and D. M. Zwelonke's semi-fictionalized *Robben Island* describe rage at a world of arbitrary violence and the continual confrontation of prisoners with warders. Contemporary reports in *Sechaba*, the ANC's magazine, by prisoners such as the poet Dennis Brutus, have a similar emphasis.[36] Writing produced in the late 1980s and retrospectively, in contrast, after the release of Mandela, tends to contextualize such violence within a narrative of survival, self-development, and community formation as it holds out the possibility— even if remote—of reconciliation.

Certainly by the 1980s, conditions at Robben Island, especially for the "Rivonia group" of prisoners, had improved markedly because of pressure from the prisoners themselves and external pressure on the South African regime. This explains the diminution of violence in later accounts but not the curious convergence of different narratives. Skimming published accounts by Mandela, Michael Dingake, Eddie Daniels, and Ahmed Kathrada, and unpublished transcripts of interviews with figures such as Mac Maharaj, Laloo Chiba, and Walter Sisulu, the reader frequently has a sense of déjà vu: the same incidents are recounted, and often from a very similar perspective.[37] Many accounts, for instance, mention the visit of Progressive Party member of Parliament Helen Suzman, and Mandela's raising with her the issue of "Suitcase" van Rensberg, a particularly brutal guard who sported a swastika tattoo.[38] Yet none—including Mandela's—mention the visit of Labour politician Denis Healey in 1970, despite the fact that Mandela had met Healey while in London in 1962.[39] This parallelism of exclusion and inclusion extends to incidents that happened before the arrest of the protagonist, even if these are casual anecdotes. Kathrada, for instance, tells a story about Helen Joseph's refusal to give her age in the 1956–61 Treason Trial identical to that in *Long Walk to Freedom;* Sisulu's recollection of his first meeting with Mandela is very similar to Mandela's protagonist's description, despite the fact that both men are recalling events that happened over a half a century previously (293–94, 79).[40]

Some of this coincidence of memory is explicable through the dynamics of writing and imprisonment. Mandela, Kathrada, Sisulu, Chiba, and Maharaj all collaborated surreptitiously on the manuscripts of Mandela's and then Sisulu's autobiographies at Robben Island; discussions, editing work, and, perhaps most important, the many acts of pooling and sharing memories would surely have led to a common narrativization of the past in which one version of an incident became solidified as a group memory, shelved and available for later recall. Yet at a deeper level the narratives share something else: the retrospective plotting of events so that they tell narratives converging on the future social imaginary of a new South Africa. Suzman's visit, for instance, is not only mentioned in many narratives, but is given the same significance. The authorities attempt to forestall Mandela's complaints to her as spokesman for the prisoners by moving him to a cell at the far end of the corridor, assuming that all her time will be taken in dealing with the individual complaints of prisoners in the other cells. The prisoners counter by each telling Suzman that he has many complaints, but that she should talk to Mandela, who is the spokesman. Group solidarity wins out over immediate personal needs, and Suzman is soon brought face to face with Mandela.

Given the prevalence of incidents like this, it is tempting to describe Mandela's autobiography as representing the privileging of collective history and identity over individual ones. David Schalkwyck thus writes of attempts of South African prison writing to constitute "community" in the face of the deprivations of solitary confinement; Paul Gready tells of the production of a "collective and political identity and mission" through the articulation of "we" instead of "I" so as to suggest a shared resistance.[41] Oliver Lovesey, taking a larger perspective, sees much African prison writing as producing a "counter-discourse," allegorizing imprisonment as that of the nation, and, through the mechanism of allegory insisting on the private as public, producing "works [that] violate the convention of private, introspective 'self-writing.'"[42] In a similar, but more critical vein, Sarah Nuttall has noted the exclusions in Mandela's autobiography's production of a collective self: "Individual or private self is vulnerable to being ignored, or seen as 'unpolitical.'"[43] This is true for not just *Long Walk to Freedom* but also many other struggle autobiographies.

These accounts are certainly correct in that the later Robben Island imprisonment narratives are clearly allegories of a new South Africa; they prefigure, or—in more belated publications such as Daniels's autobiography, reinscribe—the self-discipline required of citizens for nation-building and hold out the possibility of reconciliation. One notable feature of *Long Walk to Freedom,* for example, is its protagonist's learning to see Afrikaner nationalism not simply as racism but as an anticolonial nationalism in its own right, containing within it seeds of common experience from which reconciliation may grow. Yet the opposition between individual and collective, private and public narratives is perhaps too simplistic: it is not so much that *Long Walk to Freedom* urges a submersion of the individual in the collective through its recounting of prison life as that the narrative encourages new forms of individuation.

Mandela's narrative of imprisonment on Robben Island, indeed, returns to some of the tropes of self-fashioning present in the initial part of the book. We again have a sense of being placed in a history that exceeds the boundaries drawn by those in power at present; the difference is that apartheid, not colonialism, is challenged. On first learning that he will be imprisoned on the island, Mandela recalls his predecessors held there by the Dutch and then the British, taking courage from the example of heroic resistance by figures such as Autshumao and the Xhosa commander Makanna. Just as the cultures of the Great Place and the schoolroom parallel each other, so in a paradoxical manner the disciplinary regime instituted by the prisoners mimes and yet exceeds that of the prison itself. Robben Island becomes a "university," and the medium of education succeeds in transforming the lives of its inmates in a very different direction from that which the guards or warders might wish. As with Nehru and Nkrumah, we might see party discipline as preparing the ground for the disciplinary practices of the nation-state. Govan Mbeki noted that the "political education" carried out in Robben Island served not only "to maintain a high level of unity amongst the ANC membership" but also had a transformative moral function, aiming to inspire prisoners "with a high sense of discipline to withstand the evil social problems which arose from the presence of the common law prisoners. Such are, for example, sodomy, brewing of intoxicating concoctions, and stealing the meager rations of the prisoners to trade with other prisoners."[44] This discipline was also shot through with questions about its own incorporation of tradition in modernity, which again prefigured struggles in the formation of the nation-state. On Robben Island circumcision was practiced but much debated; Mandela himself would defend the ritual against arguments by his comrades, stating that it was a "reversion to . . . tribalism" and emphasizing its beneficial "psychological effect" (510–11).

Despite the unanimity of most sources, it is possible to gain insight into how the narrative of *Long Walk to Freedom* shapes the experience of incarceration to fit its goal of miming citizen-formation through self-governance. One key event of Mandela's imprisonment in Robben Island is the arrival in the 1970s of young male prisoners who are influenced by Black Consciousness ideology and thus embody a struggle masculinity that refuses any cooperation with the state. Mandela's protagonist does not agree with their ideas but also is eager not to judge them. In a discussion among the prisoners after a film featuring Hell's Angels, Mandela is startled to find that a "Black Consciousness member," Strini Moodley, identifies with the bikers as true social rebels, while the older ANC men see them as "amoral sociopaths" (597). Mandela listens to Moodley and defends his right to speak, the narrator commenting that he does so to keep an open mind and not become a "political fossil" (598). At the same time, a larger narrative logic tends to disqualify Moodley's views, since *Long Walk to Freedom* illustrates how many younger radicals renounce confrontation and submit themselves to study and self-improvement.

Moodley's own recollection of the incident, however, is framed very differently. The movie Mandela describes, he notes, was a B movie about Green Berets who were fighting in Vietnam; Black Consciousness members naturally all supported the Vietcong. One of the soldiers heard that his sister had been killed by Hell's Angels, and in vengeance took a battalion of Green Berets back to the United States. Thus Moodley objected when the "old men" burst into applause when the Hell's Angels were captured at the end of the movie, but his objection was to the political context, which was not based on identification with the bikers themselves.[45] In discussing the movie, Moodley also raises the possibility that, contrary to the rhetoric of *Long Walk to Freedom,* it was the studied defiance of BCM prisoners, not the persuasion and example of the older Rivonia group, which prompted a softening of the regime at Robben Island.[46] It is difficult, of course, to make a definitive judgment on whether this assessment is correct; what is more interesting is that Moodley's own narrative is not driven by an imperative toward national reconstruction and reconciliation, as Mandela's is, and he is thus free to view an incident through a very different interpretative lens, radically altering both its meaning and the trajectory of the wider narrative of which it is part.

Finally, we should not forget the obvious: Robben Island is a gendered space, more exclusively so than the Great Place of Mqhekezweni or the campus of Fort Hare. Women in *Long Walk to Freedom* are conjured through visits and letters, inevitably coming to represent the domestic and private; through the circulation of photographs, they become the object of the gaze of male prisoners. The community imagined and formed in Robben Island as a response to the harshness of prison life cannot, of course, be anything but fraternal: as an allegory of the nation, equally, it cannot but be partial.

Theaters of Modernity

Long Walk to Freedom ends in a tribute to its predecessors. As in both Nehru's and Nkumah's autobiographies, politics displace the personal narrative as the plot propels us toward the narrative present. Like *Ghana, Long Walk to Freedom* ends with the realization of freedom on a national scale and yet with the sense of commencing, not completing, a new journey. Nkrumah's vision of himself at the helm of a ship is now replaced with Mandela's vision of a "long walk" on the "road to freedom," an image ultimately derived from Nehru.[47]

As we have seen, *Long Walk to Freedom* is certainly readily readable within a national context as reflecting and assisting in producing the gendered social imaginary of the nation. It is thus part of the 1990s explosion of South African life writing as a cultural activity, through not only through published biography and autobiography but also a number of public performances ranging from television and radio talk shows to the harrowing testimonies given to the Truth and Reconciliation Commission.[48] Indeed, it perhaps distills a tendency that Cheryl-Ann Michael and Sarah Nuttall identify from the 1980s onward, in which most autobiographies remake the past in the hope of the future, sublimating the individual in preparing for "the emergence of the non-racial and post-apartheid nation"; not until the middle of the 1990s, in this reading, does South African autobiography begin to negotiate with tensions between individual and community (300). The readings of Mandela's autobiography in this chapter largely support Michael and Nuttall's assertion, and indeed the latter part of the narrative tends to submerge the private in the public. Mandela's separation from Winnie is described only briefly, and events such as the protagonist's return visit to Qunu, the scene of his childhood, bear heavy allegorical weight. Politics have now seeped into previously apolitical, remote, village society, but the village is "unswept, the water polluted and the countryside littered with plastic bags and wrappers" (696). There is no longer "pride in the community" and yet Mandela's memories that the village has not always been as it is now provide hope for regeneration in the future (696).

We have also seen, however, that *Long Walk to Freedom* is not simply a South African text; the majority of its readers are not South Africans, and, given sales patterns, most are probably citizens of countries in the developed North who would have little investment in South African nationalism. Its international popularity is not unprecedented: Nkrumah's *Ghana* was widely read by an audience larger than simply anticolonial activists, while an abridged version of Nehru's *Autobiography* achieved great popularity in the United States. Yet the scale of Mandela's autobiography's appeal does seem unique, especially if it is set within the context of a worldwide "Mandela industry" of the 1990s. Many of Mandela's older readers in the 1990s would have made no formal political identification with his struggle in the early 1980s; the freedom for which they search in the text is different from the one sought by the protagonist.

To understand the international appeal of the text, we might return to a subject touched on earlier in this study: the manner autobiography enables not just authors, but also readers, to construct a narrative of their lives. Discussions of autobiography since the 1990s have stressed its performative and constitutive elements—"recapitulating the fundamental rhythms of identity formation"—rather than its transparently referential functions.[49] Thus autobiography becomes a "cultural act of a self reading" rather than simply "the private act of a self writing."[50] The writer of the autobiography is engaged in reading a life, placing it—even if sometimes awkwardly or even oppositionally—on a larger cultural horizon. The reader of autobiography, Jane Varner Gunn notes, undergoes two forms of interpretative activity. First, he or she encounters a "participatory" discovery of self, encountering a "vulnerability which makes it possible to celebrate the finitude of his or her own selving"; second, the he or she is distanced, forced to "look at the universe of common experience from a perspective different from his or her own" (19, 20). Gunn argues that a reader's response requires an effort to integrate these perspectives, one that "acknowledges and makes productive use of the tension between the text and the reader" (21). Jerome Bruner makes a parallel argument that emphasizes the importance of reception in autobiography: an autobiographical text "can only enter the 'conversation of lives' when it achieves localness" as part of a community of readers.[51] Autobiography is "a constitutive act, one designed to construct a reality about a life in a place or time, one that can be negotiated with somebody," and its negotiation is with the "interlocutors who constitute the dialogic imagination of the teller" (44). What these perspectives share, then, is an understanding of autobiography as a socially symbolic act concerned with establishing the relationship of an individual subject and a larger community or series of communities.

All autobiographies, by definition, participate in these forms of self-making, and it would initially seem that there is nothing unique about Mandela's *Long Walk to Freedom:* indeed, it would be plausible to suggest that the world Mandela describes has little "common experience" with those of its readers. Nehru's autobiography might be seen as prophetic, preceding the age of decolonization after World War II and the concomitant faith in the powers of the developmental state; Nkrumah's, riding the high tide of Ghana's decolonization, is timely, expressing the spirit of an age. In 1994, Mandela's continued faith in the narrative of the nation and the transformative powers of the state seems at best misguidedly nostalgic, and at worst dangerously misplaced. In the South, in those areas of the world that, in Chatterjee's words, have not historically been "participants in the history of the evolution of the institutions of modern capitalist democracy," narratives of nation and modernity still continue to have power, and one might be skeptical of a claim that a widespread "incredulity towards metanarratives" indicates that the condition of postmodernity is now evenly globalized.[52] Yet international cultural, population, and capital flows, enabled by information, communication, and transport technologies have eroded the nation's sovereignty: a global economic order encircles the political kingdom ever more tightly. In the North, too, politics seem increasingly corporatized: voter participation has declined in most democracies, and the triumph of neoliberalism after the end of the cold war has frequently resulted in a convergence of economic policies between right- and left-wing parties.

Yet some of the success of Mandela's text with an international audience can perhaps be understood through features of industrialized societies in the late twentieth and early twenty-first centuries. From the 1980 onward, social theorists have explored the transformations occurring in these societies not as postmodern—not signifying an epistemic break—but rather as symptomatic of late modernity, in which the contradictions and tensions of modernity rise to the surface. Various—and indeed competing— descriptions have been given of the economic forces leading to such changes: "disorganized capitalism," "flexible . . . accumulation," "post-Fordism," or indeed "globalization."[53] Most agree, however, on "the empowerment of finance capital *vis-à-vis* the nation state," and indeed the nation-state's transformation from the "'subsidy' state/city," engaged in transformative social engineering to "the 'entrepreneurial' state/city" that relies on the common sense of individualized entrepreneurial activity.[54]

To describe the experience of those living through social transformations in late or, as he would call, it "reflexive modernity," German sociologist Ulrich Beck has coined the phrase "risk society." As Anthony Giddens clarifies, Beck does not mean that everyday life in such societies is more risky in an absolute sense—indeed, the actual prevalence of life-threatening dangers in industrialized societies has declined markedly through improvements in health care, food supply, and the provision of electrical power. Rather, because of the changes discussed above, there is a general climate in which "thinking in terms of risk and risk assessment is a more or less ever-present exercise": a job is unlikely to last for life, pensions and investments are increasingly self-managed, treatment of a chronic disease will involve choosing between contradictory advice from experts, dietary choices may involve attempts to avoid invisible toxins.[55] Both Beck and Giddens note that a response to risk is "self-actualisation" through individualized "narrative[s] of the self"—what Beck calls "biographies"—in which subjects attempt to balance opportunity and risk, and to achieve "authenticity": hence the growing popularity of self-help books.[56]

If we return to *Long Walk to Freedom* armed with this insight, we might note a feature that the text develops from latent suggestions in its predecessors: its theatricality and the way it proceeds not simply chronologically but through frequent rehearsals and retellings of its own story. The most interesting of these are its protagonist's testimonies at the Treason Trial of 1956–61 and, most crucially, the Rivonia Trial of 1963–64: in the latter case an edited version of Mandela's famous statement from the dock is interwoven with narrational commentary (432–38). The intercutting of previously published documents into the autobiography is, of course, a generic feature of national autobiography: Nehru does it silently, Nkrumah overtly, and Mandela toward the end of the narrative, reproducing, for example, extracts from his 1989 letter to P. W. Botha proposing a meeting (653–54). Yet it is arguable that the recapitulations of narrative in the courtroom—and in particular that at the Rivonia trial—occupy a much more prominent place in the narrative and deserve a special focus.

There are, of course, two contexts to these incidents that are not directly related to the late modern readership of *Long Walk to Freedom*. First, Mandela—as he and others testify—was flamboyantly theatrical in court, making use of props such as a woman's underwear or a leopard skin kaross as counsel and as defendant respectively (176–77).[57] Second, this awareness of the court as theater was deeply imbued with knowledge of the power of representation. Of all the writers of autobiographies discussed in chapters 3–7 of this study, only two—Garvey and Nkrumah—were not lawyers; this fact is surely significant. Mandela is right when he notes that justice could not be had in a South African court in a society that practiced legislated racial discrimination; yet for Gandhi, Nehru, Nkrumah, and Mandela, the courtroom provided an important space for self-articulation. In a sense, the courtroom in a colonial or racialist state becomes a theater of modernity: if justice cannot be granted, the limited but real autonomy of the courtroom allows exposure of the contradictions of a regime that claims to be an heir to the Enlightenment and yet denies its inhabitants equality because of a written or unwritten rule of difference.

There is, however, a third context that may explain the appeal of such autobiographical rehearsal to an international audience. In a recent discussion of life writing and the legal profession, Jerome Bruner notes that testimony in a court of law depends ultimately on narratives, on "opposing stories" about what happened that must be evaluated for consistency and plausibility. Legal narratives by the prosecution and defense, Bruner notes, rely on precedent, in which the "legal storyteller appeals principally to the likeness between her interpretation of the relevant facts in the present case and interpretations of what she claims are similar cases in the past."[58] This process, Bruner notes, is similar to the function of a critic in placing a story within a genre.

For Mandela, of course, testimony does not admit the legitimacy of the court: there is no pretence that, as in Bruner's model, the legal apparatus "must . . . be seen as fair and disinterested" (37). His protagonist appeals to a natural justice beyond that offered by the courtroom, embedding himself in a history larger than that of the state. Extending Bruner's analogy, we might say that Mandela's legal story at the Rivonia trial, then, mimes not so much the function of the critic as of the lay reader: it works because it fits the unarticulated horizons of expectation of its audience. In *Long Walk to Freedom,* the text of the address is pruned from the original; twenty-three pages become six, and what is reproduced is a mixture of direct quotation and summary.[59] Much of the specific context drops out: Mandela's direct address to the Justice Quartus de Wet as "My lord," for instance, is missing, as are substantial passages concerning the history of the ANC and its move from nonviolence toward considering guerilla warfare as a means of resistance. Two substantial areas of content that remain—a defense of the ANC's decision to work with the South African Communist Party, and of its decision to prepare for, but not yet implement, guerilla warfare—are necessary to the speech's immediate place in the plot of *Long Walk to Freedom.* Yet two others have a more subtle rhetorical function. The summary of the speech given in the book preserves an introduction in which Mandela talks of his "youth in the Transkei" listening to the stories of Thembu elders. It also preserves, in its dramatic conclusion, an indictment of apartheid as causing "the breakdown of family life," with the family again conceived as an idealized nuclear family: "Both parents (if there be two) have to work to keep the family alive. This leads to a breakdown in moral standards, to an alarming rise in illegitimacy" (437).

Within the context of South Africa, Mandela's words are prescient: the legacy of the disruptions of apartheid would be a high level of social violence and an erosion of various forms of community authority that persist into the new, democratic nation-state. And yet to a wider audience, Mandela's speech as edited within the text of *Long Walk to Freedom* rehearses a commonsense narrative on which the autobiography as a whole relies. Modernity is seen as a return to the natural values of the past, which is enacted through a narrative of an individual who is always already seeking autonomy, and then a parallel self-realization through romantic love and family. Various commentators have noted how a fetishization of the family becomes a way to manage tensions within late modernity between community and individual responsibilities. John D'Emilio notes that since the early twentieth century the family has become less an economic unit and increasingly an affective one.[60] Even as changing modes of production have removed the economic glue from the extended family, what D'Emilio terms "capitalist ideology" "has enshrined the family as the source of love, affection, and emotional security, the place where our need for stable, intimate human relationships is satisfied" (473). Beck identifies a similar tension in what he characterizes as "reflexive modernity": "People count on the pathos of the nation to undo and unseat individualized society. Marriage, parenthood, love, living together and maintaining a household drift apart; the result of this is none the less squeezed into the comforting little word 'family' with all the unabashed ease provided by blindness to history."[61] We might thus say that focus on family, the production of the father of the nation as a family man in *Long Walk to Freedom,* manages some of the crises of its late-modern readers, crises very different from those of its protagonist. Mandela's protagonist is menaced by immediate threats—discrimination, arbitrary arrest, state violence—but has conviction of his place within a larger, stable movement of history. Mandela's late-modern readers may well live lives from which immediate perils have been removed and yet perceive a greater, more abstract, environment of risk. *Long Walk to Freedom*'s reification of the vulnerability of its protagonist as family man moving through history provides an overall reassurance of common experience, makes sense of history through the "common sense" of the family.

It is impossible to know how much this text represents Mandela and how much the demands placed on autobiography by an international publishing industry. In a sense, such inquiry is futile: the autobiography is clearly situational, a key element of a wider production of a public self on a national and international stage by Mandela since 1994. Strategically, this public production with its associated familiality has achieved much, notably resulting in Mandela becoming one of the first major public figures in South Africa to publicly acknowledge that the death of a close relative—his son, Makgatho, in 2005—was caused by complications from AIDS. Yet it is also not without irony, if we wish to search for modernity's incompleteness.

If Mandela is celebrated as a father of the nation, it is always with regret that he is still unable to fulfill the role of father to his children: the demands of national and individual narratives conflict, even after the founding of the new South Africa.

7

A Man and an Island

Lee Kuan Yew's The Singapore Story

> Memoirs are always, to a certain degree, an act of revenge on history.
> Georges Gusdorf

When Nelson Mandela walked out from Victor Verster prison in 1990, the mantle of the world's longest-serving political prisoner passed briefly to another figure, hidden in a much darker recess of history. Former Singaporean opposition member of Parliament Chia Thye Poh had marked the twenty-third year of his imprisonment in 1989 by being released technically but in practice confined to the tourist island of Sentosa; full restrictions on his movements and actions would not be removed until 1998. Like Mandela, Chia had been offered early remission of his sentence if he agreed to governmental conditions; just as Mandela refused P. W. Botha's offer of freedom if he gave up armed struggle, so Chia refused either to confirm to the Singapore government that he had been a member of the Malayan Communist Party or renounce its actions. Yet there the similarities ended. Mandela had been convicted in the high drama of a series of court cases; Chia was simply detained indefinitely under the Internal Security Act that the new nation-state of Singapore had inherited from its colonial predecessor. If Mandela seemed the protagonist of a narrative of world history, Chia resembled at best a footnote. And Chia was released into a society extraordinary in many ways: to a developmental state that had delivered on its promise of modernization. The city in which Chia walked in the 1990s had undergone a radical transformation during his thirty years of imprisonment. Boat Quay, the dirty, busy, lighter-infested heart of the colonial entrepôt, was now silent, its gleaming shops and godowns renovated into pubs, restaurants, and coffee bars. Immediately behind them, the skyscrapers of Shenton Way, the city-state's financial district, proclaimed an economic transformation that had seen Singapore in the 1990s match the per-capita GDP of the United Kingdom, its former colonial power.

This modern Singapore, to a greater extent even than India, Ghana, or South Africa, is personified by a national father, Lee Kuan Yew. By the 1990s Lee had stepped down as prime minister after three decades in office, leaving behind a state apparatus that in many ways fulfilled the dreams of both late-colonial and post-independence modernizing projects. While popular international images of Singapore often stress authoritarianism— clean streets, no crime, caning, death penalty for drugs and petty regulations forbidding the sale of chewing gum—the reality is somewhat different. Lee's political party, the People's Action Party (PAP), has achieved legitimacy through elections held at regular intervals. The Internal Security Act has been used strategically yet sparingly, as have lawsuits for defamation against political opponents. Thus it would be inappropriate to see Singapore—as popular representation in the international media sometimes shows it—as reverting to some form of pre-modern, sovereign power. Much of Lee's success, and the continued survival of the regime that he instituted, has come through the deployment of a peculiarly modern power, through a governmentality that works not only through state ministries and organs, but also through the vast number of parastatal organizations that have, often with increased efficiency but substantially less autonomy, substituted most of the functions of independent civil society.

Central to this disciplinary power, and yet to some extent hidden from surface view because of the extent that it has been naturalized, has been an identification of the Singapore state apparatus with Lee himself. There are no public statues of Lee in Singapore as there were of Nkrumah in Accra before his fall, and no roads or major public buildings named after him; his most prominent monument is perhaps the recently-founded Lee Kuan Yew School of Public Policy, nestled modestly out of sight near the National University of Singapore campus. Despite popularly circulated Singaporean gossip regarding the activities of the Lee family, it would be a mistake to see Singapore as a personal fiefdom or a personal appendage in the way that Ato Quayson has noted, some "African leaders perceive the bureaucratic state apparatus as an extension of themselves."[1] Yet, in a different sense Quayson's remark is appropriate: as Lee himself recedes from the political scene, the postcolonial mode of governmentality that he established works without him but still bears his imprint. Lee's own self-fashioning through self-discipline, pragmatism, and ceaseless devotion to work in service of the nation are very much part of a wider social imaginary enabled by the state. And if Singapore's modernity is materially impressive, it also appears to many commentators empty or subject to lack, shorn of the poetry of the visions of the Bandung generation, variously described as "a sort of hyper-modern petit-bourgeois modernity," or "modernisation . . . without modernity."[2] Furthermore, it appears in many ways to be self-consuming: forty years after Singapore's independence, its social imaginary is still reliant on a sense of anxiety at not yet being a nation, continually re-inventing itself to keep pace with a global narrative of change that seems, in Anthony Giddens's memorable phrase, symptomatic of a "runaway world" in which individuals and nations are "propelled into a global order that no one fully understands."[3]

Lee's autobiography, *The Singapore Story*, published in 1998, is thus, as its title emphasizes, about more than merely an individual's life.[4] Like the autobiographies of Nkrumah, Nehru, and Mandela, it also writes a national narrative, constituting a national autobiography. As its predecessors do, *The Singapore Story* draws parallels between the making of a nation and the writing of a life, between disciplinary technologies of power and technologies of the self, between the governing of a city-state and the governing of a male body through a certain style of masculinity. In its stress on a gendered, disciplinary modernity, it also attempts to interpellate subject-citizens of a new Singapore: it serves as a portable machine for the production of such national subjects.[5] Yet it is also the product of a very different historical moment from its predecessors. Nehru wrote his autobiography as a forerunner of a coming wave of history, before the achievement of the Indian nation-state. Nkrumah produced *Ghana* at the wave's crest, at the high noon of decolonization, the moment of Ghana's independence from colonial power. Mandela, writing earlier in the same decade as Lee, summoned the memories and hopes of previous generations of anticolonial activists in a vision of a possible future. In each case a personal past embedded within a larger history projects an unrealized narrative of future progress after the founding of the nation. Lee, in contrast, looks back from the vantage point of more than thirty years of Singapore's existence as an independent nation-state. The history of the nation is thus not simply one of arrival, but rather of repeated management of crises, and national autobiography has become much less the "out-law" genre, in Caren Kaplan's terms, of the life devoted to the anticolonial struggle, transforming itself instead into an "in-law" genre, interpellating citizens into a particular configuration of tradition and modernity.[6]

The trope of crisis central to Lee's autobiography is in many ways not new; Geraldine Heng and Janadas Devan have noted that People's Action Party rule has often been legitimated by the discovery—sometimes retrospectively—of crises and the heroic administration of their solution.[7] At times this leads to unconscious bathos: deprived by his relative youth of a role in the anticolonial struggle, Singapore's new Prime Minister in 2004, Lee Hsien Loong, was forced to recount his own story of struggle against the odds in defying inclement weather while marching as part of a high school band in the 1968 National Day Parade.[8] As we shall see, Lee Kuan Yew's autobiography emerges from a particular series of historical and cultural contexts that need amplification. Yet it also tactically reuses elements from previous national autobiographies, forming its protagonist in relation to colonial, "oriental" and anticolonial masculinities in turn. If Mandela's *Long Walk* retrospectively naturalizes his protagonist as a family man, *The Singapore Story* seems driven by another retrospective desire: to embed the protagonist's actions in a naturalization of the "entrepreneurial self" of neo-liberalism.

The story that Lee tells in the first volume of his memoirs undoubtedly expresses a Gramscian common-sense narrative of Singapore's national history.[9] In a text that features an intrusive and heavily retrospective narrator, Lee describes how his protagonist grows up in an affluent comprador class family in colonial Singapore in the 1930s and attends the premier Anglophone educational institutions in the colony, Raffles Institution and Raffles College, largely unaware of the inequities of the colonial world. His disillusionment, and that of many other Malayans, corresponds with the surrender of British forces to the Japanese on 15 February 1942 and his own experience of the brutalities and privations of the Japanese occupation. After the end of the Second World War, Lee studies Law in the United Kingdom and returns, politically radicalized, to practice his profession in Singapore. His growing involvement in representing union members and anticolonial activists, in a series of recollections strongly guided by retrospective interpretation, leads to his being drawn further into politics and his participation in the founding of the People's Action Party in 1954.[10] The bulk of Lee's memoirs, however, cover the decade from the Party's formation to Singapore's independence in 1965, and deal with the PAP's election victory in 1959, the city-state's aborted membership of the Malaysian Federation for two brief years from 1963 to 1965, and, above all, the manner in which the PAP pragmatically "rode the tiger" of the Malayan Communist Party and its affiliates, appropriating its methods and eventually suppressing it in the context of establishing a "democratic and non-communist and socialist" state.[11] As with other texts of this genre, the chronology of *The Singapore Story* slows to a crawl as the narrative approaches its denouement—yet it never halts, as Nkrumah's *Ghana* does. The reflective element of the earlier narrative is now completely submerged: unlike Nehru or Nkrumah, Lee suffers little doubt, being concerned only with political instrumentality in managing the various political challenges that confront him. In their only significant departure from a conventional chronology, Lee's memoirs begin on 9 August 1965, throwing the reader into the unlooked-for trauma of separation from Malaysia in the first chapter: the second circles back to his childhood and begins a chronological narrative that concludes on the day of Singapore's independence.

Contexts

To understand the purchase of *The Singapore Story* as an individualizing narrative, we consider two contexts: the immediate historical context of its publication and also the larger context of the People's Action Party's molding of a Singaporean social imaginary from 1959 onward, and particularly after independence in 1965.

The publication of *The Singapore Story,* indeed, coincided with a moment of crisis in Singapore, a reconfiguration of the Singaporean national imaginary in the late 1990s in which discourses of Asian values prominent in the first half of the 1990s were superseded by a sense of isolation and a more assertive nationalism. Externally, the late 1990s were marked by the Asian crisis triggered by the collapse of the Thai baht in 1997, provoking capital flight that threatened stability of the Association of Southeast Asian Nations (ASEAN) "tiger" economies such as Thailand and Malaysia, which had seen rapid growth from the 1980s onward. In Singapore, a sense of unease was increased by a "haze" caused by forest fires in Indonesia, which sent pollution indices to record level and affected the tourism industry, and by the political uncertainty surrounding the fall of Indonesian president Suharto. To the North, the situation was little better. The late 1990s were marked by a series of disputes between Singapore and its neighbor Malaysia over custom controls, water rights and airspace violations.

A little before the Asian crisis broke, Singapore had been gripped by a social panic from 1996 onward in response to a poll by Singapore tabloid *New Paper* that suggested young Singaporeans were profoundly ignorant of their history. In response, the Ministry of Education introduced a compulsory program in National Education in all schools. In 1998, a $10 million multimedia production, entitled *The Singapore Story—Overcoming the Odds,* was shown at the Suntec City exhibition and conference center, and

500,000 free tickets were distributed; an internal return to history thus confronted an increased perception of external threats.[12]

In this context, Lee's memoirs enjoyed strong sales in Singapore, and indeed the work was immediately put to use, in both full and abridged form in schools as part of the national education initiative.[13] One of the major thrusts of Lee's memoirs is a revaluation of Singapore's separation from Malaysia in 1965, and the text received its most vocal criticism from Malaysia, which shares a common past with Singapore that is placed within a very different nationalist historiography. Clearly Lee's manipulation of crisis is at one level instrumental; just as in 1965, so the Singapore at the autobiography's time of writing stands alone in the world. In the words of one of the early National Education messages, "nobody owes Singapore a living."[14]

Yet the fact that Malaysian response to Lee's text focused less on issues of factual inaccuracy than on misrepresentation through character portrayal indicates that the text is also driven by more covert and less conscious rhetorical strategies than simply instrumental crisis management. Then Malaysian prime minister Mahathir bin Mohamad commented acidly that Lee's description of events before separation showed that Singapore's leaders were still living in the past, while the youth wing of his party attempted to get the book banned in Malaysia, charging that it promoted disrespect for the country's first two prime ministers, Tunku Abdul Rahman and Tun Abdul Razak. The focus here on character is crucial.[15] Lee's memoirs work to bind present to past, to align narrator, protagonist, and author in a trajectory of rational progress and self-discovery that mimes the nation's. As such, they are part of a disciplinary project to direct the energies of anticolonial nationalism into the service of work for the nation that extends back much further than the 1990s. The People's Action Party's early rule in Singapore was marked by disciplinary projects aimed to cleanse and then fortify a social body. The campaign against "yellow culture" from 1959 designed to produce a purified national body by expelling pornography, prostitution, and what one new member of the Legislative Assembly called "feudalistic, corrupted, Colonial bacteria,"[16] and to incite a new, nationalist subjectivity. After independence in 1965, the government stressed the creation of a "rugged resolute, highly trained, highly disciplined community," formed in such institutions as the Vigilante Corps and Community Centres. Lee wrote, "If we develop a 'soft' society, then we cannot survive."[17] At the same time, Singapore would have found it difficult, had its leaders wished, to close its economy and promote national

self-reliance and import-substitution; earlier than many newly independent nation-states, it had to submit to the rigors of globalization and in
many ways to continue the colonial narrative of free trade that began with
Stamford Raffles's establishment of Singapore as a "commercial empor-
ium."[18] The discipline of service to the party-state urged by Nehru and
Nkumah was transformed into something else, a blissful submission to
work for the nation, often in the factories of multinational corporations.

Yet there was a further element to this disciplinary self-fashioning. As
a colonial entrepôt, Singapore was postmodern avant la lettre—a world
of radical discontinuities, varied cultural communities, and competing
worldviews that the colonial state sought to manage through a vision of a
colonial "plural society" in which communities lived separate lives yet met
through the marketplace.[19] Since self-rule in 1959, successive People's Action Party governments have managed ethnicity through tools inherited
from those of the colonial state.[20] From the mass of different communities
under colonialism, four have been designated under the "multiracialism"
that constitutes one of the nation's core values. Singaporean multiracialism's racial categories have been neatly summed up by Sharon Siddique as
CMIO—Chinese, Malay, Indian, Other (Eurasian)—representing the
various communities, in descending order of size. Each citizen has his or
her race inscribed on an identity card: if the parents are of different races,
the child follows the father's racial designation. Race matters: it influences
the language that the young Singaporean will be taught as a "mother
tongue" at school, the ethnic self-help group to which he or she makes regular salary contributions, and the choices of cultural affiliation that the citizen is encouraged to make. Thus a Chinese Singaporean will study Mandarin at school, despite the fact that this language is unlikely to have been
the language spoken at birth by his or her mother and will be encouraged
to make an affiliation with a Chinese cultural tradition based on North
Chinese high culture despite the fact that the majority of Singaporean Chinese trace their ancestry to the Southern Chinese provinces of Guangdong
and Fujian. Racialized traditions are thus inscribed on citizen's bodies in
frequent contradiction to family and community histories of hybridity. In
events such as national day, multiculturalism is ritually displayed, each race
represented through the wearing of "traditional" costume: Indian women,
for instance, dress in saris, Chinese women in *qi pao* or cheongsam, Malay
women in the *baju kurong,* Others (Eurasians) often in hastily synthesized
"traditional" garments.

The Singapore Story clearly subscribes to, and indeed is instrumental in
reiterating, a national consciousness based on multiculturalism. Thus the

chapter describing Singapore's departure from Malaysia is entitled "Talak, Talak, Talak (I divorce thee)," identifying Islam with Malayness and using the archaic vocabulary common in colonial writings about Malay culture. The text also makes frequent references to typically "Chinese" behavior, and Lee's acquisition of political maturity is paralleled to his re-sinicization; his abandonment of his English name, Harry; and his painful attempts to learn Mandarin and Hokkien. A reading strategy, then, needs to move be-yond taking the autobiography at face value—seeing it, for example as part of an essentially Chinese autobiographical tradition in which the private is effaced—but rather requires that we explore the hybrid social context from which it emerges, a context in which Chineseness and Confucianism are rewritten as signs of tradition in modernity.[21]

Racial Masculinities

One mode of entry into *The Singapore Story* is to explore an element of the narrative that combines discipline and racialization: the manner in which it constructs the masculinity of its protagonist. The text transforms Singa-pore's extreme vulnerability into a national narrative of autonomy, of sur-vival through discipline, and manages it by a peculiar rhetorical sleight of hand. While Lee's—and hence Singapore's—story appears autonomous, it is in fact profoundly relational. Yet the relational self here is different from those of Nkrumah, Nehru, and Mandela: it is formed in relation not to women but to men. The book is dedicated to Lee's wife, Kwa Geok Choo, a lawyer, and Lee does mention her role in its composition, in its preface calling her a "powerful critic and helper," yet she is increasingly relegated to the realm of the private as the text's narrative loses its reflexivity; unlike Nehru's Kamala, she does not return to haunt the text (9). Rather Lee de-fines himself and a national masculine subjectivity in relation to other, nonnational racialized masculinities. While the narrative seems at first sight autonomous, almost a "model of an imperial masculinity" it is, as Nancy Miller notes of many male autobiographies, marked by "the self's passionate, vulnerable attachment to the other."[22]

Fallen Colonial Masculinity

The content of many of Lee's early postindependence speeches, replete with references to "legends that the Battle of Waterloo was won on the playing fields of Eton" provides a ready hint at the first of these others. In a certain sense, *The Singapore Story* is a work of mourning.[23] Paradoxically, and yet certainly not uniquely in texts by anticolonial leaders, Lee's memoirs simultaneously celebrate and mourn British imperial masculinity. Figures such as William Goode, governor of Singapore, Alan Lennox-Boyd, U.K. secretary of state for the colonies, and Anthony Head, British high commissioner in Kuala Lumpur at the time of Singapore's separation, are described admiringly by Lee as representatives of an empire now in decline. The discursive features of such a masculinity are familiar to us: somatic continence, sang froid, discipline, breeding, and rationality. Like Kipling's Creighton and Strickland, the exemplars of British masculinity in Lee's narrative can emotionally absent themselves from the crises they inevitably face. Having informed Head of Singapore's decision to leave the Federation, Lee writes: "Head's bearing impressed me. His demeanour was worthy of a Sandhurst-trained officer in the Life Guards. . . . He was British upper class, good at the stiff upper lip" (19–20). Later in his narrative, Lee pictures William Goode strolling through the Victoria Memorial Hall when the ballot papers of the 1957 election were being counted in imagery that could almost be taken from Conrad:

> At about 11 pm, I saw a tall figure of a white man in shorts strolling through the crowd into the hall. It was Bill Goode, the governor. He was brave. True, the crowd was not yet in an excited mood. Nonetheless, he had been the chief secretary when the first wave of arrests was carried out in October 1956, and governor when the second clean-up of the pro-communists took place. But he showed no trace of fear. My respect for him increased. (272)

The image Lee presents of Goode, a white man calmly moving through a sea of Asians, protected only by his own self-confidence, his whiteness set against a background of engulfing darkness, is a staple of colonial fiction and biography. Lee's description reminds one of Joseph Conrad's Jim at Patusan, and of pivotal scenes of hagiographic imperial biographies such as Demetrius Boulger's *The Life of Sir Stamford Raffles* (1897) and thinly fictionalized memoirs such as Hugh Clifford's *In a Corner of Asia* (1899).[24] There are some changes here—Lee himself usurps a role usually played by an anonymous British narrator, gazing upon the scene from some height and distance: Goode's shorts might seem infantilizing and out of place. Yet, above all, in *The Singapore Story* Lee mourns a fallen imperial masculinity, most apparent perhaps in the bagpipe playing of the Argyll and Sutherland Highlanders, the last British troops to cross the causeway between Singapore and the mainland, which leaves the protagonist "with a life-long impression of British courage in the face of impending defeat" by the Japanese (45–46).

In contrast to this aristocratic masculinity, Lee the narrator sees the British Empire being sapped from within by the bad faith of the middle and working classes. The "hysteria" of "white civilians and government officers" in the evacuation of Penang, Lee suggests, undermined "all assumptions of the Englishman's superiority" (52). Such emphasis on failure to regulate the body as a symptom of imperial decline continues in Lee's description of "the unabashed promiscuity of some 40 or 50 servicewomen, non-commissioned officers and other ranks" on the Cunard liner *Britannic* on which he traveled to England after the war (99). This discursive construction of the West as undermined from within, grown flabby and effete and therefore falling gasping by the wayside in the quest for disciplinary modernity, was to have a long life, becoming a staple of the discourse of Asian values in the early 1990s.

"Oriental" Masculinity

Many commentators on the cultures of colonialism, however, have noticed that the colonizer's identities are profoundly relational. British imperial masculinity is thus formed by a comparison with feminized—or at times hypermasculine—others. Curiously, perhaps, in a text written by a political leader whose goal since his political awakening was the ending of colonialism, *The Singapore Story* repeats this gesture, defining the ruins of imperial masculinity in contrast to an oriental masculinity marked by dandyism, surrender to the body, emotions and appetite, and a lack of taste and other cultural capital.

Lee's representation of this oriental masculinity is nowhere more apparent than in his characterization of David Marshall, the first chief minister of Singapore, and Lee's major opponent during his early years in politics. Lee introduces Marshall as "a mercurial, flamboyant Sephardic Jew," "a prima donna who loved to be center stage and would be uncontrollable" (177). Marshall is portrayed as narcissistic, "too involved in his own emotional processes," loquacious, and lacking in self-control (235). A key moment in *The Singapore Story* is the encounter between Lennox-Boyd and Marshall during the constitutional talks in London in 1956, between imperial and oriental masculinity. Marshall, as the narrator of *The Singapore Story* pictures him, becomes agitated when he is making an "impassioned" speech and Lennox-Boyd begins to write on correspondence passed to him by a secretary, apparently concerning a completely different matter:

> Marshall was miffed. He stopped in mid-sentence, and in a high-pitched voice that showed he was really angry, said "Secretary of State, we know that you have many important possessions around the world, but we have come 8,000 miles to London to present our case and we demand that you give us your attention."
>
> Without lifting his eyes from the cable, Lennox-Boyd continued writing and said, "Chief Minister, let me assure you that of all our valuable possessions around the world, Singapore is one of our most valuable. It is a precious jewel in the British Crown. I am all ears. You were saying, Chief Minister"—and he repeated verbatim Marshall's last three sentences. It was a virtuoso performance, very British, quite devastating. Marshall was livid and speechless, an unusual state for him. (236)

Here British imperial masculinity is defined by its emotional reticence, in contrast to Marshall's lack of self-governance, which is conspicuously feminized.

Marshall is perhaps the most prominent, but certainly not the only, exemplar of oriental masculinity in *The Singapore Story*. While *The Singapore Story* has been vetted to avoid causing offence to minority races, it is clear that the typology of race that underpins multiculturalism persists in the memoirs.[25] Lee notes in narrating his time in England that he later came to realize "performance varied substantially between the different races in Singapore, and among different categories of the same race": at least a proportion of this was due to "natural abilities" (105). Most exemplars of oriental masculinity in *The Singapore Story* are either Indian or Malay: James Puthucheary, Lee describes, talks too much and is "superficially clever but unreliable," later dismissing him and S. Woodhull as "political dilettantes who enjoyed the cocktail circuit," while he depicts erstwhile PAP secretary-general T. T. Rajah as a "left-wing poseur" (159, 514, 270). Lee's portrayal of Malaysia's prime minister, Tunku Abdul Rahman, is more cautiously sympathetic but implicitly critical of the Tunku's capriciousness and lack of self-control.[26] What these portraits share is the portrayal of Indian and Malay men as effete, governed by emotion and appetite, unable to apply the disciplinary practices necessary for the founding of a new nation.[27]

Anticolonial Masculinity

Masculine self-fashioning in *The Singapore Story*, however, does not involve merely the appropriation of an aristocratic British masculinity defined in opposition to a decadent Oriental lack of manliness. Lee does appropriate some aspects of colonial masculinity, notably panoptic vision, from the British, in such claims as "I knew the Malays better" (20) Yet he also envisages a new Asian masculinity as the foundation for the nation, a mode of self-discipline that he finds most clearly represented in the leftist anticolonial activists he identifies as communists. One of the most vividly described figures in *The Singapore Story* is Lim Chin Siong, the leftist who was detained by both the British and Lee's own government, before leaving Singapore after writing a letter of recantation in 1969.[28] In *The Singapore Story*, Lim often figures as Lee's other. He, like Lee, becomes one of the PAP's first elected members of the Legislative Assembly (MLAs) in 1955, and like Lee, he is a powerful orator. Lim's connection to the Chinese-speaking world also makes him a powerful representative, in Lee's eyes, of an anticolonial disciplinary system whose power he wishes to turn to another use. In an extraordinary passage recollecting Lim's accompanying him to constitutional talks in London, Lee turns Lim's gaze upon his body, and this transforms the narrator into an exemplar of the decadent masculinity from which he is so eager to distance himself:

> He had a new suit and had bought himself a trilby because he was advised to, but he never wore it except to go to the airport. He was modest, humble and well-behaved, with a dedication to his cause that won my reluctant admiration and respect. I wished I had cadres like him. He was a Gurkha warrant officer in the British army—totally loyal, absolutely dependable, always ready to execute orders to the best of his ability.
>
> He probably did not know what to make of me. I was a golf-playing, beer-swilling bourgeois, but he must also have sensed that I was not without a serious purpose. (233)

For Lee, "Lim Chin Siong and [his comrade] Fong Swee Suan were the exact opposite of Marshall and company"; they represented the "puritanical zeal" of a nationalism based upon the ideals, if not the actual practice of "a clean, honest, dynamic, revolutionary China," and anticolonial nationalism whose disciplinary energy the People's Action Party government sought to appropriate (178, 326–27).

In *The Singapore Story*, then, the narrative frequently makes Lim a center of attraction and desire, "young, slim, of medium height with a soft baby face. . . . The girls adored him" (186). This desire, as Lee's reference to his playing the very British game of golf in the paragraph above shows, is also one for cultural authenticity and roots. Lim represents, for Lee the narrator, the possibility of immersion in Chinese culture outside of the "sedate parlour game politics" of the limited franchise under the colonial state. He stands for a tradition that can "quote proverbs, use metaphors and allegories or traditional legends to illustrate contemporary situations" that can hold out "the prospect of Chinese greatness" (186). In terms of Chinese conceptions of masculinity that Lee the narrator is eager to reclaim, Lim represents a fusion of *wen* and *wu,* combining a scholarly purity of motive with a masterly martial command of strategy.[29]

For all Lim's discipline, he cannot accede to a Confucian category of which Lee would make much use in the late 1980s and 1990s, that of *junzi,* or righteous man, which Lee himself, in a reinscription Confucianism under the lens of Victorian masculinity, clearly regards as synonymous with the bourgeois category "gentleman." Lim's discipline is separated from the interests of the nation. He is portrayed as ultimately lacking in autonomy, willing to sacrifice Singapore's national interests for the interests of "communism," manipulated by the "faceless men" of the MCP who stand behind the publicly visible "united front supporters" (247, 246). Lim's hesitancy in London, Lee's protagonist suggests, may be less a result of culture shock than a fear "of being away from his mentors" (230). In contrast, the disciplinary practices that Lee urges are in service of the nation, involving what his colleague in arms S. Rajaratnam would describe as the transformation of anticolonial nationalism's project to "inculcate among its adherents an anti-authority and anti-government attitude" into an attempt to "re-introduce into Asian society a sense of social discipline and social responsibility" through a "modernising nationalism" committed to the nation-state.[30] The story of self-discipline becomes the nation's story, asceticism now pressed into the service of capital and Singapore's industrial development.

The Entrepreneurial Self, Race, and the Nation's Modernity

Some of the relational self-fashioning in Lee's text is, of course, not unique. We have seen how colonial masculinity attracted the interest of life writing as diverse as Gandhi's and Mandela's, and noted how these narratives appropriate elements of it at both a conscious and unconscious level, as well as at times defining their protagonists in opposition to it. Nor is the feminization and orientalization of political opponents unheard of. Nkrumah uses a similar trope to Lee's both in his autobiography and extratextually, describing his erstwhile ally J. B. Danquah as "noisily" bursting into tears when held with the autobiography's protagonist in Kumasi jail; on receiving news of the 1966 coup while in Beijing he would criticize the accompanying ministers who would later desert him as "old women."[31] In Nkrumah's portrayal of his opponents as overly emotional and unreliable, one can certainly see orientalist—if one may apply the word to representations of Africa—discourse at work, the narrator strategically redeploying critiques made by Lugard and others of the "character and temperament" of the Gold Coast native.[32] Yet Lee's rejection of the idealism of radical anticolonial nationalism in the person of Lim Chin Siong seems unique and indeed is part of a larger retrospective disillusionment with postcolonial national fathers in the text.

Singapore's independence in 1965 meant that it came later to the Afro-Asian table than many countries, but Lee's statements, speeches and writings in the 1960s indicate a strong identification with anticolonial nationalism and the stories of national fathers who went before him. In 1964, on the occasion of Nehru's death, Lee paid tribute to him as "the first of the Afro-Asians" who "gave his unceasing support to all the anticolonial revolutions elsewhere in Asia and Africa," including Singapore's own struggle, and would later recall having been inspired by this *Glimpses of World History* as a schoolboy in Singapore.[33] In 1989 he would still laud Nehru as "one of Asia's great revolutionaries."[34] Lee's relationship with Nkrumah was less close, but he praised the Ghanaian president's "vision and leadership" in correspondence after Nkrumah was ousted in the 1966 coup.[35]

In 1963, indeed, Lee embarked on a tour of African countries in order to gain support and recognition for the new Federation of Malaysia, which Sukarno had denounced as a neocolonial ploy: at this moment the support of Afro-Asia and the Non-Aligned movement was crucial. Yet Lee's recollection of his visit to Africa, as narrated in *The Singapore Story*, is already tainted with disillusionment. Lee is not contemptuous of leftist governments alone: he finds Tubman's pro-American Liberia to be "a parody of a state," an ersatz copy of the United States that preserves the form, but not the substance, of American institutions (528). Yet he reserves his greatest disillusionment for those leaders he identifies as "talking in Socialist terms of the distribution of wealth": noting that the economic systems embraced by Sekou Touré, Nkrumah, and Julius Nyerere, even if well-meaning, will result in their peoples becoming "paupers," reduced to "unnecessary poverty" (532, 533).[36]

The most powerful expression of Lee's narrational disillusionment comes in a proleptic episode in which he first recounts a visit to Lusaka on the eve of Zambian independence, staying as a guest in what was then Government House as "the guest of the last British governor of Northern

Rhodesia, Sir Evelyn Hone" (538). The house here seems to be a transparent synecdoche for the country on independence: it is "well-furnished and well-maintained" (538), and Lee is delighted to find abundant African wildlife in its grounds. The narrative now moves forward in time:

> I was to go back to Lusaka in 1970 for the Non-Aligned Conference, and again in 1979 for the Commonwealth Conference. Each time was a saddening experience. I remembered the flowers, shrubs, trees and greenery at the side of the roads and at roundabouts when I was driven in from the airport in 1964. Roses grew in abundance. Six years later, the roses had gone and the weeds had taken over. Nine years after that, even the weeds had given up; the roundabouts were covered with tarmac. And there seemed to be fewer animals and birds in the grounds of Government House, now the President's Lodge. I wondered why. (538)

Lee as narrator does not wonder too long: his "lesson in decolonization" is that "effective government" is needed, pragmatic, turning its back on "half-digested theories of socialism and redistribution of wealth" (539).

Clearly what Lee witnesses is not all ideological interpretation: developmental states did fail in Africa, and for a variety of reasons, of which poor governance was at times no doubt one; Singapore, in contrast, succeeded in maintaining a high level of economic growth, with only the occasional hiccup caused by external factors, well into the 1990s. Yet, in detaching Singapore from a narrative of anticolonial nationalism and detaching himself from the idealism of a previous generation of national fathers, Lee is engaging in a "pragmatism" that, as Chua Beng Huat has noted, is clearly ideological.[37] What seems to underlie these statements, and indeed the whole narrative itself, is a view of the modern subject as an "entrepreneurial self," acting selfishly within the market. This narrative logic is present covertly very early in *The Singapore Story*. Lee does not, for instance, attempt to show instances of anti-Japanese resistance on his part during the Japanese occupation of Singapore; rather, he devotes most of his account to a description of how he survived financially by making a "decent profit" from the sale of gum he and a friend manufactured (67). As Lee's protagonist grows intellectually both and in terms of experience, he comes to learn the truth of the market, already exemplified by the world in which he lives, and to cast idealism aside. As protagonist, for instance, he is impressed by the "fairness" of the new National Health Service of postwar England, from which he obtains free glasses and dental treatment. Yet the rather visible hand of the retrospective narrator intrudes: Lee as protagonist is "too young, too idealistic to realize that . . . under such an egalitarian system each individual would be more interested in what he could get out of the common pool than in striving to do better for himself, which had been the driving force for progress through human evolution" (129). The protagonist thus naturally abandons idealism for a pragmatic acceptance of the market as a transcendent signified.

Lee's naturalization of an entrepreneurial self might at first sight seem to be a return to the origins of autobiography itself, to the cautious accumulation of the bourgeois subject in Daniel Defoe's pseudo-autobiographical *Robinson Crusoe*, or Benjamin Franklin's "gaining money by my industry and frugality."[38] John Sturrock, indeed, has argued that autobiography is "a robustly capitalist genre" in which autobiographers "come before us as successful bankers of their past" transforming the losses of narrative setbacks "smoothly into gain and work toward the one, profitable end" of denouement.[39] Certainly, within the Singapore context, Lee's production of an entrepreneurial self enables a linking back to a history that traverses the watershed of the anticolonial struggle, reaching back to the free trade of the East India Company's Stamford Raffles, whom post-independence historiography in Singapore has continued to celebrate as the "founder" of the city-state's modernity.[40]

Lee's naturalization of an entrepreneurial self, however, looks forward as much as it looks back. Toby Miller has explored the complex manner in which the state in late modernity has to "forge two kinds of subjectivity; the selfless, active citizen who cares for others and who favors a political regime that compensates for losses in the financial domain; and the selfish, active consumer who favors a financial regime that compensates for losses in the political domain."[41] This split produces a crisis for the liberal subject, contradictorily caught between the role of a citizen seeking democratic participation for the common good and that of a consumer seeking maximum utility in the market, yet it also offers the state the possibility of managing the split through the creation of "citizen-consumers" — "not citizens who exist to act politically inside or outside the state; not citizens concerned with questions of policy or of political ideology," but rather "users of public services who are being offered a limited power of redress when those services are delivered unsatisfactorily" (135). Citizenship, in effect, becomes consumption.

Miller's study addresses transformations in the state in Australia, the United Kingdom, and the United States from the 1980s onward, and in particular the establishment of a neoliberal orthodoxy that, after the Reagan and Thatcher years, was accepted as doxological by leftist parties that came to power in the 1990s. Yet it is possible to see Lee's Singapore as pioneering the notion of the citizen consumer much earlier, and more consistently. In *The Singapore Story*, Lee as a young protagonist expresses admiration at the self-confident anticolonialism of the Indonesian nationalist Mohammed Razif, later Indonesian ambassador to Malaysia, whom he meets on a ship returning to Singapore from Europe. Almost instantly, however, the retrospective narrator intervenes. Only later, we are told, would Lee realize that a "nation needed more than a few dignified and able men at the top to get it moving." Rather, the "people as a whole" would need the "self-respect and the will to strive to make a nation of themselves" (132). Leadership thus required the creation of an economy of desire, in which entrepreneurial subjects would engage in a cycle of production and consumption, bound by "a strong framework within which they [could] learn, work hard, be productive and be rewarded accordingly" (132).

Such an economy of desire, with devotion to production matched by the citizen functioning as consumer, has been a central feature of Singaporean governmentality from the 1960s onward. Two examples might suffice. A public housing project of perhaps unprecedented scale has transformed the built environment of the city-state in the last half-century, replacing the untidiness of rural villages and squatter camps with the modernist symmetry of well-planned new towns. Yet, well before Margaret Thatcher's sale of council housing to its tenants in the 1980s in Britain, Singapore's parastatal Housing Development Board (HDB) made its tenants into consumers, encouraging them to buy their homes through low-interest mortgages, which could from 1968 onward be paid from worker's compulsory Central Provident Fund salary deductions also intended to provide for retirement. Chua Beng Huat has noted that the effect of public housing policy in Singapore has been the "'depoliticizing' of housing provision," through a framing of the terms of public debate so that "public complaints [concerning housing] are overwhelmingly of the type that attempt to make government agencies more efficient in serving the population, rather than involving issues of principle."[42] Second, while independent civil society in Singapore has certainly increased in vitality since the early 1990s, its rise has been shadowed by the mushrooming of semiautonomous organs of state that encourage citizenship as consumption. In response to electoral reverses in the 1980s, for instance, the government set up the Feedback Unit in 1985 with the dual function of receiving feedback regarding the efficiency of public services and explaining policies to citizens. Citizens approach the unit as individual consumers of the state's services, and indeed in the recent years the unit's current Web site has developed into a comprehensive resource that encourages citizens to register as members of a citizens' forum and receive "membership privileges" that mirror those of commercial sites. Whereas the site does offer the possibility of eventually influencing policy, the citizen can only achieve this if he or she adopts the role of a client of the state and accepts its governing rationality; much "feedback" is consequently about the provision of services, and there is no direct political contestation.[43]

Yet in one detail Singapore does not resemble Miller's model. If Lee and the early PAP believed in "gradual integration and the blurring of the racial divide," Lee's pragmatism would later dictate an acceptance of the persistence of race, and, through the tightening of multiracialism from the late 1970s onward, a reworking of the governmental targeting and solidification of racial communities by the colonial state (563). Under multiracialism, Singaporeans have increasingly addressed the state not simply as citizens but as racial selves. The Feedback Unit, for instance, holds feedback sessions on issues in different languages; with the implementation of mother tongue policies in education from the 1980s onward, such groups are increasingly racially homogenous, and the views sought are often seen as representative of the views of a racial "community." Newspapers regularly celebrate not only the top students in school examinations, but also the best Malay student and the best Indian student, as if the achievement somehow emerges from and gives credit to the community. The ethnic self-help organizations—Chinese Development and Assistance Council (CDAC), Yayasan Mendaki, Singapore Indian Development Association (SINDA), and, through the incorporation of an older community group, the Eurasian Association—address the Chinese, Malay, Indian and Eurasian (Other) communities respectively. The organizations address issues such as unemployment, retraining, and social integration through racial community rather than through such perspectives as class, which might result in a more politicized response.

Partha Chatterjee is surely right that such attention to "population group[s] produced by governmentality" reprises the actions of the colonial state.[44] Again, however, we might see such a strategy as looking forward as much as backward, as a means of managing the contradictions of late capitalism rather than a simple return to the origins of colonial modernity. Singapore's multiculturalism acknowledges and trains the demands of community rather than attempting to simply "reassert the utopian politics of classical nationalism" that would simply repudiate ethnic chauvinism (23). In so doing, it manages, through an illiberal multiculturalism, many of the paradoxes and contradictions that have faced the former colonial metropolitan powers in their adoption of liberal multicultural policies from the 1960s onward. In Singapore, the act of "'recognizing' the 'culture' that constitutes a minority as a distinct group" is centrally situated within the apparatus of the state; the liberal supposition that an individual should be free to disaffiliate from any group, or to challenge the authority of the group's "representatives," which has vexed multicultural politics in Europe and North America, is solved by ceding some of this decision-making power to a state envisioned as a neutral player, managing a multitude of selfish communities.[45] Vijay Mishra is right: discussions should move beyond seeing "multiculturalism as a purely Western phenomenon requiring urgent academic analysis and attention in the context of a largely post-1965 immigration of non-white peoples into Western nation-states."[46] Yet Singapore's example shows that what might be found in looking at "postcolonial nations made up of two or more 'historically subordinate (ancestral) groups'" is a model that, disturbingly, may prove attractive to nation-states eager to manage the contradictions of nation, capital, and community, rather than to confront them (199).

Conclusion

To reprise, then, Lee's national masculinity expressed in his national autobiography is both representative and unique. It is representative, we have seen, in that its stress upon disciplinary practices applied to a male body as a metaphor for nationhood is a central element in anticolonial self-fashioning in national autobiographies in the twentieth century. It is unique in that Lee writes his narrative retrospectively, more than three decades after independence in a Singapore that has prospered in its situation as a key hub in a very persistent world economic order anticolonial movements had hoped to displace. Nehru, Nkrumah, and Mandela all wrote their autobiographies to bring a nation into being, to incite their readers to become citizen-subjects and throw off the colonial rule or its legacies. Lee writes his autobiography with hindsight, dismissing the socialism that motivated many of his predecessors as impractical and inducing "unnecessary poverty" and accepting neoliberalism as common sense (533). National autobiography's individualizing impulses here mold the citizen-subject to serve a neo-liberal order, while its reference to a community of readers as citizens has the effect of legitimizing the nation as the community that demands ultimate loyalty. The nation thus becomes the protector of the social: in return for disciplined work and channeled consumption, it "can be invoked and deployed to contest community destruction by liberal capitalism."[47] Through a racialized governmentality targeting populations, the nation-state can make use of and indeed harden the boundaries of racially constituted communities, position itself as guardian of traditions and communities even as it molds them, and represent unmolded communities as dangerously antinational.[48]

Yet for all this, Lee's autobiography has been unsuccessful in recreating or redefining an international social imaginary. The paratext of *The Singapore Story* works earnestly to emphasize its subject's importance, with four pages of approving comments solicited from politicians from all around the world. Yet Lee's book, while popular among United States neoconservatives and some lay readers, has never achieved the international sales of Mandela's *Long Walk;* Lee himself has never reached the international prominence of Mandela. If his book's common sense represents one of the ends of modernity—the neoliberal subject held in an economy of desire and a cocoon of community by a corporatized state—it is an end that readers perhaps still do not wish to recognize.[49] Indeed, internationally recently disseminated images of Singapore's hypermodernity—if we move beyond caning and chewing gum—have tended to be dystopian, rather than utopian. Cyberpunk author William Gibson has famously described Singapore as "Disneyland with the Death Penalty"; Bruce Sterling in *Islands in the Net* portrays it as an island of stiflingly over-regimented order menaced by terrorism in a chaotic world; Dutch architect Rem Koolhaas has influentially described it as a "Potemkin metropolis," a series of theatrical stage fronts of modernity with little intrinsic content.[50] When positive images of Singapore are deployed, it is usually in the service of extremely focused local critique—for instance, in the aftermath of the chaotic scenes in New Orleans after hurricane Katrina, in Thomas L. Friedman's praise of a country where the "head of Civil Defense . . . is not simply someone's college roommate."[51]

Yet there is perhaps one further international context to Lee's identification of his life history with the story of Singapore nationhood. In 1997 Nelson Mandela visited Singapore, giving the Sixteenth Singapore Lecture, sponsored by the Institute of Southeast Asian Studies on the theme "South and Southern Africa into the Next Century." His welcome stressed economic connections rather than a shared history of anticolonial struggle and largely involved public contact with the generation of leaders who had succeeded Lee: a preparatory visit by then prime minister Goh Chok Tong to South Africa was followed, during Mandela's trip to Singapore, by a state banquet that featured an address by President Ong Teng Cheong, which praised South Africa as Singapore's "largest economic partner on the African continent."[52] Yet there was a story told in Singapore regarding

Mandela's Singapore lecture speech. On the way to the podium, Mandela paused to greet veteran opposition leader J. B. Jeyaretnam—who had doggedly survived bankruptcy through defamation suits mounted against him by various governing politicians, including Lee himself—whispering private words into his ear before the dutiful public performance of his speech and question-and-answer session.[53] The story, like many political rumors in Singapore, may be accurate, hold a germ of truth, or, in fact, be completely inaccurate—but its dissemination through coffee-shop conversations, telephone discussions, and cyberspace testifies to the continued circulation and indeed oppositional power of narratives that connect "character" and to nation-building. Strategic appropriation of the tropes of national autobiography may still hold potential in the ongoing reconfiguration of social imaginaries, in local contestations of national inscriptions of modernity.

Conclusion

Every page a victory.
Who cooked the feast for the visitors?
Every ten years a great man.
Who paid the bill?

So many reports
So many questions.

Bertolt Brecht,
"Questions from a Worker Who Reads"

The publication of Lee's *Singapore Story* and *From Third World to First* perhaps signals the exhaustion of a genre. New nations, such as Timor Leste, will certainly emerge, and, barring a revolution in transnational gender regimes, narratives will presumably continue to be written by their founding fathers; yet such events are likely to have regional rather than global significance. The historical period of decolonization as a global movement—strongest in the two decades or so after the Second World War—is now over, and most of those who participated in it as actors are no longer with us or are now unable to write. In contemplating a genre's end, indeed, we might add technology to chronology. The end of the twentieth century and the beginning of the twenty-first have witnessed a proliferation of electronic and visual media, which have both created new possibilities for narrative and reworked older traditions: the singular print autobiography of the nation's life is unlikely to occupy the position of prominence it once did. Members of the generation that produced national autobiography at its height, we have seen, shared much, not least the humanist discipline of the colonial schoolroom and the theater of the colonial court, both intimately concerned with processes of narrativization. Later generations of politicians in Asia and Africa would have different backgrounds, often educations in engineering or in public or business administration. The network of emulative self-fashioning of the writers of national autobiographies in the process of decolonization has vanished, and later generations of leaders may well not turn to a prose narrative as a means of memorializing their lives.

To conclude this study, we look at a subject elided in this book so far: the possibility of resistance, or of using the form of the national autobiography to make a new, transformative intervention into the social imaginaries that underpin the nation. In examining national autobiographies under decolonization, I have consciously emphasized how they make social worlds, whether through inciting the creation or transformation of social imaginaries, or participating in the production of a Gramscian common sense of the everyday life of the nation. The manner in which the nation and the state are imagined, I have argued, is closely related to the subject-formation of individual citizens through the reading of narrative, and indeed the construction of their own life narratives. Much of this occurs at a level not consciously registered or theorized by subjects themselves: one might say that narratives of nation and state constitute elements of the habitus that surrounds most citizens in the postcolony. Yet it is surely possible for individual writers to use available material to construct narratives that take new directions, challenging elements of the social imaginaries that the texts discussed in this book played a key role in creating.

In discussing resistance or rewriting, however, we need to express some caution. Much criticism concerning life writing and globalization, we have seen, tends to oppose individual micronarratives of belonging to the grand narratives of nationalism. Postmodern narratives featuring "performative dialogism" and "openness, mobility, transcultural hybridity" are viewed as challenging the monologism of "Western subjects, Western cultures, and Western concepts of nation."[1] Frequently, the subject position of a writer marginalized through ethnicity or gender is viewed as enabling such a critique, in that this allows a view of the authorized narrative from a new and often unflattering angle. Individual readings of texts in this mode are frequently persuasive, but we need to negotiate with care what almost amounts to a fetishization of the small, insurgent narrative. Postcolonial nationalism's attention to populations already trains subjects to speak through an ethnic or a gendered identity: simply writing as an ethnic minority, for instance, will not automatically challenge a national narrative that emplaces ethnicity. Similarly, postmodern aesthetics in themselves are not resistant; indeed, if they are not precisely located within a context of reading and writing, they may well produce a text that gains global critical attention but has little specific historical or social purchase within the context it represents.

To explore these issues, this chapter analyzes two pairs of recently published texts from different contexts, which might be felt to rewrite the narratives of their respective national fathers. In the case of South Africa, Njabulo Ndebele's innovative prose novel *The Cry of Winnie Mandela* is discussed in conjunction with the more conventional *In Our Lifetimes,* Elinor Sisulu's biography of her parents-in-law, Walter and Albertina Sisulu. We then return to Singapore and Malaysia to compare Lau Siew Mei's postmodern novel *Playing Madame Mao,* which contains a portrait of Lee, with *Alias Ching Peng,* the autobiography of Malayan Communist Party secretary general Chin Peng (Ong Boon Hua), one of the former Singapore prime minister's erstwhile political adversaries. I argue here that transformations within the genre of national autobiography through a careful reworking of its parameters may frequently promote a greater contestation and questioning of social imaginaries than that provoked by more consciously literary texts more experimental in form. In the concluding section of the chapter, we will move from writing to reading, considering how the insights gained from the genre of national autobiography and its discontents in this study might suggest a historicized reading practice for the larger field of postcolonial writing.

South African Narratives

As Sarah Nuttall and Cheryl-Ann Michael have noted, life writing in its various forms—from the Truth and Reconciliation Commission to confessional television shows (now, indeed, supplemented by reality television)—has been a central element of public culture in the new South Africa from 1994 onward. In chapter 6, we saw the way Nelson Mandela's *Long Walk to Freedom* narrated the story of nationalism for both a South African and an international audience. Despite its superficial fulfilling of Lejeune's autobiographical pact, we noted the composite—if still to some degree occluded—genesis of the text, and the manner in which this might cause us to interrogate the referentiality of the autobiographical narrative. A powerful case might, indeed, be made that the carefully assembled research and interviews underpinning Anthony Sampson's monumental *Mandela: The Authorized Biography* provide a greater sense of interiority of its subject than does *Long Walk to Freedom.*

One ready means of questioning Mandela's narrative would appear to be life writing concerning a figure whose life story followed a very different trajectory from that of the ANC leader: his former wife, Winnie Madikizela-Mandela. Winnie's autobiographical testimony from the 1980s, despite the layers of mediation through which it passed, had power to illuminate some of the gaps and inconsistencies in the "master text" of *Long Walk to Freedom*. At first sight, it might seem that a classical autobiography telling Winnie's story—with emphasis on her life after the separation from her famous husband—might provide a useful counter-narrative of South African modernity. Yet the three conventional biographies of Madikizela-Mandela fail to rise to the challenge. Nancy Harrison's *Winnie Mandela: Mother of a Nation* was produced early enough to be able to weld Winnie and Nelson's stories comfortably together, concluding with the assurance to a reader that its subject was "passionately committed to an ideal for which, like Nelson, she is prepared to die if need be."[2] Emma Gibley's *The Lady: The Life and Times of Winnie Mandela* focuses on the events of the later 1980s in Soweto, including the disappearance and murder of the fourteen-year-old "Stompie" Seipi, that were eventually to lead to Winnie's trial, her divorce from her husband, and her—albeit temporary—resignation from positions of authority in the ANC; at a crucial point, the connections between Winnie's own narrative and that of the achievement of a new South Africa are suddenly cut. Written in 2003, Anné Mariè du Preez Bezdrob's *Winnie Mandela: A Life* offers greater retrospective possibilities, but its romanticization of its protagonist also fails to address the deeply contradictory ways she has been represented in a national narrative.

Njabulo Ndebele's *The Cry of Winnie Mandela* takes a consciously different approach from these predecessors; rather than attempting a historically accurate reconstruction of the past, the novel plays with the way Madikizela-Mandela has become an overdetermined symbol of tensions within a South African narrative of nation. The text is subtitled "a novel," and a "note to the reader" insists that the book is "a work of fiction, with quotations from some non-fiction texts listed at the end of the book."[3] Ndebele clearly draws on several autobiographical and biographical sources concerning Madikizela-Mandela (including *Long Walk to Freedom*, *Part of My Soul*, and the biographies by Gibley and Harrison) but frames his novel as a series of fictionalized but representative autobiographical narratives. In the first section of the text, Ndebele assembles four narratives of "Penelope's descendants," representative South African women who have been separated from husbands or partners because of the effects of apartheid, global capitalism, and postapartheid nationalism. In the second section of the novel, the four women meet for an *ibandla labafazi,* a gathering of women, and decide each to enter into a conversation with a woman who epitomizes their situation: Winnie Mandela. They do so in short narrative sections that now bear not numbers, but the names of the individual women themselves. In a fifth section, Winnie herself now speaks at length to the women, at one point addressing a *bizo,* a namesake, calling her on a cell phone and taking her through the long narrative of separation from Nelson, his return, and the Truth and Reconciliation Commission (TRC) hearings. In a final scene, the four women and Winnie travel in a Volkswagen Caravelle from Johannesburg to Durban; they stop to pick up a hitchhiker who is revealed as the Penelope of Greek mythology, pursuing a "pilgrimage of reconciliation" since Odysseus returned home and left again, so that the "world learns to become more aware of [her] not as Odysseus's moral ornament on the mantelpiece, but as an essential ingredient in the definition of human freedom" (145). Penelope travels with the women for a short while, and then is dropped off in "the middle of nowhere" to continue her journey (146).

Ndebele is perhaps best known as a critic for a previous intervention the politics of narrative: his urging, in the 1980s, that South African literature should move beyond being trapped in a simple binary opposition to apartheid, "reflecting the situation of oppression."[4] Rather, Ndebele argued, such literature should participate in the "rediscovery of the ordinary," portraying not victims but autonomous, agential individuals and communities, exploring the "nooks and crannies" of social formations which offer "no obvious political insight" that can immediately be read off (55). In *The Cry of Winnie Mandela,* we might see a similar strategic shifting of the terms of debate: rather than concerning himself with adjudicating competing—and ultimately irreconcilable—accounts of Madikizela-Mandela's life, Ndebele investigates what is at stake in the telling of her narrative, and how questioning her story becomes the occasion for other women to assemble and interpret their own life narratives.

Ndebele's attention to gender politics is clearly crucial here. The novel is dedicated to Sara or Saartjie Baartman, the so-called Hottentot Venus, a Khoisan woman brought to Europe in the early nineteenth century, and whose brain and sexual organs were subsequently put on display after her death in the Musée de l'Homme in Paris in order to prove racist theories about black sexuality. The repatriation and burial of Baartman's remains in 2002 was welcomed by South African president Thabo Mbeki as an act of reparation for historical injustices now made possible by the existence of a new South African nation.[5] Ndebele's narrative seems to suggest something further: Baartman, like Winnie, was represented as part of many narratives, largely constructed by men, that were not her own. And, like Winnie, these narratives ultimately focused on a representation of female sexuality deemed inappropriate and then made into a public spectacle. In a sense, Ndebele takes Ramphela Mamphele's notion of the "political widow" and amplifies it to describe a gender regime in South Africa, in which women must support various male narratives enacted by their partners—the bildungsroman of the foreign student, the romance of the activist, the sojourn in the mines of Gauteng—while being expected to remain in narrative suspension themselves. Winnie clearly has agency here, and her interlocutors admire her "legendary defiance," yet it is achieved at the cost of standing in for an absent husband, of "absorbing his political image into" herself, a strategy only tenable until his release (92, 71).

Perhaps the most incisive rewriting of the text of *Long Walk* occurs in a passage later in the novel, when Winnie is in dialogue with her alter ego. We are given a long quotation from *Long Walk to Freedom,* describing an incident when Nelson teaches Winnie how to drive in Orlando, their quarrelling finally forcing him to storm out of the car and return home on foot. Winnie continues to drive around the township for a further hour before returning home; this occasions narrational reflection from Mandela on the difficulty she had in forming "her own identity in my shadow," and how he made every effort to "let her bloom in her own right, and she soon did so without any help from me" (116). The anecdote is then subject to two readings by Winnie in Ndebele's text; in the first, she admits the seductiveness of the narrative, the "cloud of love" that surrounds the two protagonists, and how the narrator cedes power to the female character, allowing her to gain "victory" in the argument, to drive the streets of the township as "the queen of highways" (116). Yet in the second reading, she notes that the way the narrative is framed means that Nelson "ultimately wins, on another terrain," retaining the ability to use the signs of "maturity" and "the authority of wisdom" to make narrational comments about his wife that have the quality of pronouncements by an "oracle" (116–17). Crucially, Ndebele emphasizes that this ability is not simply confined to Mandela's role as the narrator of *Long Walk to Freedom*. Rather, subject formation has multiple sites: this gendered construction of self is manifest in many texts and signs produced by Mandela and others, not simply in an autobiographical text.

Yet if Ndebele's text is useful in making its readers aware of the gendered sleights of hand and exclusions of national autobiography, its investment in the smaller narratives of individual women does not necessarily place it in opposition to all grand narratives. Rather, Ndebele seems concerned to write these smaller narratives back into a history that is still progressive and may still be enabled by the formation of an ideal nation. Penelope, on departing from her sisters, speaks to them in terms drawn from the Enlightenment. Her journey, she tells them, will follow "the path of the unfolding spirit of the world as its consciousness increases": release from "unconditional fidelity" is "an essential ingredient in the definition of human freedom" (145). And in ending with a motif of a journey, Ndebele seems to seek a narrative of reparation, of convergence, rather than fragmentation.

The manner in which Ndebele's narrative excavates the centrality of gender to national autobiography may usefully be compared to a parallel exploration in Elinor Sisulu's *Walter and Albertina Sisulu: In Our Lifetime.* Sisulu's narrative is superficially a far less innovative text than Ndebele's: it is a biography published by a major international publishing house, with a foreword by Mandela himself. The narrative, unlike Ndebele's, is firmly referential, assembled through interviews and archival research, and supported with copious endnotes. Yet there are two features of the biography that do make a significant intervention in and response to the tradition of national autobiography. First, the author, Elinor Sisulu, is not an invisible narrator but enters the narrative of the biography through her marrying into the Sisulu family: the manner in which the lives of the protagonists are narrated tends to increase the author's visibility, rather than diminish it, and thus to foreground the process of storytelling and assembling of narrative that classical biography and autobiography frequently seek to elide. Second, the narrative makes a consciously feminist intervention into the tradition of "public" political life writing in South Africa in its refusal to produce a single monolithic masculine protagonist. Sisulu's biography is an account of two lives that are woven together into a single "lifetime," neither gaining absolute priority. Walter Sisulu's narrative—which in many ways resembles that of Mandela's in terms of childhood, imprisonment, and release—is paralleled by that of his wife, Albertina, who does not, as does Winnie in *Long Walk,* serve merely as a relational accessory in the protagonist's self-fashioning.

Walter & Albertina Sisulu: In Our Lifetime begins not with the birth or ancestry of its protagonists but with a brief prologue in which Elinor Sisulu describes her emotional distress on a first encounter with Walter during a visit to Pollsmoor prison. While a strategy of beginning with a moment of crisis is not uncommon in popular biographies, serving as a narrative hook to draw in the reader, Sisulu's prologue does enable a framing that introduces elements that will be significant later in the text. First, it allows an introduction of both Walter and Albertina as actors who mediate between public and private selves. Second, it allows Elinor to foreground an important motivation for the writing of their biography: the memory of the death of her father and her realization then that there was much she did not know about his and thus her own past.[6] We see here a powerful illustration how the writing of biography—and, through the many interviews that Elinor has conducted, the "reading" of autobiographical texts—is important to the self-construction of not just the protagonists, but also the biography's author. Elinor now vanishes from the text, only reappearing when the narrative reaches 1985, when her relationship with the Sisulus' son, Max, commences; from this point onward, fragments of personal narrative are interspersed with much longer sections continuing the larger narrative of the biography (419). The effect of such interpolations is to emplace, but never quite submerge, Elinor Sisulu's own narrative within that of her two protagonists. The narrative itself does not stop, and indeed much of the common sense of a narrative of self-realization and national progress that is a feature of national autobiography is preserved. At the same time, however, Elinor's presence as actor and narrator calls attention to the discourse of the text in narratological terms, the process of telling, recording, and remembering. Such awareness is also raised by references to and discussion of autobiographical practice in the text itself, for instance in Elinor's quotation from Ciraj Rasool that such records are "a species of biography, an instance of biographical attention to an individual, as a mode of surveillance, regulation and terror," and her conscious foregrounding of the use of police records of Walter's activities (143).

The narrative of *Walter and Albertina Sisulu* in many ways resembles Mandela's. The early narrative stresses Walter's public role and Albertina's more private one, epitomized by Anton Lembede's warning Albertina at her wedding that she is "marrying a man who [is] already married to the nation" (78). Yet the trajectory of the narrative soon changes; Albertina is placed in the public narrative through emphasis on her work in the Federation of South African Women (FEDSAW) and the ANC Women's League (152–53). At times, indeed, the biography gently contests the text of *Long Walk*. In recounting the imprisonment of Albertina Sisulu, Winnie Mandela, and many other women after a women's protest against the Sophiatown removals in 1958, for instance, Elinor Sisulu gives two different versions of how the women eventually came to be released: Mandela's account that many women demanded that they be bailed out because they were unprepared for prison and Helen Joseph's that the ANC bailed them despite their determination to serve full sentences because "their husbands wanted them to come out because of the care of their homes and their children" (167). Neither account is given full narrational endorsement, but the effect of Joseph's unrefuted supplementary narrative is to cast doubt on Mandela's account in *Long Walk to Freedom*. The intertwining of Walter and Albertina's lives, indeed, tends to eat away at the monolithic and monologic nature of national autobiography; *In Our Lifetime*, for instance, notes the tensions between Govan Mbkei and Mandela on Robben Island, which *Long Walk to Freedom*, in its production of a unified national story, elides (307).

The greatest transformation of Mandela's narrative, however, occurs in the representation of family in *In Our Lifetime*. Mandela's narrative, we have seen, opposes an idealized nuclear family to the ravages of apartheid; Mandela as protagonist is a family man unable to achieve his goal because of the deformations of an unjust political system. While the text briefly acknowledges Winnie's political involvement and their children's activism, it tends to downplay these elements, concentrating on the way the family is victimized by the state. *In Our Lifetime*, perhaps partly under the influence of its author's own experience of entering the Sisulu family, adopts a very different strategy. The narrative indicates how each member of a large, extended family was caught up as an actor in the struggle. There is no overriding impulse toward unity at the expense of diversity here; the text, for instance, gives a sympathetic account of Walter and Albertina's nephew Gerald's defection from Umkhonto we Sizwe in Tanzania because of his dissatisfaction with the guerrilla movement's leadership (292–93). Readers of the Sisulu narrative see the victimization of the family by the apartheid state, but they also see clear expressions of agency through, for example, the protagonist's son, Zwelakhe, and his involvement in activist journalism. The interweaving of Albertina's narrative with Walter's has a further effect: it reduces the monolithic masculinity of Mandela's narrative. Walter frequently appears conciliatory and nonconfrontational—in a sense he is "feminized"—while Albertina at times takes on roles that in Mandela's text are the prerogative of men exhibiting Unterhalter's "heroic masculinity." Albertina's transformation does not reach the extent of Judith Halberstam's "female masculinity," but it does begin the process of detaching the normatively masculine from male bodies, challenging an identification that national autobiography has worked hard to make.[7] Through these mechanisms, then, *In Our Lifetimes* begins to pull apart or complicate some of the homologies on which national autobiographies such as Mandela's are founded.

Other Singapore Stories

Ndebele's and Sisulu's narratives suggest, then, that the form of the text alone, to paraphrase Adorno, cannot resist the course of the world: conventional (auto)biographies may provide possibilities of challenge to or transformation of received narratives as great as or perhaps greater than more formally innovative ones do.[8] This fact is perhaps more starkly illustrated by two recent Singapore narratives: Lau Siew Mei's novel *Playing Madame Mao,* and Chin Peng's *Alias Ching Peng: My Side of History,* one of a number of recently published "autobiographies of defeat" written by those who were marginalized politically by the way Singapore and Malaysian nationalism developed in the second half of the twentieth century.

Lau's text initially seems to make a more radical intervention into the politics of the city-state. It is set against the background of the last security crisis managed by Lee as prime minister, the "Marxist Conspiracy" of 1987, in which a number of activists were arrested, detained without trial under the Internal Security Act, and accused of attempting to establish a Marxist "network" in Singapore through forming front organizations through which "they surreptitiously disseminated their Marxist ideas and agitated against the government."[9] Further rounds of arrests were followed by confessions, and then claims by released detainees that the confessions had been forced; the last detainee, alleged plot leader Vincent Cheng, was not released from custody until June 1990. Rather than write a thinly fictionalized account of the events of 1987–88, however, Lau instead writes a fragmentary, postmodern narrative, with multiple narrators, which commences in Singapore and ends in Brisbane, Australia. This trajectory follows Lau's own migration to Australia as a young woman and perhaps illustrates her indifference to being classified as a Singaporean writer or as an Australian one, and her conscious attempts to write for a transnational audience. Lau's reply to an interviewer when asked about how her writing should be classified—"Do I belong anywhere? Should it bother me?"—seems, indeed, to represent a challenge to the boundaries of national narratives, an insistence on the performative, hybrid subjectivity exemplified in her novel.[10]

Playing Madame Mao's protagonist is an actor named Chiang Ching who gains critical acclaim for playing the part of her namesake, the wife of Mao Zedong, in what appears to be a contemporary opera staged in Singapore. Her husband, who is also active in theatre, is arrested in a course of events that has many parallels to the Marxist conspiracy: he is imprisoned by the authorities and made to confess, retracts his confession on release, is made to confess again, and finally commits suicide. Yet this narrative, which is broadly realist in terms of its parameters, intersects with others in which many of the codes of realism are suspended. One narrative, for instance, concerns a parallel world of monstrous mirror people, drawn from Chinese mythology. These creatures, imprisoned behind mirrors by the mythical Yellow Emperor, attempt to break the glass that separates them from the real world; sightings in Singapore confirm that some have succeeded, bring social chaos to the city-state. Finally, the narrative also tells elements of the life story of Jiang Qing (Chiang Ching), the real-life wife of Mao Zedong, who became a scapegoat for Mao's excesses after his death. The identical names of the actor Chiang Ching and the character she represents, permits considerable play on two "chairmen," Chairman Mao of Chinese history and the chairman who governs the city in which Ching lives, an "intellectual, meticulous, a tough opponent" who is "not one to look too deeply into matters of heart"—a transparent representation, indeed, of Lee Kuan Yew himself.[11]

Lau's novel is certainly innovative in terms of form. However, it seems to have little discursive purchase on Lee's national narrative: indeed, although it critiques Lee, it does so within the parameters laid down by *The Singapore Story*. In the preceding chapter, we saw how a key component to Lee's welding of national and personal narratives is the production of "race" as an essential truth of self, and how this is also manifest through the multiracialism of post-independence governmentality. While Lau critiques the "Chairman," the comparison of Lee to Mao Zedong tends to diagnose the problem in Singapore's polity as unchanging patriarchal and authoritarian tendencies within Chinese culture itself. In a key early passage in the text, Mao Zedong's authoritarianism is compared to that of the first emperor of China, Qin Shi Huang, and his desire to "define space and territory" through the construction of the Great Wall of China; a few pages later, the voices of the Red Guards of the Chinese Cultural Revolution merge with the officers of Singapore's Internal Security Department (17, 26–27). An ensuing scene in which Chiang Ching meets the chairman brings elements of Chinese culture characteristic of Southeast Asia (rattan chairs, *pong piah*—a Hokkien [*minnan hua*] "dialect" word for a kind of biscuit) together with a formal scene of tea-drinking in an apparently classical Chinese garden. The cumulative effect of these scenes is to compose a picture of an unchanging essence of Chinese culture as authoritarian and patriarchal; the only response that Lau's protagonist can make is flight.[12] What the narrative does not do is to challenge the imposition of the template of race onto hybrid communities, or indeed to delegitimize Lee's culturalist constructions of Chineseness.

The fault here, of course, is not entirely Lau's: her novel is published in Australia, and thus participates in another national narrative through its negotiation with identity politics. Yet its lack of critical purchase on Lee's narrative may be compared with a group of more conventionally auto/bio-graphical narratives published in the last decade. In recent years, several auto/biographical works have been published concerning political figures who were active in Singapore and the region in the period between the end of the Second World War in 1945 and independence in 1965. Lee's own memoirs have thus been supplemented and challenged by a number of accounts by those excluded from the "Singapore story" that founds the national social imaginary: opposition politicians, exiles, and those with a radically different and in many ways more nuanced understanding of the travails of modernity and modernization. The publication of these mem-oirs has been facilitated by two further factors. First, since the majority of these figures were leftist and were labeled by the colonial and succeeding national states as communists, the removal of this particular external threat to Singapore after the end of the Cold War has produced a changed climate in which Marxism can be publicly discussed.[13] A final agreement between the Malaysian Government and the Communist Party of Malaya in 1989 and Singapore's establishing of diplomatic relations with the People's Re-public of China in 1990 are perhaps two significant public markers of this process. Second, many of the key protagonists in the struggle are, if still alive, now in their seventies. Some have felt a need to testify, to tell "the other side of the story,"[14] while the premature passing of others has led to their friends, relatives, colleagues, or concerned fellow citizens to publish accounts that memorialize their place in history.

Many of these narratives, although interesting, are perhaps weakened by their primary attention to a key element of national autobiography: the construction (and here rehabilitation) of the "character" of their protago-nist. Said Zahari's *Dark Clouds at Dawn*, for example, devotes much of its energy to demonstrating that its protagonist, the fiercely independent edi-tor of the Malay newspaper *Utusan Melayu* who was imprisoned in Singa-pore over three decades, was not, as he was accused of being, a communist. The narrative rehabilitates its subject's own personal integrity, attacking Lee's labeling him as "nefarious" and "vengeful," but it does not challenge the overall shape of Lee's national narrative (175). If *Dark Clouds at Dawn* makes a place for its protagonist in one of the valleys of a national social imaginary, then, it does not attempt to storm the commanding heights overlooking them.

The new millennium, however, has seen the publication of autobiographical texts that engage in a more successful remapping of the historical common sense that underlies a national social imaginary. The only one to be published in English is a classical autobiography, Communist Party of Malaya's General Secretary Chin Peng's *Alias Chin Peng: My Side of History* (2003).[15] The acknowledged product of "collaboration" between its author, former *Daily Telegraph* columnist Ian Ward and writer and editor Nora Miraflor, the text, like Mandela's, still maintains Lejeune's autobiographical pact in its insistence on identity between author, narrator, and protagonist. Chin's autobiography, indeed, has a greater task of rehabilitation to do than Said's. From 1948 to 1989, Chin led a guerrilla army based initially in the Malayan jungle and later across the border in southern Thailand in a conflict first against the British colonial and later against successive independent Malayan and Malaysian governments. Discursively positioned as a terrorist by colonial and postcolonial public history in both Malaysia and Singapore, Chin remains in exile to this day. While at first sight Chin's autobiography might be felt to address Malaysians rather than Singaporeans, the fact that the majority of its narrative is set before Singapore's separation from the Malaysian federation in 1965 means that it responds to received histories in both countries.

As a response to the manner in which its protagonist has been discursively positioned, Chin's autobiography makes full use of a key feature of autobiography: the split between a protagonist who experiences events and a narrator, in the narrative present, who recalls them. The life of Chin's protagonist is thus suffused with the commonplace. His description of a childhood in Sitiawan, Perak, in what is now Malaysia is portrayed as unexceptional, "typical of any Chinese boy growing up in a rural township in colonial Malaya."[16] In this level of the narrative, an awareness of the "poverty of the power of money," Chinese nationalism expressed through resistance to Japanese aggression against China, a love of Chinese classics such as the "story of the Three Kingdoms" that depict "[t]he poor fighting the tyrants" and a growing skepticism regarding the legitimacy of British colonialism lead naturally to the protagonist's growing politicization (37). The terminus of this process is a "personal passage to communism" that the protagonist experiences as "strong as a religious conversion" (47). Chin Peng's narrator respectively locates the moment of conversion during a month-long vacation in Lumut in 1938. Asked to help out at a branch of the family shop, his protagonist reads books on Marxist philosophy for hours at a stretch in a room on the first story of the shop house, followed by "the palliative of cooling contemplation" in the evening on a jetty by the river (49). In a manner reminiscent of the early part of Mandela's *Long Walk,* this period of conversion is retrospectively embedded by the narrator into a much wider movement of history: the advance of Japan in East Asia, and Germany's Anschluss in Austria and later occupation of the Sudetenland. Thus the protagonist's embracing of Marxism results from a relentless quest to discover how he should live and act within history, his wondering "where a Chinese teenager from Sitiawan might fit into the scheme of things at such a tumultuous time" (49).

A further and more powerful respective element to *My Side of History* is added by Chin Peng's use of documents from the colonial archive. The text's narrator frequently stitches accounts gleaned from Foreign and Colonial Office records from the Public Record Office in London together with personal reminiscences. At one level, such documentation serves to legitimize Chin Peng's account by placing it within publicly recorded history, much as footnoted references do in an academic history article or monograph. Indeed, the narrator endorses this view at times, noting that access to both a lifetime of personal experience and to colonial archives give him a uniquely "levitated view of history" (329). Yet the use of declassified documents has further effects in the text. It introduces doubt into an imperial narrative of counter-insurgency that was then appropriated by hegemonic national histories in both Singapore and Malaysia: Chin Peng illustrates disagreement between colonial officials, and indeed their awareness of the fundamental contradictions in policy. And by reaching back beyond the Emergency to the World War II alliance between the British and his guerrillas, Chin Peng shows that his own narrative and the public narrative of which Lee's is perhaps the most prominent retelling are not simply the inverse of each other: each shares common elements with the other, and at times they run parallel, before sharply diverging.

This ability of Chin Peng's autobiography to question the received historical narrative of both the colonial and national state is enhanced by the manner in which its narrative is constructed. Like Lee's *The Singapore Story, My Side of History* begins *in medias res.* Lee begins his story with the reluctant declaration of Singapore's independence in 1965; Chin, in contrast, chooses to commence his narrative with the events leading up to the signing of a cooperation agreement between the British and CPM to resist the Japanese in 1943. The incident is crucial because it reveals the mutability of historical narrative. When negotiations are over, Chin's protagonist reflects on the irony that changed circumstances have brought: Lai Te, the Secretary General of the CPM and "the most wanted man in pre-War Malaya" is now working out "conditions for cooperation with the very people who would normally be enforcing our illegal status, incarcerating and banishing us" (24). The negotiations themselves turn on the precise "semantics of history": a sticking point is, for instance, the British use of the words "reoccupation" to describe their projected return to Malaya, and Chin and Lai's proposal of the word "re-taking," without any connotation of legitimacy or permanence (25). The narrative then returns to Chin Peng's birth, but the emphasis on the construction of historical narrative as a site of struggle is also evident in the narrative's detailed emphasis on two other sets of negotiations: the peace talks at Baling in 1955, and the 1989 peace negotiations in Phuket, Thailand. Both of these episodes occupy far more discourse time than story time in *My Side of History*.

A further tactic that *My Side of History* employs in order to rework received historical narratives is its use of photographs. Photographs are a staple of much popular autobiography, and often serve to anchor or materialize elements of the narrative: they are a key feature, indeed, of Mandela's and Lee's autobiographies. Those in *My Side of History* perhaps have two other functions. First, working in a manner similar to the opening scene, they point out the fact that history is open to reinterpretation and reinscription. The autobiography reprints several photographs of the ceremony at which Chin and his comrades received medals from Louis Mountbatten, then Supreme Allied Commander, South East Asia Region, after the conclusion of World War II. The first of these has Singapore's Municipal Building—now City Hall—in the background, and thus indicates a second purpose of the photos: the reinscription of Chin Peng and his comrades within a widened and contested national history. Apart from pictures of archival records, the autobiography also incorporates contemporary pictures taken at sites in Malaysia to which Chin Peng refers in his narrative: the shop where he was born, or the place where he and a senior comrade, Yeung Kuo, met in Penang to discuss how to unmask their Secretary General's spying activities for the British. Since few photographs taken by the guerrillas themselves survive from early in the emergency, some photographs of colleagues such as Yeung Kuo in the earlier part of Chin Peng's narrative are taken from sources such as high school records, again embedding them into a larger story of Chinese education and culture in Malaya.

Like Lee's narrative, and unlike that of Said Zahari, *My Side of History* makes its protagonist a metonym for a larger historical narrative. The question of the reinterpretation of a history written by the victors is thus manifest through the personal. Chin Peng's narrative, after its initial prolepsis, begins with the a revelation: "Several months after my 25th birthday I discovered that I was, in fact, only 23 years old" (29). The occasion is his attempt to apply for a passport for travel on CPM duties, and the difference in birthdates is explained by reference to Chinese customary practice, yet the tension introduced between public and private narratives will never be quite erased. And the next sentence further adds to the confusion: the narrator names himself, for the first time, as "Ong Boon Hua." This breaks Lejeune's pact—the book is written by "Chin Peng" (with the addition of "alias" in a small font on the front cover as, apparently, part of the title, although not in the title page or the prefatory matter). And the narrator has already noted in his first chapter during his protagonist's negotiations with the British that "I introduced myself as Chen Chin Seng" and that other negotiators—Lai Te and the Chinese Nationalist and translator for the British, Lim Bo Seng—also made use of aliases (17). Even the basic building blocks of identity are here malleable: they may be used by others to ascribe identity, to fix oneself within a story that is not one's own, yet they may also be deployed creatively, in order to rewrite or transform history.[17]

The manner in which Chin Peng's narrative uses the personal to question larger historical narratives is perhaps best illustrated in his treatment of Lim Bo Seng. As a non-communist Chinese who resisted the Japanese occupation at the cost of his own life, Lim has been inscribed into popular national history in Singapore as a national hero: there is a substantial monument to him on the Esplanade in central Singapore, and his grave is located in a prominent area of the more remote but popular recreation area at MacRitchie Reservoir. Yet Lim died at the hands of the Japanese in 1944, when the prospect of an independent Singapore had been never imagined.[18] Lim himself was born in China and left Malaya for the Chinese Nationalist wartime capital of Chongqing after the fall of Singapore to the Japanese. He was sent back by the Nationalist government to assist the British in operations in the Malaya theatre, and it is thus likely that he saw himself as fighting more for China than for an independent Malaya. The inscription on the memorial at the Esplanade, erected by a memorial committee in 1954, three years before Malayan independence, describes Lim "as a martyr to the cause of a liberated Malaya," and with renewed emphasis on national education from the 1990s onward, popular Singapore television programs such as *War Diary* have presented him implicitly as a Singaporean patriot and national hero *avant la lettre*. Chin Peng's narrative does not explicitly address these questions, but rather describes the protagonist's own experience of working with Lim. Rather than being exposed to the Japanese by Lai Te as most colonial and national narratives emphasize, Chin suggests, he was most likely betrayed by one of his own men.[19] There is, of course, no independent corroboration whether Chin's suggestion is accurate or not, but through a studiedly neutral presentation of Lim as a character, Chin's begins to ask questions. Why is Lim's martyrdom now remembered as central to a national narrative when the deaths of anti-Japanese fighters who were communists are willfully forgotten? *My Side of History* thus quietly makes individual characters metonymic of historical processes, while avoiding excursions into personalized attack and defense that punctuate *Dark Clouds at Dawn.*

For all its questioning of popular historiography, however, Chin's narrative is not in any way postmodern. The narrative retains a central concern with referentiality, and indeed makes use of much of the vocabulary of a Rankean view of history. Chin has waited for a long time before writing the memoirs, he notes in conclusion, out of a need to "gain perspective," passing his thoughts "through a sieve" in order to choose those which give access to a wider meaning (516). Telling history "how it was" corrects the "lopsided" view we have inherited from other accounts, making more refined judgment possible (516).

From the perspective of contemporary auto/biography studies, Chin's claim to tell history "how it was" might initially seem absurd. The narrative is clearly elaborately constructed: as we have noted, a key feature in it is the split between active—and sometimes too impulsive—protagonist and reflective narrator. *My Side of History* is clearly also influenced by other narrative models. Its celebration of insurgent life on the margins of society owes much to another classic Chinese novel read by its author while still a young man, *The Water Margin,* and its sense of movement through history, with the individual as a metonym for social change owes much to Nehru.[20] When interviewed about his own recollections of events during the Emergency by a group of academics at Australian National University in 1999, Chin made it clear that he had read many other historical accounts of the Emergency based on testimony from those on the opposite side of the conflict, and he frequently used them to supplement, confirm or restore his memory of events that he had witnessed.[21] Finally, we have Chin's collaboration with Ward and Miraflor that, while not foregrounded in the text itself, has surely radically transformed the way in which the book addresses its reader. Clearly, Chin's is a constructed text, which selects historical events, orders, and links them causally according to narrative principles, even while it claims a transparent representation of history.

Reading the Multicultural Social Imaginary

Yet Chin's injunction to tell history "how it was" may be a useful touchstone through which we can draw critical insights from the reading of national autobiography as a genre in this study. It is now somewhat of a critical truism to note that history, and indeed the nationalism that underlies many common-sense historical accounts, are themselves narratives. Yet narratives also have histories, emerging from precise circumstances of production, and in response to other narratives. Individual subjects form themselves through the consumption of such narratives and, through using templates that come to hand, constructing narratives of their own which may be either obedient or truculent, pushing against and at times breaking the framework that surrounds them.

In describing autobiographies written by such subjects, and consumed, read, and adapted by countless others, I have consciously attempted to avoid a determinist reading, preferring Taylor's conception of a social imaginary or Gramsci's flexible notion of common sense to the more determinist approach of Marxist ideology or the many (mis)uses of Foucauldian notions of discourse which petrify an originally flexible term. Yet I also wish to emphasize how individuals are still socially constrained, how they work through a series of acquired dispositions in narrative practice, how self-construction through gender and ethnicity is frequently guided by larger structures which derive from a governmentality that acts upon these categories. In a sense, the appropriate model here might be Pierre Bourdieu's notion of "field" and "habitus," in which an overall constraint on the "structure of the possibilities" is matched by an individual's "'feel for the game' [that] excludes and bypasses any calculation."[22]

In the four texts we have explored in this chapter we have seen that such games may be played on many terrains: the formal nature of the narrative itself, and the identifications made by its author and narrator(s) are important, but largely in terms of how they are used within an overall strategy, how they place the narrative within the historical field it seeks to disturb. We have also seen in previous chapters how national autobiographies participate in the formation of such fields and how, through a careful reading of these texts in comparison with other narratives, we may become aware of the gaps and contradictions in the stories they tell us, of the shaping of the specific histories that inform the texts. Yet, as we saw in particular in our discussion of *Long Walk to Freedom,* such historical embedding needs to extend beyond the scene of writing to the scene of consumption, the manner in which these texts appeal to not only a specifically national, but also a transnational reading public.

In the case of Mandela's text, indeed, we saw how the narrative serves to manage some of the contradictions of late capitalism, in particular some of the contradictions between citizenship and consumption embodied in the notion of an entrepreneurial, frequently masculinized self. It is perhaps now time to return to the question of cultural identities in late capitalism, and the manner in which this is reflected in the continued consumption not simply of autobiographical texts such as Mandela's, but also in terms of literary texts which have, from the late 1980s onward, been variously described as postcolonial, diasporic, transnational, or symptomatic of globalization.

The rise of the postcolonial literary text in the contexts of both literary studies and of popular readership in the former metropolitan colonial powers and their settler colonies has developed in parallel with transformations in these societies which might be grouped together under the rubric "multiculturalism." Britain has seen the migration of many subjects of its former colonies to the metropolitan centre in the past half-century, resulting in an interrogation and revision of British identity; Australia and Canada, in a similar time period, having abandoned explicitly racist immigration policies, have witnessed increased immigration from Asia, Africa, and South and Central America. Many literary texts written during this period have attempted to restore to visibility those marginalized by a national narrative. Joy Kogawa's *Obasan,* for instance, raised awareness of the internment of Japanese Canadians during World War II, and the popularity of recent British novels such as Monica Ali's *Brick Lane* or Andrea Levy's *A Small Island* perhaps results from the manner in which they foreground still occluded histories of Bangladeshi and Jamaican immigrants in London. Several commentators have noted, however, the problematic way that such a demand for recognition is addressed by the state through governmental multiculturalism in which a subject's ethnicity becomes a component of her or his performance of the role of citizen. This, Slavoj Žižek, notes, is "a reverse process to that of the early modern constitution of a Nation: in contrast to the 'nationalization of the ethnic'—the de-ethnicization, the 'sublation' . . . of the ethnic into the national—we are now dealing with the 'ethnicization of the national,' with a renewed search for (or reconstitution of) 'ethnic Roots.'"[23]

As Arif Dirlik has demonstrated, this process of recognition by the state places a particular burden on writers who are perceived as "ethnic" in that their works are taken to express an "ethnic collectivity."[24] Thus for a

Chinese British or Chinese American writer, ethnic identification is thought of as giving authority to "speak for something called Chinese" but it also has the effect of making everything the writer utters as a product of "Chineseness": here "an oppressive and hegemonic culturalism becomes barely distinguishable from a liberal and benign multiculturalism," since both are based on an abstraction of the concept of culture (219). Orientalism, Dirlik argues, is now replaced by a valorization of ethnicity within the state that nonetheless still persists in taking culture out of a political or historical context.

Multiculturalism is, of course, as Robert Stam and Ella Shohat note, "protean": it may be "top-down or bottom-up, hegemonic or resistant, or both at the same time."[25] As a state project in those nation-states that, in Chatterjee's formulation, were "participants in the history of evolution of the institutions of modern capitalist democracy,"[26] it is clearly belated, and indeed contested. After the events of 11 September 2001, many local interventions have shown that Žižek's "nationalization of the ethnic" has not been wholly discarded; indeed, there has been "a retreat from official multiculturalism policies" in nation-states such as the Netherlands, the United Kingdom and Australia in recent years.[27] Yet Dirlik is surely right that one continued effect of contemporary invocations of multiculturalism and their concomitant "fixing" of identity politics in such nation-states is a dehistoricization of ethnicity. While cultural politics increasingly insists on the authenticity of cultural identities, academic analysis frequently acknowledges that cultural identity is ambiguous and the historical materials out of which it is constructed are invented yet stops there, as though merely demonstrating this fact was in itself an important intervention.[28]

In following Dirlik's lead, and thinking how ethnicity and cultural belonging might be historicized, the texts and contexts associated with national autobiography offer a powerful heuristic. In a perceptive argument originating from his own experience of Fiji, Vijay Mishra has observed that a new understanding of multiculturalism can be gained by moving beyond "a tendency to read multiculturalism as a purely Western phenomenon requiring urgent academic analysis and attention in the context of a largely post-1965 immigration of non-white peoples into Western nation-states."[29] When we look at the situation of many postcolonies outside the West, Mishra argues, "made up of two or more 'historically subordinate (ancestral) groups' we discover features that show resistance to many of the idealistic presumptions inherent in current multicultural policy" (199). Through colonialism and anti-colonial nationalism, the nations of "most of the world" have struggled with the contradictions of multicultural governmentalities for much longer than those of the former metropolitan centre; the texts in this study document—in a way that many "postcolonial" literary texts do not—the complex manner in which culture has been reformulated under the sign of modernity. For this reason alone they are worthy of further study.

When I talk about my own experience in Singapore over the past decade with colleagues at conferences abroad, I frequently pull out my blue Singapore identity card; my racial designation of "Caucasian" produces reactions that range from amusement to horror. Yet historical inquiry into the conditions of emergence of the card, this artifact of an illiberal multiculturalism, leads to a history that is not easily reducible to a struggle between constructionism and essentialism, between colonialism and anti-colonialism, or between a grand narrative and local resistance. National autobiographies offer much more than this, as artifacts that repay careful reading. They offer particular possibilities to a critical reader: displaying the manner in which culture becomes gendered, and embedded within the bodies of citizen-subjects: they make us aware of histories of culture, and the manner in which cultural identities are bound up with the stories of development, modernization, and capitalism. They offer us, wherever we live, the possibility of writing a history of our present, of coming to know the ways in which narrative can make and unmake social imaginaries, so that what seems solid now may not always be so.

Notes

Introduction

1. Kee, *Just in So Many Words,* 240.
2. Holden, "Paper Tiger," 13.
3. Chatterjee, *The Politics of the Governed,* 4.
4. Spivak, *A Critique of Postcolonial Reason,* x.
5. See the following reports in the *Straits Times:* Walter Fernandez, "National Education Exhibition: Don Glasses to See Future Challenges," 6 July 1998, http://www.factiva.com (accessed 16 November 2006); "S'pore Story Show Extended," 29 July 1998, http://www.factiva.com (accessed 16 November 2006); "Singapore Story Show Goes to the People," 25 November 1998, http://www.factiva.com (accessed 16 November 2006).
6. The genre still has some life, however. Lee's book was followed by the publication in 2000 of *To Resist Is to Win!* the autobiography of Xanana Gusmao, the leader of Timor Leste's independence struggle.
7. It could be argued that the genre is more extensive. Texts examined in this study are largely autobiographies in a classical sense, telling the story of an individual life. Yet others, such as Jomo Kenyatta's *Facing Mount Kenya* and Nehru's own *The Discovery of India,* following different generic conventions—here anthropology and cultural history, respectively—also engage in a gendered construction of a national social imaginary.
8. Boehmer, *Stories of Women,* 70.
9. Chatman, *Story and Discourse,* 9.
10. Eakin, *How Our Lives Become Stories,* 101 (emphasis in original).
11. Muslow, "History and Biography," 1.
12. Hutcheon, *The Politics of Postmodernism,* 65; Lyotard, *The Postmodern Condition,* xxiv.
13. Cultural studies has long attempted a more socially situated reading practice. Yet the problem remains: close readings of a single work may lead to unsupported generalizations about its effect on the social field in which it is published and read. More careful work on reading communities through questionnaires and

interviews, such as Ien Ang's pioneering work in *Watching Dallas,* makes convincing arguments regarding the connection between textual and social worlds but inevitably sacrifices close reading practices in doing so.

14. Fanon, *The Wretched of the Earth,* 199.
15. Taylor, *Modern Social Imaginaries,* 23.
16. Du Bois, *The Souls of Black Folk,* para. 3 (online edition).
17. Lejeune, "The Autobiographical Contract," 202.
18. Casely Hayford, Introduction, ii.
19. Wright, *The Color Curtain,* 208.
20. Morrell and Swart, "Men in the Third World," 92.

Chapter 1. Starting Points

1. Aquino, *In the Name of Democracy and Prayer,* 55.
2. Bhutto, *Daughter of the East,* 16.
3. Ramphele, "Political Widowhood in South Africa," 101.
4. Rajan, "Subversive-Subaltern Identity," 201.
5. Chatterjee, *The Politics of the Governed,* 3.
6. Taylor, *Modern Social Imaginaries,* 23. It remains to be seen whether the election of Ellen Johnson-Sirleaf and Luisa Dias Diogo as president of Liberia and prime minister of Mozambique respectively marks the beginning of a wider trend. Several African nations have a high proportion of elected representatives who are women; the presence of a particular social imaginary does not necessarily signify an absence of other symbolic resources on which women in politics may draw.
7. Chatterjee, *The Politics of the Governed,* 4.
8. Lejeune, "The Autobiographical Contract," 193. Joshua Mostow and Richard Bowring both explore the court diaries of women in Hei'an Japan, Mostow as part of a larger discussion of the Japanese nikki or "day record" brought originally from China ("Japanese *Nikki* as Political Memoirs," 108). Wu Pei-Yi, describing various forms of autobiographical writing in pre-nineteenth-century China in *The Confucian's Progress,* notes in passing that the personal nature of the Hei'an diarists may result from the fact that their writers were women, and thus not trained in classical Chinese and not bound by generic constraints. Doireann MacDermott's edited collection *Autobiographical and Biographical Writing in the Commonwealth* contains several brief, if rather sketchy, attempts to survey non-Western autobiographical traditions; Wimal Dissanayake's "Introduction/Agency and Cultural Understanding: Some Preliminary Remarks" is more sophisticated, as are many of the essays in his edited collection *Narratives of Agency.* The conclusion of most of this literature is that while autobiographical traditions have existed in many societies, modern autobiography of the type written in Western Europe and North America from approximately the nineteenth century onward does seem a definably different genre. With regard to earlier texts now incorporated into a western tradition, Martin Danahay makes a very useful distinction between confession

and autobiography. Confession is predicated upon reproducibility, and thus the text of Augustine's *Confessions* is a "self-duplicating machine intended to produce conversion in its reader" (*A Community of One*, 41) and then to generate a new series of confessional texts. Autobiography, in contrast, has inscribed at its heart a Romantic notion of individualism, and thus "is founded on the basis of the redefinition of community as society and the creation of a space for the autonomous individual" (46).

9. Lejeune, "The Autobiographical Contract," 193.

10. Weintraub, "Autobiography and Historical Consciousness," 830.

11. Weintraub's seminal essay concentrates on the evolution of "Western man" and proposes as part of its motor Christianity's encouraging of a "turn toward an inner-directed personality" (836). Yet it is possible to trace parallel developments in other societies, looking for not so much unique cultural elements as a confluence of external social factors. For Anderson's discussion, see his *Imagined Communities*, 24.

12. I am here using the schema proposed by Sidonie Smith and Julia Watson in their *Reading Autobiography:* a "first modern generation" established a canon of representative writings, while "second-wave" responses called attention to the problematics of self-construction, while still maintaining "an ideology of . . . autonomous selfhood" (128). "Third wave" theorizing, under the influence of poststructuralism, has stressed the performative nature of autobiography, and the concepts of positionality and polyvocality (142, 145). As the later discussion in this chapter shows, I find Smith and Watson's taxonomy of autobiography criticism very useful but have reservations about the manner in which critical and life writing practices are conflated, despite the authors' attempt to make a clear distinction between the two in the chapter organization of their study. For a more complete account, see chapter 2.

13. Weintraub, "Autobiography and Historical Consciousness," 838.

14. Gusdorf, "Conditions and Limits of Autobiography," 29.

15. Berryman, "Critical Mirrors," 73.

16. Watson and Smith, "De/Colonization and the Politics of Discourse," xvii.

17. Danahay, *A Community of One*, 3.

18. Weber, *The Protestant Ethic*, 123.

19. Broughton, *Men of Letters, Writing Lives*, 9.

20. Broughton and Danahay note the complexities of canonical male autobiographical texts. Paul John Eakin's *How Our Lives Become Stories* demonstrates that such canonical texts can be read through a feminist-derived lens as exhibiting some of the features of relationality formerly thought to be the exclusive property of women's autobiographies (48–50), while Françoise Lionnet, in a study largely concerned with "métissage and creolization" (*Autobiographical Voices*, 6) in women's texts, makes "a feminist reappropriation of the covertly maternal elements of . . . [Augustine's] *Confessions*" and implies that it might be plausibly be seen as exhibiting the same ambiguity about writing in a borrowed tongue that is present in many postcolonial texts (19). See also the concluding discussion in chapter 3.

21. Smith and Watson, *Reading Autobiography,* 135.

22. Hornung and Ruhe, *Postcolonialism and Autobiography,* 2; Bergland, "Postmodernism and the Autobiographical Subject," 162.

23. Ahmad's famous—and vitriolic—critique was directed at "the growing number of 'Third World intellectuals' . . . based in the metropolitan university" who could represent "the *postcolonial* Other . . . without much examining of their own presence" (*In Theory,* 93 [emphasis in original]). Dirlik's criticism was slightly more nuanced, noting the way in which a critical methodology formed by a specific politics of location (postcolonialism) sought to recreate the world after its own image (postcoloniality or the postcolonial condition) ("The Postcolonial Aura," 523–24). It is fair to say that some of the targets of Dirlik's and Ahmad's attacks—Gayatri Spivak and Edward Said, for example—have been scrupulous about interrogating the location from which they speak in a manner which Ahmad himself has perhaps not.

24. Zhou, *Historicizing Online Politics,* 9–10.

25. Cooper, *Colonialism in Question,* 95.

26. Ofosu-Appiah, *Joseph Ephraim Casely Hayford,* 20.

27. C. W. Watson's *Of Self and Nation,* for example, looks at a series of autobiographies to plot "the way in which the idea of an Indonesian nation is conceived and the way in which individuals come to think of themselves as Indonesian," from Raden Ajeng Kartini's *From Darkness to Light* to young contributors to *Mencari Islam* a century later (2–3). Kartini would have not thought of herself as Indonesian: the contributors to *Mencari Islam* are considering their membership of a wider Islamic community beyond the nation, but they write in Indonesian as people beginning to think beyond the nation (4). It is difficult to think of any of these texts within the rubric of postmodernity, especially if postmodernity is identified with texts that in some way resist hegemonic national discourses: all these make use of the narrative of the nation in different ways, but they are neither simply resistant nor compliant.

28. Horkheimer and Adorno, *Dialectic of Enlightenment,* 4.

29. Lyotard, *The Postmodern Condition,* xxiv; Baudrillard, *Simulacra and Simulation,* 2.

30. Hardt and Negri, *Empire,* 76; Beck, *Reinvention of Politics,* 35.

31. Bauman, *Liquid Modernity,* 8.

32. Cooper, "Conflict and Connection," 24.

33. Cooper, *Colonialism in Question,* 114.

34. Gandhi, *An Autobiography,* 156.

35. Gyekye, *Tradition and Modernity,* 279.

36. Appadurai, *Modernity at Large,* 3.

37. See Anderson's chapter entitled "The Origins of National Consciousness" (*Imagined Communities,* 37–46).

38. Foucault, "Technologies of the Self," 18.

39. Weber, *The Protestant Ethic,* 30.

40. Chatterjee, *Nationalist Thought and the Colonial World,* 42.

41. Chatterjee, *The Politics of the Governed,* 36.

42. Foucault, *The History of Sexuality,* 139.

43. Foucault, "Technologies of the Self," 18.

44. Chatterjee, *The Politics of the Governed,* 37. Nick Thomas (*Colonialism's Culture,* 105–42), David Scott (*Refashioning Futures,* 23–52), and Chatterjee himself in "The Disciplines in Colonial Bengal" provide useful considerations of the manner in which Foucauldian concept of governmentality may be applied to colonialism. David Cannadine's *Ornamentalism,* from a very different critical perspective, provides convincing illustrations of how class, as much as race, structured colonial governance.

45. Chatterjee, *The Politics of the Governed,* 37.

46. One could, of course, argue that this movement between "I" and "we" is central to all nationalist discourse: Bina Toledo Freiwald makes this point regarding the uses of autobiography in Québec nationalism ("Nation and Self-Narration," 33). But, unlike in Freiwald's example, in many of the postcolonial polities I examine, narratives exploring membership of an ethnic or a linguistic community do not necessarily problematize the nature of the national community; "the politics of heterogeneity" may well have already found a place for such expression.

47. Chatterjee, *The Nation and Its Fragments,* 10.

48. Prakash, *Another Reason,* 230; Nyerere, *Freedom and Unity,* 164.

49. Rofel, *Other Modernities,* xii.

50. Gaonkar, "On Alternative Modernities," 17; Gikandi, "Cultural Translation and the African Self," 363.

51. Chatterjee, *Nationalist Thought in the Colonial World,* 30.

52. Chatterjee, *The Politics of the Governed,* 3.

53. Gaonkar, "On Alternative Modernities," 17. An example that supports my point here is Sandra Greene's careful study of social changes from the 1850s to the 1950s in the Ewe polity of Anlo, in now what is Southeastern Ghana. Greene is supportive of an effort to critique the notion of a single, monolithic modernity (*Sacred Sites and the Colonial Encounter,* 5). However, she notes that while it was possible for the colonized to take "advantage of the cracks and fissures, the contradictions that existed within the beliefs imposed on them," colonialism also profoundly transformed the manner in which the colonized comprehended themselves (6). The notion of "alternative modernities" needs careful exploration in specific social contexts: it cannot remain simply a utopian wish. We should also recognize that many anticolonial nationalists believed in modernity in the singular, although they recognized the need for different paths to it. See, for example, Julius Nyerere's comment that "the destination of all true socialists is probably the same, but the path will be largely determined by the starting point" (*Freedom and Unity,* 18).

54. Schneer gives an account of some of the connections made between Asian and African proto-nationalist movements in London around 1900; Boehmer in *Empire, the National, and the Postcolonial* makes some interesting, if tentative,

explorations of "cross-nationalist" connections between various actors who imagined—and indeed laid the foundations for—national communities in the years 1890 through 1920.

55. Boehmer, *Stories of Women*, 14.

56. Ibid., 8. McClintock gives a more generous reading of Fanon's gender politics than Boehmer, noting how "Algeria Unveiled" explores the manner in which colonialism makes colonized women its object and how thus for male nationalists women become representative of the nation because of a "colonial rescue fantasy" ("'No Longer in a Future Heaven,'" 97). Fanon, in this reading, shows how colonialism targets the family and then attempts to think of the family as a place of resistance. However, in doing so, McClintock notes, he subordinates feminist agency to the overall movement of nationalism—women can only enter history through the nation and the notion of "a distinctive feminist agency is never broached" (98).

57. Stratton, *Contemporary African Literature and the Politics of Gender*, 41.

58. Boehmer, *Stories of Women*, 8.

59. Yuval-Davis, *Gender and Nation*, 1; Mayer, "Gender Ironies of Nationalism," 5; Ranchod-Nilsson and Tétreault, "Gender and Nationalism," 5.

60. McClintock, "'No Longer in a Future Heaven,'" 91.

61. Ray, *En-gendering India*, 9.

62. See in particular Bannerji, "Pygmalion Nation"; De Mel, *Women and the Nation's Narrative*; Jayawardena, *Feminism and Nationalism in the Third World*; Kandiyoti, "Identity and Its Discontents."

63. Boehmer, *Stories of Women*, 6.

64. De Mel, *Women and the Nation's Narrative*, 2.

65. Alarcón, Kaplan, and Moallem, "Introduction: Between Woman and Nation," 10.

66. Kandiyoti, "Identity and Its Discontents," 380.

67. Ranchod-Nilsson and Tétreault, "Gender and Nationalism," 3; De Mel, *Women and the Nation's Narrative*, 5.

68. Bannerji, Mojab, and Whitehead, "Introduction," 20.

69. Rajan, *The Scandal of the State*, 30, 25.

70. Mayer, "Gender Ironies of Nationalism," 5.

71. Connell, *The Men and the Boys*, 43.

72. Louie and Edwards, "Chinese Masculinity," 138.

73. Connell, "Globalization, Imperialism, and Masculinities," 74.

74. Mosse, *The Image of Man*, 17.

75. Davidoff and Hall, *Family Fortunes*, 412–13, 234.

76. Sussman, *Victorian Masculinities*, 10, 11.

77. Mosse, *The Image of Man*, 26.

78. Haley gives a useful account of Victorian notions of health and bodily integrity and their employment in other, apparently unrelated, areas of culture, such as literary criticism, in which the "Victorian critic believed that he should diagnose

a work, looking for signs of disease or soundness, then looking further for causes of the disclosed condition" (*The Healthy Body and Victorian Culture,* 46). For Spencer, see *Education,* 131.

79. Connell, *The Men and the Boys,* 41; Connell, *Masculinities,* 77–78, 164.

80. D'Emilio, "Capitalism and Gay Identity," 470.

81. Said develops the notion of the feminization of the Orient largely through readings of individual writers such as Gustave Flaubert's description of Kuchuk Hanem (*Orientalism,* 186–88) and his general comments on Gérard de Nerval and Flaubert's valorization of "female figures such as Cleopatra, Salomé, and Isis" (180).

82. Chatterjee, *The Nation and its Fragments,* 10; Hyam, *Empire and Sexuality,* 202–3; Sinha, *Colonial Masculinity,* 1–22.

83. Gartrell, "Colonial Wives," 169.

84. Phillips, *Mapping Men and Empire,* 45, 89. Phillips notes that such discursive norms were, however, not monolithic and were challenged by, for example, girls' adventure stories (90–91).

85. Dawson, *Soldier Heroes,* 167–72; Aldrich, *Vestiges of the Colonial Empire,* 158.

86. Connell, "Globalization, Imperialism, and Masculinities," 73.

87. Stoler and Cooper, "Between Metropole and Colony," 20.

88. Nordau, "Jewry of Muscle," 547.

89. Lim Boon Keng, "Physical Culture," 121; Gandhi, *An Autobiography,* 107.

90. Gandhi, *Hind Swaraj,* 66.

91. Nandy, *The Intimate Enemy,* 48, 52.

92. Nehru to Gandhi, 11 January 1928. Gandhi, *The Collected Works,* 4:487–91.

93. Fanon, *The Wretched of the Earth,* 180; Pramoedya, *Footsteps,* 294.

94. Pateman, "The Fraternal Social Contract," 104 (emphasis in original).

95. Said, *Culture and Imperialism,* 288–89.

96. Nehru, *An Autobiography,* 178.

97. Powell, *Private Secretary,* 35. On Mugabe, see Phillips, *Sex, Politics, and Empire.* Phillips is right to urge caution in simply dismissing contemporary African leaders such as Mugabe as homophobes without realizing how Mugabe's attack on homosexuality is part of a larger politics "between Zimbabwe and former colonial or neo-colonial powers" that is based on attempts to fashion discourses of morality through the figuration of the male body (226). However, Phillips is wrong to simply suggest that gay and lesbian identity politics "does not 'travel' well to . . . other parts of the world" and that a "gay and lesbian organisation" might be seen as "alien in Southern Africa" in societies where "the gender of one's sexual partner(s) is not necessarily the defining feature of one's sexuality" (226–27). In fact, most societies in Asia and Africa have seen a series of complex social interactions in which new individualized notions of sexuality have been mapped onto older structures; this has been further addressed by a recent stress on queer rather than "homonormative" sexualities in both activist and academic work. Against Mugabe's example, one might contrast the constitutional prohibition of discrimination against homosexuals in the new South Africa.

Chapter 2. Missing in Action

1. Smith and Watson, *Reading Autobiography*, 128.

2. I use "non-Western" here in response to its use in autobiography theory and criticism. Paradoxically, many of the immigrant or migrant writings used as examples of non-Western cultural production are often centrally concerned with Western polities and social structures, and the claiming of a place within them for marginalized subjects. I thus use "non-Western" provocatively to indicate texts written outside the West which tell stories that do not end in the West: they do not, obviously, embody uncontaminated non-Western subjectivities.

3. The phrase is Caren Kaplan's. Kaplan notes that "out-law genres" exist "on the borders between colonial and neocolonial systems, where subjectivity, cultural power, and survival are played out in the modern era" ("Resisting Autobiography," 133).

4. Imperialism and Colonialism are closely related, but not identical. In this study, I follow Jürgen Osterhammel's distinction, in which the "imperial" is seen as an ideological position emanating from an imperial center, in contrast to the "colonial," which describes material conditions and discursive fields within European colonies (*Colonialism*, 21–22).

5. In the ensuing analysis, I have chosen to use the Barthesian distinction between "lisible" and "scriptible" or readerly and writerly texts in Richard Miller's translation (*S/Z*, 4) rather than Lyotard's distinction between modern and postmodern, in order to indicate my uneasiness with a celebratory rhetoric that conflates the postmodern with contemporary globalization and thus implicitly sees colonialist rhetoric as unproblematically modern. It is interesting in this regard that Lyotard himself is more cautious, at least in retrospect: he remarks that "the essay (Montaigne) is postmodern" in attempting to give a more precise definition of postmodernity as a disruptive element within the modern (*The Postmodern Condition*, 81).

6. Lugard, *The Dual Mandate*, 618.

7. Quoted in Miller, *"Benevolent Assimilation,"* 134.

8. Green, *Dreams of Adventure*, 20.

9. Bristow, *Empire Boys*, 58.

10. Sinha, *Colonial Masculinity*, 40.

11. Rosen, "The Volcano and the Cathedral," 30.

12. Kirk-Greene, *Britain's Imperial Administrators*, 9.

13. Cain and Hopkins, *British Imperialism*, 34.

14. Kirk-Greene, *Britain's Imperial Administrators*, 212.

15. Aldrich, *Colonialism and Homosexuality*, 93.

16. This was edited and published by his friend W. E. Stead as *The Last Will and Testament of Cecil John Rhodes* (London: Review of Reviews Office, 1902).

17. Lejeune, "The Autobiographical Contract," 214.

18. Marjorie Perham persuaded Edward Lugard to allow the publication of expurgated versions of his brother's diaries of his travels in East Africa from 1889

until 1892 and of two expeditions to the Niger region in 1894–95 and 1898. Edward Lugard would not, however, permit the publication of the first diary, recounting Lugard's first voyage to Nyasaland in 1888–89. See Perham, "Editor's Preface," 11.

19. Perham, *Lugard,* 2:700–701.

20. Goradia, *Lord Curzon,* 24.

21. The notes are preserved as MSS Eur F112/362 and F112/363, Curzon Papers, India Office Library, British Library.

22. Curzon's authorized biography was written by his former assistant in India, Lawrence Dundas, Earl of Ronaldshay and later Marquess of Zetland.

23. Holden, *Modern Subjects,* gives a fuller account of Clifford's career and literary output, and the tensions in his work among exemplary masculinity, imperial rule, and the structural demands of genre.

24. Clifford to Henry Clodd, 2 August 1916. Henry Clodd Papers, Brotherton Library, University of Leeds.

25. Clifford to Henry Clodd, 5 May 1917. Brotherton Library.

26. Clifford to Henry Clodd, 8 February 1918 (emphasis in original). Brotherton Library.

27. Notes by Curzon on his early life and education are found in the Curzon Papers. Internal evidence suggests that the earliest possible time of composition of the narrative notes would be a few years after Curzon's stepping down as Viceroy in 1905: he mentions that he has now reconciled with St John Brodrick after the dispute which led to his demise (20 verso, 210). (The manuscript's pages are numbered only on front sides: to give complete page references I have thus adopted the notation "recto" for front side and "verso" for back side.)

28. Neuman, "Autobiography, Bodies, Manhood," 415, 416.

29. Curzon, *Tales of Travel,* 159.

30. Curzon, *Leaves from a Viceroy's Notebook,* 269.

31. Curzon, *Tales of Travel,* 4.

32. Clifford, *In a Corner of Asia,* vi.

33. Lejeune, "The Autobiographical Contract," 202.

34. Clifford, *In a Corner of Asia,* 65.

35. See especially the *Annual Report on the State of Pahang for the Year 1898,* Public Record Office, Colonial Office [PRO, CO] 437.

36. Clifford, annotations made between 24 and 26 December 1924, to a copy of *Bush-Whacking and Other Sketches* (London: Blackwood, 1901), ix. National University of Singapore Library, Rare Books Room.

37. Clifford, *The Further Side of Silence,* 299.

38. The story would seem to predate the new resident John Rodger's account of new agreements made through increased British power in Pahang in 1889; according to his *Annual Report on the State of Pahang for the Year 1889* (PRO, CO 437): "The periodic raids on girls and female children, by means of which the Sultan's harem was formerly replenished, entirely ceased from the date of my arrival in Pahang, and the recent Slavery and Forced Labour Regulations, as well as an

arrangement with the Sultan that weapons shall only be carried by his Body-guard and immediate personal attendants, will obviate many of the difficulties formerly incidental to the Sultan's residence at Pekan" (9).

39. Clifford, "Report on Certain Matters Relating to the Current State of Pahang," 3 August 1887, PRO, CO 273.

40. "H.H." is an abbreviation for His Highness, that is, Sultan Ahmad of Pahang.

41. Clifford, "Report on Certain Matters Relating to the Current State of Pahang," 3 August 1887, PRO, CO 273.

42. Clifford, *Report on the State of Pahang for the Year 1893,* PRO, CO 437.

43. Fabian, *Time and the Other,* 143.

44. Clifford, *The Further Side of Silence,* 299–300.

45. Clifford, "In Chains," 173.

46. Bhabha, "Of Mimicry and Man," 131.

47. Scott, *Refashioning Futures,* 47–48; Guha, *Dominance without Hegemony,* 25.

48. Ranger, "The Invention of Tradition," 212.

49. Chatterjee, *The Nation and Its Fragments,* 18.

50. Weintraub, "Autobiography and Historical Consciousness," 824; Gusdorf, "Conditions and Limits of Autobiography," 31.

51. Fabian, "Time, Narration," 4.

52. This feature of colonial writing, indeed, forms the basis of Robert Young's interrogation of the work of Bhabha. "Is Bhabha," Young asks, "describing a forgotten moment of historical resistance, or does that resistance remain inarticulate until the interpreter comes a hundred and seventy years later to 'read between the lines' and rewrite history? And precisely what reality can such a reading between the lines hope to change?" (*White Mythologies,* 149). Here I am describing an example of the first of Young's alternatives.

53. Weintraub, "Autobiography and Historical Consciousness," 833.

54. Nehru, *An Autobiography,* xii.

55. Smith and Watson, *Reading Autobiography,* 135.

56. Sturrock, *The Language of Autobiography,* 18–19.

57. Miller, "Representing Others," 1–2.

58. Eakin, *How Our Lives Become Stories,* 55.

Chapter 3. Absent States

1. Gandhi, *An Autobiography,* 263.

2. Lejeune, "The Autobiographical Pact," 193; Ofosu-Appiah, *Joseph Ephraim Casely Hayford,* 20.

3. Casely Hayford, *Ethiopia Unbound,* 71 (hereafter cited in text).

4. See, for example, Newell's discussion of the "multiplicity of reading practices" in the colonial Gold Coast (*Literary Culture in Colonial Ghana,* 3) and the importance of missionary presses (8–9), or Gareth Griffiths's exploration of the

manner in which exemplary Christian life narratives might be subverted (*African Literatures in English,* 68–69).

5. The most comprehensive account of this process is still David Kimble's monumental *Political History of Ghana.*

6. Edmund D. Morel, "Editorial," *African Mail,* 9 July 1909, 391.

7. Woolf, *The Common Reader,* 189.

8. For literary impressionism, see Peters, *Conrad and Impressionism,* 7–34. Watt describes "delayed decoding" as descriptive passages combining "the forward temporal progression of the mind, as it receives messages from the outside world, with the much slower reflexive process of making out their meaning" (*Conrad in the Nineteenth Century,* 175). In common with many modernist literary devices, it thus calls attention to the levels of mediation involved in any act of representation.

9. See, for example, Newell's discussion of the text in *Literary Culture in Colonial Ghana,* 136–49.

10. Anderson, *Imagined Communities,* 24.

11. Casely Hayford, "Patriotism," 157.

12. Gusdorf, "Conditions and Limits of Autobiography," 35.

13. Casely Hayford, "Toast Proposed to His Excellency the Governor," 159, 160.

14. Kimble discusses the application in the Gold Coast of colonial notions of appropriate dress for women (*A Political History of Ghana,* 134) and missionary condemnation of polygamy (157–61). In this regard, it is interesting that condemnations of the "scholar" or "educated native" made by the colonial state frequently stressed character or morality (87–93). Casely Hayford, *Ethiopia Unbound,* 2.

15. In *Nationalist Thought,* Chatterjee explores how anticolonial nationalism "simultaneously rejects and accepts the dominance, both epistemic and moral, of an alien culture" (11). Chatterjee explains how it does this by using two concepts derived from Jean-Paul Sartre: the "thematic" and the "problematic": the former is the basic principles of an ideological system expressed as both epistemology and ethics, while the latter represents "concrete statements" that are only made possible by an underlying thematic. Thus, while the problematic—statements about what should be done—is exactly the reverse in nationalist thought from colonialism, the thematic is the same (38). Hence nationalist thought becomes a "different discourse, yet one that is dominated by another" (42).

16. Priestley, *West African Trade and Coast Society,* 187.

17. Kimble, *A Political History of Ghana,* 157, 164. Adelaide Cromwell notes, for instance, stories within the Casely Hayford family that the author of *Ethiopia Unbound*'s separation from his second wife, Adelaide Smith, may well have resulted from his practicing polygyny: whatever the truth of these rumors, he certainly was very much part of an Akan lifeworld that she found difficult to enter (*An African Victorian Feminist,* 212n34).

18. Vellenga, "Who Is a Wife?" 146–47. As Audrey Gadzekpo indicates, the situation is clearly complex; women in Akan, Ga, and other African societies in the precolonial Gold Coast in many ways had greater autonomy than Victorian

housewives—they might live separately from men in family compounds, for instance, and engage in independent economic activity (Gadzekpo, "Women's Engagement with Gold Coast Print Culture," 54). However, among the Gold Coast elites in the late nineteenth and early twentieth centuries a different struggle took place. Elite men defended polygamy as a "cultural issue," while elite women preferred "monogamy because it gave them security in marriage" through property rights, even though they would then need to fight against the relegation to a domestic sphere incited by "marriage of the European kind" (220, 218, 54). We thus need to be cautious of Kwamankra's simple endorsement of polygyny as tradition, especially since much of the rest of *Ethiopia Unbound* is marked by a very Victorian gender politics.

19. Newell, *Literary Culture in Colonial Ghana,* 169–70.

20. Casely Hayford's descriptions of exemplars of a distinctly African masculinity are often messianic in nature. He describes Blyden as "the greatest living exponent of the true spirit of African nationality and manhood" (Introduction, ii) and also wrote a brief biography of the West African evangelist William Wadé Harris, praising him as a "wonder of God" who bypassed the blandishments of colonialism and brought "into current thought a phenomenon appalling, strange, arresting" (*William Waddy Harris,* 15, 19).

21. Alter, *Gandhi's Body,* 50–51.

22. Much analysis concentrates on the paradox that while Gandhian politics did enable the participation of women, many of Gandhi's discussions of women were conservative in nature and endorsed discursive constructions of women as embodiments of domesticity and tradition: if Ghandian politics gave women "localized power" it did not make significant "interventions in patriarchal order or political power" (Katrak, "Indian Nationalism, Gandhian 'Satyagraha,' and Representations of Female Sexuality," 403). Suresht Bald in "The Politics of Gandhi's 'Feminism'" argues that Gandhi's mobilization of women was strategic in that he wished to encourage women's involvement in the nationalist movement but that his essential ideas concerning women's place in society remained conservative. Richard Fox is more optimistic, noting that Gandhi's view of women was essentialist but constituted an "affirmative essentialism" that did not substantially work against feminism and at times allied itself with feminist activism ("Gandhi and Feminized Nationalism in India," 41).

23. Nandy, *The Intimate Enemy,* 48.

24. The tendency to oppose Gandhi's "traditionalism" to Nehruvian modernity in Indian historiography has been questioned in recent years, and discussion of Gandhi's modernity is a key feature of much contemporary writing about him. Few of Gandhi's contemporaries—least of all Nehru, as we shall see—thought of him as simply embodying tradition. Robert Young notes how Gandhi made strategic use of modern media and campaigning methods to produce a "counter-modernity" that was "the most modern of all those of anti-colonial activists" (*Post-colonialism,* 334), while Sunil Khilnani, with typical perspicacity, describes Gandhi

as leading and writing "a very modern life—perhaps, most of all, in its judgment that there was more to life than just being modern" (Introduction, 11). Gyan Prakash, following Ashis Nandy, suggests that Gandhi "was not opposed to science and technology, but espoused plural concepts of science and technology" (*Another Reason*, 217) and sees both Gandhi and Nehru as modern figures who embarked on different but parallel critiques of Western modernity.

25. The text was translated by Mahadev Desai, apart from the last few chapters. Gandhi carefully revised Desai's text for subject matter and had Mirabehn (Madelaine Slade) check the English usage carefully. The second edition of the English translation was further revised by Desai and a "revered friend who, among many other things, has the reputation of being an eminent English scholar." In Gandhi's *Collected Works* this friend is identified as V. S. Srinivasa Sastri, but Sunil Khilnani identifies the reviser as the British anthropologist Verrier Elwin (Introduction, 3). See Gandhi, *The Collected Works* (44:88) for a full account of the translation's textual history. The extent of Gandhi's involvement in the translation is shown in correspondence from the *Modern Review* published in *Young India* in 1927 relating to Gandhi's description of Sister Nivedita (Margaret Noble) as "volatile." Gandhi here notes, "as a rule I revise these translations, and I remember having discussed the adjective with Mahadev Desai" (*The Collected Works*, 39:135). Like Nkrumah's and Mandela's autobiographies, Gandhi's thus has a complex textual history before publication.

26. Gandhi was remarkably consistent in denying the text's status as an autobiography from his 1925 preface onward. See, for example, his 1946 note: "I never really wrote an autobiography. What I did write was a series of articles narrating my experiments with truth which were later published in book form" (*The Collected Works*, 90:1).

27. For example, Gandhi, *An Autobiography*, 415 (hereafter cited in text).

28. The simplest explanation for the sudden ending is perhaps the most plausible—Gandhi's inability to find time to devote to the project. Gandhi commenced the autobiography in Yeravda jail, and his precipitate release prevented him from continuing as rapidly with it as he would have liked. Twenty years later, Gandhi noted that he had found no "time to bring the remainder of my experiments with truth up to date" (*The Collected Works*, 90:1). In the last section of the book, Gandhi also mentions the need to maintain "a sense of propriety" in his relationships with Congress leaders as a further reason for discontinuing the narrative (*An Autobiography*, 467).

29. Anderson, *Imagined Communities*, 24.

30. Weintraub, "Autobiography and Historical Consciousness," 830, 832.

31. Gusdorf, "Conditions and Limits of Autobiography," 29.

32. In the voluminous literature on the uneven nature of non-Western (and indeed all) modernities, see, for instance, see Probst, Deutsch, and Schmidt's discussion of "modernity as contingency" ("Introduction: Cherished Visions and Entangled Meanings," 10–11) or Partha Chatterjee's description of the actual space of

modern life for most of the world as marked by a series of heterotopias and by time that is "heterogeneous, unevenly dense" (*The Politics of the Governed,* 7).

33. Gandhi, *The Collected Works,* 10:168.

34. Parekh, *Gandhi's Political Philosophy,* 30–32.

35. Gandhi's engagement with various Indian and non-Indian philosophical systems is an important area of study and indeed one regarding which there is substantial debate. As Brown notes, Gandhi was born a Hindu and indeed claimed that he was a *sanatani,* or an orthodox Hindu. Yet he rejected orthodoxy on the issue of untouchability and interpreted the scriptures in a way "both radical and modern," as not literally true but depicting "fundamental truths" through allegory (Gandhi, *Prisoner of Hope,* 196, 197).

36. Foucault, "Technologies of the Self," 18.

37. Gandhi, *An Autobiography,* 129.

38. Gandhi, "*Ahimsa* and Other Animals," 136.

39. Gandhi, *Hind Swaraj,* 66.

40. Gandhi, *An Autobiography,* 131–32.

41. Yeoh, *Contesting Space,* 81–83, and Harrison, "A Question of Locality."

42. Manderson, *Sickness and the State,* 230.

43. Government of the Gold Coast, *Report on Achimota College,* 4; Kerr, *Fort Hare 1915–48,* 240.

44. Neuman, "Autobiography, Bodies, Manhood," 415.

45. Rao and Pierce, "Discipline and the Other Body," 160.

46. Examples of this from Gandhi's published and unpublished writings are numerous. See, for example, his letter to Harjivan Kotak, 10 November 1927, in which he links "involuntary discharges," constipation, and the drinking of milk; he apparently felt that the latter matter had a great enough significance to warrant a chapter in the *Autobiography* (*The Collected Works,* 40:350).

47. Nandy, *The Intimate Enemy,* 52–53.

48. See, for example, Kandiyoti, "Identity and Its Discontents," 378–80.

49. Garvey, "Autobiography," 103 (hereafter cited in text).

50. Garvey, qtd. in Hill and Bair, *Marcus Garvey,* xxvi.

51. For a more extended discussion of these autobiographies of defeat, see the concluding chapter of this book.

52. Domingo, "Appendix," 113.

53. Eakin, *How Our Lives Become Stories,* 43.

54. Emphasis in original. Eakin does not use Barthes's terms, which I have used here for brevity and clarity: his distinction is rather between "narrative" and "nonnarrative."

Chapter 4. Nehru and the National Sublime

1. Pandit, *The Scope of Happiness,* 43.

2. Chatterjee, *The Nation and Its Fragments,* 117.

3. Nanda, *Jawaharlal Nehru,* 16.

4. Nehru, *An Autobiography,* 64 (hereafter cited in text).

5. Gandhi, *An Autobiography,* 263.

6. See Jawaharlal Nehru to Motilal Nehru, 16 September 1926, Motilal Nehru Papers, Jawaharlal Nehru Memorial Museum and Library, Teenmurti House, New Delhi, India. Here Nehru recounts attempts to have Indian dress—here a "dark blue—almost black—sherwani" recognized by the hotel management as "evening dress" at the Savoy Hotel, Mussorie, when he went down for dinner with his wife, Kamala. For more on the self-fashioning of Indian political elites, see Khilnani, *The Idea of India,* 7–8. On ornamentalism, and the social hierarchy material structures in the empire embodied, see Cannadine, *Ornamentalism,* 3–24.

7. In his 1936 preface to the *Autobiography,* Nehru notes, "If I thought of an audience, it was one of my own countrymen and countrywomen" (xi). However, he first published the *Autobiography* in London and defended this choice in a letter to a student leader in 1937 by stating, "I wanted a world audience" (Jawaharlal Nehru to Shayum Sunder Lal, 6 September 1937, *Selected Works,* 8:856). At the end of his text, finally, Nehru gives a much more personal motivation for writing. "Most of this has been written under peculiarly distressing circumstances when I was suffering from depression and emotional strain. Perhaps some of this is reflected in what I have written, but this very writing helped me greatly to pull myself out of the present with all its worries. As I wrote, I was hardly thinking of an outside audience; I was addressing myself, framing questions and answering them for my own benefit, sometimes even drawing amusement from it. I wanted as far as possible to think straight, and I imagined that this review of the past might help me to do so" (*An Autobiography,* 559–60).

8. The retrospective shaping of a life performed in *An Autobiography* seems to have a lasting effect on Nehru's own self-construction. When interviewed by Michael Brecher in 1956 and asked to name key formative elements in his life, he listed only events that had taken place before 1935: India's then prime minister listed the Amritsar Massacre, his work with the kisans, and the first "close contact" with Gandhi, as well as the 1929 Lahore Congress, his various terms of imprisonment, and—after a little thought—his visit to Europe in 1926–27 (Brecher, *Nehru,* 28–29).

9. See Jawaharlal Nehru to V. K. Krishna Menon, 9 December 1935, *Selected Works,* 7:15.

10. See Wolpert, *Nehru,* 200. Nehru cabled his dedication of the autobiography to Kamala to Krishna Menon from Baghdad on his return to India in March 1936.

11. Nehru, *The Discovery of India,* 563.

12. "History Sheet (February 1928) of Jawahar Lal Nehru, son of Pandit Moti Lal Nehru," India Office Records, India Office: Public and Judicial Department Records, 1795–1950, 12/292: Scotland Yard Reports on Visits of Nehru to Europe and Activities in India between February 1926 and December 1935, India Office Library, British Library, London, p. 22.

13. Lord Willingdon to Samuel Hoare, 18 September 1933, European Manuscripts [Mss. Eur.] E240/6: 361, Templewood Collection, India Office Library; Carl Heath to Marquess of Zetland, 18 December 1935, India Office Records, India Office: Public and Judicial Department Records, 1795–1950, 7/547: Release of Pandit Jawahar Lal Nehru—Further Arrest & Prosecution, India Office Library.

14. Boehmer also makes the same point (*Stories of Women*, 75).

15. Anonymous review of *An Autobiography* by Jawaharlal Nehru, *Times* (London), 28 April 1936, 10.

16. The review was by M. G. Hallett: file 121/36, "Publication by Messrs. John Lane, London, of a book by Pt. Jawahar Lal Nehru entitled 'Jawaharlal Nehru—an Autobiography,'" Home Department, Political Section 1936, National Archives of India, Janpath, New Delhi 110001, pp. 10–11.

17. Comment on intercepted correspondence by Lithlingow. National Archives of India, file 121/36, Home Department, Political Section 1936, National Archives of India.

18. Nehru, "Whither India?" *Selected Works*, 6:3.

19. Nehru, *Glimpses of World History*, 683, 665–66.

20. See Gobind Behari Lal to Jawaharlal Nehru, 30 July 1936, letter 1785; and Jean Frost to Jawaharlal Nehru, 15 April 1941, letter 1354; both in Jawaharlal Nehru Correspondence, Jawaharlal Nehru Papers, Jawaharlal Nehru Memorial Museum and Library, Teenmurti House, New Delhi, India.

21. Gopal, *Jawaharlal Nehru*, 79.

22. See J. Wilson Johnston to A .B. Minchin, 24 September 1923, file 401, Home Department, Political Section 1924, National Archives of India, p. 201, and ensuing correspondence.

23. Motilal Nehru, "Note" attached to J. Nehru's "Written Statement," personal file 105, "Papers Relating to J. N.'s Trial and Conviction at Nabha, 1923," Jawaharlal Nehru Papers.

24. Nehru, "Statement in Court," *Selected Works*, 1:380.

25. See J. Wilson Johnston to A. B. Minchin, 22 September 1923, file 401, Home Department, Political Section 1924, National Archives of India, p. 198.

26. Jawaharlal Nehru, "Draft Statement to be Read in Court at Nabha," *Selected Works*, 1:375.

27. See, for example Motilal's letter to Jawaharlal dated 28 September (*A Bunch of Old Letters*, 28–29) and Jawaharlal's reply (Jawaharlal Nehru to Motilal Nehru, 30 September 1923, *Selected Works*, 1:381).

28. Guha, *Elementary Aspects*, 335, 334.

29. Nehru, "Draft Statement to be Read in Court at Nabha," 374, and "Statement in Court," 380 (see note 24).

30. Nehru to Indira [Gandhi], 22 February 1935, in *Freedom's Daughter*, ed. Sonia Gandhi, 146.

31. Bernal, *Black Athena*, 209.

32. Dyer, *White*, 21.

33. See Prakash for an account of how this strand of thought develops in Nehru's later work, *The Discovery of India,* into a conviction that India's tradition equipped it naturally "to redirect science and fashion a true scientific temper that would impart a moral intent to scientific and technical progress" (211).

34. Burke, *On the Sublime and Beautiful,* pt. 1, sec. 7 (online edition).

35. Kant, *The Critique of Judgement,* no. SS26 (online edition).

36. Nehru to Krishna Nehru Hutheesing, 30 October 1934, in *Nehru's Letters to His Sister,* 50.

37. Nehru to Indira, 23 March 1932, in *Freedom's Daughter,* ed. Sonia Gandhi, 56, 57.

38. Nehru to Indira, 29 January 1938, in *Freedom's Daughter,* 363.

39. Nehru to Indira, 20 October 1937, in *Freedom's Daughter,* 338.

40. Nehru to Indira, 15 October 1936, in *Freedom's Daughter,* 286.

41. Nehru to Indira, 15 May 1941, *Selected Works,* 11:592.

42. Gandhi, *Hind Swaraj,* 66.

43. Nehru to Aldous Huxley, 1 September 1933, *Selected Works,* 5:511.

44. See, for instance, Gandhi's two letters to Nehru on 4 January and 17 January 1928, in which the senior nationalist leader accuses his comrade of "encouraging mischief-makers and hooligans" and proposes that Nehru's best course of action would be to "carry on open warfare against me and my views" (Nehru, *A Bunch of Old Letters,* 58–59).

45. See also Chatterjee's chapter "The Moment of Arrival: Nehru and the Passive Revolution" in *Nationalist Thought and the Colonial World,* especially pages 147–57, in which he describes Nehru's "wondrous and yet condescending" appropriation of Gandhi's thought into the "monistic progression of real history" (157).

46. Nehru to Indira, 5 July 1935, in *Freedom's Daughter,* 182.

47. Nehru to Indira, 15 March 1938, in *Freedom's Daughter,* 387.

48. Rao and Pierce, "Discipline and the Other Body," 163.

49. Anand, "Self-Actualization in the Writings of Nehru," 10.

50. Arnold, "The Self and the Cell," 45.

51. Nehru, Prison Diary entry dated 15 March 1931, *Selected Works,* 5:369.

52. Motilal Nehru to Jawaharlal Nehru, 28 September 1923, in *A Bunch of Old Letters,* 28.

53. Nehru to Vijaya Lakshmi Pandit, 4 October 1932, *Selected Works,* 5:414.

54. Foucault, *Discipline and Punish,* 304.

55. Nehru to Indira, 15 May 1941, *Selected Works,* 11:593.

56. Review by M. G. Hallett, file 121/36, Home Department, Political Section 1936, National Archives of India, p. 14. Ellen Wilkinson's review of *An Autobiography* ("This Hero Chose Prison," *Bombay Chronicle,* 7 May 1936) is enclosed as a clipping in the same file. See, for example, Mary E. Stanton to Jawaharlal Nehru, 1 June 1942, letter 5725, Jawaharlal Nehru Correspondence, Jawaharlal Nehru Papers. Stanton, an Irish-American reader in New York, is responding to *Toward Freedom,* the abridged American version of the text and confesses she has always

been fascinated by India, although has never visited. In particular, she enjoyed the "bout with the centipede in Alipore jail. . . . Your sudden understanding of Pavlov's reflexes especially amused me."

57. Nehru to Indira, 15 May 1941, *Selected Works*, 11:593.

58. See subject file 415, "Notes Prepared for 'Toward Freedom,'" Jawaharlal Nehru Papers. Despite the title given to the file, these are actually working notes for the continuation of the autobiography, written in Dehradun jail in August 1941.

59. Subject file 415, "Notes Prepared for 'Toward Freedom.'"

60. Ray, *En-gendering India*, 9.

61. Nehru, Prison Diary entry for 21 February 1935, *Selected Works*, 6:320.

62. Nehru, Prison Diary entry for 1 February 1935, *Selected Works*, 6:312–13.

63. Nehru, Letter to Padmaja Naidu, 26 January 1926, *Selected Works*, 2:226.

64. Nehru, "The Rashtrapati," *Selected Works*, 8:520.

65. Nehru, Prison Diary, 21 April 1941, *Selected Works*, 11:576.

66. See "Postscript to the Autobiography." The notebook written by Nehru in 1941 (see note 58) contains a much-revised schema for "Continuations of Autobiography," in which chapter 10, "The Discovery of India," ends up consuming the whole work. Subject file 415, Jawaharlal Nehru Papers.

67. Nehru, "The Meaning of Words," 445.

68. Nkrumah, "The Impact That Lasts," 93–94.

69. Lee, "First of the Afro-Asians," 356; Lee, "Always a Revolutionary," 96.

Chapter 5. Modernity's Body

1. Application of F. Nyakofi Nkrumah of Admission to Lincoln University, 1 March 1935, Lincoln University Archives.

2. James, *Nkrumah and the Ghana Revolution*, 187. The other three men James lists are Lenin, Gandhi, and Mao.

3. Watson Commission, 5th Hearing, Cross-examination of Kwame Nkrumah, United Kingdom Public Record Office, Colonial Office [PRO, CO] 964/27: 58.

4. "Fragmentary Autobiography," SC21/1/119, National Archives of Ghana, p. 1.

5. Nkrumah, *Ghana*, 198 (hereafter cited in text).

6. Smith and Watson, *Reading Autobiography*, 135; Rhodes is, of course, a key item of evidence for Weber, who notes that "so many of the greatest capitalistic entrepreneurs—down to Cecil Rhodes—have come from clergyman's families" (*The Protestant Ethic*, 9).

7. "Reply of the Hon'ble Dr. Kwame Nkrumah, Prime Minister of Ghana," Kwame Nkrumah Papers, Moorland-Spingarn Research Center, Howard University, box 154-15, file 3.

8. Jomo Kenyatta's *Facing Mount Kenya*, published under the influence of Malinowski in 1935 does autoethnographical work which resembles that of Nkrumah's Ph.D. doctoral dissertation and the content of the early part of *Ghana*. However, most of the major Anglophone autobiographies by national leaders or

leaders of independence movements were published after Nkrumah's text. This is true both of Nkrumah's contemporaries (such as Kenneth Kaunda) and his seniors; Albert Luthuli's *Let My People Go* was published in 1962, and Nnamdi Azikiwe's *My Odyssey* in 1970.

9. Chatterjee, *The Nation and Its Fragments*, 11.

10. Powell, *Private Secretary,* 101. See Nkrumah's acknowledgement (*Ghana,* xii). Powell describes her role as one of helping Nkrumah write the autobiography and fitting "together the bits of scattered mosaic" that made up his life (*Private Secretary,* 83). David Birmingham notes that Powell "was responsible for writing [Nkrumah's] biography" (*Kwame Nkrumah,* 37). While Birmingham has noted in an 8 September 2001 email to me this judgment is a "surmise" drawn from "reading between the lines," Powell did read and correct the manuscript of Birmingham's study and did not question his attribution of the writing of the book to her. Like many other national autobiographies of its type—Mandela's *Long Walk to Freedom* being another example—the text's genesis is clearly complex.

11. Correspondence concerning the trip, including Nkrumah's and Powell's substantial bar and cigarette bills, is preserved in the National Archives of Ghana, SC/BAA/125.

12. Nehru, *An Autobiography,* xii.

13. Lugard, *The Dual Mandate,* 80, 88.

14. Casely Hayford, *Ethiopia Unbound,* 75.

15. Griffiths's account of African writing under missionary influences gives useful background to this feature of Casely Hayford's text. See *African Literatures,* 50–70.

16. Notes on the WANS and United Gold Coast Convention, Public Record Office, Colonial Office [PRO, CO] 537/3566, item 26: 1.

17. Watson Commission, 4th Hearing, Cross-Examination of Dr. J. Danquah, PRO, CO 964/26: 133.

18. Watson Commission, 5th Hearing, Cross-Examination of Kwame Nkrumah, PRO, CO 964/27: 44–45. Nkrumah's explanation was that he was using the cards as models for membership cards for the UGCC.

19. Official Report of the Watson Commission, PRO, CO 964/32: 18, 89.

20. "Parties and Personalities of the New Order," *Times* (London), 4 June 1951, 5.

21. Sir C. Arden-Clarke to W. L. Gorell Barnes reporting his discussions with Dr. Nkrumah on future prospects, 24 September 1952, PRO, CO 554/371: 31. Reprinted in Rathbone, *Ghana,* 2:4.

22. Report of the Gold Coast Intelligence Committee on the Allegations Made by T. M. Kodwo Mercer, August 1956, Public Record Office, Dominions Office [PRO, DO] 35/6178, no. 4. Reprinted in Rathbone, *Ghana,* 2:301–2.

23. "Secret: Dr. the Right Honorable Kwame Nkrumah, M.P.," 1959, PRO, DO 195/415, 87633, no. 3:1; "Ghana. Osagyefo Dr. Kwame Nkumah, President of the Republic of Ghana. (Prepared for the Commonwealth Prime Ministers' Meeting

1961)," PRO, DO 195/415, 87633, no. 7; letter from T. W. Keeble, Deputy High Commissioner, 5 Dec. 1962, PRO, DO 195/415, 876333, no. 37.

24. C. M. Le Quesne to Sir Roger Stevens, PRO, DO 195/415, 87633, no. 19. Nkrumah is here identified as one of five West African "prima donnas"—the others are given as Houpouet-Boigny, Sekou Touré, Modibo Keita, and Yameogo.

25. John Hare, "Visit to Commonwealth Capitals in Africa, June–July 1961," Secret Memorandum by the Minister of Labour, Cabinet C (61) 96, 11 July 1961, PRO, DO 195/415, 87633, no. 8, 2; Geoffrey De Freitas to G. W. St. J. Chadwick, PRO, DO 195/415, 87633, no.17, 2.

26. Rathbone, *Nkrumah and the Chiefs*, 23–24.

27. My discussion here necessarily elides a larger exploration of Nkrumah's role in within Ghanaian nationalism and the cultural milieu from which it emerged. Useful accounts of the background to nationalism in the Gold Coast are given by Kimble and, in terms of cultural milieu, Newell. George Padmore's *The Gold Coast Revolution* gives a contemporary account. The five most significant biographies of Nkrumah are Bankole Timothy, *Kwame Nkrumah: His Rise to Power;* Basil Davidson, *Black Star: A View of the Life and Times of Kwame Nkrumah;* David Birmingham, *Kwame Nkrumah: The Father of African Nationalism;* June Milne, *Kwame Nkrumah: A Biography;* David Rooney, *Kwame Nkrumah: The Political Kingdom in the Third World.* Of these, Birmingham's is the most concise and focused overview, but Timothy's is unique because it was written before the publication of Nkrumah's *Ghana* and with access to his personal papers. Marika Sherwood's *Kwame Nkrumah: The Years Abroad 1935–1947* is the best-researched account of crucial years of Nkrumah's life. Ebenezer Obiri Addo's *Kwame Nkrumah: A Case Study of Religion and Politics in Ghana* and Kwame Arhin's edited collection *The Life and Work of Kwame Nkrumah* provide useful additional discussion. Rathbone's *Nkrumah and the Chiefs* is an important reassessment of the manner in which Nkrumah engaged with and made use of "tradition."

28. Nordau, "The Jewry of Muscle," 547. For Muscular Confucianism, see Holden, "The Beginnings of 'Asian Modernity' in Singapore." Gyan Prakash, among others, discusses muscular Hinduism in his account of the "modern discourse of *brahmacharya*" (*Another Reason*, 156).

29. For this and other strategies of self-construction by Nkrumah as a political leader, see Monfils, "Kwame Nkrumah's Exgtrinsic Rhetorical Strategies."

30. Hagan, "Nkrumah's Leadership Style," 188; Monfils, "Kwame Nkrumah's Extrinsic Rhetorical Strategies," 325.

31. See Rathbone, *Nkrumah and the Chiefs,* for the manner in which progressive nationalism critiqued chieftaincy and associated "tribalism" (3–6). The classic elaboration of indirect rule, Lugard's *The Dual Mandate in British Tropical Africa* was, as its title suggests, drawn largely from the author's experience of West Africa.

32. Gikandi, "Cultural Translation and the African Self," 365.

33. *Report of the Committee Appointed in 1932 by the Governor of the Gold Coast Colony to Inspect the Prince of Wales' College and School, Achimota* (London: Crown Agents for the Colonies, 1932), 36–37.

34. Government of the Gold Coast, *Report on the Achimota College for the Year 1929–30* (Accra: Government Printing Department, 1930), 25.

35. *Report of the Achimota Third Educational Conference Held on 20th and 21st December, 1928* (Accra: Government Printing Office, 1929), 38.

36. *Achimota Social Service: A Review and Forecast* (Achimota: College Press, 1931), 14–15.

37. See Viswanathan, *Masks of Conquest.* For a cogent critique of this position, which still does not resolve the issue of agency, see Trivedi, *Colonial Transactions.*

38. *Report of the Committee Appointed in 1932,* 63.

39. Azikiwe, *My Odyssey,* 280; J. E. K. Aggrey, "Ideals and Principles of Education in the Gold Coast," 6; A. G. Fraser, *An Address,* 10.

40. Government of the Gold Coast, *Report on Achimota College, 1928–1929* (Accra: Government Printing Office, 1929), 4.

41. Circular Letter as General Secretary of the Nzima Literary Association, 10 May 1935, SC 21/1/27, National Archives of Ghana.

42. For instance, see Azikiwe's account of his time at the Wesleyan Boys' High School in Lagos (*My Odyssey,* 20–23).

43. *Report of the Achimota Third Educational Conference Held on 20th and 21st December, 1928* (Accra: Government Printing Office, 1929), 38.

44. Kwame Nkrumah, "Mind and Thought in Primitive Society: A Study in Ethno-Philosophy, with Special Reference to the Akan Peoples of the Gold Coast, West Africa," SC21/10/1, National Archives of Ghana, p. 212. The document appears to be a close to final draft of Nkrumah's Ph.D. dissertation, which apparently was rejected by the University of Pennsylvania because it was too politicized. See Sherwood (*Kwame Nkrumah,* 62–65) for a discussion of the possible status of this and other documents in the National Archives of Ghana.

45. See, for example, Nkrumah's letter from America to a friend in the Gold Coast in 1935, stating: "No African student who visits this country . . . can return home without being determined to help liberate Mother Africa from imperialist chains of exploitation and from ignorance and poverty" (qtd. in Timothy, *Kwame Nkrumah,* 25). The use of the trope of "Mother Africa" would persist throughout Nkrumah's career, for instance in his discussion of the "African Personality" in *I Speak of Freedom* (126).

46. "Aggrey Memorial Celebrations," *The African Interpreter* 1, no. 1 (February 1943): 9, SC21/5/1, National Archives of Ghana.

47. Wright, *Black Power,* 345, 347.

48. "Osagyefo Dr. Kwame Nkrumah's Directions for the Running of the Convention People's Party and the *Evening News* from James Fort Prison, Accra, 22nd Jan. 1950–12th Feb. 1951," SC21/8/23, National Archives of Ghana.

49. "Osagyefo Dr. Kwame Nkrumah's Directions."

50. "Osagyefo Dr. Kwame Nkrumah's Directions."

51. James, *Nkrumah and the Ghana Revolution,* 62.

52. [Anon.], "Nationalism on the Gold Coast," *Times* (London), 2 July 1949, 5.

53. Text of Broadcast made by G. Creasy, 13 March 1948, PRO, CO 537/3559, 87633, no. 14, 1–2.

54. See Powell, *Private Secretary,* 91–93, for Charles Arden-Clarke's claim that no one was present when Nkrumah was released from jail, and that photographs of a mass rally purporting to be taken at the time of his release were actually taken on a later occasion.

55. Fraser, *An Address,* 5. Nkrumah's ascetic daily routine is independently described by several people who knew him, including Powell (*Private Secretary,* 76–80) and Marais (*Kwame Nkrumah as I Knew Him,* 35). The Conakry Papers at the Moorland-Spingarn Center contain a typescript of notes—possibly made by June Milne—taken from a short biography of Nkrumah apparently written by A. K. Barden, director of Ghana's Bureau of African Affairs; these give a similar account of a very ascetic lifestyle (p. 9). Kwame Nkrumah Papers, box 154-31, file 35.

56. Dabu Gizenga, interview with J. Newton Hill, 4 January 1976. Gizenga Papers, box 128-27 (Taped Interviews), T-19; W. Beverly Carter to Jessie Dickson [Dabu Gizenga], 29 November 1973, Gizenga Papers, box 1, file 2.

57. See Portia D. Duhart to Nkrumah, 23 June 1944, SC 21/3/48, National Archives of Ghana, 3. In this letter, Portia comes close to proposing marriage, writing, "God has given us to each other" (5). The file SC/BAA/516 also contains a letter written to Nkrumah in 1957 by "Zander," a friend in Philadelphia who is a mutual acquaintance of both Nkrumah and Portia, referring to the couple as "two yearning longing hearts made by God to compliments [*sic*] each the other" (4) and noting that "the full potential of neither can be realised till that which God has joined in creation is not assundered [*sic*]" (5).

58. Portia Duhart to Nkrumah, 23 June 1944.

59. Dabu Gizenga, interview with Florence Manley, 28 June 1973, Gizenga Papers, Box 128-27 (Taped Interviews), T-10.

60. Florence Manley to Nkrumah, 6 January 1948, PRO, Co 964/24: Watson Commission—Gold Coast Commission of Enquiry—Exhibits (Vol. 1): Exhibit 46.

61. Watson Commission, 5th Hearing, Cross-examination of Kwame Nkrumah, PRO, CO 964/27: 110. Nkrumah's lack of emphasis on his private life may also well have been tactical. Much of the evidence presented at the Watson Commission regarding Nkrumah's "girl friends" in London had only peripheral relationship to the matters under investigation, and was presumably intended to introduce doubts about the nationalist leader's character.

62. Florence Manley to Dabu Gizenga, 7 October 1973, MSC, Gizenga Papers, box 128-4, file 77.

63. Kwame Nkrumah to Erica Powell, 6 January 1969; Powell to Nkrumah, 16 August 1970, Kwame Nkrumah Papers, Conakry Correspondence, box 154–7, folder 68: Powell, Erica.

64. Nkrumah to Powell, 6 December 1966, Kwame Nkrumah Papers, Conakry Correspondence, box 154–7, folder 68: Powell, Erica.

65. Nkrumah to Reitsch, 21 June 1967, Kwame Nkrumah Papers, Conakry Correspondence, box 154–7, folder 82: Reitsch, Hanna.

66. Powell, *Private Secretary*, 89.

67. Cabral, "The Cancer of Betrayal," 300.

68. Lee to Nkrumah, 11 March 1966, Kwame Nkrumah Papers, Conakry Correspondence, box 154–9, folder 35: Yun, Lee Kuan [*sic*].

69. Nkrumah to Lee, 16 April 1966, in *Kwame Nkrumah: The Conakry Years*, 35.

70. Lee, *From Third World to First*, 399; Lee, *The Singapore Story*, 532.

71. I am here drawing on Neil Lazarus's use of the term to describe the writings of Frantz Fanon. In Lazarus's analysis, Fanon thought of decolonization and social revolution occurring simultaneously: "decolonization was interpreted as a *revolutionary* process and the independence ceremony was taken to signal that the revolution had been won, rather than merely begun" (12). If Fanon's messianism is appealing to contemporary postcolonial thought in that his early death prevented his—and our—facing this contradiction, it is less easy for us to avoid seeing contradictions in Nkrumah's identification of decolonization with social revolution. In this sense, Nkrumah's text provides us with a much more powerful heuristic than Fanon's *The Wretched of the Earth*.

Chapter 6. Nelson Mandela's Long Walk

1. The independence of the Portuguese colonies of Mozambique and Angola in 1975, and 1980 elections that ended fifteen years of independent white minority rule in Rhodesia, made South Africa the last representative of colonial-style regime based on a restricted and discriminatory franchise. Yet, as Mandela himself was very much aware, Afrikaner nationalism saw itself as anticolonial, as achieving victory after a long struggle against the colonial power in the manner or Ireland or the United States. Indeed, one of Mandela's most powerful rhetorical strategies in *Long Walk to Freedom* is his cutting across the grain of historical narrative in comparing the struggle of the ANC and its allies to an earlier generation of Afrikaner nationalists seeking independence from the British.

2. See Nixon, "Mandela, Messianism, and the Media," 43–44. In 1990 the British Mandela Reception Committee (itself with headquarters in the newly renamed Mandela Street in the Borough of Camden, London), collected a list of the honors Mandela had received in Britain alone. These included two honorary degrees, the freedom of nine cities or regions, and a four-page list of buildings,

rooms, and public spaces named in his honor. See "Nelson Mandela International Reception Committee," Oliver Tambo Papers C3.11.12.1, African National Congress (ANC) Archives, Liberation Archive at the University of Fort Hare, Alice.

3. Nixon, "Mandela, Messianism, and the Media," 45.

4. Ngũgĩ, "Mandela Comes Home," 18.

5. Terreblanche, *A History of Inequality in South Africa*, 96–112.

6. The title of the Robben Island manuscript is not given in *Long Walk to Freedom*, presumably in an effort to encourage the reader to identify the manuscript as *Long Walk* itself. Mandela gives the original title in what is apparently a draft of his memorandum addressed to P. W. Botha in March 1989: "My political beliefs have been explained in the course of several political trials in which I was charged, in the policy documents of the ANC, and in my autobiography 'The Struggle is My Life' which I wrote in prison in 1975" (653, 9). See the document entitled "Mandela Document (South)," Robben Island General Recreational Committee Archive, University of the Western Cape–Robben Island Mayibuye Archives, MCH 64–80. This autobiographical text should not be confused with the collection of speeches and miscellanea (also entitled *The Struggle Is My Life*) published on the occasion of Mandela's sixtieth birthday in 1978.

7. In a prefatory section to the book Mandela writes that he began the manuscript "clandestinely in 1974 during . . . imprisonment on Robben Island," that the text was smuggled out, and that he "resumed work on it after . . . release from prison in 1990" ([ix]). *Long Walk to Freedom* also contains an account of the writing of the memoirs (567–72) and of Mac Maharaj carrying a concealed copy out when he was released in December 1975. This account is independently corroborated by Maharaj, Ahmed Kathrada, Laloo Chiba, and Walter Sisulu, all of whom were involved in the editing and transcription of the manuscript. Maharaj typed up the manuscript and presented it to Oliver Tambo, but it was never published. However, the manuscript produced in Robben Island bears little resemblance to the final text of *Long Walk to Freedom*. Anthony Sampson, one of the few to view the original typescript, describes it as partially consisting of letters to his daughter, Zeni, in the style of Nehru's *Glimpses of World History*, and the quotations he gives from it bear little recognizable relation to any sections of *Long Walk* (*Mandela*, 242–43). Richard Stengel's PBS interviews make it clear that many of the anecdotes in the early sections of *Long Walk* arose from interviews with Mandela; and an anonymous source who has seen the Robben Island document has indicated to me that its total length was about 15,000 words, roughly 10 percent of the length of the published volume. The importance of the Robben Island manuscript should not be underestimated: the act of working on it together clearly bonded Kathrada, Sisulu (who was later to write his own autobiography on Robben Island), and Mandela. The process of constructing this narrative likely cemented the recollections of all three men to such an extent that their narratives of the past frequently feature the same incidents. Yet it is equally important not to think of *Long Walk to Freedom* as simply an updated version of the Robben Island manuscript. Unpublished

accounts of the genesis of the manuscript include transcripts of interviews with Maharaj. See interviews with Mac Maharaj, Robben Island Audio Transcripts HA.AUD.109, and Laloo Chiba, Robben Island Audio Transcripts MCA 6 258, University of the Western Cape–Robben Island Mayibuye Archives. Sisulu's comments are given in "Interview with Walter Sisulu on 20 September 1995," Records, box 37—Transcripts, Sisulu Papers, ANC Archives, Liberation Archive at the University of Fort Hare, Alice.

8. Mandela, *Long Walk to Freedom,* 24 (hereafter cited in text).

9. Nelson Mandela to Fatima Meer, 25 February 1988. Nelson Mandela, Correspondence, 1978–1989, Tambo Papers C11–C11.2, ANC Archives, Liberation Archive at the University of Fort Hare, Alice.

10. Ngũgĩ, "The Language of African Literature," 443.

11. Kerr, *Fort Hare 1915–48,* 239–40.

12. See Massey, "The History of Fort Hare and Its Student Activists," in particular chapter 7, "From Black Englishmen to African Nationalists, Student Politics at Fort Hare to 1955" (61–81). Correspondence regarding the protests is preserved in the Fort Hare Papers, "Strikes in 41/42." The college did not have everything its own way: since it was not a degree-granting institution but rather prepared students for University of South Africa examinations, it could expel students but could not prevent them from sitting the examinations.

13. Daniels, *There and Back,* 8.

14. Sampson, *Mandela,* 215, 563. Mandela did study English Literature during his time at Fort Hare, but the 1940 syllabus makes no mention of Henley, although it does include a selection of Wordsworth's poems. "Invictus" was, however, an extremely popular poem in the Edwardian and Georgian schoolroom, and it is likely that Mandela first came across it at Clarkebury, Healdtown, or Fort Hare. See the English syllabi in the *South African Native College Calendar for 1940* (Alice: Lovedale Press, 1940), 28–29. These include Wordsworth and Arnold, but not Henley. An intriguing alternative possibility is that Mandela came across the poem via the writings of Marcus Garvey, which were influential in South Africa between the wars, and which Mandela specifically mentions as an influence at times in *Long Walk.* "Invictus" was a favorite poem of Garvey's. For an account of Garveyism in South Africa and its connection with early ANC politics, see Hill and Pirio, "'Africa for the Africans.'"

15. Mager, "Youth Organisations," 653.

16. Foucault, *History of Sexuality,* 3–13.

17. Kenyatta, *Facing Mount Kenya,* 159.

18. Mager, "Youth Organisations," 660.

19. The reference is to the famous opening lines of the first book of *The Social Contract:* "Man is born free; and everywhere he is in chains" (1:1).

20. Massey, "The History of Fort Hare and Its Student Activists," 61–81.

21. Morrell, "The Times of Change," 14.

22. Carton, "Locusts Fall from the Sky," 130, 139.

23. Extract from letter from Nelson to Winnie Mandela, 6 May 1971, qtd. in Mandela, *Part of My Soul*, 137.

24. Dubow, "Race, Civilisation, and Culture," 78–80; Morrell, "The Times of Change," 13; Bonner, "The Transvaal Native Congress, 1917–1920," 272.

25. See, for instance, Mandela's recollection of expressing regret at his daughter Zindzi's wedding over having to sacrifice his family for the nation: "To be the father of a nation is a great honour, but to be the father of a family is a greater joy. But it was a joy I had far too little of" (720). Gillian Slovo, daughter of Joe Slovo and Ruth First, recalls Mandela telling a story at Slovo's funeral of his hugging his grown-up daughter and her flinching and telling him that he was the father to the South African people but had never had time to be her father. "This, he said, was his greatest, perhaps his only regret: the fact that his children, and the children of his comrades, had been the ones to pay the price of their parents' commitment" (*Every Secret Thing*, 214).

26. Unterhalter, "The Work of the Nation," 167, 169.

27. Both Evelyn—before her death in 2004—and Mandela have been extremely reticent in recalling details of the end of the marriage, Evelyn refusing to talk to the media in the frenzy preceding her former husband's release, and simply telling them, "It hurts my soul." See "Mandela a 'No-no' for Ex-wife Eveline [*sic*]," *South* (Cape Town), 15 February 1990.

A possible clue occurs in a 1988 letter from Mandela to Fatima Meer, in which he begins conventionally, describing Evelyn as "a pleasant and charming person," noting that it would be "quite unfair to blame her for the breakdown." He continues, however, by revealing that his sister Leabie blames "two persons for the collapse of the marriage" and remarks, "in my present position, it would be quite indiscreet to attempt a thesis on the exciting adventures of more than 30 yrs ago," while confessing, "I would be lacking in chivalry if I were to dismiss the allegations altogether." Assuming that Mandela himself is one of the "two persons" who are to blame, it would seem that the second person is either Winnie or another woman with whom Mandela was romantically involved: in either case, the autobiography elides this element of the separation and divorce. See Nelson Mandela to Fatima Meer, 25 February 1988. Nelson Mandela, Correspondence, 1978–1989, Tambo Papers C11–C11.2, ANC Archives, Liberation Archive at the University of Fort Hare, Alice. In Meer's biography of Mandela, *Higher Than Hope*, she explores at some length Evelyn's doubts about her husband's fidelity (78–79).

28. Mandela, *Part of My Soul*, 65, 68, 65–66. In its introduction Ann Benjamin clarifies that *Part of My Soul*, published in the United States in 1985, is not "an autobiography in the conventional sense" (7). It arises from lengthy tape-recorded interviews by Benjamin with Winnie and was compiled outside South Africa. While "Mrs Mandela was fully informed about the project, she could not see the manuscript in detail before it went into print," and Benjamin sought further input and editorial advice from Mary Benson, who worked on a biography of Mandela with his full support (7). *Part of My Soul* is nonetheless useful in that it

was produced before the couple split in the early 1990s. Winnie's comments are thus interesting—and arguably more reliable—because they work against the overt rhetorical goal of the text, which is to promote empathy for both her and her husband in their struggle against the apartheid regime.

29. Unterhalter, "The Work of the Nation," 169.

30. Ramphele, "Political Widowhood in South Africa," 113.

31. See Sampson, *Mandela* (452–54), especially his discussion of the 1992 publication of an incriminating letter by Winnie to her lover Dalie Mpofu.

32. "Biography of Nelson Rolihlahla Mandela, Deputy President of the African National Congress of South Africa." Folder "Individuals—NM: 2–3," Washington Mission, box 11, ANC Archives, Liberation Archive at the University of Fort Hare, Alice.

33. Quoted in Erlank, "Gender and Masculinity in South African Nationalist Discourse," 653.

34. Schalkwyk, "Writing from Prison," 282.

35. Alexander, *Robben Island Prison Dossier,* viii.

36. Brutus, "Robben Island," 10.

37. Kathrada's *Letters from Robben Island* are, of course, not a retrospective narrative, but their selection—partly perforce, given the restrictions on writing letters in operation at Robben Island in the early years of his incarceration—tends to emphasize letters written in the 1980s. Many of the later ones are retrospective: they refer to previous events, and they are similar in tone to Mandela's and other later Robben Island narratives. In a letter from Pollsmoor Prison in 1987, for instance, Kathrada describes the influx of young activists to Robben Island from 1976 onward, and the efforts he made to persuade them to study rather than resist through total noncooperation with their jailers (215).

38. See, for example, Dingake, *My Fight against Apartheid,* 149, Mandela, *Long Walk to Freedom,* 518–20.

39. See "Nelson Mandela Confident of Victory, Says Denis Healey," *Sechaba* 5.1 (January 1971): 14–16.

40. Kathrada to Helen Joseph, 1 March 1985 (Kathrada, *Letters from Robben Island,* 174). See "Interview with Walter Sisulu on 20 September 1995," FA, ANC Papers, Sisulu, W. Records, box 37—Transcripts.

41. Schalkwyck, "Writing from Prison," 280–81; Gready, "Autobiography and the 'Power of Writing,'" 515, 520.

42. Lovesey, "Chained Letters," 32.

43. Nuttall, "Telling 'Free' Stories," 77.

44. See "How They Came to Be," Govan Mbeki Papers, 48-2-3.11, University of the Western Cape-Robben Island Mayibuye Archives. The document is apparently an early draft of a preface for a collection of prison writings.

45. See interview with Strini Moodley, Robben Island Audio Transcripts, HA.AUD.143, University of the Western Cape-Robben Island Mayibuye Archives, 41.

46. Interview with Strini Moodley, 34.

47. Mandela admitted in an interview with Anthony Sampson in 1997 that he was heavily influenced by Nehru, sometimes using his ideas without acknowledgement in early speeches. The image embodied in the title of *Long Walk to Freedom* can be traced to Mandela's first important speech as president of the Transvaal ANC in 1953, which he concluded with a quote from Nehru: "You can see that there is no easy walk to freedom anywhere, and many of us will have to pass through the valley of the shadow of death again and again before we reach the mountaintops of our desires" (Sampson, *Mandela,* 85).

48. Nuttall and Michael, "Autobiographical Acts," 298.

49. Eakin, *Fictions in Autobiography,* 9.

50. Gunn, *Autobiography,* 8.

51. Bruner, "The Autobiographical Process," 44.

52. Chatterjee, *The Politics of the Governed,* 3; Lyotard, *The Postmodern Condition,* xxiv.

53. Offe, *Disorganized Capitalism,* 6; Harvey, *The Condition of Postmodernity,* 124.

54. Harvey, *The Condition of Postmodernity,* 165 (emphasis in original), 178.

55. Giddens, *Modernity and Self-Identity,* 124.

56. Beck, *Risk Society,* 132; Beck, *The Reinvention of Politics,* 12; Giddens, *Modernity and Self-Identity,* 76, 78–79.

57. See also, for example, the testimony of Godfrey Pitje, who served as Mandela's articled clerk in the late 1950s. Pitje notes that Mandela's court performances were famous—once in a Kempton Park case "he bowed to the public gallery, rather than the bench" while on another occasion he walked through a door marked "Blankes" ["Whites"] in the magistrate's court. See "Mandela? Hell, He was a Tough Boss," *Weekly Mail,* 15 July 1988.

58. Bruner, *Making Stories,* 39.

59. Locating the original speech is more difficult than might at first sight appear. Versions disseminated abroad in pamphlet form during the antiapartheid struggle—for example, *I Am Prepared to Die*—are much longer than the extracts given in *Long Walk to Freedom* but still bear signs of editing to increase their rhetorical power, as does the version given on the ANC Web site. The transcripts preserved in the Percy Yutar Papers, National Archives of South Africa, seem largely accurate but their comparison to the transcripts of still-extant sound recordings of the trial shows that Yutar, as prosecutor, has edited his own comments to make them appear more coherent. See 1962–1963 Rivonia Trial; MS 385/6 NAN, 52 Vol. 4, Percy Yutar Papers, National Archive Repository, Pretoria. Definitive recordings and transcripts of the speech from original dictabelts are now available through the British Library: Rivonia Trial, South Africa, 1963–4: Nelson Mandela Dictabelt Dubbings, C985, National Sound Archive, London.

60. D'Emilio, "Capitalism and Gay Identity," 470.

61. Beck, *The Reinvention of Politics,* 13.

Chapter 7. A Man and an Island

1. Quayson, *Calibrations,* 49. Lee's eldest son, Lee Hsien Loong, became Singapore's third prime minister in 2004. His younger son, Lee Hsien Yang, was chief executive officer of Singapore Telecom, one of Singapore's largest government-linked companies, for more than ten years. As of June 2007 his daughter Lee Wei Ling is director of the National Neuroscience Institute, and daughter-in-law Ho Ching is executive director of Temasek Holdings, the company that oversees government investment. The Lee family has been extremely sensitive to charges of nepotism, and various family members have successfully pursued defamation cases in Singapore Courts against publications that have made such accusations.

2. Wee, "Forming an Asian Modern," 13; Tay, "The Problem of Aesthetics in Contemporary South East Asia," para. 25.

3. Giddens, *Runaway World,* 25. All national narratives, of course, have their denouements projected into an always receding future, yet the pace of social change and the transformation of its built environment has made Singapore particularly expressive of the gathering pace of modernity. This is reflected in policy documents and campaigns: the 1991 PAP Manifesto, for instance, was entitled *The Next Lap,* while periodical government-initiated projects such as *The Remaking Singapore Committee* have solicited feedback on ways of coping with the need for continuous social transformation. Thirty-four years after Singapore achieved independence, then prime minister Goh Chok Tong could still note that Singapore was not yet "a nation" and urge citizens to participate in the "never-ending challenge" of nation-building. See Goh Chok Tong, "Will a Singapore Tribe Emerge?" *Straits Times,* 6 May 1999, http://www.factiva.com/ (accessed 6 November 2006).

4. In this chapter I will use the phrases "autobiography" and "first volume of Lee's memoirs" interchangeably to describe *The Singapore Story.* The second volume of Lee's memoirs, *From Third World to First,* was published in 2000. While it deals with the story of Singapore's national development from 1965 onward, rather than as a narrative, it is structured largely as a series of thematic chapters and thus does not constitute life writing in the manner of the first volume.

5. Simon During notes the use of the Ossian poems by many different nineteenth-century nationalisms in Europe. While concerned with creating "Celticness," the poems, During notes, could in fact easily be "appropriated by . . . deterritorialising and artificial techniques for producing subjective intensities": they thus became "portable machines" that could be used anywhere in the context of emerging nations. I am viewing Lee's text as a machine in During's sense of the word ("Postcolonialism and Globalisation," 44).

6. Kaplan, "Resisting Autobiography," 119.

7. Heng and Devan, "State Fatherhood," 343.

8. Peh Shing Huei, "S'pore Spirit has Brought Nation to Where It Is Today," *Straits Times,* 22 August 2005, http://www.factiva.com/ (accessed 15 November 2006).

9. I have been using "common sense" in a Gramscian context to indicate the "diffuse, unco-ordinated features of a general form of thought common to a particular period and a particular popular environment" (Gramsci, *Selections from the Prison Notebooks*, 330n). In terms of this discussion in this final chapter, we might note that while Gramsci emphasizes the conservative nature of common sense, he also postulates that it contains "a healthy nucleus" of "good sense" that could, under the influence of specific ideological commitment, acquire greater coherence and a potentially transformative social function (328).

10. An example of the manner in which the narrative apparently imposes a retrospective instrumentality on its protagonist's actions is in its description of Lee serving as the election agent to his boss, John Laycock, who stood as a candidate for the Progressive Party in the Legislative Council elections held under a limited franchise in 1951. Lee describes the Progressive Party leaders as "overawed and overwhelmed by English values" and "emotionally and psychologically incapable of fighting for freedom" (138). Yet it would seem unlikely that Lee would have taken on so major a role in the election simply, as the narrative argues, to gain "an idea of conditions and practices in Singapore" if he felt so alienated by the leaders whose election he was working for; it is perhaps more likely that his disillusionment in part arose from his experiences working in the election, and his later radicalization (140). Without surviving contemporary documentation, this interpretation is, of course, speculative, but Lee was not alone in working with the Progressive Party and then leaving it to move further left—a similar trajectory was charted by David Marshall, Singapore's first chief minister.

11. Lee, *The Singapore Story*, 310 (hereafter cited in text).

12. Samantha Santa Maria, "Free Exhibition Tickets Are a Hit," *Straits Times*, 8 June 1998, http://www.factiva.com/ (accessed 15 November 2006).

13. Published in September 1998, the first volume of Lee's memoirs sold out within a few days and was reprinted the following month. By the time the book was issued in abridged form in 2000, it had sold 340,000 copies. Of these, 250,000 were Singaporean sales: thus one copy was sold per ten adult Singapore residents, and the total readership was presumably larger than this. Jason Leow, "Reprint of SM's Book Out," *Straits Times*, 2 October 1998, http://www.factiva.com/ (accessed 15 November 2006). Lydia Lim, "Sept Launch for Sequel to SM's Singapore Story," *Straits Times*, 13 May 2000, http://www.factiva.com/ (accessed 15 November 2006).

14. Tan and Chew, "Moral and Citizenship Education as Statecraft," 603.

15. See Ashraf Abdullah, "Singapore Exploits Neighbours' Weaknesses, Says PM," *New Straits Times*, 15 September 1998, http://www.factiva.com/ (accessed 15 November 2006); and [anon.], "Umno Youth: Ban Kuan Yew's Book," *New Straits Times*, 18 September 1998, http://www.factiva.com/ (accessed 15 November 2006). One might dismiss these responses in part as self-interest on the part of Mahathir's party, the United Malays National Organisation, in response to Lee's presentation of UMNO secretary-general Ja'afar Albar's "racist agitation" as being responsible

for communal riots in Singapore in 1964 (666). Other reactions, however, had less overt political self-interest. Tan Siok Choo, the daughter of Malayan Chinese Association (MCA) president Tan Siew Sin, wrote to Singapore's *Straits Times* to protest not only small inaccuracies but a personal characterization of her father that seemed at variance with Lee's other recorded statements and her father's own recollections. Lee's response, via his press secretary, Yeong Yoon Ying, was to argue that no contradictions existed. While the struggle here is often over historiographic interpretation, it is interesting to note the degree to which most discussions eventually return to the issue of character. Tan Siok Choo, "Memoirs Cast Aspersions," *Straits Times,* 30 September 1998, http://www.factiva.com/ (accessed 15 November 2006). Yeong Yoon Ying, "S.M.'s Views Are Not Contradictory," *Straits Times,* 5 October 1998, http://www.factiva.com/ (accessed 15 November 2006).

16. Teo Hock Guan, Speech to the Legislative Assembly, 138.

17. Lee, "Discipline for Survival," 1.

18. [Thomas], Stamford Raffles to Addenbrooke, 10 June 1819, reprinted in *Memoir of the Life* by Sophia Raffles, 379.

19. J. S. Furnivall describes the "plural society" of colonialism as one in which members of distinct communities meet as individuals only through the market place, but then must address the state as communities (Furnivall, *Colonial Policy and Practice,* 304). It is important to stress that this is a project of certain colonial regimes that may also filter doxological perceptions of, and yet not adequately describe, a lived social reality.

20. For an account of racial classification under colonialism in Singapore and Malaya, see Hirschman, "The Making of Race in Colonial Malaya." Noting that Singapore's system of racial classification was derived from colonialism is not, of course, tantamount to asserting that the essential purpose of classification remains unchanged in the new nation-state.

21. Di, "The Craft of Chinese Historical Biography," 17. Cultural contexts are, of course, crucial, but it is important to see them as socially constituted and contested rather than resorting to culturalist explanations. In Lee's memoirs, it is quite clear that Lee as narrator reevaluates his life—and that of the nation—according to a conscious engagement with notions of Confucian capitalism and Asian values that have become part of contemporary political discourse. It is much less clear that Lee's memoirs are in some way deeply "Chinese" or conform to, for instance, the tradition of Confucian autobiography identified by Wu Pei-yi, and indeed a quest for such a cultural unconscious takes Singaporean multiculturalism at face value. C. W. Watson makes a similar criticism of culturalist readings of the autobiography of the Indonesian anticolonial leader Tan Melaka that view the autobiography as simply a "Minangkabau view of the world" modified and glossed with "Western" Marxism (*Of Self and Nation,* 101), rather than as a text engaging with the social context of a modern Indonesian nation.

22. Miller, "Representing Others," 14.

23. Lee, "Schools Must Have Character," 393.

24. One scene with which Lee's account has clear parallels is Boulger's description of Raffles's meeting with the Sultan of Jogjakarta in 1811, in which the "energetic and impressive form of Raffles," remains "calm, unmoved" while hemmed in by the "disturbed and threatening scene" of a crowd of armed Malay retainers. See Boulger, *The Life of Sir Stamford Raffles,* 80. Clifford similarly dramatizes his own experiences when acting as political agent in Pahang in thinly fictionalized stories such as "At the Court of Pelesu." See Clifford, *"At the Court of Pelesu" and Other Malayan Stories,* 40–92.

25. In his acknowledgements section, Lee notes that he has had "all . . . draft chapters relating to Malays" read by several prominent Malay Singaporeans in order to "avoid being unwittingly insensitive on Malay issues" (11).

26. Lee describes the Tunku as a "bon vivant," and he reports Harold Macmillan depicting the Malaysian leader as being like a "Spanish grandee," his lifestyle implicitly contrasted with the asceticism of the British and of Lee himself (440, 443). Later in *The Singapore Story* the comparison becomes more explicit. Lee notes how "Singapore ministers were not pleasure-loving" in contrast to those in Malaysia, and recounts an incident in which the Tunku tried to tempt economic czar Goh Keng Swee and himself by bringing them to a club "where attractive call girls and even starlets were available. We had a good meal, and when they played poker afterwards, I joined in. But as soon as the girls arrived, Keng Swee and I pleaded pressing engagements and made ourselves scarce" (656–57).

27. Michael D. Barr has exhaustively documented Lee's views on race in his chapter "Culture, Race and Genes" in his *Lee Kuan Yew: The Beliefs Behind the Man* (185–210). While Barr's documentation is impressive, he imputes a philosophical coherence to Lee's beliefs that is probably present only in retrospect. When Lee's ideas of race become part of public discourse in the late 1970s, they do so as part of a much larger civilizational discourse about East Asian modernity and the Confucian work ethic. Barr's analysis often leads back to race alone when racial and civilizational discourses are actually articulating—and occluding— discussions of capitalism, gender, and modernity; and at times his discussion becomes ensnared by the very categories he seeks to critique. For instance, he concludes his study by noting that Lee is "Chinese at a very deep level of his psyche" and that "at a very young age he internalised the basic precepts of Chinese culture and its view of the world" (221). Thus in Lee's "worldview lay a Chinese cultural element that, when he entered politics, led him instinctively to act upon traditional Chinese precepts" (222). Barr is right that Lee's later appropriation of Confucianism is not merely cynical instrumentality but surely wrong in a culturalist interpretation that reads out the hybridity of Lee's milieu, on indeed the complexities of Nanyang Chinese identity. In postulating a singular "Chinese . . . view of the world" or Chineseness as a deep psychic structure, he takes Lee's self-representation at face value.

28. Wee's "The Vanquished" gives a sympathetic reappraisal of Lim's neglected place in the history of Singapore's transition to nationhood.

29. For an influential account of Chinese masculinity, see Louie and Edwards, who argue that "the Chinese tradition of machismo represented in terms such as *yingxiong* (hero) and *haohan* (good bloke) will be seen to be counterbalanced by a softer, more cerebral male tradition that is not found to the same degree in the secular West" (138). Whereas I am wary of seeing Lee's autobiography as having a "cultural unconscious" formed by ethnic affiliation, notions of Chinese identity and Chinese difference have clearly been important to his self-conception in the last fifteen years, and this interest is clearly inscribed in the retrospective self-representation of *The Singapore Story.*

30. "The Modernising Nationalism," 1.

31. Nkrumah, *Ghana,* 82; Nkrumah, *Dark Days in Ghana,* 11.

32. Lugard, *The Dual Mandate,* 88.

33. Lee, "First of the Afro-Asians," 357, 356.

34. Lee, "Always a Revolutionary," 112.

35. See chapter 5, this volume.

36. Paradoxically, Lee critiques Nkrumah after mentioning a visit to the construction sight of the High Volta dam, one of Ghana's developmental projects that, far from being socialist in inspiration, was heavily—and perhaps fatally—reliant on investment by private foreign capital.

37. See Chua, *Communitarian Ideology,* 57–78. Writing in the early 1990s, Chua sees a stress on communitarianism replacing survivalism and pragmatism; the experience of the ensuing decade after Chua's text was published suggests that survivalism and pragmatism do not vanish but are rather shuffled into new permutations.

38. Franklin, *His Autobiography,* para. 49 (online edition).

39. Sturrock, *The Language of Autobiography,* 212–13.

40. Governmental speeches in the 1980s and 1990s frequently cited Singapore's modernity—and indeed history—as commencing with Raffles's arrival in 1819. S. Rajaratnam, the first foreign minister of an independent Singapore, developed a more nuanced view of the rationale for this in a 1984 speech. Singapore's genealogy, Rajaratnam noted, went back to 1819. It would certainly be possible to construct a longer historical account, but "the price we would have to pay for this more impressive genealogical table would be to turn Singapore into a bloody battleground for endless racial and communal conflict and interventionist politics by the more powerful and bigger nations from which Singaporeans had emigrated" (*The Prophetic and the Political,* 149). Rajaratnam's understanding of multiracialism was different from Lee's in that he stressed the diminution of ethnic boundaries, but this statement noticeably preserves the governmental function of the state as being above ethnicity and of managing the potential of conflict that proceeds from differing ethnic pasts.

41. Miller, *The Well-Tempered Self,* 129–30.

42. Chua, *Political Legitimacy and Housing,* 151.

43. In October 2006 the Feedback Unit was renamed REACH ("Reaching Everyone for Active Citizenry @ Home") in a further refinement of the

interpellation of active citizen as consumer. The organization's URL is now http://www.reach.gov.sg/.

44. Chatterjee, *The Politics of the Governed*, 75.

45. Joppke, "The Retreat of Multiculturalism," 238.

46. Mishra, "Multiculturalism," 199.

47. Chua, "'Asian-Values,'" 588.

48. See Heng and Devan for an account of how women's interests in Singapore have been seen as "always and already anti-national" ("State Fatherhood," 356). In parallel, a proposal by the Association of Muslim Professionals, a nongovernmental organization, for a collective Malay community leadership was dismissed by the government as encouraging communalism, despite the fact that the state itself manages ethnicity through the communally based ethnic self-help group Mendaki.

49. If we compare popular reviews of Lee's and Mandela's autobiographies on a retail Web site such as Amazon.com, for instance, key differences emerge. When I checked the information (21 September 2005) there were many more reviews of Mandela's *Long Walk to Freedom* than of *The Singapore Story* (103 to 56), and while negative criticism of Mandela's book largely focuses on its length, many critiques of Lee's notes that it gives only a partial reading of history. Even reviews very supportive of Lee tend to acknowledge in prefatory remarks that he is a controversial figure and anticipate readers' unfavorable disposition toward him. Amazon.com reviewers are, of course, predominately based in the United States, but a similar pattern seems to hold for readers identifying as coming from other countries.

50. It is important to note that Koolhaas and Gibson, for all their rhetorical passion, tend to confuse the surface of a project with a much more complex and indeed contested social reality. Koolhaas's assertion that Singapore "represents the ideological production of the past three decades in its pure form, uncontaminated by surviving contextual remnants" would be recognized by few inhabitants of the city-state ("Singapore Songlines," 1011). Indeed, assertions such as that Singapore "is the brainchild of one man: Lee Kuan Yew" tend to repeat, rather than contest, ideological parameters (1013).

51. Thomas L. Friedman, "Singapore and Katrina," *New York Times*, 14 September 2005, http://www.factiva.com (accessed 15 November 2006).

52. Ong Teng Cheong, "Speech by President Ong Teng Cheong," 2.

53. Mandela spoke diplomatically in his speech and the following question-and-answer session. When told by a member of the audience, "in this country there are voices and particularly one voice which says that democracy is not for Singaporeans, not for Asians" (and asked to comment), he replied that Asians needed to decide on their own interpretation of democracy depending on "specific conditions existing in their country"; he also, however, emphasized that a key demonstration of South African democracy had been an instance in which he, as president, was overruled by the constitutional court (*South and Southern Africa into the Next Century*, 20, 22, 21).

Conclusion

1. Smith and Watson, *Reading Autobiography,* 109, 108.
2. Harrison, *Winnie Mandela,* 180.
3. Ndeble, *The Cry of Winnie Mandela,* [v] (hereafter cited in text).
4. Ndebele, *Rediscovery of the Ordinary,* 49.
5. See Mbeki, "Address of the President," particularly his endorsement of the return of Baartman's remains in the context of the production of national symbols. Mbeki made a similar point in his regular "Letter from the President" column in *ANC News* in May 2002.
6. Sisulu, *Walter and Albertina Sisulu,* xxiii (hereafter cited in text).
7. The tradition of "female masculinity" that Halberstam explores is mostly concerned with European and American cultural production which consciously foregrounds masculinity in women. While there are few obvious parallels with this in the texts covered in this book, Halberstam's text does suggest possibilities for further inquiry: in particular, the detaching of masculinity from male bodies offers possibilities in rewriting texts which insist on the body as a metonym for a state apparatus. Queer theory, working within historicized contexts, may well offer a useful purchase on the gendered self-fashioning of national autobiography, which is founded on notions of respectable sexuality.
8. In Adorno's famous critique of Jean-Paul Sartre's endorsement of art with a direct political "message" in his essay "Commitment," he writes, "It is not the office of art to spotlight alternatives, but to resist by its form alone the course of the world, which permanently puts a pistol to men's heads" (180).
9. Lee Boon Yang, "Speech at the Jalan Besar Youth Group," 4.
10. Lau, "A New Voice in Singaporean Literature," 444.
11. Lau, *Playing Madame Mao,* 22 (hereafter cited in text).
12. For a more extended elaboration of this argument, see Holden, "Writing Conspiracy."
13. The change of climate has proceeded at an uneven pace. The staging of a season of Forum Theatre by The Necessary Stage in 1993, for example, provoked a *Straits Times* article noting that Haresh Sharma and Alvin Tan, two of the moving forces behind the productions, had been "trained at Marxist workshops" (Devan 243). This led to a withdrawal of National Arts Council support from unscripted performances, and a tightening of licensing requirements. However, since late 1990s, security focus in Singapore has shifted decisively away from alleged Marxist infiltration to a concern with terrorist organizations which call themselves Islamic: the most recent detentions under the Internal Security Act have all been of persons connected to Jemaah Islamiyah, an organization allegedly dedicated to the formation of an "Islamic" state encompassing many of the countries of Southeast Asia.
14. Said, *Dark Clouds at Dawn,* xvii.

15. Fang Chuang Pi, the so-called Plen or plenipotentiary sent by the CPM to negotiate with Lee Kuan Yew, published three related autobiographical accounts in Chinese in 2000. Eu Chooi Yip, Secretary of the Malayan Democratic Union and CPM cadre who spent four decades in exile in Indonesia and China, completed an oral history recording at the National Archives of Singapore in the early 1990s, and his family has now published an edited version of this. Plans are currently being made to translate Fang's and Eu's memoirs into English. Several accounts of CPM guerrilla life have also recently been published in Chinese by writers with less political connection to Singapore.

16. Chin, *My Side of History*, 32 (hereafter cited in text).

17. As Chin and Hack point out, CPM activists often adopted pseudonyms within the party, which might then be misremembered by others, or pronounced in a number of Chinese dialects, radically transforming the manner in which they would be transliterated into English. The name "Chin Peng" was in fact a British construction, resulting from a combination of two pseudonyms used by the protagonist at different times. (Chin and Hack, *Dialogues with Chin Peng*, 338).

18. From 1826 until the Japanese occupation in 1942, Singapore was part of the Straits Settlements, a series of islands and littoral territories that became a Crown Colony in 1867. Post-war nationalism in Malaya saw the Straits Settlements as becoming part of an independent Malaya, and there was little sense of and no agitation for Singapore's viability as a nation state before it left the Federation of Malaysia in 1965.

19. Chin, *My Side of History*, 106.

20. See Chin Peng's accounts of reading Chinese novels (Chin and Hack, *Dialogues with Chin Peng*, 71) and Nehru's *The Discovery of India* (ibid., 66), and his conscious modeling of his life on the former.

21. For example, when trying to recall the number of times he had met Lai Te, Chin Peng notes that "[t]o recall what happened over fifty years ago, even for me, I have to refer to [F. Spencer] Chapman's book, *The Jungle is Neutral*" (ibid., 103).

22. Bourdieu, *The Field of Cultural Production*, 189.

23. Žižek, "Multiculturalism," 42.

24. Dirlik, "Literature/Identity," 218.

25. Stam and Shohat, "Traveling Multiculturalism," 296.

26. Chatterjee, *The Politics of the Governed*, 3.

27. Joppke, "The Retreat of Multiculturalism," 238.

28. Dirlik, *Postmodernity's Histories*, 205.

29. Mishra, "Multiculturalism," 199.

Bibliography

Archival Sources

African National Congress (ANC) Archives, Liberation Archive, University of Fort Hare, Alice, Eastern Cape, South Africa.

Clodd, Henry. Papers. Brotherton Library, University of Leeds, United Kingdom.

Curzon, George Nathaniel, Marquess. Papers. India Office Library, British Library, Euston Rd, London, U.K.

Fort Hare Papers, University of Fort Hare, Alice, Eastern Cape, South Africa.

Gizenga, Dabu. Papers. Moorland-Spingarn Research Center, Howard University, Washington, D.C., USA.

India National Archives. Janpath, New Delhi 110001, India.

India Office Library, British Library, Euston Road, London, U.K.

Lincoln University Archives, Lincoln University, 1570 Baltimore Pike, Lincoln University, Pa., USA.

Mbeki, Govan. Papers. University of the Western Cape–Robben Island Mayibuye Archives, University of the Western Cape, Modderdam Road, Bellville, Cape Town, South Africa.

National Sound Archive, British Library, Euston Road, London, U.K.

Nehru, Jawaharlal. Papers. Jawaharlal Nehru Memorial Museum and Library, Teenmurti House, New Delhi, India.

Nehru, Motilal. Papers. Jawaharlal Nehru Memorial Museum and Library, Teenmurti House, New Delhi, India.

Nkrumah, Kwame. Papers. Moorland-Spingarn Research Center, Howard University, Washington, D.C., USA.

Public Records and Archives Administration Department (National Archives of Ghana). Castle Road, Accra, Ghana.

Sisulu, Walter. Papers. ANC Archives, Liberation Archive at the University of Fort Hare, Alice, Eastern Cape, South Africa.

South Africa. National Archives Repository, National Archives and Records Service of South Africa, 24 Hamilton Street, Arcadia, Pretoria, South Africa.

Tambo, Oliver. Papers. ANC Archives, Liberation Archive at the University of Fort Hare, Alice, Eastern Cape, South Africa.

United Kingdom. Public Record Office [now National Archives], Ruskin Avenue, Kew, Richmond, Surrey, U.K.

University of the Western Cape–Robben Island Mayibuye Archives, University of the Western Cape, Modderdam Road, Bellville, Cape Town, South Africa.

Yutar, Percy. Papers. National Archives Repository, National Archives and Records Service of South Africa, 24 Hamilton Street, Arcadia, Pretoria, South Africa.

Published Material

Abdullah bin Abdul Kadir, Munshi. *The Hikayat Abdullah: The Autobiography of Abdullah Bin Abdul Kadir, 1797–1854,* translated by A. H. Hill. Singapore: Oxford University Press, 1969.

Achimota Social Service: A Review and Forecast. Achimota: College Press, 1931.

Addo, Ebenezer Obiri. *Kwame Nkrumah: A Case Study of Religion and Politics in Ghana.* Lanham: University Press of America, 1997.

Adorno, Theodor. "Commitment." In *Aesthetics and Politics,* by Ernst Bloch et al., 177–95. London: New Left Books, 1977.

Aggrey, J. E. Kwegyir. "Ideals and Principles of Education in the Gold Coast." In *Notes of Lecturers Given at the Teachers' Refresher Course—July 8 to 21st, 1926,* 6–18. Accra: Achimota College, 1926.

Ahmad, Aijaz. *In Theory: Classes, Nations, Literatures.* London: Verso, 1992.

Alarcón, Norma, Caren Kaplan, and Minoo Moallem. "Introduction: Between Woman and Nation." In *Between Woman and Nation: Nationalisms, Transnational Feminisms, and the State,* edited by Caren Kaplan, Norma Alarcón, and Minoo Moallem, 1–18. Durham, N.C.: Duke University Press, 1999.

Aldrich, Robert. *Colonialism and Homosexuality.* London: Routledge, 2003.

———. *Vestiges of the Colonial Empire in France: Monuments, Museums, and Colonial Memories.* Basingstoke, England: Palgrave Macmillan, 2005.

Alexander, Neville. *Robben Island Prison Dossier, 1964–1974.* Rondebosch, South Africa: University of Cape Town Press, 1994.

Alter, Joseph S. *Gandhi's Body: Sex, Diet, and the Politics of Nationalism.* Philadelphia: University of Pennsylvania Press, 2000.

Anand, Mulk Raj. "Self-Actualization in the Writings of Nehru." In *Jawaharlal Nehru: Centenary Volume,* edited by Sheila Dikshit et al., 6–12. Delhi: Oxford University Press, 1989.

Anderson, Benedict. *Imagined Communities: Reflections on the Origin and Spread of Nationalism.* Rev. ed. London: Verso, 1991.

Ang, Ien. *Watching Dallas: Soap Opera and the Melodramatic Imagination.* London: Methuen, 1985.

Appadurai, Arjun. *Modernity at Large: Cultural Dimensions of Globalization.* Minneapolis: University of Minnesota Press, 1996.

Aquino, Corazon. *In the Name of Democracy and Prayer: Selected Speeches of Corazon C. Aquino.* Pasig City, Philippines: Anvil, 1995.

Armah, Ayi Kwei. *The Beautyful Ones Are Not Yet Born.* Boston: Houghton Mifflin, 1968.

Arnold, David. "The Self and the Cell: Prison Narratives as Life Histories." In *Telling Lives in India: Biography, Autobiography, and Life History,* edited by David Arnold and Stuart Blackburn, 29–53. Bloomington: Indiana University Press, 2004.

Azikiwe, Nnamdi. *My Odyssey: An Autobiography.* London: Hurst, 1970

Bald, Suresht R. "The Politics of Gandhi's 'Feminism': Constructing 'Sitas' for *Swaraj.*" In *Women, States, and Nationalism: At Home in the Nation?* edited by Sita Ranchod-Nilsson and Mary Ann Tétreault, 81–97. London: Routledge, 2000.

Bannerji, Himani. "Pygmalion Nation: Towards a Critique of Subaltern Studies and the 'Resolution of the Women's Question.'" In *Of Property and Propriety: The Role of Gender and Class in Imperialism and Nationalism,* edited by Himani Bannerji, Shahrzad Mojab, and Judith Whitehead, 34–84. Toronto: University of Toronto Press, 2001.

Bannerji, Himani, Shahrzad Mojab, and Judith Whitehead. Introduction to *Of Property and Propriety: The Role of Gender and Class in Imperialism and Nationalism,* edited by Himani Bannerji, Shahrzad Mojab, and Judith Whitehead, 3–33. Toronto: University of Toronto Press, 2001.

Barthes, Roland. *S/Z,* translated by Richard Miller. New York: Hill and Wang, 1974.

Baudrillard, Jean. *Simulacra and Simulation,* translated by Sheila Faria Glaser. Ann Arbor: University of Michigan Press, 1994.

Bauman, Zygmunt. *Liquid Modernity.* Cambridge: Polity, 2002.

Beck, Ulrich. *The Reinvention of Politics: Rethinking Modernity in the Global Social Order.* Cambridge: Polity, 1997.

———. *Risk Society: Towards a New Modernity.* London: Sage, 1992.

Bergland, Betty. "Postmodernism and the Autobiographical Subject: Reconstructing the 'Other.'" In *Autobiography and Postmodernism,* edited by Kathleen Ashley, Leigh Gilmore, and Gerald Peters, 130–66. Amherst: University of Massachusetts Press, 1994.

Bernal, Martin. *Black Athena: The Afroasiatic Roots of Classical Civilization.* Vol. 1, *The Fabrication of Ancient Greece, 1785–1985.* New Brunswick, N.J.: Rutgers University Press, 1987.

Berryman, Charles. "Critical Mirrors: Theories of Autobiography." *Mosaic* 32 (1999): 71–84.

Bhabha, Homi. "Of Mimicry and Man: The Ambivalence of Colonial Discourse." *October* 28 (1984): 125–33.

Bhutto, Benazir. *Daughter of the East: An Autobiography.* London: Hamish Hamilton, 1988.

Birmingham, David. *Kwame Nkrumah: The Father of African Nationalism.* Rev. ed. Athens: Ohio University Press, 1998.

Boehmer, Elleke. *Empire, the National, and the Postcolonial, 1890–1920: Resistance in Interaction*. Oxford: Oxford University Press, 2002.

———. *Stories of Women: Gender and Narrative in the Postcolonial Nation*. Manchester: Manchester University Press, 2005.

Bonner, Philip. "The Transvaal Native Congress, 1917–1920: The Radicalization of the Black Petty Bourgeois on the Rand." In *Industrialisation and Social Change in South Africa: African Class Formation, Culture and Consciousness, 1870–1930,* edited by Shula Marks and Richard Rathbone, 270–313. London: Longman, 1982.

Boulger, Demetrius. *The Life of Sir Stamford Raffles*. 1897. London: Knight, 1973.

Bourdieu, Pierre. *The Field of Cultural Production: Essays on Art and Literature,* edited by Randal Johnson. Cambridge: Polity Press, 1993.

Bowring, Richard. "The Female Hand in Heian Japan: A First Reading." In *The Female Autograph: Theory and Practice of Autobiography from the Tenth to the Twentieth Century,* edited by Domna C. Stanton, 49–56. Chicago: University of Chicago Press, 1987.

Brecher, Michael. *Nehru: A Political Biography*. London: Oxford University Press, 1959.

Bristow, Joseph. *Empire Boys: Adventures in a Man's World*. London: HarperCollins, 1991.

Broughton, Trev Lynn. *Men of Letters, Writing Lives: Masculinity and Literary Auto/Biography in the Late Victorian Period*. London: Routledge, 1999.

Brown, Judith M. *Gandhi: Prisoner of Hope*. New Haven, Conn.: Yale University Press, 1989.

Bruner, Jerome. "The Autobiographical Process." In *The Culture of Autobiography,* edited by Robert Folkenflik, 38–56. Stanford: Stanford University Press, 1993.

———. *Making Stories: Law, Literature, Life*. New York: Farrar, Straus and Giroux, 2002.

Brutus, Dennis. "Robben Island." *Sechaba* 2.12 (December 1968): 10–11.

Burke, Edmund. *On the Sublime and Beautiful*. Harvard Classics, Vol. 24, Part 2. New York: P. F. Collier & Son, 1909–14. Bartleby.com, 2001. http://www.bartleby.com/24/2/107.html.

Cabral, Amilcar. "The Cancer of Betrayal Speech Made by Amilcar Cabral on Nkrumah Day, Conakry, 13 May 1972." In *Kwame Nkrumah,* edited by June Milne, 296–301. Panaf Great Lives Series. London: Panaf, 1974.

Cain, Peter. J., and Anthony. G. Hopkins. *British Imperialism: Innovation and Expansion 1688–1914*. London: Longman, 1993.

Cannadine, David. *Ornamentalism: How the British Saw Their Empire*. Oxford: Oxford University Press, 2001.

Carton, Benedict. "Locusts Fall from the Sky: Manhood and Migrancy in KwaZulu." In *Changing Men in Southern Africa,* edited by Robert Morrell, 129–40. Pietermaritzberg, South Africa: University of Natal Press, 2001.

Casely Hayford, Joseph Ephraim. *Ethiopia Unbound: Studies in Race Emancipation.* 1911. 2nd ed. London: Cass, 1969.

——. Introduction to *West Africa before Europe and Other Addresses Delivered in England in 1901 and 1903,* by Edward Wilmot Blyden, i–iv. London: C. M. Phillips, 1905.

——. "Patriotism." In *West African Leadership: Public Speeches Delivered by the Honourable J. E. Casely Hayford,* edited by Magnus J. Sampson, 153–57. Ilfracombe, U.K.: Arthur Stockwell, 1948.

——. "Toast Proposed to His Excellency the Governor, Sir Hugh Clifford. . . ." In *West African Leadership: Public Speeches Delivered by the Honourable J. E. Casely Hayford,* edited by Magnus J. Sampson, 158–60. Ilfracombe, U.K.: Arthur Stockwell, 1948.

——. *William Waddy Harris, the West African Reformer: The Man and His Message.* London: C. M. Phillips, 1915.

Chatman, Seymour. *Story and Discourse: Narrative Structure in Fiction and Film.* Ithaca, N.Y.: Cornell University Press, 1978.

Chatterjee, Partha. "The Disciplines in Colonial Bengal." In *Texts of Power: Emerging Disciplines in Colonial Bengal,* edited by Partha Chatterjee, 1–29. Minneapolis: University of Minnesota Press, 1995.

——. *The Nation and Its Fragments: Colonial and Postcolonial Histories.* Princeton, N.J.: Princeton University Press, 1993.

——. *Nationalist Thought and the Colonial World: A Derivative Discourse?* Minneapolis: University of Minnesota Press, 1993.

——. *The Politics of the Governed: Reflections on Popular Politics in Most of the World.* New York: Columbia University Press, 2004.

Chin, C. C., and Karl Hack. *Dialogues with Chin Peng: New Light on the Malayan Communist Party.* Singapore: Singapore University Press, 2004.

Chin Peng [Ong Boon Hua]. *Alias Ching Peng: My Side of History.* Singapore: Media Masters, 2003.

Chua Beng Huat. "'Asian-Values' Discourse and the Resurrection of the Social." *Positions* 7 (1999): 573–92.

——. *Communitarian Ideology and Democracy in Singapore.* London: Routledge, 1995.

——. "Living with Capitalism in Asia, Uncomfortably." In *"We Asians": Between Past and Future,* edited by Kwok Kian-Woon et al., 136–53. Singapore: Singapore Heritage Society, 2000.

——. *Political Legitimacy and Housing: Stakeholding in Singapore.* London: Routledge, 1997.

Cleaver, Frances. "Men and Masculinities: New Directions in Gender and Development." In *Masculinities Matter: Men, Gender, and Development,* edited by Frances Cleaver, 1–27. London: Zed Books, 2002.

Clifford, Hugh Charles. *The Further Side of Silence.* Garden City, N.J.: Doubleday, 1923.

———. *"At the Court of Pelesu" and Other Malayan Stories,* edited by William R. Roff. Kuala Lumpur: Oxford University Press, 1993.

———. *In a Corner of Asia, Being Impressions of Men and Things in the Malay Peninsula.* London: Unwin, 1899.

———. "In Chains." *Blackwood's Magazine* 166 (1899): 160–73.

Connell, R. W. "Globalization, Imperialism, and Masculinities." In *Handbook of Studies on Men and Masculinities,* edited by Michael S. Kimmel, Jeff Hearn, and R. W. Connell, 71–89. Thousand Oaks, Calif.: Sage, 2005.

———. *Masculinities.* Cambridge: Polity, 1995.

———. *The Men and the Boys.* St. Leonards, Australia: Allen and Unwin, 2000.

Cooper, Frederick. *Colonialism in Question: Theory, Knowledge, History.* Berkeley: University of California Press, 2005.

———. "Conflict and Connection: Rethinking Colonial African History." In *The Decolonization Reader,* edited by James D. Le Sueur, 23–44. New York: Routledge, 2003.

Cromwell, Adelaide M. *An African Victorian Feminist: The Life and Times of Adelaide Smith Casely Hayford, 1868–1960.* London: Frank Cass, 1986.

Curzon, George Nathaniel. *Leaves from a Viceroy's Notebook and Other Papers.* London: Macmillan, 1926.

———. *Tales of Travel.* London: Hodder and Stoughton, 1923.

Danahay, Martin. A. *A Community of One: Masculine Autobiography and Autonomy in Nineteenth-Century Britain.* Albany: State University of New York Press, 1993.

Daniels, Eddie. *There and Back: Robben Island, 1964–1979.* 3rd ed. Cape Town: Eddie Daniels, 2002.

Davidoff, Leonore, and Catherine Hall. *Family Fortunes: Men and Women of the English Middle Class, 1780–1850.* Chicago: University of Chicago Press, 1987.

Davidson, Basil. *Black Star: A View of the Life and Times of Kwame Nkrumah.* London: Allen Lane, 1973.

Dawson, Graham. *Soldier Heroes: British Adventure, Empire, and the Imagining of Masculine Communities.* London: Routledge, 1994.

De Mel, Neloufer. *Women and the Nation's Narrative: Gender and Nationalism in Twentieth-Century Sri Lanka.* New York: Rowman and Littlefield, 2001.

D'Emilio, John. "Capitalism and Gay Identity." In *The Lesbian and Gay Studies Reader,* edited by Henry Abelove, Michèle Aina Barale, and David M. Halperin, 467–76. New York: Routledge, 1993.

Di Feng. "The Craft of Chinese Historical Biography." In *Life Writing from the Pacific Rim: Essays from Japan, China, Indonesia, India, and Siam, with a Psychological Overview,* edited by Stanley Schab and George Simson, 13–18. Honolulu: University of Hawai'i and the East-West Center, 1997.

Dingake, Michael. *My Fight against Apartheid.* London: Kliptown, 1987.

Dirlik, Arif. "Literature/Identity: Transnationalism, Narrative and Representation." *Review of Education, Pedagogy and Cultural Studies* 24 (2002): 209–34.

———. "The Postcolonial Aura: Third World Criticism in the Age of Global Capitalism." In *Dangerous Liaisons: Gender, Nation and Postcolonial Perspectives,* edited by Anne McClintock, Aamir Mufti and Ella Shohat, 501–27. Minneapolis: University of Minnesota Press, 1997.

———. *Postmodernity's Histories: The Past as Legacy and Project.* Lanham, Md.: Rowman and Littlefield: 2000.

Dissanayake, Wimal. "Introduction—Agency and Cultural Understanding: Some Preliminary Remarks." In *Narratives of Agency: Self-Making in China, India, and Japan,* edited by Wimal Dissanayake, ix–xxi. Minneapolis, University of Minnesota Press, 1996.

Dlamini, Moses. *Hell-Hole, Robben Island: Reminiscences of a Political Prisoner in South Africa.* Trenton, N.J.: Africa World Press, [n.d.].

Domingo, W. A. "Appendix: W.A. Domingo to the Editor of the *Pittsburgh Courier.*" 1930. In *Marcus Garvey: Life and Lessons. A Centennial Companion to the Marcus Garvey and Universal Negro Improvement Association Papers,* edited by Robert A. Hill and Barbara Bair, 111–13. Berkeley: University of California Press, 1987.

Du Bois, W. E. B. *The Souls of Black Folk.* Chicago: A. C. McClurg, 1903. Bartleby .com, 1999. http://www.bartleby.com/114/1.html.

Du Preez Bezdrob, Anné Mariè. *Winnie Mandela: A Life.* Cape Town: Zebra, 2003.

Dubow, Saul. "Race, Civilisation, and Culture: The Elaboration of Segregationist Discourse in the Inter-War Years." In *The Politics of Race, Class and Nationalism in Twentieth- Century Africa,* edited by Shula Marks and Stanley Trapido, 71–94. London: Longman, 1987.

During, Simon. "Postcolonialism and Globalisation: A Dialectical Relation after All?" *Postcolonial Studies* 1 (1998): 31–47.

Dyer, Richard. *White.* London: Routledge, 1997.

Eakin, Paul John. *Fictions in Autobiography: Studies in the Art of Self-Invention.* Princeton, N.J.: Princeton University Press, 1985.

———. *How Our Lives Become Stories: Making Selves.* Ithaca, N.Y.: Cornell University Press, 1999.

Egan, Susanna. *Mirror Talk: Genres of Crisis in Contemporary Autobiography.* Chapel Hill: University of North Carolina Press, 1999.

———. "'True North' in Transit: Some Thoughts on Autobiography and Globalisation." In *Selves Crossing Cultures: Autobiography and Globalisation,* edited by Rosamund Dalziell, 22–38. Melbourne: Australian Scholarly Publishing, 2002.

Erlank, Natasha. "Gender and Masculinity in South African Nationalist Discourse, 1912–1950." *Feminist Studies* 29 (2003): 653–71.

Fabian, Johannes. *Time and the Other: How Anthropology Makes Its Object.* New York: Columbia University Press, 1983.

———. "Time, Narration and the Exploration of Central Africa." *Narrative* 9 (2001): 3–20.

Fanon, Frantz. *The Wretched of the Earth,* translated by Constance Farrington. London: MacGibbon and Kee, 1965.

Foucault, Michel. *Discipline and Punish: The Birth of the Prison,* translated by Alan Sheridan. New York: Vintage, 1979.

———. *The History of Sexuality.* Volume 1, *An Introduction,* translated by Robert Hurley. New York: Vintage, 1990.

———. "Technologies of the Self." In *Technologies of the Self: A Seminar with Michel Foucault,* edited by Luther H. Martin, Huck Gutman, and Patrick H. Hutton, 16–49. Amherst: University of Massachusetts Press, 1988.

Fox, Richard G. "Gandhi and Feminized Nationalism in India." In *Women Out of Place: The Gender of Agency and the Race of Nationality,* edited by Brackette F. Williams, 36–49. New York: Routledge, 1996.

Franklin, Benjamin. *His Autobiography.* Harvard Classics, Vol. 1, Part 1. New York: P. F. Collier & Son, 1909–14. Bartleby.com, 2001. http//:www.bartleby.com/1/1/.

Fraser, A. G. *An Address Delivered at the Fifth Meeting of the Achimota College Council on November 17th, 1931.* Accra, Ghana: College Press, 1931.

Freiwald, Bina Toledo. "Nation and Self-Narration: A View from Québec/Quebec." *Canadian Literature* 172 (Winter 2002): 17–38.

Furnivall, J. S. *Colonial Policy and Practice: A Comparative Study of Burma and Netherlands India.* New York: New York University Press, 1956.

Gadzekpo, Audrey Sitsofe. "Women's Engagement with Gold Coast Print Culture from 1857 to 1957." Ph.D. diss., University of Birmingham, 2001.

Gandhi, Indira. *India: The Speeches and Reminiscences of Indira Gandhi, Prime Minister of India.* London: Hodder and Stoughton, 1975.

———. *The Years of Endeavour: Selected Speeches of Indira Gandhi, August 1969–August 1972.* New Delhi: Ministry of Information and Broadcasting, 1975.

Gandhi, Mohandas Karamachand. *An Autobiography; or, The Story of My Experiments with Truth,* translated by Mahadev Desai. In *The Collected Works of Mahatma Gandhi,* 44:88–511.

———. *The Collected Works of Mahatma Gandhi.* 100 vols. Delhi: Government of India Publications Division, 1994.

———. *Hind Swaraj.* In *The Penguin Gandhi Reader,* edited by Rudrangshu Mukherjee, 3–66. New Delhi: Penguin, 1993.

Gandhi, Leela. "*Ahimsa* and Other Animals: The Genealogy of an Anarchist Politics." Keynote Address, *Interventions* Conference 2005: The Postcolonial State: Decolonization and After, Nottingham Trent University, 26 May 2005.

Gandhi, Sonia, ed. *Freedom's Daughter: Letters between Indira Gandhi and Jawaharlal Nehru 1922–1939.* London: Hodder and Stoughton, 1989.

Gaonkar, Dilip Parameshwar. "On Alternative Modernities." In *Alternative Modernities,* edited by Dilip Parameshwar Gaonkar, 1–23. Durham, N.C.: Duke University Press, 2001.

Gartrell, Beverley. "Colonial Wives: Villains or Victims?" In *The Incorporated Wife,* edited by Hilary Callan and Shirley Ardener, 165–85. London: Croom Helm, 1984.

Garvey, Marcus [Malcus Mosiah]. "Autobiography: Articles from the *Pittsburgh Courier.*" In *Marcus Garvey: Life and Lessons. A Centennial Companion to the Marcus Garvey and Universal Negro Improvement Association Papers,* edited by Robert A. Hill and Barbara Bair, 33–110. Berkeley: University of California Press, 1987.

Gibley, Emma. *The Lady: The Life and Times of Winnie Mandela.* London: Cape, 1993.

Gibson, William. "Disneyland with the Death Penalty." *Wired* 1, no. 4 (September–October 1993). http://www.wired.com/wired/archive/1.04/gibson.html

Giddens, Anthony. *Modernity and Self-Identity: Self and Society in the Late Modern Age.* Stanford: Stanford University Press, 1991.

———. *Runaway World: How Globalization Is Reshaping Our Lives.* New York: Routledge, 2000.

Gikandi, Simon. "Cultural Translation and the African Self: A (Post)colonial Case Study." *Interventions* 3 (2001): 355–75.

Gopal, Sarvepalli. *Jawaharlal Nehru: A Biography.* Vol 1, *1889–1947.* London: Cape, 1975.

———, ed. *Selected Works of Jawaharlal Nehru.* First Series. 15 vols. New Delhi: Orient Longman, 1972–1986.

Goradia, Nayana. *Lord Curzon: Last of the British Moghuls.* Delhi: Oxford University Press, 1993.

Government of the Gold Coast. *Report on Achimota College, 1928–1929.* Accra: Government Printing Office, 1929.

Gramsci, Antonio. *Selections from the Prison Notebooks of Antonio Gramsci,* edited by Q[uintin] Hoare and Geoffrey Nowell Smith. London: Lawrence and Wishart, 1971.

Gready, Paul. "Autobiography and the 'Power of Writing': Political Prison Writing in the Apartheid Era." *Journal of Southern African Studies* 19 (1993): 498–523.

Green, Martin. *Dreams of Adventure, Deeds of Empire.* London: Routledge and Kegan Paul, 1980.

Greene, Sandra E. *Sacred Sites and the Colonial Encounter: A History of Memory and Meaning in Ghana.* Bloomington: Indiana University Press, 2002.

Griffiths, Gareth. *African Literatures in English: East and West.* Harlow, U.K.: Longman, 2000.

Guha, Ranajit. *Dominance without Hegemony: History and Power in Colonial India.* Cambridge, Mass.: Harvard University Press, 1997.

———. *Elementary Aspects of Peasant Insurgency in Colonial India.* Delhi: Oxford University Press, 1983.

Gunn, Janet Varner. *Autobiography: Toward a Poetics of Experience.* Philadelphia: University of Pennsylvania Press, 1982.

Gusdorf, Georges. "Conditions and Limits of Autobiography," translated by James Olney. In *Autobiography: Essays Theoretical and Critical,* edited by James Olney, 28–47. Princeton, N.J.: Princeton University Press, 1980.

Gusmao, Xanana. *To Resist Is to Win! The Autobiography of Xanana Gusmao with Selected Letters and Speeches.* Ringwood, Australia: David Lovell, 2000.

Gyekye, Kwame. *Tradition and Modernity: Philosophical Reflections on the African Experience.* New York: Oxford University Press, 1997.

Hagan, George P. "Nkrumah's Leadership Style—An Assessment from a Cultural Perspective." In *The Life and Work of Kwame Nkrumah,* edited by Kwame Arhin, 177–206. Trenton, N.J.: Africa World Press, 1993.

Halberstam, Judith. *Female Masculinity.* Durham, N.C.: Duke University Press, 1998.

Haley, Bruce. *The Healthy Body and Victorian Culture.* Cambridge, Mass.: Harvard University Press, 1978.

Hardt, Michael, and Antonio Negri. *Empire.* Cambridge, Mass.: Harvard University Press, 2000.

Harrison, Mark. "A Question of Locality: The Identity of Cholera in British India, 1860–1890." In *Warm Climates and Western Medicine: The Emergence of Tropical Medicine, 1500–1900,* edited by David Arnold, 133–59. Amsterdam: Rodopi, 1996.

Harrison, Nancy. *Winnie Mandela: Mother of a Nation.* London: Gollancz, 1985.

Harvey, David. *The Condition of Postmodernity: An Enquiry into the Origins of Cultural Change.* Oxford: Blackwell, 1989.

Heng, Geraldine, and Janadas Devan. "State Fatherhood: The Politics of Nationalism, Sexuality, and Race in Singapore." In *Nationalisms and Sexualities,* edited by Andrew Parker et al., 343–64. New York: Routledge, 1992.

Henley, William Ernest. "Invictus." In *Modern British Poetry,* edited by Louis Untermeyer. New York: Harcourt, Brace and Howe, 1920. Bartleby.com, 1999. http://www.bartleby.com/103/7.html.

Hill, Robert A., and Barbara Bair, eds. *Marcus Garvey, Life and Lessons. A Centennial Companion to the Marcus Garvey and Universal Negro Improvement Association Papers.* Berkeley: University of California Press, 1987.

Hill, Robert A., and Gregory A. Pirio. "'Africa for the Africans': The Garvey Movement in South Africa, 1920–1940." In *The Politics of Race, Class, and Nationalism in Twentieth-Century Africa,* edited by Shula Marks and Stanley Trapido, 209–53. London: Longman, 1987.

Hirschman, Charles. "The Making of Race in Colonial Malaya: Political Economy and Racial Ideology." *Sociological Forum* 1 (1986): 330–60.

Holden, Philip. "The Beginnings of 'Asian Modernity' in Singapore: A Straits Chinese Body Project." *Communal/Plural* 7 (1999): 59–78.

———. *Modern Subjects/Colonial Texts: Hugh Clifford and the Discipline of English Literature in the Straits Settlements and Malaya 1895–1907.* Greensboro, N.C.: ELT Press, 2000.

———. "Writing Conspiracy: Race and Rights in Two Singapore Novels." *Journal of Postcolonial Writing* 42 (2006): 58–70.

Horkheimer, Max, and Theodor Adorno. *Dialectic of Enlightenment*, translated by John Cumming. London: Allen Lane, 1972.

Hornung, Alfred, and Ernstpeter Ruhe. Preface to *Postcolonialism and Autobiography: Michelle Cliff, David Dabydeen, and Opal Palmer Adisa*, edited by Alfred Hornung and Ernstpeter Ruhe, 1–5. Amsterdam: Rodopi, 1998.

Hutcheon, Linda. *The Politics of Postmodernism*. London: Routledge, 1989.

Hyam, Ronald. *Empire and Sexuality: The British Experience*. Manchester, England: Manchester University Press, 1990.

James, C. L. R. *Nkrumah and the Ghana Revolution*. London: Allison and Busby, 1977.

Jansen, G. H. *Afro-Asia and Non-Alignment*. London: Faber, 1966.

Jayawardena, K. *Feminism and Nationalism in the Third World*. London: Zed, 1986.

Joppke, Christian. "The Retreat of Multiculturalism in the Liberal State: Theory and Policy." *British Journal of Sociology* 55 (2004): 237–57.

Kandiyoti, Deniz. "Identity and Its Discontents: Women and Nation." In *Colonial Discourse and Post-Colonial Theory: A Reader*, edited by Patrick Williams and Laura Chrisman, 376–91. New York: Harvester, 1993.

Kant, Immanuel. *The Critique of Judgement*, translated by James Creed Meredith. 1790. Adelaide Library Electronic Texts Collection, 2004. http://etext.library .adelaide.edu.au/k/kant/immanuel/k16j/.

Kaplan, Caren. "Resisting Autobiography: Out-Law Genres and Transnational Feminist Studies." In *De/Colonizing the Subject: The Politics of Gender in Woman's Autobiography*, edited by Sidonie Smith and Julia Watson, 115–38. Minneapolis: University of Minnesota Press, 1992.

Kathrada, Ahmed. *Letters from Robben Island: A Selection of Ahmed Kathrada's Prison Correspondence, 1964–1989*. Edited by Robert D. Vassen. Cape Town: Mayibuye Books, 1999.

Katrak, Ketu H. "Indian Nationalism, Gandhian 'Satyagraha,' and Representations of Female Sexuality." In *Nationalisms and Sexualities*, edited by Andrew Parker et al., 395–406. New York: Routledge, 1992.

Kee Thuan Chye. *Just in So Many Words: Views, Reviews, and Other Things*. Singapore: Heinemann Asia, 1993.

Kenyatta, Jomo. *Facing Mount Kenya: The Tribal Life of the Gikuyu*. London: Secker and Warburg, 1938.

Keren, Michael. "Biography and Historiography: The Case of David Ben-Gurion." *Biography* 23 (2000): 332–51.

Kerr, Alexander. *Fort Hare 1915–48: The Evolution of an African College*. London: Hurst, 1968.

Khilnani, Sunil. *The Idea of India*. New Delhi: Penguin, 1999.

———. Introduction to *An Autobiography; or, The Story of My Experiments with Truth*, by M. K. Gandhi, 1–10. London: Penguin, 2001.

Kimble, David. *A Political History of Ghana: The Rise of Gold Coast Nationalism, 1850–1928.* Oxford: Clarendon, 1963.

Kirk-Greene, Anthony. *Britain's Imperial Administrators, 1858–1966.* Basingstoke, England: Macmillan, 2000.

Koolhaas, Rem. "Singapore Songlines: Portrait of a Potemkin Metropolis . . . or Thirty Years of Tabula Rasa." In *S, M, L, XL,* by Rem Koolhaas and Bruce Mau, 1009–89. New York: Monacelli Press, 1995.

Lau Siew Mei. "A New Voice in Singaporean Literature: Interview with Lau Siew Mei." By Mohammad A. Quayum. In *Singaporean Literature in English: A Critical Reader,* edited by Mohammad A. Quayum and Peter Wicks, 443–46. Serdang: Universiti Putra Malaysia Press, 2002.

———. *Playing Madame Mao.* Rose Bay: Brandl and Schlesinger, 2000.

Lazarus, Neil. *Resistance in Postcolonial African Fiction.* New Haven, Conn.: Yale University Press, 1990.

Lee Boon Yang. "Speech at the Jalan Besar Youth Group Biennial General Meeting at Jalan Besar Community Centre On Sunday, 19 July 1987." Singapore Government Press Release No. 48/Jul 87-Lby-6 Ll-2/87/07/19. Speech-Text Archival and Retrieval System, National Heritage Board, Singapore. http://stars.nhb.gov.sg/stars/public/.

Lee Kuan Yew. "Always a Revolutionary." In *A Study of Nehru,* edited by Rafiq Zakaria, 96. Bombay: Times of India, 1960.

———. "Discipline for Survival." *The Mirror: A Weekly Almanac of Current Affairs* 2.30 (25 July 1966): 1.

———. "First of the Afro-Asians." In *Jawaharlal Nehru: Centenary Volume,* edited by Sheila Dikshit et al., 356–57. Delhi: Oxford University Press.

———. *From Third World to First: The Singapore Story, 1965–2000.* Singapore: Times Editions, 2000.

———. "Schools Must Have Character." In *Lee Kuan Yew: The Man and His Ideas,* edited by Han Fook Kwang, Warren Fernandez, and Sumiko Tan. Singapore: Times, 1998.

———. *The Singapore Story: Memoirs of Lee Kuan Yew.* Singapore: Times Editions, 1998.

———. "Speech by Singapore Prime Minister and Secretary-General of the People's Action Party, Mr. Lee Kuan Yew, in the Debate on East-West Relations at the Socialist International Conference Council on 3rd September, 1964 in Brussels." 1964. In *Republic of Singapore Prime Minister's Speeches, Press Conferences, Interviews, Statements, etc.* (Singapore: Prime Minister's Office, n.d.).

———. "Text of Speech by the Prime Minister, Mr. Lee Kuan Yew, At a Rally to Pay Homage to Pandit Nehru at the Jalan Besar Stadium on Saturday, May 30th, 1964, at 5.00 p.m." 1964. In *Republic of Singapore Prime Minister's Speeches, Press Conferences, Interviews, Statements, etc.* (Singapore: Prime Minister's Office, n.d.).

Lejeune, Philippe. "The Autobiographical Contract," translated by R. Carter. In

French Literary Theory Today: A Reader, edited by Tzvetan Todorov, 192–222. Cambridge: Cambridge University Press, 1982.

———. *On Autobiography,* translated by Katherine Leary. Minneapolis: University of Minnesota Press, 1989.

Lim Boon Keng [as W. C. Lin]. "Physical Culture." *Straits Chinese Magazine* 8 (1904): 117–21.

Lionnet, Françoise. *Autobiographical Voices: Race, Gender, Self-Portraiture.* Ithaca, N.Y.: Cornell University Press, 1989.

Louie, Kam, and Louise Edwards. "Chinese Masculinity: Theorizing *Wen* and *Wu.*" *East Asian History* 8 (1994): 135–48.

Lovesey, Oliver. "Chained Letters: African Prison Diaries and 'National Allegory.'" *Research in African Literatures* 26, no. 4 (Winter 1995): 31–45.

Lugard, Frederick. *The Dual Mandate in British Tropical Africa.* 1922. 5th ed. London: Frank Cass, 1965.

Luthuli, Albert. *Let My People Go: An Autobiography.* London: Collins, 1962.

Lyotard, Jean François. *The Postmodern Condition: A Report on Knowledge,* translated by Geoff Bennington and Brian Massumi. Minneapolis: University of Minnesota Press, 1984.

MacDermott, Doireann, ed. *Autobiographical and Biographical Writing in the Commonwealth.* Barcelona: Editorial AUSA, 1984.

MacIntyre, Angus. *In Search of Megawati Sukarnoputri.* Monash Asia Institute Working Paper 103. Clayton: Monash Asia Institute, 1997.

Mager, Anne. "Youth Organisations and the Construction of Masculine Identities in the Ciskei and Transkei, 1945–1960." *Journal of Southern African Studies* 24 (1998): 653–67.

Mandela, Nelson R. "'I Am Prepared to Die': Nelson Mandela's Statement from the Dock at the Opening of the Defence Case in the Rivonia Trial." African National Congress. http://www.anc.org.za/ancdocs/history/mandela/1960s/rivonia.html.

———. *Long Walk to Freedom: The Autobiography of Nelson Mandela.* London: Abacus, 1994.

———. *No Easy Walk to Freedom,* edited by Ato Quayson. 1965. London: Penguin, 2002.

———. *South and Southern Africa in the Next Century.* Singapore: Institute of Southeast Asian Studies, 1997.

———. *Why I Am Prepared to Die. . . .* Christian Action Pamphlet. Kent, U.K.: Bishop and Sons, n.d.

Mandela, Winnie [Madikizela-Mandela, Nomzamo Winifred Zanyiwe]. *Part of My Soul Went with Him,* edited by Anne Benjamin. New York: Norton, 1985.

Manderson, Lenore. *Sickness and the State: Health and Illness in Colonial Malaya, 1870–1940.* Cambridge: Cambridge University Press, 1996.

Marais , Genoveva Esther. *Kwame Nkrumah as I Knew Him.* Chichester: Janay Publishing, 1972.

Massey, Daniel. "The History of Fort Hare and Its Student Activists, 1933–1973." MA thesis, University of Fort Hare, 2001.

Mayer, Tamar. "Gender Ironies of Nationalism: Setting the Stage." In *Gender Ironies of Nationalism: Sexing the Nation,* edited by Tamar Mayer, 1–22. London: Routledge, 2000.

Mbeki, Thabo. "Address of the President, Thabo Mbeki, at the Opening of the 51st National Conference of the African National Congress." Stellenbosch, 16 December 2002. African National Congress. http://www.anc.org.za/ancdocs/speeches/2002/sp1216.html.

———. "Letter from the President." *ANC Today* 2, no. 19 (10–16 May 2002). African National Congress. http://www.anc.org.za/ancdocs/anctoday/2002/text/at19.txt.

McClintock, Anne. "'No Longer in a Future Heaven': Gender, Race and Nationalism." In *Dangerous Liaisons: Gender, Nation, and Postcolonial Perspectives,* edited by Anne McClintock, Aamir Mufti, and Ella Shohat, 89–112. Minneapolis: University of Minnesota Press, 1997.

Meer, Fatima. *Higher Than Hope: A Biography of Nelson Mandela.* London: Hamish Hamilton, 1988.

Miller, Nancy K. "Representing Others: Gender and the Subjects of Autobiography." *Differences* 6 (1994): 1–27.

Miller, Stuart Creighton. *"Benevolent Assimilation": The American Conquest of the Philippines, 1899–1903.* New Haven, Conn.: Yale University Press, 1982.

Miller, Toby. *The Well-Tempered Self: Citizenship, Culture, and the Postmodern Subject.* Baltimore: Johns Hopkins University Press, 1993.

Milne, June. *Kwame Nkrumah: A Biography.* London: Panaf, 1999.

Mishra, Vijay. "Multiculturalism." *The Years Work in Critical and Cultural Theory* 11 (2003): 179–202.

"The Modernising Nationalism." *Mirror: A Weekly Almanac of Current Affairs* 6, no. 16 (20 April 1970): 1.

Monfils, Barbara S. "Kwame Nkrumah's Extrinsic Rhetorical Strategies." *Journal of Black Studies* 7 (1977): 313–30.

Morrell, Robert. "The Times of Change: Men and Masculinity in South Africa." In *Changing Men in South Africa,* edited by Robert Morrell, 3–37. Pietermaritzberg, South Africa: University of Natal Press, 2001.

Morrell, Robert, and Sandra Swart. "Men in the Third World: Postcolonial Perspectives on Masculinity." In *Handbook of Studies on Men and Masculinities,* edited by Michael S. Kimmel, Jeff Hearn, and R. W. Connell, 90–113. Thousand Oaks, Calif.: Sage, 2005.

Mosse, George L. *The Image of Man: The Creation of Modern Masculinity.* Oxford: Oxford University Press, 1996.

Mostow, Joshua. "Japanese *Nikki* as Political Memoirs." In *Political Memoir: Essays on the Politics of Memory,* edited by George Egerton, 106–20. London: Cass, 1994.

Muslow, Alun. "History and Biography: An Editorial Comment." *Rethinking History* 7 (2003): 1–11.

Nairn, Tom. *The Break-Up of Britain: Crisis and Neo-Nationalism.* London: New Left, 1977.

Nanda, B. R. *Jawaharlal Nehru: Rebel and Statesman.* Delhi: Oxford University Press, 1995.

Nandy, Ashis. *The Intimate Enemy: Loss and Recovery of Self under Colonialism.* Delhi: Oxford University Press, 1983.

Ndebele, Njabulo S. *The Cry of Winnie Mandela.* Banbury, U.K.: Ayebia, 2004.

———. *Rediscovery of the Ordinary: Essays on South African Literature and Culture.* Johannesburg: Congress of South African Writers (COSAW), 1991.

Nehru, Jawaharlal. *An Autobiography.* 1936. Delhi: Allied Publishers, 1962.

———. *A Bunch of Old Letters, Written Mostly to Jawaharlal Nehru and Some Written by Him.* 2nd ed. Bombay: Asia Publishing House, 1960.

———. *The Discovery of India.* 1946. Delhi: Oxford University Press, 1985.

———. *Glimpses of World History: Being Further Letters to his Daughter, Written in Prison, and Containing a Rambling Account of History for Young People.* 1934. Bombay: Asia Publishing House, 1962.

———. *Nehru's Letters to His Sister,* edited by Krishna Nehru Hutheesing. London: Faber, 1963.

———. *Selected Works of Jawaharlal Nehru,* edited by Sarvepalli Gopal. First Series. 15 vols. New Delhi: Orient Longman, 1972–1986.

"Nelson Mandela Confident of Victory, Says Denis Healey." *Sechaba* 5.1 (January 1971): 14–16.

Neuman, Shirley. "Autobiography, Bodies, Manhood." In *Women, Autobiography, Theory,* edited by Sidonie Smith and Julia Watson, 415–24. Madison: University of Wisconsin Press, 1998.

Newell, Stephanie. *Literary Culture in Colonial Ghana: "How to Play the Game of Life."* Bloomington: Indiana University Press, 2002.

Ngũgĩ wa Thiong'o. "The Language of African Literature." In *Colonial Discourse and Post-colonial Theory: A Reader,* edited by Patrick Williams and Laura Chrisman, 435–55. New York: Columbia University Press, 1994.

———. "Mandela Comes Home." *Emerge Magazine* 1, no. 6 (April 1990): 16–21.

Nixon, Rob. "Mandela, Messianism, and the Media." *Transition* 51 (1991): 42–55.

Nkrumah, Kwame. *Dark Days in Ghana.* New York: International Publishers, 1968.

———. *Ghana: The Autobiography of Kwame Nkrumah.* 1957. New York: International, 1979.

———. *I Speak of Freedom: A Statement of African Ideology.* London: Heinemann, 1961.

———. "The Impact That Lasts." In *A Study of Nehru,* edited by Rafiq Zakaria, 93–95. Bombay: Times of India, 1960.

———. *Kwame Nkrumah: The Conakry Years—His Life and Letters,* edited by June Milne. London: Panaf, 1990.

Nordau, Max. "Jewry of Muscle." 1903. In *The Jew in the Modern World: A Documentary History,* edited by Paul R. Mendes-Flohr and Jehuda Reinharz, 546–47. 2nd ed. Oxford: Oxford University Press, 1995.

Nuttall, Sarah. "Telling 'Free' Stories: Memory and Democracy in South African Autobiography since 1994." In *Negotiating the Past: The Making of Memory in South Africa,* edited by Sarah Nuttall and Carli Coetzee, 75–88. Cape Town: Oxford University Press, 1998.

Nuttall, Sarah, and Cheryl-Ann Michael. "Autobiographical Acts." In *Senses of Culture: South African Cultural Studies,* edited by Sarah Nuttall and Cheryl-Ann Michael, 298–317. Cape Town: Oxford University Press, 2000.

Nyerere, Julius K. *Freedom and Unity / Uhuru na Umoja: A Selection from Writings and Speeches, 1952–65.* London: Oxford University Press, 1967.

Offe, Claus. *Disorganized Capitalism: Contemporary Transformations of Work and Politics,* translated by John Keane. Cambridge, Mass.: MIT Press, 1985.

Ofosu-Appiah, L[awrence] H[enry]. *Joseph Ephraim Casely Hayford: The Man of Vision and Faith.* Accra, Ghana: Academy of Arts and Sciences, 1975.

Ong, Aihwa. "'A Momentary Glow of Fraternity': Narratives of Chinese Nationalism and Capitalism." *Identities* 3 (1997): 331–66.

Ong Teng Cheong. "Speech by President Ong Teng Cheong at the State Banquet Hosted in Honour of his Excellency Mr Nelson Mandela, President of the Republic of South Africa, at Raffles Hotel on 5 March 1997." Istana Press Release No.: 09/MAR 02–1/97/03/05. Speech-Text Archival and Retrieval System, National Heritage Board, Singapore. http://stars.nhb.gov.sg/public/.

Osterhammel, Jürgen. *Colonialism: A Theoretical Overview,* translated by Shelley L. Frisch. Princeton, N.J.: Markus Weiner, 1997.

Padmore, George. *The Gold Coast Revolution: The Struggle of an African People from Slavery to Freedom.* London: Dennis Dobson, 1953.

Pandit, Vijaya Laskshmi. *The Scope of Happiness: A Personal Memoir.* New Delhi: Vikas, 1979.

Parekh, Bhikhu. *Gandhi's Political Philosophy: A Critical Examination.* Houndmills, U.K.: Macmillan, 1989.

Pateman, Carole. "The Fraternal Social Contract." In *Civil Society and the State: New European Perspectives,* edited by John Keane, 101–27. London: Verso, 1988.

———. *The Sexual Contract.* Cambridge: Polity, 1988.

Perham, Margery. "Editor's Preface." In *The Diaries of Lord Lugard.* Volume 1, *East Africa, November 1889 to December 1890,* 11–14. London: Faber, 1959.

———. *Lugard: The Life of Frederick Dealtry Lugard.* Vol. 1, *The Years of Adventure, 1858–1898.* London: Collins, 1956.

———. *Lugard: The Life of Frederick Dealtry Lugard.* Vol. 2, *The Years of Authority, 1898–1945.* London: Collins, 1960.

Peters, John G. *Conrad and Impressionism.* Cambridge: Cambridge University Press, 2001.

Phillips, Richard. *Mapping Men and Empire: A Geography of Adventure.* London: Routledge, 1997.

——. *Sex, Politics, and Empire: A Postcolonial Geography.* Manchester: University of Manchester Press, 2006.

Powell, Erica. *Private Secretary (Female)/Gold Coast.* New York: St. Martin's, 1984.

Prakash, Gyan. *Another Reason: Science and the Imagination of Modern India.* Princeton, N.J.: Princeton University Press, 1999.

Pramoedya Anata Toer. *Footsteps,* translated by Max Lane. 1985. Ringwood, Australia: Penguin, 1990.

Priestley, Margaret. *West African Trade and Coast Society: A Family Study.* London: Oxford University Press, 1969.

Probst, Peter, Jan-Georg Deutsch, and Hieke Schmidt. "Introduction: Cherished Visions and Entangled Meanings." In *African Modernities: Entangled Meanings in Current Debate,* edited by Jan-Georg Deutsch, Peter Probst, and Heike Schmidt, 1–17. Oxford: James Currey, 2002.

Quayson, Ato. *Calibrations: Reading for the Social.* Minneapolis: University of Minnesota Press, 2003.

Raffles, Lady Sophia. *Memoir of the Life of and Public Services of Sir Thomas Stamford Raffles.* 1830. Singapore: Oxford University Press: 1991.

Rajan, Gita. "Subversive-Subaltern Identity: Indira Gandhi as the Speaking Subject." In *De/Colonizing the Subject: The Politics of Gender in Woman's Autobiography,* edited by Sidonie Smith and Julia Watson, 196–221. Minneapolis: University of Minnesota Press, 1992.

Rajan, Rajeswari Sunder. *The Scandal of the State: Women, Law, and Citizenship in Postcolonial India.* Durham, N.C.: Duke University Press, 2003.

Rajaratnam, Sinnathamby. *The Prophetic and the Political: Selected Speeches and Writings of S. Rajaratnam,* edited by Chan Heng Chee and Obaid ul Haq. Singapore: Graham Brash, 1987.

Ramphele, Mamphela. "Political Widowhood in South Africa: The Embodiment of Ambiguity." In *Social Suffering,* edited by Arthur Kleinman, Veena Das, and Margaret Lock, 99–117. Berkeley, University of California Press, 1997.

Ranchod-Nilsson, Sita, and Mary Ann Tétreault. "Gender and Nationalism: Moving beyond Fragmented Conversations." In *Women, States, and Nationalism: At Home in the Nation?* edited by Sita Ranchod-Nilsson and Mary Ann Tétreault, 1–17. London: Routledge, 2000.

Ranger, Terence. "The Invention of Tradition in Colonial Africa." In *The Invention of Tradition,* edited by Eric Hobsbawm and Terence Ranger, 211–62. Cambridge: Cambridge University Press, 1983.

Rao, Anupama, and Steven Pierce. "Discipline and the Other Body: Correction, Corporeality, and Colonial Rule." *Interventions* 3 (2001): 159–68.

Rathbone, Richard, ed. *Ghana.* 2 vols. British Documents on the End of Empire, Series B. London: HMSO, 1992.

———. *Nkrumah and the Chiefs: The Politics of Chieftaincy in Ghana, 1951–60.* Oxford: James Currey, 2000.

Ray, Sangeeta. *En-gendering India: Woman and Nation in Colonial and Postcolonial Narratives.* Durham, N.C.: Duke University Press, 2000.

Rhodes, Cecil John. *The Last Will and Testament of Cecil John Rhodes,* edited by W. T. Stead. London: Review of Reviews Office, 1902.

Rofel, Lisa. *Other Modernities: Gendered Yearnings in China after Socialism.* Berkeley: University of California Press, 1999.

Ronaldshay, Earl [Lawrence John Lumley Dundas]. *The Life of Lord Curzon.* 3 vols. London, E. Benn: 1928.

Rooney, David. *Kwame Nkrumah: The Political Kingdom in the Third World.* London: Tauris, 1988.

Rosen, David. "The Volcano and the Cathedral: Muscular Christianity and the Origins of Primal Manliness." In *Muscular Christianity: Embodying the Victorian Age,* edited by Donald E. Hall, 17–44. Cambridge: Cambridge University Press, 1994.

Rousseau, Jean-Jacques. *The Social Contract.* 1762. University of Adelaide E-Texts Library, 2000. http://etext.library.adelaide.edu.au/r/r864s.

Said, Edward W. *Culture and Imperialism.* London: Vintage, 1994.

———. *Orientalism.* London: Routledge, 1978.

Said Zahari. *Dark Clouds at Dawn: A Political Memoir.* Petaling Jaya: Institute of Social Analysis (INSAN), 2001.

Sampson, Anthony. *Mandela: The Authorized Biography.* London: HarperCollins, 1999.

Schalkwyk, David. "Writing from Prison." In *Senses of Culture: South African Cultural Studies,* edited by Sarah Nuttall and Cheryl-Ann Michael, 278–97. Cape Town: Oxford University Press, 2000.

Schneer, Jonathan. *London 1900: The Imperial Metropolis.* New Haven, Conn.: Yale University Press, 1999.

Scott, David. "Colonial Governmentality." *Social Text* 43 (Fall 1995): 191–220.

———. *Refashioning Futures: Criticism after Postcoloniality.* Princeton, N.J.: Princeton University Press, 1999.

Sherwood, Marika. *Kwame Nkrumah: The Years Abroad, 1935–1947.* Legon, Ghana: Freedom Publications, 1996.

Sinha, Mrinalini. *Colonial Masculinity: The "Manly Englishman" and the "Effeminate Bengali" in the Late Nineteenth Century.* Manchester: Manchester University Press, 1995.

———. "Nationalism and Respectable Sexuality in India." *Genders* 21 (1995): 30–57.

Sisulu, Elinor. *Walter and Albertina Sisulu: In Our Lifetime.* Cape Town: David Philip, 2002.

Slovo, Gillian. *Every Secret Thing: My Family, My Country.* Boston: Little, Brown, 1997.

Smith, Sidonie, and Julia Watson. *Reading Autobiography: A Guide for Interpreting Life Narratives.* Minneapolis: University of Minnesota Press, 2001.

Spencer, Herbert. *Education: Intellectual, Moral, and Physical.* 1861. London: Watts, 1949.

Spivak, Gayatri. *A Critique of Postcolonial Reason: Toward a History of the Vanishing Present.* Cambridge, Mass.: Harvard University Press, 1999.

Stam, Robert, and Ella Shohat. "Traveling Multiculturalism: A Trinational Debate in Translation." In *Postcolonial Studies and Beyond,* edited by Ania Loomba et al., 293–316. Durham, N.C.: Duke University Press, 2005.

Stengel, Richard. Interview by John Carlin. *Frontline: The Long Walk of Nelson Mandela.* PBS Online. http://www.pbs.org/wgbh/pages/frontline/shows/mandela/interviews/stengel.html.

Sterling, Bruce. *Islands in the Net.* New York: Arbor House, 1988.

Stoler, Ann Laura, and Frederick Cooper. "Between Metropole and Colony: Rethinking a Research Agenda." In *Tensions of Empire: Colonial Cultures in a Bourgeois World,* edited by Frederick Cooper and Ann Laura Stoler, 1–56. Berkeley: University of California Press, 1997.

Stratton, Florence. *Contemporary African Literature and the Politics of Gender.* London: Routledge, 1994.

Sturrock, John. *The Language of Autobiography: Studies in the First Person Singular.* Cambridge, Cambridge University Press, 1993.

Sussman, Herbert. *Victorian Masculinities: Manhood and Masculine Poetics in Early Victorian Literature and Art.* Cambridge: Cambridge University Press, 1995.

Tan Tai Wei and Chew Lee Chin. "Moral and Citizenship Education as Statecraft in Singapore: A Curriculum Critique." *Journal of Moral Education* 33 (2004): 597–606.

Tay Kheng Soon. "The Problem of Aesthetics in Contemporary Southeast Asia." 3 January 2000. http://www.akitektenggara.com.

Taylor, Charles. *Modern Social Imaginaries.* Durham, N.C.: Duke University Press, 2004.

Teo Hock Guan. Speech to the Legislative Assembly, 16 July 1959. *Legislative Assembly Debates: State of Singapore—Official Report* 11 (1959): cols. 137–38.

Terreblanche, Sampie. *A History of Inequality in South Africa, 1652–2002.* Pitermaritzburg, South Africa: University of Natal Press, 2002.

Thomas, Antony. *Rhodes.* London: BBC Books, 1996.

Thomas, Nicholas. *Colonialism's Culture: Anthropology, Travel, and Government.* Cambridge: Polity, 1994.

Timothy, Bankole. *Kwame Nkrumah: His Rise to Power.* 2nd ed. London: Unwin, 1963.

Trivedi, Harish. *Colonial Transactions: English Literature and India.* Manchester: Manchester University Press, 1995.

Unterhalter, Elaine. "The Work of the Nation: Heroic Masculinity in South African Autobiographical Writing of the Apartheid Struggle." *European Journal of Development Research* 12 (2000): 157–79.

Vellenga, Dorothy Dee. "Who Is a Wife? Legal Expressions of Heterosexual Conflicts in Ghana." In *Female and Male in West Africa*, edited by Christine Oppong, 144–55. London: Allen and Unwin, 1983.

Viswanathan, Gauri. *Masks of Conquest: Literary Study and British Rule in India.* New York: Columbia University Press, 1989.

Watt, Ian. *Conrad in the Nineteenth Century.* London: Chatto & Windus, 1980.

Watson, C. W. *Of Self and Nation: Autobiography and the Representation of Modern Indonesia.* Honolulu: University of Hawaii Press, 2000.

Watson, Julia, and Sidonie Smith. "Introduction: De/Colonization and the Politics of Discourse in Women's Autobiographical Practices." In *De/Colonizing the Subject: The Politics of Gender in Woman's Autobiography*, edited by Sidonie Smith and Julia Watson, xiii–xxxi. Minneapolis: University of Minnesota Press, 1992.

Weber, Max. *The Protestant Ethic and the Spirit of Capitalism*, translated by Talcott Parsons. 1930. London: Routledge, 2001.

Wee, C. J. W[an]-L[ing]. "Forming an Asian Modern: Capitalist Modernity, Culture, 'East Asia,' and Post- Colonial Singapore." *Identity, Culture, and Politics* 5 (2004): 1–18.

———. "The Vanquished: Lim Chin Siong and a Progressivist National Narrative." In *Lee's Lieutenants: Singapore's Old Guard*, edited by Lam Peng Er and Kevin Y.L. Tan, 169–90. St. Leonards: Australia: Allen and Unwin, 1999.

Weintraub, Karl. "Autobiography and Historical Consciousness." *Critical Inquiry* 1 (1975): 821–48.

Werbner, Pnina. "Introduction: The Materiality of Diaspora—Between Aesthetic and 'Real' Politics." *Diaspora: A Journal of Transnational Studies* 9 (2000) 5–20.

Wolpert, Stanley. *Nehru: A Tryst with Destiny.* New York: Oxford University Press, 1996.

Woolf, Virginia. *The Common Reader.* 2nd ed. London: Hogarth Press 1925.

Wright, Richard. *Black Power: A Record of Reactions in a Land of Pathos.* New York: Harper, 1954.

———. *The Color Curtain: A Report on the Bandung Conference.* Cleveland: World Publishing, 1956.

Wu Pei-Yi. *The Confucian's Progress: Autobiographical Writings in Contemporary China.* Princeton, N.J.: Princeton University Press, 1990.

Yeo Kim Wah. *Political Development in Singapore, 1945–55.* Singapore: Singapore University Press, 1973.

Yeoh, Brenda S. A. *Contesting Space: Power Relations and the Urban Built Environment in Colonial Singapore.* Kuala Lumpur: Oxford University Press, 1996.

Young, Robert J. C. *Postcolonialism: An Historical Introduction.* Oxford: Blackwell, 2001.

―――. *White Mythologies: Writing History and the West.* London: Routledge, 1990.

Young, Sandra. "Narrative and Healing in the Hearings of the South African Truth and Reconciliation Commission." *Biography* 27 (2004): 145–62.

Yuval-Davis, Nira. *Gender and Nation.* London: Sage, 1997.

Zhou Yongming. *Historicizing Online Politics: Telegraphy, the Internet, and Political Participation in China.* Stanford: Stanford University Press, 2006.

Žižek, Slavoj. "Multiculturalism; or, the Cultural Logic of Multinational Capitalism." *New Left Review* 225 (September–October 1997): 28–51.

Zwelonke, D. M. *Robben Island.* London: Heinemann, 1973.

Index

Wisconsin Studies in Autobiography

William L. Andrews
General Editor

Robert F. Sayre
The Examined Self: Benjamin Franklin, Henry Adams, Henry James

Daniel B. Shea
Spiritual Autobiography in Early America

Lois Mark Stalvey
The Education of a WASP

Margaret Sams
Forbidden Family: A Wartime Memoir of the Philippines, 1941–1945
Edited with an introduction by Lynn Z. Bloom

Charlotte Perkins Gilman
The Living of Charlotte Perkins Gilman: An Autobiography
Introduction by Ann J. Lane

Mark Twain
Mark Twain's Own Autobiography: The Chapters from the North American Review
Edited with an introduction by Michael Kiskik

Journeys in New Worlds: Early American Women's Narratives
Edited by William L. Andrews, Sargent Bush, Jr., Annette Kolodny, Amy
Schrager Lang, and Daniel B. Shea

American Autobiography: Retrospect and Prospect
Edited by Paul John Eakin

Caroline Seabury
The Diary of Caroline Seabury, 1854–1863
Edited with an introduction by Suzanne L. Bunkers

Marian Anderson
My Lord, What a Morning
Introduction by Nellie Y. McKay

American Women's Autobiography: Fea(s)ts of Memory
Edited with an introduction by Margo Culley

Frank Marshall Davis
Livin' the Blues: Memoirs of a Black Journalist and Poet
Edited with an introduction by John Edgar Tidwell

Joanne Jacobson
Authority and Alliance in the Letters of Henry Adams

Cornelia Peake McDonald
*A Woman's Civil War: A Diary with Reminiscences of the War,
    from March 1862*
Edited with an introduction by Minrose C. Gwin

Kamau Brathwaite
The Zea Mexican Diary: 7 September 1926–7 September 1986

Genaro M. Padilla
My History, Not Yours: The Formation of Mexican American Autobiography

Frances Smith Foster
Witnessing Slavery: The Development of Ante-bellum Slave Narratives

Native American Autobiography: An Anthology
Edited with an introduction by Arnold Krupat

American Lives: An Anthology of Autobiographical Writing
Edited with an introduction by Robert F. Sayre

Carol Holly
*Intensely Family: The Inheritance of Family Shame and the Autobiographies
    of Henry James*

People of the Book: Thirty Scholars Reflect on Their Jewish Identity
Edited by Jeffrey Rubin-Dorsky and Shelley Fisher Fishkin

G. Thomas Couser
Recovering Bodies: Illness, Disability, and Life Writing

José Angel Gutiérrez
The Making of a Chicano Militant: Lessons from Cristal

John Downton Hazlett
My Generation: Collective Autobiography and Identity Politics

William Herrick
Jumping the Line: The Adventures and Misadventures of an American Radical

Women, Autobiography, Theory: A Reader
Edited by Sidonie Smith and Julia Watson

Carson McCullers
Illumination and Night Glare: The Unfinished Autobiography of Carson McCullers
Edited with an introduction by Carlos L. Dews

Marie Hall Ets
Rosa: The Life of an Italian Immigrant

Yi-Fu Tuan
Who Am I?: An Autobiography of Emotion, Mind, and Spirit

Henry Bibb
The Life and Adventures of Henry Bibb: An American Slave
Introduction by Charles J. Heglar

Suzanne L. Bunkers
Diaries of Girls and Women: A Midwestern American Sampler

Jim Lane
The Autobiographical Documentary in America

Sandra Pouchet Paquet
Caribbean Autobiography: Cultural Identity and Self-Representation

Mark O'Brien, with Gillian Kendall
How I Became a Human Being: A Disabled Man's Quest for Independence

Elizabeth L. Banks
*Campaigns of Curiosity: Journalistic Adventures of an American Girl
    in Late Victorian London*
Introduction by Mary Suzanne Schriber and Abbey L. Zink

Miriam Fuchs
The Text Is Myself: Women's Life Writing and Catastrophe

Jean M. Humez
Harriet Tubman: The Life and the Life Stories

Voices Made Flesh: Performing Women's Autobiography
Edited by Lynn C. Miller, Jacqueline Taylor, and M. Heather Carver

Loreta Janeta Velazquez
The Woman in Battle: The Civil War Narrative of Loreta Janeta Velazquez,
    Cuban Woman and Confederate Soldier
Introduction by Jesse Alemán

Cathryn Halverson
Maverick Autobiographies: Women Writers and the American West, 1900–1936

Jeffrey Brace
The Blind African Slave: Or Memoirs of Boyrereau Brinch, Nicknamed Jeffrey Brace
as told to Benjamin F. Prentiss, Esq.
Edited with an introduction by Kari J. Winter

Colette Inez
The Secret of M. Dulong: A Memoir

Before They Could Vote: American Women's Autobiographical Writing, 1819–1919
Edited by Sidonie Smith and Julia Watson

Bertram J. Cohler
Writing Desire: Sixty Years of Gay Autobiography

Philip Holden
Autobiography and Decolonization: Modernity, Masculinity, and the Nation-State

Jing M. Wang
When "I" Was Born: Women's Autobiography in Modern China

www.ingramcontent.com/pod-product-compliance
Lightning Source LLC
Chambersburg PA
CBHW070910100426

42814CB00003B/122